Mod
edit
Pet
Uni
Sar

VENEZUELA AND PARAGUAY
Political modernity
and tradition in conflict

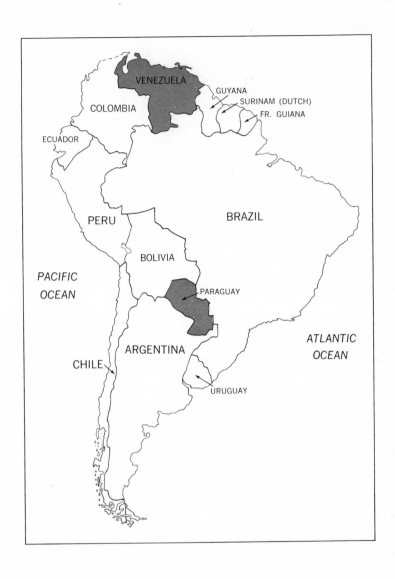

VENEZUELA AND PARAGUAY

**Political modernity
and tradition in conflict**

Leo B. Lott
University of Montana

HOLT, RINEHART AND WINSTON, INC.
New York   Chicago   San Francisco   Atlanta
Dallas   Montreal   Toronto   London   Sydney

To Katharine and Christopher

FOREWORD TO THE SERIES

This new series in comparative politics was undertaken in response to the special needs of students, teachers, and scholars that have arisen in the last few years, needs that are no longer being satisfied by most of the materials now available. In an age when our students seem to be getting brighter and more politically aware, the teaching of comparative politics should present a greater challenge than ever before. We have seen the field come of age with numerous comparative monographs and case studies breaking new ground, and the Committee on Comparative Politics of the Social Science Research Council can look back proudly on nearly a decade of important spade work. But teaching materials have lagged behind these changing approaches to the field. Most comparative government series are either too little coordinated to make systematic use of any common methodology or too conventional in approach. Others are so restricted in scope and space as to make little more than a programmatic statement about what should be studied, thus suggesting a new scholasticism of systems theory that omits the idiosyncratic richness of the material available and tends to ignore important elements of a system for fear of being regarded too traditional in approach.

In contrast to these two extremes, the Modern Comparative Politics Series attempts to find a happy combination of rigorous, systematic methodology and the rich sources of data available to area and country specialists. The series consists of a core volume, *Modern Comparative Politics* by Peter H. Merkl, country volumes covering one or more nations, and comparative topical volumes.

Rather than narrowing the approach to only one "right" method, the core volume leaves it to the teacher to choose any of several approaches he may prefer. The authors of the country volumes are partly bound by a framework common to these volumes and the core volume, and are partly free to tailor their approaches to the idiosyncrasies of their respective countries. The emphasis in the common framework is on achieving a balance between such elements as theory and application, as well as among developmental perspectives, sociocultural aspects, the group processes, and the decision-making processes of government. It is hoped that the resulting tension between comparative approaches and politicocultural realities will enrich the teaching of comparative politics and provoke discussion at all levels from undergraduate to graduate.

The group of country volumes is supplemented by a group of analytical comparative studies. Each of these comparative volumes takes an important topic and explores it cross-nationally. Some of these topics are covered in a more limited way in the country volumes, but many find their first expanded treatment in the comparative volumes—and all can be expected to break new scholarly ground.

The ideas embodied in the series owe much to the many persons whose names are cited in the footnotes of the core volume. Although they are far too numerous to mention here, a special debt of spiritual paternity is acknowledged to Harry Eckstein, Gabriel A. Almond, Carl J. Friedrich, Sidney Verba, Lucian W. Pye, Erik H. Erikson, Eric C. Bellquist, R. Taylor Cole, Otto Kirchheimer, Seymour M. Lipset, Joseph La Palombara, Samuel P. Huntington, Cyril E. Black, and many others, most of whom are probably quite unaware of their contribution.

P. H. M.

Santa Barbara, California

PREFACE

This book is intended to serve as an introduction to the political systems of Venezuela and Paraguay. I selected these countries because I felt they offered an excellent case study in contrast and similarity. Basically similar in many ways, sharing the same type of political culture and heritage, they are now at somewhat different stages of economic, political, and social development. The task I set myself in this book was to account for this fact.

For the most part, I have not tried to hold consistently to any particular theoretical model of analysis, except to conform with the structure of the series of which this volume forms a part. I think this is a virtue since the instructor who uses the book can mold the information contained in it to his own theoretical preference.

I am strongly convinced that if a student has to read a paragraph three or four times to extract meaning from it, the author has failed in his essential task of intelligently communicating with his reader. The basic purpose of a textbook is to present material in a form the student can readily comprehend and use. To this end I have deliberately avoided a good deal of the jargon of comparative analysis and have tried to keep my writing as clear and accessible as possible.

With the exception of certain portions on Venezuela, I have drawn heavily on the works of my colleagues in political science, anthropology, sociology, and history. The student will soon discover that the Venezuelan system has received greater in-depth treatment in almost every chapter. One reason for this is that I know more about Venezuela, having lived and studied there. Another reason is that Paraguay has been neglected by serious students of Latin American affairs and literature on it is scarce. That scarcity is reflected in my volume. Statistical details and reliable data on Paraguay are extremely difficult to come by. I have yet to receive a response from an official agency of the Paraguayan government to any of my inquiries. Several excellent studies have been made on various aspects of Paraguay, and I am indebted to them for much of the factual and, indeed, interpretative material. Some of them are Harris G. Warren's *Paraguay, an Informal History,* Elman R. and Helen S. Service's *Tobatí, Paraguayan Town,* and George Pendle's *Paraguay, a Riverside Nation.* Particularly useful and timely articles are Byron Nichols' "Paraguay—A Future Democracy?" "Las Espectativas de Los Partidos Politicas en el Paraguay," and Frederick Hicks's "Politics, Power and the Role of the Village Priest in Paraguay."

Based upon the available literature, I have sought to present as accurate a picture as possible of the society, culture, political development, the political actors, and the political process of Venezuela and Paraguay. There are gaps in certain areas, notably in the field of local government and judicial structures. Where detailed factual information has not been available, I have relied upon the bare bones of the constitution and the law, which, while shedding little light on the true nature of political institutions and phenomena, at least reveal desired goals in the system.

The gap between constitutional theory and practice is wide indeed. Research in many neglected areas of Latin American politics is now underway, however. In a decade or so it will be possible to write more meaningfully of the entire political environment in Latin America.

L. B. L.

Missoula, Montana
September 1971

CONTENTS

Foreword to the series   vii

Preface   ix

INTRODUCTION   Progress and traditionalism in the
    Latin American setting   1

Geographic Bases of Politics **6/** Economic Bases of
Politics **14/** Social Bases of Politics **22/** Summary **26**

1. THE DEVELOPMENT OF VENEZUELA AND
    PARAGUAY   28

The Colonial Epoch: Foundations of Nationhood **28/**
Summary **55/** Independence and Nationhood **56/**
Summary **93**

2. AUTHORITARIANS, INNOVATORS, AND RESISTORS   95

Political Socialization, Recruitment, and Participation **95/**
Summary **135**

3. VARIATIONS ON THE THEME OF HISPANIC
    HERITAGE   Ingredients of the political culture   138

Political Man: Spanish Views and Values **139/** Politics and
Theology: The Catholic Influence **145/** Ideologies and
Politics: Authoritarianism and Democracy **148/** Politics of

Consent and Command: Elections and Force **153/** Politics
of Militarism: The Praetorian Guard **157/** Politics of
Power and Restraint: Constitutional Traditions **165/**
Summary **185**

4. **NATIONAL, STATE, AND LOCAL GOVERNMENT**
   Federal and unitary systems   **186**

   Federalism in Venezuela: Ideal and Reality **186/** The
   Unitary System of Paraguay **203/** The Communications
   Resources **206**

5. **THE PARTY SYSTEM   Multiparty coalition**
   democracy and status quo one-party rule   **213**

   Historical Perspectives **213/** The Contemporary Legal and
   Political Milieu **216/** The Political Party Spectrum **222/**
   The Party Structure and Campaign Techniques **236/**
   The Electoral Process **241**

6. **OLIGARCHICAL AND INSTITUTIONAL PLURALISM:**
   INTEREST GROUPS   **250**

   Men of the Cloth: The Catholic Church **251/** Men on
   Horseback: The Military Establishment **256/** Men at Desks:
   The Bureaucracy **262/** The Intellectual Community:
   The University and Student Organizations **264/** The
   Proletarian Community: Industrial and Agricultural
   Organizations **269/** The Business Community: Industrial
   and Commercial Groups **275/** Summary **280**

7. **STRUCTURES AND ROLES IN THE CONVERSION**
   PROCESS   The national government   **282**

   The Executive Branch of the Government **283/** The
   Legislative Branch of the Government **303/** Public Policy
   Problems **316/** Summary **317**

8. **THE SPIRIT OF SPANISH LAW   The individual and**
   the courts   **318**

   The Nature of the System **318/** Judicial Structures and
   Roles **321/** The Citizen and the Law **333/** Summary **337**

9. **ISOLATIONISM, NATIONALISM, AND**
   INTERNATIONALISM   Foreign policy   **339**

   Conditioning Influences and Trends **339/** Regional
   Organization: The Inter-American System **348/**
   Participation in International Organizations: The League
   of Nations and the United Nations **360**

10. SUMMARY AND CONCLUSIONS   365

Progress Toward Democracy **365**/ Progress in the
Utilization of Natural Resources **370**/ Progress in the
Distribution of Goods and Services **375**/ Progress in
Responding to Demands of Society **377**/ The Citizen and
Symbolic Values **378**/ Conclusion **374**

Additional Bibliography   382

Index   385

TIME LINE FOR VENEZUELA

1498	Venezuelan mainland visited by Columbus on his third voyage.
1528–1548	Duration of the Crown's commercial monopoly grant to the German banking family of Welser.
1567	Founding of Caracas.
1728–1785	Duration of the Crown's commercial monopoly grant to the Royal Guipuzcoa Company of Caracas.
1777	The Provinces of Venezuela became a Captaincy-General.
1811	Venezuela declared its independence.
1811	Venezuela wrote its first constitution.
1812	Caracas suffered a devastating earthquake.
1819	Venezuela wrote its second constitution.
1821	Venezuela achieved victory and independence of Spain at the Battle of Carabobo.
1821–1830	The period of the Republic of *Gran Colombia* of which Venezuela was a member with Colombia and Ecuador.
1830	Venezuela became an independent nation, separating from the Republic of *Gran Colombia*. A new constitution was proclaimed.
1830–1846	General Antonio Páez dominated the country during these years. Period known as the Conservative Oligarchy.
1848–1858	Venezuela was dominated by the Mongas brothers, José and Gregorio. New constitutions were promulgated in 1857 and 1858.
1858–1864	The Federal War. During this period there was civil war between partisans for federalism and unitary government. The unitary forces were defeated.
1864	End of the Federal War and the promulgation of a new federal constitution.
1870–1888	Antonio Guzmán Blanco seized power in 1870 and governed or controlled the country until 1888. During this time the constitutions of 1874 and 1881 were promulgated.
1888–1898	A period of rebellion and political unrest. Two more constitutions were written: 1891, 1893.
1889	Political power passed from the *Llanos* to the Andes when General Cipriano Castro seized power.

1899–1907   Castro dominated Venezuela. Constitutions of 1901 and 1904 were proclaimed.

1908–1935   Juan Vicente Gómez deposed Castro in 1908 and ruled until 1935. He was responsible for the constitutions of 1909, 1914, 1921, 1925, 1928, 1929, and 1931.

1914   Oil was first pumped from Lake Maracaibo.

1936–1940   Presidency of General Eleazar López Contreras, Constitution of 1936 adopted.

1941   *Acción Democrática* legalized and allowed to run candidates for public office.

1941–1945   Presidency of General Medina Angarita.

1945   President Medina Angarita was deposed by the military with the support of *Acción Democrática*. Country governed by a junta composed of men from both forces.

1947   A new constitution was adopted. Elections were held and *Acción Democrática* emerged as the majority party. Rómulo Gallegos, renowned novelist was elected president, in November.

1948   A military coup deposed President Gallegos who had taken office in February.

1948–1950   A military junta governed Venezuela under the presidency of Lieutenant Colonel Delgado Chabaud.

1950   Junta president Chabaud was assassinated in November.

1950–1952   A new government junta under a civilian figurehead governed the country.

1952   Elections held for delegates to a Constitutional convention.

1952   Colonel Marcos Pérez Jiménez, dominant member of the government junta, dissolved the Junta and proclaimed himself provisional president.

1953   Constitutional convention met from January to March and wrote a new constitution. It also elected Pérez Jiménez as constitutional president.

1957   Pérez Jiménez conducts a fraudulent plebiscite which enabled him to enter a second five-year term as president.

1958   Pérez Jiménez was overthrown in January in the wake of a popular and military uprising.

1958   New elections were held in December. *Acción Democrática* assumed power under Rómulo Betancourt.

1958–1963   Presidency of Rómulo Betancourt.

1961   A new constitution was adopted, Venezuela's twenty-sixth. It is presently in effect.

1963   National and state elections were held in December. AD continued in control of the government with power passing from President Rómulo Betancourt to his party colleague Raul Leoni.

1963–1968   Presidency of Raul Leoni.

1968   New elections were held. Power passed to COPEI with the victory of Rafael Caldera.

TIME LINE FOR PARAGUAY

1524	The first white man visited the territory of what is now Paraguay.
1537	Asunción, capital city of Paraguay, was founded by Juan de Ayala.
1536–1616	Asunción was the seat of Spanish authority in southern South America until power was transferred in 1616 to Buenos Aires.
1720	Beginning of the Comunero revolt.
1776	Paraguay was placed under the jurisdiction of the newly created Viceroyalty of Rio de la Plata.
1811	Paraguay proclaimed and achieved independence from both Spain and Argentina.
1816–1840	Dictatorship of José Gaspar Rodríguez de Francia.
1840–1862	Dictatorship of Carlos Antonio López.
1844	Paraguay's first constitution was promulgated. It was largely ignored.
1862–1870	Dictatorship of Francisco Solano López.
1865–1870	War of the Triple Alliance. Paraguay was defeated by Brazil, Argentina, and Uruguay and was occupied for six years.
1870	Paraguay's second constitution was promulgated.
1870–1940	Period governed by the constitution of 1870.
1874–1904	Conservative elites controlled Paraguay for thirty years.
1886–1904	Sale of public lands took place. Much of Paraguay's land passed into private and foreign hands.
1887	Paraguay's two great parties, the Colorado and the Liberal were founded.
1904–1936	Liberal elites controlled Paraguay for thirty-two years.
1932–1935	The Chaco War. Paraguay defeated Bolivia in a dispute which involved ownership of part of the *Gran Chaco*.
1936	The Febreristas under Colonel Rafael Franco deposed President Eusebio Ayala.
1937	The Febreristas were driven from power in August and a period of political instability existed until 1939.
1939	General José Felix Estigarribia was elected president. He was a member of the Liberal party.
1940	Paraguay's third constitution was promulgated in February. President Estigarribia was killed in a plane

	accident on September 7. General Higinio Morínigo succeeded to the presidency on the death of the president.
1940–1967	Period governed by the constitution of 1940.
1943	General Morínigo elected for a five-year term as president.
1947	Civil war broke out in March as dissidents tried to oust Morínigo. The rebels were defeated in August and driven from Paraguay.
1948	Juan Natalicio Gonzalez, the personal choice of Morínigo, was elected president. Later in the year Gonzalez was overthrown and both he and Morínigo went into exile.
1948–1949	A period of confusion and political instability followed the overthrow of Gonzalez. It ended when power passed into the hands of Federico Chaves.
1953	Federico Chaves elected to a five-year term as president.
1954	General Alfredo Stroessner overthrew Chaves in May. He has governed Paraguay since then.
1967	Paraguay's fourth constitution was promulgated.
1968	President Stroessner was elected to a third five-year term.

VENEZUELA AND PARAGUAY
Political modernity
and tradition in conflict

INTRODUCTION
Progress and traditionalism in the Latin American setting

Stretching 7000 miles southward from continental United States to the remote, storm-swept Tierra del Fuego at the tip of Argentina is the great land mass of Central and South America, collectively known as Latin America. It covers 14 percent of the total land surface of the world and claims 8 percent of the world's population. Its present (mid-1969) population of about 276 million people is increasing at the rate of about 3 percent a year, making it the fastest growing region of the world. If the present rate continues, by 1990 only China, Europe, and India will have larger populations.[1]

The civilization of this burgeoning area of the world is overwhelmingly Spanish and Portuguese in origin. Other national cultures, however, are also represented. The Caribbean island states of Jamaica, Trinidad, Barbados, and Tobago, once under British control, naturally reflect Anglo-Saxon cultural influences, as do Guyana (formerly British Guiana) on the northeastern coast of South America, and British Honduras in Central America. French influence is found in island dependencies in the Caribbean Sea and in French Guiana; it predominates in Haiti. Dutch culture prevails in Curaçao and Dutch Guiana and in some minor islands.

[1] *Statistical Abstract of Latin America 1966,* C. Paul Roberts and Takako Kohda, eds., 10th ed. (Berkeley, Calif.: University of California Press, 1966), p. 5.

Although these European influences have provided the dominant value patterns, other ethnic influences are at work as well. Large, unassimilated masses of Indians, descendents of the brilliant Inca civilization, make up 63 percent of the Bolivian, 30 percent of the Ecuadorean, and 46 percent of the Peruvian populations. About one-half of Guatemala's people are pure-blooded Indians, mostly of the Mayan strain. Mexico's rural life is still greatly influenced by Indian customs, traditions, and dialects. Eight percent of Mexico's people are Indians. Negroes account for 10 percent or more of the populations of Venezuela, Nicaragua, Panama, Cuba, the Dominican Republic, and Brazil. In Haiti, almost everyone is a Negro or mulatto.

In view of the variety of cultures represented, it may be argued that the term "Latin America" is inappropriate, since it does not take non-Hispanic influences into account. A more accurate generally acceptable term, however, has not been found.

Students of the Hispanic regions of Latin America employ the designation in a narrow sense that includes only those countries which derive their culture from Spain or Portugal or, in the case of Haiti, France. Within the scope of this definition, Latin America includes Mexico, the six republics of Central America (Guatemala, Honduras, Nicaragua, El Salvador, Costa Rica, and Panama), the ten republics of South America (Venezuela, Colombia, Ecuador, Peru, Chile, Bolivia, Argentina, Uruguay, Brazil, and Paraguay), and the three island republics (Haiti, Cuba, and Santo Domingo).

Having narrowed our definition of Latin America, we must hasten to warn that it is impossible to treat it as an integrated cultural unit and certainly not as a social or political unit. There is no such thing as a unified Latin American reality, nor a "typical" Latin American republic. Justice may be done to the twenty nations of Latin America only by studying in detail their individual developments, their departures from and adherence to their Iberian origins, their adaptations of French, Swiss, Anglo-Saxon, and American political philosophies, and the direction of their economic growth and aspirations.

Different influences are more strongly at work in some countries than others. An example would be that of religion. Catholicism predominates in all of the Hispanic countries, at least formally. It is a particularly powerful force in Colombia and Ecuador. The Church and its impact is far weaker in Uruguay, which in 1867 dissolved the bonds between church and state and suppressed monasteries and convents with the injunction that their inmates ought to marry and increase Uruguay's population!

While it is possible to make generalizations concerning Latin America as a whole, each such generalization must be qualified by one or more exceptions. Consider, for example, the statement that the population of Latin America is predominantly a mixture of Indian and European strains (*mestizo*). Such a generalization would not be true of Uruguay, Costa Rica, and Argentina, each of which claims to be at least 95 percent Caucasian. Or consider the generalization that Latin America in its political development has reflected the authoritarian tradition of Spain. Yet some of the nations, such as Uruguay and Costa Rica, have clearly demonstrated their attachments to non-Hispanic political institutions and practices.

Other countries are steadily undergoing changes as the result of immigration. Buenos Aires, the capital city of Argentina, has taken on a distinct Italian flavor. German influences may be found in Argentina, Colombia, and Chile, among others. American influences are stronger in the Caribbean and northern South America than they are farther south. These few examples could be joined by others to show the continuing cultural flux.

What we see in Latin America today is a collection of independent nations in varying stages of development: economic, political, and social. There are great contrasts between those who have made the most progress in these fields and those who are lagging far behind. Starting with basically similar features and faced with similar geographical obstacles, the twenty republics, while adhering for the most part to their Hispanic values, have evolved national societies that are distinguished as much by their dissimilarities as by their common characteristics.

This common yet distinctive pattern of cultural evolution is found in Venezuela and Paraguay, the subjects of this volume. There are certain characteristics shared by these two countries that would lead us to expect a parallel development. First, both nations use Spanish as their official language. Paraguay, however, is a bilingual country, its second language being Guaraní, the language of the original Indian population of the land. Second, the Roman Catholic Church is nominally the paramount religious institution in both. Third, each was colonized, socialized, and ruled by Spain for over 300 years, and each achieved independence from Spain at about the same time, although under quite different circumstances. Fourth, both have been greatly affected by their geography and topography. Fifth, both have suffered from the effects of civil wars, and in the case of Paraguay, an international war.

We must take other points of resemblance into account. Both countries have suffered long periods of dictatorship and corrupt rule by unscrupulous *caudillos* (leaders, or bosses, usually of military rank) who had little regard for the legislative or judicial branches of the government. The economic systems of Venezuela and Paraguay were, until the discovery of oil in Venezuela in 1914, both based on feudalistic estates called *latifundia* or *haciendas* that were maintained by tenant farmers and peons. (The plantation system was far more widespread in Venezuela than it was in Paraguay, however).

The political cultures of Paraguay and Venezuela have been and still are characterized to a considerable degree by a subject and parochial population. This means that only a small minority of the people have been involved in an effective way in the input process of the political system or have identified themselves meaningfully with their political structures.

Some of the differences that will be considered relate more fully to social forces, forms of government, and geographic locations. Paraguay has one of the most homogeneous populations in Latin America; Venezuela has a more mixed population. Paraguay is a landlocked country; Venezuela faces both the Atlantic Ocean and the Caribbean Sea. Paraguay has always been governed under a unitary system of government, while Venezuela has shown a distinct preference for the federal form. Both, however, operate under a unitary system.

In spite of the numerous similarities, Venezuela and Paraguay today present considerable contrasts in terms of social development, economic progress, and political stability. Venezuela is the richest country in Latin America, Paraguay one of the poorest. Venezuela has a gross national product of $7.1 billion and an annual income of $6.6 billion. Its average per capita income is $865, the highest in Latin America. Paraguay is much worse off with a gross national product of only $457 million, an annual income of $334 million, and an average per capita income of $174.

Venezuela is undergoing tremendous economic changes and social and political upheaval as a result of government-directed attacks on traditional bases of power. Giving way to the reforms of the Betancourt and Leoni administrations are antiquated educational and economic philosophies, illiteracy, grossly unequal patterns of landownership, and widespread unemployment. Three peaceful, fair elections since 1959 indicate that authoritarian political patterns are also beginning to change. For the first time in 133 years of independence, the political leadership was able in 1964 to transmit power peacefully from one constitutionally elected president to another. Opposition parties are now relatively free to organize and to participate in the electoral process and in the actual governing of the nation. Indeed, coalition government has become a necessity because the ruling party does not enjoy a majority in either house of the national congress. This situation is a new development for Venezuela, where the president has traditionally had complete control of a subservient congress.

Venezuela has entered the twentieth century determined to take advantage of all the industrial and technological advances of the times. It is endeavoring to bring into congruity its democratic ideals (as expressed in the 1961 constitution) and its traditional political culture. The task will be a long and painful one, for many traditional and parochial attitudes persist that will impede progress toward formation of a truly participant, allegiant culture. The considerable progress already achieved in such areas as education and land reform speak well for future progress. We must not, however, discount the possibility of a new eruption of violence and a forceful overthrow of government, for there is a high degree of potential instability within the system as old values and goals are challenged by forces that are only beginning to articulate their demands in the freer political atmosphere that now prevails.

By way of contrast, Paraguay, on the basis of observable

progress, must be considered a relatively static country. George Pendle, an authority on Paraguay, revisiting the country in 1966 after an absence of ten years, observed that practically nothing had changed during that decade. Paraguayans took a longer view. They felt the problems of Paraguay in 1966 were those of 400 years ago.[2] Paraguayan political orientations remain largely subject-centered. The political system continues to be dominated by one man (as it has been throughout its history), and by the same elite groups that have controlled the country since independence. It may be said, therefore, that Paraguay, in spite of almost yearly attempts by its citizens in exile to unseat the government, is a politically stable country in the sense that there is order and continuity in government.

President Alfredo Stroessner has been in power since 1954 and rules the country with a firm hand. Paraguay has never been free of dictatorships. No fundamental changes are being undertaken, although there are plans on paper for them. Opposition parties do not play a significant role in the political process; educational facilities are inadequate and about one-third of the Paraguayan people live in exile in Uruguay, Argentina, and Brazil. Social and economic forces bent on change are not allowed expression. Paraguay has not yet entered the twentieth century.

Thus we may observe that in the third quarter of the present century two countries of Latin America with similar backgrounds and institutions are at very different stages of development. The task of this book is to account for the dissimilar paces of evolution. The theme of the book will be a study of contrasts: Venezuela is a dynamic, prosperous, volatile country engaged in democratizing both her economic and political system. Paraguay is a backward, slow-moving, impoverished nation under the control of a military dictator whose goals are strongly influenced by his desire to preserve his own power base.

GEOGRAPHIC BASES OF POLITICS

The terrain and topography of South America have almost everywhere created severe problems for the political, cultural, and

[2] George Pendle, *Paraguay, A Riverside Nation,* 3d ed. (London: Oxford, 1967), p. v.

commercial life of most of the countries on the continent. Great mountain walls between three and four miles high on the west coast, vast rain forests and jungles in the interior and on the eastern coast, hot and inhospitable deserts, extensive featureless plains, and cold dreary stretches of land, such as those of Patagonia to the south, have all been major factors that block the integrating forces within the individual countries. In Brazil's 3.2 million square miles, for example, lie the world's largest swamp area, the world's most extensive river system, and the world's largest and densest rain forest. Landlocked Bolivia is sliced into three different regions: the intermountain valleys of the high Andes, the lower eastern slopes of these mountains, and the rain forests stretching toward Brazil. The list could be extended to all twenty republics.

Features such as these have created and prolonged the basic problem of internal isolation that plagues the communities of most of the Latin American nations, even to this day. Communications between regions of the same country, as well as between countries themselves, have been difficult to achieve. Regions are isolated from regions, and communities from communities.

Venezuela and Paraguay are good examples of the above generalization. Their geographical position on the continent of South America, their internal physical diversities and peculiarities, and the presence or absence of important natural resources all have affected the historical development of the two republics.

The different rates of economic development experienced by Venezuela and Paraguay can in part be assigned to their geographic location and their access to the sea. A map of Latin America (see Fig. 1) reveals a transcendental difference between the two countries. Paraguay is landlocked, whereas Venezuela stretches around the northern coast of South America for more than 1700 miles, facing both the Caribbean Sea and the Atlantic Ocean. Venezuela's advantageous location presents it with few problems of external communication and transportation. Direct shipping lines now connect it with the major commercial capitals of the world, and a well-developed airline network facilitates travel and commerce to all parts of the globe.

At the opposite end of the South American continent lies the riverside nation of Paraguay, wholly within the underdevel-

Figure 1 **Geographic divisions of the Republic of Venezuela**

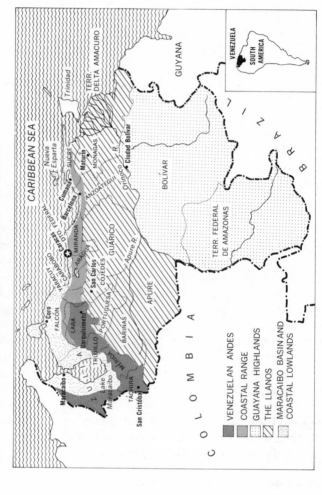

oped interior, cut off from any easy access to the outside world except through the territory of neighbors who have not always been friendly. Asunción, the capital city, lies 1000 miles from the Atlantic Ocean. To reach it and the Argentine markets with their international connections, Paraguayan trade and commercial interests must utilize the Paraguay-Paraná river system, 800 miles of which flows through Argentine territory. The river normally is deep enough to permit small ocean vessels to reach Asunción during the fall and winter months of March through October, but during the remaining four months the water level is so low that river traffic practically ceases. There are times, too, during the fall and winter months when the water level suddenly drops, stranding vessels in transit. International trade and travel are thus subject to the caprices of the river.

Because of its dependence on the river system, Paraguay must maintain friendly relations with its large and powerful neighbor, Argentina, through which most of the river runs. Not only does Argentina control the Paraguayan water routes and carry most of the Paraguayan imports and exports in its ships, but it also exercises a potential stranglehold on the sole railway connection Paraguay has with the outside world. Two-thirds of the 928 miles of railway between Asunción and Buenos Aires, the capital of Argentina, are in Argentine territory. These economic facts of life mean that Paraguay is essentially at the mercy of Argentina, and, indeed, the latter has for centuries had a preponderant influence on its affairs. This unfortunate situation has exacerbated the historical Paraguayan jealousies and suspicions of Argentina. The little country is, however, making some progress in freeing itself from Argentine domination by developing new transportation routes, mainly with Brazil. The establishment of air lines with other countries is gradually bringing some changes to Paraguay, especially to that segment of society which participates in the cultural and political life of the capital city. It has left the rural masses largely untouched.

Major geographical regions of Venezuela

Venezuela has an area of 352,000 square miles and is about 1.5 times the size of Texas. It supports a population of 9.7 million.

Although some geographers see as many as eight distinct geographical regions in Venezuela, the customary description confines itself to four principal areas: the Guayana highlands, the llanos (or plains), the Andean highlands, and the Maracaibo Basin. These regions vary greatly in size, wealth, productivity, climate, population, and influence in national affairs.

The Guayana highlands   Largest in size is the Guayana highlands, a vast, remote, upland territory extending south of the Orinoco River to the northern border of Brazil and east to the boundary of the new South American state of Guayana (formerly British Guiana). This territory is totally encompassed within the boundaries of the state of Bolívar and the federal territory of Amazonas. The country is spectacularly beautiful, with savannahs and fantastic plateaus that rise steeply from the floor of the forest. It is the country that inspired the locale of Sir Arthur Conan Doyle's famous novel *The Lost World*. It also contains Angel Falls, the highest waterfall in the world. The highlands represent 45.1 percent of the total area of Venezuela but can claim only 3 percent of its population. This great segment of land was for many years the least important portion of Venezuela. It contributed very little to the national economy; it exerted no influence in national affairs and consequently was ignored by the government.

Much of the Guayana highlands still is unexplored and inaccessible, but great strides have been made in the last decade toward opening the northern rim and incorporating it as an effective partner in the national economy. The new surge of interest results from the discovery of rich deposits of valuable natural resources. These, combined with cheap sources of water power, a fuel and a natural transportation route, make the area an attractive one for industrial development. Hydroelectric projects completed or under construction on the Caroní River (see Fig. 2) have a projected capacity three times the total 1968 electrical output of Venezuela. When completed, the great Guri Dam on the Caroní will have a capacity of 6 million kilowatts, the largest individual capacity in the world. So great is the potential, that government officials claim their plants can supply not only all of Venezuela's future needs but also will be able to transmit power to Brazil and Colombia.

The transportation route is the 1600-mile long Orinoco River. It is navigable for oceangoing vessels as far as Puerto

Figure 2   Venezuela opens a treasure chest

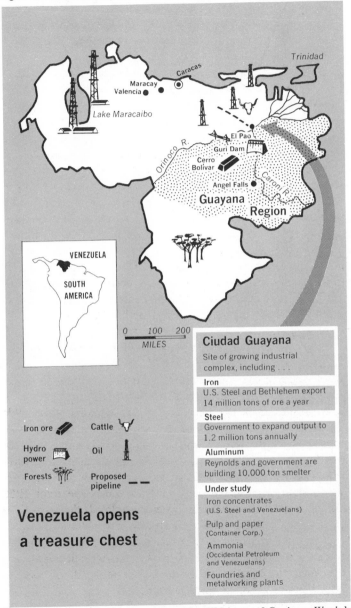

Ordaz, which lies at the juncture with the Caroní River, a distance of 220 miles from the Atlantic Ocean.

The area is rich in natural resources. Not only does the northern highland have reserves of coal (a scarce commodity in Latin America), diamonds, and bauxite, but it also contains the tremendous mountain of iron ore, Cerro Bolívar. The mountain is 2600 feet high and 7.5 miles long with a proven reserve of 1.3 billion tons of high-grade iron ore. About 35,000 tons of ore a month are shipped ninety miles by rail to Puerto Ordaz where it is loaded into vessels for shipment to the United States. Another major asset of the Guayana region is its proximity to petroleum fields north of the Orinoco River; these contain a proven reserve of some 2.2 billion barrels of oil and 11 trillion cubic feet of gas.

Such advantageous circumstances have greatly increased the government's interest in the economic possibilities of the region. To make maximum use of its potential, the Venezuelan government has created the Guayana Corporation to plan for and to supervise its economic growth. American industrial concerns are sharing in the exciting adventure of creating a new industrial giant, as are American technical experts. A whole new industrial complex is beginning to take shape. Already in operation is the Orinoco steel mill, which is well on its way to producing its second millionth ton of steel. An aluminum plant will soon be in production and eighty new additional industrial establishments are planned. When these are constructed and in operation, the area may become one of the great industrial centers of the hemisphere and of the world. To service this burgeoning complex, a whole new city, Ciudad Guayana, is being built. Together with its port, Puerto Ordaz, it had a population in 1968 of 100,000. By 1972 that population is expected to triple.

It should be clear from the above account of the Guayana highlands that its northern portion, at least, is rapidly developing into one of the most productive and influential regions in Venezuela. As population streams to the new jobs created by its industrial growth, the region will play an increasingly important role in the economic and political life of the nation. Indeed, conservative government estimates predict that by 1980 industry in the region will be contributing 20 percent of the total industrial output of Venezuela and will be manufacturing 20 percent of its total exports.

The llanos   A second major region of Venezuela, known as the *llanos,* is the great flat interior plain that lies between the Orinoco River and the narrow coastal range of mountains on the Caribbean Sea. This vast area extends from the eastern slopes of the Andes in western Venezuela to the delta of the Orinoco River on the Atlantic Ocean 600 miles away. Partly cleared savannah and partly dense jungle, its average width is 200 miles and its maximum elevation is 700 feet. The llanos take up 35.5 percent of Venezuela's national domain and supports more than 1.4 million people or 18 percent of the population of the nation. Population density is about 10 persons per square mile.

As a whole it is a disagreeable region in which the climate alternates between prolonged periods of rain and dry, dusty heat. Cattle raising has always been the principal occupation of the plains and only recently have scientific methods been introduced. The 1961 census revealed 6.4 million cattle on the plains.

Most of the native Indians avoided the harsh environment of the llanos, but those who lived there intermarried with the Spaniards and other European settlers. They produced a tough, nomadic breed of men who clung tenaciously to the land and to the great roving herds of cattle. These *llaneros,* or plainsmen, were "rough, illiterate horsemen who feared neither God nor man." [3] Contemptuous of the refinements of civilization, always ready for adventure and war, they have played an important part in the history of Venezuela. In the war of independence they provided a savage fighting force for the side that could command and hold their loyalty. The great llanero General José Antonio Páez is today revered as the father of Venezuela. Essentially men of the saddle, they were, and still are, not much given to the sedentary pursuits of agriculture. Although essential food crops are now being grown on a commercial scale (rice in Guárico and Portuguesa and cotton in Guárico and Anzoátegui), the llaneros are not enthusiastic about tilling the soil.

The population of the llanos is predominantly rural. Sixty-

[3] Hubert Herring, *A History of Latin America, from the Beginnings to the Present* (New York: Knopf, 1959), p. 265.

five percent of the people live in communities of less than 2000 persons, and a high percentage live in much smaller communities. The principal cities are, in general, capitals of the states that comprise it, such as Maturín, Barinas, Guanare, San Fernando de Apure, and San Carlos. Seven of Venezuela's twenty states lie within the boundaries of the llanos: Barinas, Portuguesa, Apure, Cojedes, Monagas, Anzoátegui, and Guárico. The federal territory of Delta Amacuro is also a part of the plains region. The llanos is economically very important to the economy of Venezuela, for it supplies about 22 percent of the crude oil production.

The culture and way of life of this fascinating region of Venezuela has been vividly portrayed by the Venezuelan novelist Rómulo Gallegos in his classic, *Doña Barbara*.

The Andean highlands   The mountain highlands constitute a third major geographical region of Venezuela. They are part of the great Andean range that dominates the western coast of South America. The chain divides in Colombia, and the easternmost cordillera branches northward almost to the border of Venezuela, where it in turn divides. One range continues almost due north and becomes the western boundary line between Venezuela and Colombia. The other arches off to the northwest and runs parallel to the northern rim of Venezuela. Between the two branches lies the Maracaibo Basin. The southernmost section of the Venezuelan Andes borders on Colombia and contains the three states of Táchira, Mérida, and Trujillo. For many years this land of high peaks, called by the Venezuelans the Sierra Nevada de Mérida, was the most inaccessible part of the Andean highlands. Because of its inaccessibility and low commercial productivity it did not attract large landowners. Smaller landholdings therefore characterized the landowning pattern. The Sierra is the most intensively cultivated area of the country, with about 12 percent of the land being farmed. In Venezuela as a whole, only 2 percent of the land is in crops.

The successful introduction of coffee as a commercial crop several decades ago ended the isolation of the Andes and has helped to integrate the area into the economic life of the country. Táchira is the largest coffee-producing state in Venezuela. The

Andean states today supply about 20–25 percent of the total agricultural output of the country.

About 1 million people live in the Sierra. The principal cities are San Cristóbal, Valera, and Mérida. Mérida is a proud, aristocratic city, the seat of a university, a cultural center, and the home of distinguished Catholic families. It has long considered itself to be the equal of Caracas, and a cultural rivalry has persisted between the two cities for years.

The Andean area is characterized by a basically white population. About 20 percent of Venezuela's people are white and the majority of them live in the Andes. In the mestizo strain in the Andes, the predominant element is Indian.

Between the Sierra Nevada de Mérida and the Caribbean coast are the Segovia highlands. Because of the scanty rainfall, recurring droughts, scrub forests, and numerous savannahs, much of the agricultural activity of the region is of the subsistence variety. There is also some cattle raising and at least one mining operation. Most of the population is found in small clusters around water sources. Venezuela's only desert is in the oil-producing state of Falcón on the Caribbean Sea. Other states of the Segovia highlands are Lara and Yaracuy.

The Andean spur that becomes the coastal range continues almost unbroken across the northern coastal area of Venezuela to the Paria Peninsula in the northeastern portion of Venezuela. In the central section of the coastal range are found the capital city of Caracas and the rich and fertile basin of Lake Valencia that contains some of the best agricultural land in the country. Here are found large coffee plantations, sugarcane haciendas, and cattle ranches. Until agrarian reform set in, the region was dominated by large estates with peon or tenant farmer labor.

The coastal range has always been the economic, social, religious, and political center of the nation. Although many of the rulers of Venezuela have come from the states of the Sierra de Mérida, political power has been exercised from Caracas. The states of Carabobo, Aragua, Miranda, and the Federal District constitute the nuclear region of Venezuela and contain 32.5 percent of the total population, or approximately 2.5 million people.

The northeastern end of the coastal range terminates in the

Paria Peninsula. It is a poor area that does not readily support a population and on the whole is of little consequence. Off the coast of Sucre is the island state of Nueva Esparta, famous for its pearl fishing.

The Andean section of Venezuela represents only 12 percent of the land area of the nation, but it supports two-thirds of Venezuela's population and produces the bulk of the national income.

The Maracaibo Basin and the coastal lowlands The final distinct geographic division of Venezuela consists of the V-shaped Lake Maracaibo Basin and the long narrow strip of land that lies between the coastal range and the Caribbean Sea. The Maracaibo Basin is encompassed totally by the state of Zulia. The steamy, unpleasantly warm climate in the basin did not attract settlers until oil transformed the economy of the region. Today the basin boasts the thriving city of Maracaibo, Venezuela's second largest metropolitan center, with a population of about 550,000. Great reserves of oil lie beneath Lake Maracaibo, and the rigs of large numbers of producing wells dot the surface of the lake. In 1965, Lake Maracaibo produced 76.5 percent of the national petroleum output. The Maracaibo Basin is also rich in excellent agricultural lands and cattle ranches.

The basin and the lowlands have a population of about 2 million people, 77 percent of whom are classified as urban. Important coastal cities and ports are La Guaíra, Puerto La Cruz, Cumaná, and Carúpano. Negro and mulatto influence is particularly strong in these areas, as it is in Caracas.

Major geographic regions of Paraguay

Paraguay has an area of 150,047 square miles and a population of about 2.1 million people. Paraguay also presents striking geographical diversities, but it concentrates them in fewer regions. The contrast between its two principal sectors is startling (see Fig. 3). Even more unusual is their abrupt separation by the Paraguay River. Nowhere else in the world does a river separate two such diverse lands.[4]

[4] Pendle, p. 2.

**Figure 3   Geographic divisions of the Republic
of Paraguay**

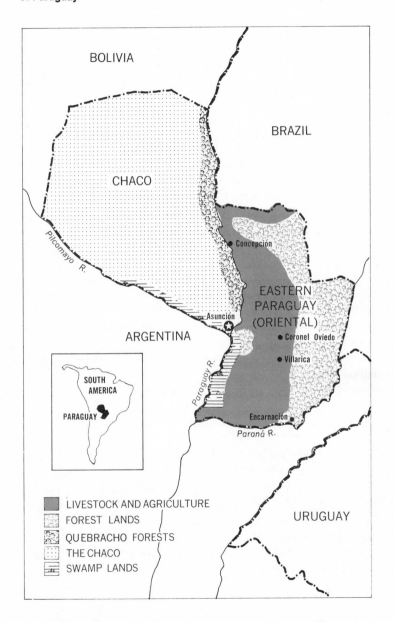

The Chaco The 96,000 square miles of Paraguayan territory lying west of the Paraguay River is a part of a larger geographical area, the Gran Chaco, which lies in Argentina, Paraguay, and Bolivia, and which is thought to have been the bed of an inland sea. Maximum elevation of this enormous territory is about 700 feet. Although there are some jungle areas in the northern portion, the region is overwhelmingly a grim, gray wilderness. Most of the vast expanse is covered with scrubby grass that grows up to three feet in height. Its natural rhythm is determined by dry and wet seasons, with dry predominating. Water drains off into sluggish, crocodile-infested streams or evaporates rapidly. Heat, dust, animal and insect life, and above all, thirst, make life a misery in most of the region. Battles were fought by Paraguayan and Bolivian forces in the Chaco War (1932–1935) over water-holes, for their control meant victory. This lonely region is a "plain with the soul of a mountain, motionless and hard as steel." [5] It is an isolated and empty land for the most part. About 30,000 Indians roam the interior, keeping apart from the dominant civilization. A few hardy religious groups, such as the Mennonites, have established colonies there and eke out a living in the inhosptiable region. The population density of the Chaco is 1.3 persons per square mile as compared with 14.2 in Paraguay as a whole.

For reasons such as these, the Chaco has remained almost completely outside the national life of Paraguay. Yet it has played an important role in the political fortunes of the country. It was here that Paraguay expended more than 39,000 of her young men and $124 million in a disastrous war with Bolivia over the ownership of the northern portion.

It can be seen that the Chaco is in many ways similar to the llanos of Venezuela, but the latter is more a part of the nation in a physical sense than is the Chaco. The llanos has sustained a population and has produced a distinct way of life. It has some fairly large cities. The Chaco has none worth mentioning. We can expect its isolation to decrease as the nation builds new roads toward its neighbor, Bolivia. Oil deposits have been found in the Chaco, and cattle raising and lumber products afford a

[5] Pendle, p. 2.

meager living for its inhabitants. In spite of these minor advances, however, the Chaco remains for the most part an unintegrated section of Paraguay.

Eastern Paraguay   Across the Paraguay River lies eastern Paraguay, or the Oriental as it is called by Paraguayans. Here are rich meadows, great grasslands, luxuriant green growth, numerous rivers, hills, and widespread forests. In the semitropical climate orchards flourish, birds sing, and life is relatively pleasant and orderly. Rainfall is adequate the year around.

There are well-defined areas in the Oriental. Some are suitable for large cattle ranches, others for orchards, sugarcane, cotton plantations, and tobacco farms. However, only 2.1 percent of the land is used for such purposes. A sizable portion (59.6 percent) of the land in the northern section of the Oriental is forested, and lumber industries produce considerable revenue.

Sixty-five percent of the Paraguayan people live in the Oriental and within a 120-mile radius of Asunción, the heart and pulse of the nation.

ECONOMIC BASES OF POLITICS

Paraguay

Unlike its northern sister republic, Paraguay is essentially devoid of most valuable minerals except limestone. Small deposits of mica, kaolin, copper, and bauxite are present, but important raw materials such as iron, tin, natural gas, manganese, nickel, and phosphates are either totally absent or present in such minute quantities as to be commercially unimportant. The extent of the Chaco oil deposits have yet to be determined.

Although Paraguay and Venezuela each have about 32 percent of their populations economically active, patterns of production and occupation are very different. In Paraguay 52 percent of the labor force is engaged in agricultural pursuits and produce 37 percent of the gross national product (compare Venezuela's 33 percent and 7 percent, respectively). Industry employs 19 percent of the labor force and produces 16 percent of the gross national product (GNP). The commercial sector absorbs 7 percent of the working population and produces 16 percent of the GNP. Three percent are in public services and the remainder in diverse occupations.[6]

Paraguay's GNP has been increasing at 4 percent a year since 1963. Government revenues in 1970 were $58.9 million, and expenditures were $60.5 million. The republic has a foreign debt of $100 million. No reliable figures are available on the amount of foreign investment in Paraguay.

In the area of transportation and communication facilities, Paraguay has the following: 309 miles of railways, 7876 miles of highways, 19,962 telephones (1.5 for every 100 persons), 8 newspapers, 19 radio stations, 160,000 radio sets, and 20,000 automobiles. Until 1967 there were no television stations or sets in Paraguay.

Much of the wealth and resources of Paraguay are in the hands of foreign owners, principally Argentine interests, which control 75 percent of the manufacturing establishment and the river transport system, as well as large amounts of land. Even the commercial activity of Asunción is dominated by first-generation immigrants from Italy, Lebanon, and Syria.

The economy of Paraguay is an agrarian one, with a majority of the population involved in agricultural pursuits. Sixty-five percent of these people are subsistence squatters who do not own their land and who contribute very little to the economic life of the nation. According to the Inter-American Development Bank

> the system of land tenure has been one of the most important limiting factors in Paraguay's agricultural development. The problem of squatters, which numbered about 65,800 in 1956 is particularly serious. About half of these occupied state-owned lands.[7]

The agricultural sector is marked by both *minifundia* (small landholdings) and *latifundia* (large landholdings). Sixty-nine percent of the farmers own 2.5 percent of the farm area in hold-

[6] *Social Progress Trust Fund: Fifth Annual Report, 1965* (Inter-American Development Bank, 1966), p. 497.
[7] *Social Progress Trust Fund: Fifth Annual Report, 1965*, p. 507.

ings of less than ten hectares (one hectare equals 2.47 acres). At the other end of the scale are the 534 estates of 5000 or more hectares each. These account for 73.5 percent of the total farm area.

Paraguay's unit of currency is the guaraní, exchangeable at the rate of 125 to the dollar.

Venezuela

Rich in natural resources, many of which are still waiting to be developed, Venezuela nevertheless has for many years been considered a monocultural country, almost entirely dependent on oil production. The discovery of iron ore in quantity has eased the situation somewhat. Most of the output of these two great industries, particularly that of oil, goes to world markets, thus tying Venezuela to the fluctuations in world prices over which she has no control. When one considers the fact that mining and petroleum provide 92 percent of the government's total yearly revenue and account for 28.5 percent of the GNP, Venezuela's concern with its lopsided economy is understandable. Diversification and industrialization are important objectives in modern Venezuela, for a stable revenue base is essential to the economic plans of the government.

Two percent of the economically active population (about 33 percent of the total population) are engaged in the oil and iron industries. Thirty-three percent, on the other hand, are employed in agricultural activities and produce only 7 percent of the GNP. This is understandable since many farmers produce no more than they can consume.

The manufacturing, construction, and power sector of the economy in 1964 accounted for 20.7 percent of the GNP, while communications, transportation, services, and commerce contributed 43.8 percent.

The unit of currency is the bolívar. It is exchangeable at the rate of 4.5 to the dollar and is considered one of the soundest currencies in the world.

The gross national product of Venezuela increased at an annual rate of 8 percent between 1950 and 1959. Since then, it has leveled off to a yearly average increase of between 6 and 7 percent. The government presented a balanced budget in 1969 in which revenues and expenditures were each estimated at $2 billion. The public debt in 1966 was $489 million.

Transportation and communication facilities in Venezuela are as follows: 220 miles of railroads, 30,000 miles of highways, 309,000 telephones (3 for every 100 persons), 36 newspapers, 170 radio stations, 1,660,000 radios, 30 television stations, and 650,000 television sets. There are some 550,000 registered motor vehicles.

SOCIAL BASES OF POLITICS

The social structures of Venezuela and Paraguay may be classified as traditional systems in that the people are polarized between a dominant and extremely small industrial and agricultural oligarchy and a massive landless and poor urban and rural proletariat. Paraguay is more traditional than is Venezuela, for it has only the rudiments of a middle class. Venezuela, on the other hand, is in a transitional stage in which a middle class is growing and acquiring an identity and a set of goals of its own.

In Paraguay only 10 percent of the population falls within the category of the upper stratum of society, which includes both the upper and middle class. In general this entire group is an urban class, with the exception of landowners and cattlemen —and even they maintain town houses. Most of the upper echelons of society live in the capital city—the center of culture, politics, and industry. Indeed, about one-fifth of the total population of Paraguay lives in Asunción or in one of the other three principal cities, none of which exceeds 20,000. Mere residence in Asunción confers status. Those who live there, regardless of their social station, clearly regard the inhabitants of the provincial areas with disdain and contempt.[8] The members of the highest social rung are ranking members of the Catholic hierarchy, eminent politicians, the elite of the military forces, university circles, commercial and industrial magnates, highly acclaimed intellectuals, and the landed gentry and cattlemen. The middle class reflects similar occupations, although on a lower level of

[8] Elman R. Service and Helen S. Service, *Tobatí: A Paraguayan Town* (Chicago: The University of Chicago Press, 1954), p. 141.

achievement: merchants and tradesmen, government workers, primary- and secondary-school teachers, shop attendants, and the lower ranks of the armed forces and the Church.[9] Both groups in the upper stratum have their own clubs and social centers and do not intermix. A significant part of the business middle class in Paraguay is made up of recent immigrant, many of whom are from the Middle East. Some also have Italian and Spanish fathers or grandfathers and thus tend to appear more European than do the rural peasants, who present an Indian appearance. The peasants regard the tradesmen of the towns with hatred, distrust, and envy and refer to them as "sons of foreigners." [10] Tradesmen's attitudes toward the peasants are hardly more complimentary, and thus significant social cleavages exist between the two groups.

The lower and by far the larger portion of the citizenry is the rural and urban proletariat. Between the lowest-ranking rural peasant—the peon, who has only his labor to sustain him —and the large landowners are those who own a few acres, those who rent land, and those who merely squat on it temporarily. About 65 percent of the Paraguayan lower class is rural. The influence of the peasant, however, has been minimal.

Venezuela's social structure is less unbalanced but it too reveals a lopsided polarization between the upper and lower classes. Today, as a result of increasing numbers of immigrants who settle in the cities, the establishment of many new small industries and businesses, growing government services, and expanding educational facilities, the urban middle class is growing steadily. It is presently estimated that 15 percent of the economically active population (about 350,000 persons) engage in occupations that place them in the middle sectors of society: [11] this includes small businessmen, professional men, government employees, teachers and professors, and, of course, the officer

[9] Cesar R. Acosta argues that the owners of between one and fifty hectares of land in Paraguay may be considered as an elemental part of an emerging rural middle class. See "La Población rural del Paraguay," *Materiales para el Estudio de la Clase Media en La América Latina,* Vol. III (Washington, D.C.: Union Panamericana, 1950), p. 104.

[10] Service and Service, p. 43.

[11] Edwin Lieuwin, *Venezuela,* 2d ed. (London: Oxford, 1965), p. 16.

class of the military establishment. The very small upper class (5 percent of the total population) is made up of the old land-owning aristocratic families and the new industrial giants and large urban property holders. The landowning class is decreasing as Venezuela moves ahead with its agrarian reforms. Except for the size of its middle classes and the larger concentration of the proletariat in the cities, the Venezuelan social division is very much like that of Paraguay.

Class determinants in both countries include race, family, wealth, occupation, and education. Although the people of Venezuela and Paraguay are relatively free of racial discrimination, white persons are almost always found in the upper sections of the social scale and blacks at the bottom. Latin Americans insist that this situation is a matter of economic status rather than one of prejudice. Inherited wealth is a vital factor in one's claims to social position. Large acreages are particularly valuable indicators of wealth, while fortunes accumulated through business acumen and industrial ventures rate slightly below land ownership. Industrial wealth is more important in Paraguay than in Venezuela as many of the landed aristocrats lost their properties during the War of the Triple Alliance (1864–1870). In Venezuela there is a tendency for the old established families, who see their wealth threatened by agrarian reforms, to ally themselves with the industrial sector through marriage—an illustrious name in exchange for new wealth.

Occupation and education, of course, depend in large part upon family position and resources. Family ties are particularly important because in Venezuela and Paraguay about 50 percent of the children born each year are illegitimate. A proper family name is therefore a considerable asset in these "who-oriented" societies.

Elman and Helen Service found in their penetrating study of a typical Paraguayan town that education as a class determinant was particularly stressed. This may be because not many Paraguayans possess much wealth. Education was broadly defined to mean "not only formal education, but also good manners, modern sophistication, cleanliness and uprightness in conduct." [12] Those who qualified were called *la sociedad* (soci-

---

[12] Service and Service, p. 136.

ety); those who did not, *la gente* (the people)—unless they had wealth enough to compensate for their educational deficiencies. The distinctions between these two groups in society in the towns of Paraguay were maintained on all social and official occasions in segregated meetings. Between those who lived in towns and the rural peasants there were also clear differences. Peasants could be distinguished by appearance, dress, speech (usually faulty Spanish and a reliance on Guaraní), manners, and an almost total ignorance of national or international affairs.

Both Venezuela and Paraguay have basically very young populations. In each country about 65 percent of the total population is under twenty-five years of age, and only 10 percent is over fifty years of age. The political ramifications of this population distribution will be discussed in later chapters. Both populations are increasing at an annual rate of 3.0–3.5 percent. Venezuela has a population density of 25 persons per square mile, Paraguay, 14.2—two of the lowest densities in Latin America. With proper land utilization far larger populations could be supported in both countries, and each is endeavoring to encourage immigration.

Ethnically, the two populations are also similar. The distribution in Venezuela is as follows: mestizo, 68 percent; white, 20 percent; Negro, 10 percent; and Indian, 2 percent. Statistics for Paraguay are more difficult to come by, but most authorities agree that the overwhelming majority of the people are descendants of the Spaniards and the indigenous Guaraní Indians. Estimates of those with mixed blood range from 75 percent to 90 percent. Thus, depending upon which figure is accepted for the mestizo element, between 10 and 20 percent of the present population is white. Negroes account for less than 1 percent and Indians for 3 percent. The white element of society has been growing in Paraguay since the end of the War of the Triple Alliance as a result of European immigration. The non-Latin immigrants (Lebanese, Syrians, Germans, Japanese, and so on) have preserved their cultural and genetic identity, while the Latin immigrants (Italians, Spaniards, Argentines, and so on) have intermarried with the mixed bloods. All are, however, ardent Paraguayan nationalists.[13]

[13] Service and Service, pp. 42–43.

SUMMARY

If there is virtue in homogeneity, then Paraguay would rate high indeed, because it is considered to be one of the most homogeneous countries in Latin America. It is, however, perfectly clear that homogeneity by itself has produced no significant results in Paraguay other than contributing to an exaggerated sense of nationalism. It has not produced clearly defined political objectives, effective economic planning, or a modern participating society.

Whatever advantage lies in homogeneity of population is offset in Paraguay by its geographical and intellectual isolation and the paucity of its natural resources essential to the development of a modern, democratic industrial state. Unless Paraguay has hidden resources awaiting discovery, it seems likely that its future will be linked to the development of its considerable agricultural potential.

Venezuela is far better endowed with physical, human, and material resources. With its rich natural resources, its willingness and wealth to explore and exploit them, and its advantageous geographical position, Venezuela is well on its way to becoming an industrial power in Latin America.

The persistence in both countries of a traditional social structure that divides the majority of the people into upper and lower classes and which results in elite concepts of government and status quo outlooks will hinder the development of mobile, participating, and socially conscious majorities. If one accepts the controversial thesis that a sizable and economically stable middle class is an essential, but by no means the only, ingredient contributing to the emergence of a modern democratic society, then one might be pessimistic about the realization of such a society in Paraguay. Venezuela's growing middle sector, although relatively small, points to a growing modernization of society in that country.

The youthfulness of their populations presents both republics with formidable challenges in the creation of jobs and housing to meet the minimum needs of the large numbers of young people who enter the adult job market each year. Not the least of the problems facing the two governments is that of trying to accommodate the rising aspirations of the youthful sector of society who are growing impatient with traditional molds and objectives. Venezuela's social and economic resources and the recent appearance of some elements of democracy in its political system will make this task easier for it than for Paraguay.

ONE
THE DEVELOPMENT
OF VENEZUELA
AND PARAGUAY

THE COLONIAL EPOCH: FOUNDATIONS OF NATIONHOOD

One aspect of the development approach to the study of political systems focuses on the problems common to all such systems: state building, nation building, participation, and distribution. State building involves the process of integration and control, that is, the creation of a police force and an administrative apparatus. Nation building concerns the problem of citizen identification with and loyalty to the system as a whole. Participation stresses the involvement of members of the society in the decision-making process of the system. And distribution is the problem of allocating the goods, services, symbols, and values of the system.[1] The latter is, of course, the essence of politics, which has been described as the process of deciding "who gets what, when, and how."

Developing systems meet these formidable challenges in varying ways and with varying degrees of success. The ability of a political system to socialize and recruit its members, to maintain and adapt itself to external and internal challenges, and to accommodate the raw demands of society, as well as the extent to which the system is secularized (that is, the extent to which it responds to rational, empirical, and analytical criteria rather than to emotional criteria) depends in part upon forces that

[1] Gabriel A. Almond and G. Bingham Powell, Jr., *Comparative Politics: A Developmental Approach* (Boston: Little, Brown, 1966), p. 314.

have played a significant role in the political evolution of the country.

Thus developmental theory stresses, among other things, the "impact of one of the most powerful sets of constraints and limitations which condition the future of political systems—their political past." [2] The theorists do not argue that history determines the future, but they do argue that it may well limit or foreclose certain alternatives as well as condition present responses to problems.

We have already pointed out the fact that although Venezuela and Paraguay began as somewhat similar entities, they are today far apart in terms of their overall development and certainly in the area of their political development. The purpose of this chapter is to explore the political past of Venezuela and Paraguay in an effort to discover how some of the restraints and limitations that now bear on their future development as political systems developed.

Discovery and settlement

Venezuela   Mainland Venezuela was discovered by Columbus on his third voyage in 1498. Venezuela's name (literally "little Venice") is attributed to the explorer Alonso de Ojeda, who was reminded of Venice when he first saw the crude houses built on stilts on Lake Maracaibo. The first Spanish settlement in the area was New Cadiz on the island of Cubagua. In 1521, what is now the city of Cumaná in eastern Venezuela was founded in the territory of the fierce Cumanagota Indians.

During most of its existence as a colony of Spain, Venezuela was a victim of Spain's indifference. The Crown made little attempt to develop it into a viable economic entity after it was clear that quick riches were not to be had in the province. The indifference became neglect, which in turn brought isolation from the cultural currents of metropolitan Spain. For a period of over thirty years in the seventeenth century not a single official Spanish ship called at Venezuelan ports. In part, this isolation from the intellectual influences of Europe can be traced to Spain's obsession with the need to keep its colonies free from the corrosive effects of foreign political and religious ideas. The

[2] Almond and Powell, p. 301.

partnership of church and state in the settlement of Latin America was a very strong one, indeed.

The neglect suffered by Venezuela (and Paraguay) cannot be attributed to the inability of the Spanish explorer to penetrate the area or maintain lines of communication with it. Indeed, the *conquistadores* were renowned for their extraordinary and heroic feats of exploration in the face of tremendous odds. It was riches they were after, but quick, spectacular, easily exploited riches were lacking in Venezuela. Consequently many Spanish explorers moved on in search of the fabled kingdom of El Dorado, whose king was reputed to bathe in gold dust.

Venezuela gradually became a Spanish possession that did not pay its way. The Crown frequently found it necessary to draw funds from the treasuries in Mexico to pay the salaries of officials in Caracas. The state of affairs was a matter of grave concern to a government that expected its colonies to yield handsome returns.

Hopeful of obtaining some revenue from the colony and its inhabitants, the Spanish king in 1528 granted an economic monopoly to a German banking family. Their unenlightened efforts ended in total failure, and the grant was revoked in 1548.

Caracas was founded in 1567 and ten years later became the provincial capital. It remained, however, a small, backward town during most of the colonial period.

Spanish indifference came to an abrupt end in 1730 when a group of Basque merchants from Spain was granted an agricultural monopoly in the colony. The Royal Guipuzcoa Company of Caracas was an unqualified success. Not only were its profits a source of joy and comfort to both the Crown and the company, but the latter's economic reforms and agricultural efforts encouraged new production in tobacco, cacao, sugar, and indigo. The import of Negro slaves was doubled from 1730 to 1739 in order to take care of increased labor demands. Important cultural developments that followed upon these advances were the creation of new schools (mostly under religious auspices) and the establishment of the University of Caracas.[3]

During the years of Spanish neglect, the inhabitants of Venezuela had grown accustomed to managing their own affairs,

[3] James Tello, "Historia del Petróleo en Venezuela," *El Farol* (January–March 1967), 36–37.

and they resented what they regarded as the despotic actions of the Guipuzcoa Company in raising the prices of its imports and refusing to pay Venezuelans adequate prices for their products. In 1749 an abortive revolt against the resident Spanish governor was led by a *criollo* judge who had been deposed in favor of a *peninsular* judge (a criollo was a Spaniard born in the colony; a peninsular, one born in Spain). Economic grievances as well as the favoritism shown to the peninsulars planted seeds of discontent that later found expression in the fight for independence. These and other activities of the company had a profound effect on the economic and political life of the country and, for all practical purposes, the long isolation of Venezuela was at an end.

The government in Spain was so impressed by the gratifying economic returns from Venezuela that it raised the colony to the level of a captaincy-general in 1777. Although nominally subject to the Viceroy of New Granada in Bogotá, the new entity was in fact almost autonomous. In 1785 the Crown withdrew the charter of the Caracas company in a rare gesture to the economic grievances of the Venezuelans.

The official policy of Spain during much of the colonial period had been to prevent economic intercourse between its colonies and between them and Spain's European competitors. Implementation of this policy proved difficult in Venezuela, for with its long coastline there were ample opportunities to trade with Dutch, French, English, and American smugglers. The traffic was not only in goods, but also in ideas. Educated Venezuelans were aware of the new revolutionary movements in America and Europe, and republican sentiment had its advocates. When the struggle for independence came, Venezuela had its articulate political thinkers, leaders, and agitators.

Paraguay   The origin of the name Paraguay is a matter of dispute. Some associate it with the Payaguas Indians, others with Lake Xarayes, a flooded lowland in which Indians believed the river to have its source.[4] The territory now encompassed by Paraguay was explored by the Spaniards early in the sixteenth century in their continuing search for gold. The city of Asunción

[4] Harris, Gaylord Warren, *Paraguay, An Informal History* (Norman, Okla.: University of Oklahoma Press, 1949), p. 3.

was founded on August 15, 1537, by Juan de Ayolas on the eastern shore of the Paraguay River. The site was chosen after an earlier attempt to consolidate a position near the present location of Buenos Aires had failed because of belligerent Indian opposition. The Guaraní Indians whom the Spaniards met in Paraguay were more friendly, however, and looked upon the white men as allies in their wars with other Indian tribes of the interior. The land, too, was friendly and yielded peanuts, potatoes, pumpkins, beans, and much variety in animal food.

Yet Paraguay suffered even more than did Venezuela from neglect by Spain and for some of the same reasons. Since it had no gold or silver to attract the conquistadores, it was passed by for the most part. It was not even on the principal trade routes between the rich mines of the Andes and ports that were later established on the Atlantic and Pacific coasts of South America. In spite of the fact that Asunción was the seat of Spanish colonial authority in the whole area of southern South America (known as the Plata Basin) from 1537 to 1617, it was never a center of vigorous Spanish administrative effort. It was simply too far distant and too poor for Spain to take an active and enthusiastic interest in it. With the transfer of government headquarters to Buenos Aires in 1617 (an action bitterly resented by the residents of Asunción, who considered themselves superior in every way to the people of Buenos Aires, a city they regarded as an offspring), Spanish interest in the area virtually ceased. No commercial companies were formed to exploit the riches of Paraguay. No period of economic growth such as that experienced by Venezuela after 1730 interrupted the stagnant tenor of life of the colony. Few travelers entered it. The difficulty of reaching Paraguay ensured an almost total immunity to the invigorating contact with new political ideas made possible by continuous commercial intercourse with other countries. Paraguay was denied even the excitement of dealing with smugglers, other than those from nearby Brazil. It is true that Paraguay was harassed by the slave raiders of Brazil, who were after the Indians in the Jesuit missions, but these contacts could hardly be called beneficial. Soon after its foundation as a colony Paraguay settled into an economy of subsistence agriculture, a way of life that still characterizes the activity of the majority of the population.

Spain's attitude of disinterest and its neglect of Paraguay produced, as it had in Venezuela, a people who had grown used to having their own way and who came to resent interference in their affairs by Spain's representatives. They were, however, proud of their status as the seat of Spanish authority in the Plata region, even though they did not wish to be too much subject to it. Their resentment flared into open rebellion in 1721 in the *Comunero* revolt, certainly one of the earliest and most serious rebellions against Spanish authority in South America.

The trouble started when an ambitious and covetous Spanish official persuaded the criollo elite of Asunción to depose a governor whose appointment most of them considered to be a violation of law and tradition and to install him in his place. The Crown, sensitive about attacks on its authority, naturally attempted to reinstate the ousted governor. Fifteen years of civil war and turmoil passed before it was finally successful.

In spite of such disturbances, cultural and commercial isolation endured as a way of life, and the coming of independence did not change matters. Paraguay on the eve of independence was a stagnant, ingrown culture.

Within the territory of what is today the Republic of Paraguay there were few obstacles in the way of the evolution of an integrated, unified, and fairly egalitarian society. Isolation, geography, and the predilection of both Spanish conquerors and the Indians disposed the people of the colony to settle in eastern Paraguay and in particular in the areas adjacent to Asunción. Thus there were no serious rival provincial jealousies to complicate the emergence of a new nation. The population grew to be remarkably homogeneous and nationalistic in its outlook toward the other areas of Spanish colonization. These and other characteristics made it easy for Dr. José Gaspar Rodríguez de Francia, Paraguay's first dictator, to set up an independent nation and for him and his successors to keep it unified and politically cohesive. These same attributes made possible the imposition of a series of long-lived dictatorships.

Social components of the colonial period

Venezuela, says Guillermo Morón, "is a country with a profoundly messianic temperament with egalitarian sentiments at the very roots of its history." [5] Today its citizens look with pride on their democratically elected government and on the visible evidences of democratic progress. Strongly motivated by feelings of social and personal equality, the people of Venezuela today are nevertheless conscious of glaring economic and political inequalities—survivals of the colonial period—and they look to their government to remedy the basic inequalities that still persist in the nation. The capability of the political system to respond to these desires is conditioned by the hard realities of the colonial period and by the events that have occurred since Venezuela gained its independence.

Paraguay is a nation with professed devotion to the concepts of equality and democracy, although without the experience of democracy at any time in its history.

Venezuela in 1970 is without doubt a far more politically mature and democratic nation than is Paraguay, but it has not always been so. At the time of independence (1811–1821) Venezuela's society was certainly undemocratic and characterized by a fairly rigid class structure. Paraguay entered its independent existence with a much more egalitarian society. Yet today it is, as it has always been, under a dictatorship. An examination of the early social structure of the two countries during their formative years will help us to understand the divergent developments following freedom from Spain.

The Spanish component   Having completed the monumental task of expelling the Moors from their homeland, the Spaniards after 1492 turned their enormous energies to creating the "greatest, most enduring, and in many respects, the most remarkable colonial empire which the world has yet seen." [6] Intrepid adventurers, idealists fired by religious and patriotic zeal and visions of wealth, they brought under the sway of Spain all the vast territories south of the Rio Grande River and even penetrated into much of what is now the United States. Their religion, their political ideals and values (for a discussion of the Spanish mentality and political personality, see Chapter Three), their social

---

[5] Guillermo Morón, "Venezuela," *Latin America and the Caribbean, A Handbook,* Claudio Vélez, ed. (New York: Praeger, 1968), p. 139.

[6] Cecil Jane, *Liberty and Despotism in Spanish America* (Oxford: Clarendon Press, 1929), p. 16.

mores, and their organization were impressed upon all the countries of Latin America except Brazil (Portuguese) and Haiti (French) in a remarkably short time.

The early conquistadores were men of action; later settlers were more sedentary. Both shared a common aversion to manual labor, which they considered—as do their descendants in Latin America today—degrading and denoting an inferior social position. To preserve their aristocratic standing, therefore, it was necessary for the Spaniards in the New World to find someone to do the physical work required for their continued survival. Indians and then imported Negro slaves were pressed into service on the plantations and in the mines of the colonies.

The conquistadores were seeking wealth through the discovery of minerals. Those who came later were content to derive sustenance from their great landed properties, even though many of them refused to live on their estates, preferring the glitter of urban life to the monotony of a bucolic, agricultural existence. Many of the large estates in Latin America today are managed for absent city-dwelling owners by resident overseers.

The colonial Spaniard was not greatly agitated by democratic notions of natural rights and equality. In Spain he had lived in a stratified and undemocratic society in which he knew his place. He transferred that concept of society to his New World possessions, where it has persisted in varying degrees in spite of the revolutions and constitutions whose goals have been to eradicate it.

The Indian component   The Spaniards found considerable diversity in the cultural levels and political organization among the Indian civilizations with which they came into contact in the New World. The Aztecs and the Incas, for example, exhibited brilliant, disciplined, and highly advanced cultures. The once-great civilization of the Mayas, on the other hand, was in the process of decay at the time of the Spanish conquest.

Most of the Indians found in Venezuela and Paraguay lived in varying degrees of primitiveness. In Venezuela they were divided by language, culture, and political and social organization. There were the gentle Arawaks on the coastal islands, the fierce, aggressive, and predatory Caribs and the Cumanagotas of the eastern mainland, the sedentary, farming Timotes of the

Andes, and the nomadic Achuagas and Guahibos of the llanos. The relations between the Spaniards and the Venezuelan Indians were generally hostile, not only because most of the latter were warlike by nature, but also because of the adverse effects on them of the slave raids carried out by the Spaniards. A number of the weaker tribes soon disappeared, victims of the alien civilization.

It has been asserted that "Indian warfare was the chief impediment to the settlement of Venezuela during the sixteenth century." [7] The many belligerent tribes presented the Spaniard with a formidable political and social challenge. The pacification of all the Indians proved to be beyond the ability of the state, and the Crown turned to the missionaries of the various religious orders for assistance. Their efforts, although considerably more successful than those of the State, did not bring about the measure of ecclesiastical and political control desired by either during the colonial period.[8]

Intermarriage occurred between the Spaniards and Indians of Venezuela, but it was naturally inhibited by the uncompromising nature of the principal tribes. As the Indians were "reduced"—that is, gathered into missions or assigned to landlords —the mixture of the races was accelerated. The decimation of the Indians through warfare, slavery, and disease made it necessary for the Spanish settlers to turn to Negro slaves as a cheap source of labor. As the latter mated readily with both the Indians and the Spaniards, the population began to take on a very mixed character.

In Paraguay, the friendly nature of the Indians made the settlement of the land far easier than had been the case in Venezuela. The ready acceptance of the Spaniards by the Guaraní Indians prevented the bloodshed and violence that marred the relations between the two peoples in Venezuela.

The Indian population of Paraguay belonged to the great Tupi-Guaraní family that occupied the Amazon and Plata basins.

[7] Donald E. Worcester and Wendell G. Schaeffer, *The Growth and Culture of Latin America* (New York: Oxford, 1956), p. 75.

[8] Mary Watters, *A History of the Church in Venezuela 1810–1830* (Chapel Hill, N.C.: The University of North Carolina Press, 1933), pp. 4–5.

Although most historians treat the Guaraní Indians as one tribe, they were in fact divided into numerous competing groups that were almost constantly at war with one another. Those that associated with the Spaniards were assisted in military ways against their enemies and thus came to dominate the others. The Guaranís had some skills in horticulture (the work of their women), but they were seminomadic.

In the early days of their occupation of Paraguay the Spaniards made little effort to enslave the Indians or to fit them into their own mold. Their attention, as was that of their compatriots in Venezuela, was fixed on the lure of great riches elsewhere. In Paraguay the Spaniards were content with the major contributions of the Indians: food and women. Being an expedient people and having brought few women with them on their explorations, the Spaniards quickly adopted a system in Paraguay that ensured them a source of labor and food as well as a position of status among the Guaraní. With the acquiescence of the Indian chiefs the Spaniards were fitted into the Indian lineage system on a kinship basis. The mutual attraction of the two races to each other, the benefits of military cooperation, and an almost complete lack of racial discrimination on the part of the Spaniard provided a fruitful environment for the miscegenation that took place. Through the kinship arrangement the Spaniards freely entered into a number of polygynous unions with many Indian women who, through their relations with the Spaniards, achieved higher status in their own society. The Services regard "the extensive polygyny of the first twenty years and the fact that the Spaniards and the Guaraní regarded each other as kinsmen after the Indian fashion . . . as two of the most important of the unusual circumstances which influenced subsequent cultural developments of colonial Paraguay." [9]

The mingling of the two races in both Venezuela and Paraguay was facilitated by the introduction of the *encomienda,* or grant, system. The encomienda was a Spanish device designed to regularize the use of the labor of the Indian population. One type of encomienda gave to the *encomendero* (the individual receiving the grant) a number of Indians to live in his household

[9] Elman R. Service and Helen S. Service, *Tobatí: A Paraguayan Town* (Chicago: The University of Chicago Press, 1954), p. 29.

or on his estate. They owed him in their personal services for an indefinite period without compensation. The encomendero was expected to care for and protect them. Another type of encomienda permitted the Indians to live in their own villages, but required them to render services to various encomenderos to whom they were assigned for specified times during the year in return for small favors. The Indian women assigned to the households often were taken in concubinage by their landlords. From time to time more Indians were brought from the villages to replenish those of the household and thus the fusion of the two races proceeded. The encomienda system was particularly useful in Venezuela, where a plantation system resting upon slave labor grew up. There it formed the basis of the modern hacienda complex as it did in many other areas in Latin America. The encomienda was never a great success in Paraguay because the plantation system did not develop there to such an extent.

In comparison with the Indian population, the Spaniards in Paraguay were a tiny but important minority. One result of the widespread interracial mating was that while the Hispanic values survived to become the dominant cultural determinants of the emerging society, the small Spanish class was not able to preserve its own racial identity, nor was it able to develop an elite socioeconomic class that could dominate the positions of power and influence (as happened in other colonies of Spain). There developed in Paraguay a high degree of internal cultural unity as a new, more egalitarian ethnic group arose from the blending of Indian and Spaniard.

The number of Negroes in colonial Paraguay was small. Because there were no great mines to exploit nor extensive plantations calling for slave labor, there was no need to import Negroes. Indians provided what labor force the Paraguayan economy needed.

The mestizo component   In most areas of Latin America when Indians and Spaniards met, there was unrestrained mating between them. The intermingling of the two people continued throughout the colonial period. This was particularly true in Paraguay, where the Spaniards eagerly adopted the Indian system of polygyny. "The *mestizo* children whom the conquerors begat in such profusion grew up about them and took over new vitality and enterprise where their fathers had left off." [10] Before many years had passed, neither Indian nor European element persisted in a pure form. The mestizos in Paraguay were legally considered white and of European origin, for the king had declared them to be Spaniards.[11] There were, of course, some persons of pure Spanish extraction in colonial Paraguayan society because the Crown persisted in its practice of sending native-born Spaniards to fill the administrative and ecclesiastical positions. The process of amalgamation of the ethnic elements in Paraguay was so thorough, however, that today the population is estimated to be between 80 and 90 percent mestizo.

In Venezuela, the Spanish aristocracy, both peninsular and criollo was able to preserve its separate identity, even while mixing with the other racial elements. Purity of blood came to be a hallmark of social distinction and position. Descendents of these people are concentrated in the Andes. Yet Venezuela, too, became a mestizo nation. There the bloodline was more complex as Indian and European mixed with Negroes, with whom they were associated in close proximity on the plantations.[12] Today the population of Venezuela is estimated to be 68 percent mestizo and mulatto, 20 percent white, 10 percent Negro, and the rest Indian.

Of the three principal ingredients in the colonial social structure, the mestizo has become the dominant one, both politically and socially, in the majority of Latin American nations. But this has not always been so. In the area in general, the mestizo throughout the colonial period was viewed with hostility, contempt, and suspicion. This "Indian caught in the skin of a Spaniard" was, in the minds of the upper classes, a disturbing and undisciplined element whose presence was deplored. The mestizo was generally regarded as having inherited the worst characteristics of his parent races. The unfortunate mestizo lived in a world of confusing values "where his mother and father lived in different cultures, had different standards of conduct,

[10] William S. Schurz, *This New World* (New York: Dutton, 1954), p. 149.
[11] Bailey W. Diffie, *Latin American Civilization, Colonial Period* (Harrisburg, Pa.: Stackpole, 1945), pp. 443–444.
[12] Carlos Siso, *La Formación del Pueblo Venezolano* (New York: Horizon House, 1941), pp. 184–185.

different notions of good and right, and different basic loyalties." [13] Most of the mestizos naturally aspired to the social position of their Spanish father. That they were unable to achieve it in most countries aroused their envy and frustration. For the most part, this was the situation that prevailed in Venezuela up to the struggle for independence from Spain.

In Paraguay, however, the mestizo enjoyed greater freedom and less social stigma than in any other Spanish colony in Latin America. The principal reason for this was that almost all Paraguayans were mestizos. Because they were regarded by law as white and European, they could hold minor government offices, command troops, pursue a military career, and were free from the tribute demanded of the Indians, opportunities denied to them elsewhere.[14] They shared with the criollos the commanding position in business and commerce, and, according to some historians, in Paraguayan society and government. Paraguay, in short, was a more democratic and egalitarian society in the colonial period than was Venezuela.

The tide began to turn for the mestizo in Venezuela after he had demonstrated his abilities as a soldier and fighter in the war for freedom. Having helped his country achieve nationhood, he was not to be denied a share in the power structure nor in the process of governing. This goal was not realized without considerable internal strife.

Class structure   As one might expect in the formation of a new society in which primitive peoples participated, social stratification was inevitable. Although the Spanish conquerors were happy to accept Indians and Negroes as sexual partners, they were not so disposed to regard them as social equals.

The social organization that the Spaniards brought with them was an aristocratic, hierarchical one in which class lines were rigidly drawn. At the apex of the colonial society were individuals of pure European descent. Within this upper stratum there was a basic undemocratic distinction between peninsulars and criollos. A high premium was attached to birth in Spain, for

[13] Frank Tannenbaum, *Ten Keys to Latin America* (New York: Knopf, 1963), p. 44.
[14] Warren, p. 134.

under established Crown policy no one born in the colonies could realistically hope to rise to the highest position in government or the Church, the chief arenas for careers. Even the humblest Spaniard born in Spain regarded those born elsewhere as inferior.

The arrogant peninsular was a transient element in colonial society because his administrative appointment was for a fixed term. After three years he ordinarily returned to Spain. The peninsulars resident in Paraguay considered themselves, as did all of their breed, superior to the Paraguayan-born Spaniard, and certainly to the mestizos. They were, however, unable to obtain the social and economic privileges and prerogatives that were accorded to them in the other Spanish colonies. Paraguay, says Warren, was altogether too democratic for their pretensions.[15] Nevertheless, they were able to make themselves obnoxious enough to bring discredit and disaster upon all Spaniards who remained behind in Paraguay after it became an independent country in 1811.

The small criollo class was composed of the permanent Spanish residents, the descendants of the original conquistadores and of peninsulars who had elected to remain in Paraguay after the expiration of their commission. The criollos were the land-owning, aristocratic, and professional class and as such sought to exercise social and political rights that they regarded as commensurate with their economic position. Spain's deliberate exclusion of them from all but the most minor government posts, and the condescending attitude of the peninsulars, evoked their hostility and resentment. In the case of Paraguay this feeling was diluted to a considerable degree because the criollo class enjoyed more political opportunities and a better social position than their counterparts in other colonies of Spain.

In Venezuela, however, hostility and ill will marred the relations between the two groups in the upper class up to and through the war of independence.

Below the white upper classes came the mestizos. Indians and Negroes forming semislave and slave castes were at the bottom of the social scale.

[15] Warren, p. 134.

Colonial political organization

The colonization of the New World by the Spaniards preceded that of the English by more than a century and thus belongs to an era that antedates the Lockean concept of the rights of man.[16] Although Spain produced such brilliant clerical theorists as Súarez, de Las Casas, and de Vitoria, who argued for limitations on the power of the ruler, it is the absolutism of the Catholic kings of Spain that was stamped on the political organization of colonial Latin America. The power and authority of the Crown, from which came all legitimate authority in Spain's overseas territories, derived not from the people but from God. Divine and natural laws were regarded as constituting limits on the sovereign's power, but these were largely matters of individual royal conscience. There were no effective institutionalized restraints on the king during most of the colonial period.

At the time of the discovery of America, Spain was experiencing a trend toward absolutism and a decay in its weak representative institutions. One consequence of this development was the transfer of authoritarian government to the new colonies, which, in the theory of the time, were regarded as personal properties of the Crown. Wholly new institutions, completely independent of those of metropolitan Spain, were created to govern the colonial empire of the king, but as devices of absolutism they were less than successful. The great distance of the colonies from Spain, and the disposition of royal officials and citizens to disregard the king's law when it was expedient and safe to do so, mitigated the authoritarian nature of the regime to some extent, as did the administrative confusion and jurisdictional disputes that were integral features of colonial government.

The basic agency by which Spain governed the New World was the Royal Council of the Indies. Resident at court and under direct supervision of the monarch, it had complete legislative, executive, and judicial power over the colonies. In its legislative capacity it produced a staggering number of detailed laws. Many of its edicts were wise and humane; others were far in advance of their time and were unenforceable, particularly those that re-

---

[16] Richard M. Morse, "Political Theory and the Caudillo," *Dictatorship in Spanish America*. Hugh M. Hamill, ed. (New York: Knopf, 1965), p. 53.

lated to the welfare of the Indians. This state of affairs contributed to the growth of disrespect for the law and for legal authority.

The economic life of the overseas possessions was subject to the House of Trade. Created in 1503, it was later placed under the overall supervision of the Royal Council of the Indies when that institution was set up in 1524. The basic purpose of the House of Trade was to maintain the Crown monopoly of trade and commerce with the colonies. Its restrictive measures were resented by the colonists, and an active contraband and smuggling trade soon arose.

Laws were made in Spain, but they had to be enforced in the colonies. The royal administrative organization set up in the overseas empire to achieve this result was confusing and complex with no clear administrative lines drawn. The New World possessions were divided into two territories called viceroyalties, each of which was headed by a viceroy, the personal representative of the king. Later there were four. The territory of a viceroyalty was divided into various units such as a presidency or a captaincy-general, depending on the unit's size and importance. A captain-general had military power over his district as well as civil and political power and was far more independent of the viceroy than was a president, who had only civil powers. Both individuals were technically subordinate to the viceroy. They were, however, appointed by the king and had the right of direct access and appeal to him.

In each of the major divisions of the empire there was also a judicial body called an *audiencia*. It, too, exercised quasi-legislative and executive powers. The principal officer of the region (president, captain-general, or viceroy) was also a member of its audiencia. To make matters more confusing, the area to which the jurisdiction of the court extended was also called an audiencia.

The presidencies and the captaincies-general were in turn subdivided, and each of the lesser units had its royal official. At the bottom of the administrative hierarchy was an individual known as a *corregidor* (magistrate), who was ultimately responsible for applying the royal law. He was often a corrupt and venal man who did little to enhance the reputation of the Crown administration. He had the power to interfere in the affairs of the cities in which he lived by exercising veto rights in the town council, the *cabildo*.

Although self-government was not a conspicuous feature in the Spanish colonies, it was by no means completely absent. A royal decree of 1560, for example, gave the towns of Venezuela the right "to govern themselves like so many little city republics to the exclusion of the *Audiencia* of Santo Domingo." [17] A similar decree conferred upon Paraguay the right to elect its own governor in the event of a vacancy. Both concessions were withdrawn after the *Comunero* uprising in Paraguay in 1721.

Spain's policy of appointing only persons born in Spain to positions of power and authority in the colonies was a source of great discontent among the criollos. The cabildo, or city council, was the only political institution in which the criollo could realistically hope to participate. Such powers as the Crown permitted the colonists to exercise were lodged in the cabildo. Its members were at first elected, but later in the colonial period when the Crown was short of money council seats were sold to the highest bidder. In the movement for independence the cabildos played an important role by sounding the cry for freedom and by directing the revolutionary effort.

Several other royal governing devices in the colonies must be mentioned before we leave the subject of colonial political structure. Many Spanish officials were attracted to the New World because of opportunities they foresaw for enriching themselves. In order to discourage this profiteering the Crown required its appointees to declare the extent of their wealth before they sailed for their New World post. A further judicial accounting took place at the end of the official's term of office in a special court called a *residencia*. An official named by the Royal Council of the Indies was sent to the colonies to conduct an examination into the record and accomplishments of the royal official who could not leave his jurisdiction until he had been cleared by the court. Anyone who had a grievance against the Crown agent could appear and make it known.

As a further check on colonial administrators, the Crown sent from time to time a *visitador* (inspector) to examine all financial records, which had to be kept in great detail. He, too,

---

[17] C. H. Haring, *The Spanish Empire in America* (New York: Oxford, 1947), p. 170.

could hear complaints against any royal official and decide what to do about them. His visits were unannounced and therefore were not enthusiastically anticipated.

The elaborate administrative apparatus just described was considered necessary to control the numerous officials and institutions who were exercising many of the same powers. The king did not generally trust his appointees, and such agencies as the residencia and *visita* were created to prevent institutions and individuals from becoming too powerful.

One effect of these precautions was to stifle individual initiative on the part of the officials. They never knew how their innovations would be received by the king nor who among his subjects would complain about them during a visita or residencia. It was better to follow the letter of the law exactly. A second effect was to encourage corruption, for visitadors and judges of the residencia were not above temptation. An official had to make three fortunes while in office: one to pay for his appointment, one to support him in office, and one to bribe the judge at the end of his term.[18]

Venezuela The colonial organization of the territory that now comprises Venezuela was partly responsible for the failure of this country to develop into a fully integrated political society following independence. Regionalism and separatist tendencies have long roots in Venezuela, dating back to the beginning of the colonial period. Indeed, it has been argued that personalism and regionalism were natural outgrowths of the peninsular culture transmitted to the colonies by Spain.[19]

Throughout most of the 300-year colonial era Venezuela existed as a group of provinces more or less independent of each other. Over the years each colony had developed its own particular culture, economy, and political views. Ingrained habits of commerce, individual development, and suspicion of the political motives of the other provinces, particularly that of Caracas, stood in the way of the development of a strong feeling of national unity or identity. Only for the last thirty-six years of

[18] Hubert Herring, *A History of Latin America* (New York: Knopf, 1959), p. 161.

[19] J. Uslar Pietri, *La Estructura Social y Política de Venezuela* (Paris: Librarie des Editions Espagnoles, 1951), p. 15.

Spain's rule did the provinces have a central political authority in Caracas. In 1777 the Crown extended the military authority of the captain-general in Caracas to the other five provinces. Succeeding reforms placed fiscal and judicial control of all six provinces in the hands of the same captain-general. In spite of these centralizing changes, a good deal of political power still remained in the hands of the governors of the separate provinces.

Their thirty-six years as an administrative unit was too short a time for the provinces to erase previous misunderstandings, and when the independence movement began, the provinces insisted upon a federal form of government. They were all suspicious of the motives and goals of the government in Caracas.

This "gremlin of disunity" did not confine itself to the provinces. Simon Bolívar, the liberator of northern South America, complained that not only did the provinces want to govern themselves, but that each "city pretended to the same prerogatives, citing the example of the provinces, and the theory that all men and all people enjoy the rights of instituting at their own pleasure the government which seems most suitable to them." [20]

Provincial loyalties and differences persisted for many years after independence and still have by no means disappeared. In the constitutional convention of 1858, for example, twenty-eight years after Venezuela terminated its association with Gran Colombia, one delegate proclaimed, "We are not yet one race; the *cumaneses* are not *merideños,* nor are the *trujillanos margariteños.* Our professions, our characters, our territories are different; in every respect we are different; the political situation of the provinces with respect to one another demands division." [21]

Venezuela's colonial experience was one of administrative confusion, regional jealousies, official indifference, and a very modest measure of self-government.

Paraguay   Paraguay was one of a number of provinces under first one jurisdiction and then another. It eventually came under the presidency of Buenos Aires, for which it had little affection.

---

[20] Victor A. Belaunde, *Bolívar and the Political Thought of the Spanish American Revolution* (Baltimore, Md.: The Johns Hopkins Press, 1938), p. 130.

[21] Venezuela, *Diario de Debates de la Convención Nacional* (Valencia: Imprenta de Jesus María Soriano, 1858), No. 222.

Its status vis-à-vis the other units of the Plata area was similar to that of one of the provinces that were collectively referred to as Venezuela. Its long isolation permitted it to develop an even more distinct culture than did any of the Venezuelan provinces. There was, of course, a Spanish governor in Asunción, but the unruly nature of the Paraguayans often made that official's life a trial. A number of governors were deposed over the course of the years. The cabildo of Asunción was, in Warren's words, "Paraguay's aggressive defender, its frustrated champion in bouts with Spain's bureaucratic colonial system." [22]

In the movement for independence the homogeneous Paraguayan people successfully resisted Argentine efforts to integrate Paraguay into a larger political unit.

Religious influences

The Church was easily the most powerful social force in Latin American history. Contributing to its vast power and authority were

> its strong organization, penetrating every part of Latin America and working in every institution; its influence over the State; the work of the Inquisition in controlling the political activity and the mental development of the people; the pioneering and educational activities of the religious orders; the intellectual monopoly of the clergy; the property holdings and economic power of the Church; and its influence on private and public morals.[23]

The Spanish empire in the New World reflected a firm partnership between the Church and state. Indeed, members of the priesthood were often recruited to fill government posts in the colonial administration. The very existence of the empire in the western hemisphere had a religious basis in that the distribution of lands was carried out under a papal bull that established the Line of Demarcation. It was on this division of territory between Spain and Portugal that Spain claimed possession of the areas that now include Venezuela and Paraguay.

It would be a mistake to underestimate the intensity of re-

[22] Warren, p. 136.
[23] Diffie, p. 567.

ligious fervor and conviction brought to their colonial ventures by the Spaniards. Religious personnel accompanied all the conquistadores. Indians were regarded as pagans to be converted as soon as possible to save their souls and remove them from the category of religious and political enemies. Almost immediately, therefore, the Crown began to concern itself with their spiritual welfare. Doubt has been cast on the genuineness of the conversion of the Indians, for it appears that in many instances they became members of the Church after having heard a statement of Church principles read to them in Spanish, a language they did not understand. The Guaraní Indians of Paraguay with their almost poetic religion that included the idea of an impersonal, abstract diety, were perhaps more sympathetic to the new religion and more truly converted to it than were the Indians in other parts of the Spanish empire.

In theory the Crown exercised a great deal of control over the Church in both Spain and the colonies. Various papal bulls had conceded to the Spanish kings the right to appoint Church dignitaries (the so-called *real patronato*) and to collect tithes and ecclesiastical revenues. The tithes were used to pay the salaries of priests and to build new churches. The Crown controlled the erection and location of all new edifices, the establishment of monasteries and convents, and the movements of all priests within the empire. Papal communications to the hierarchy in the New World were subject to royal approval before promulgation. In return for these concessions, the Crown made itself responsible for the cultivation and care of the Church.

In spite of these restrictions, the Church enjoyed a privileged status in colonial society, as seen by the number of special rights (*fueros*) extended to it. These included tax exemptions, freedom from debt imprisonment, preference for public offices, and the right to have its own courts to hear cases involving pious matters or Church interests.

The Church accumulated great wealth during the colonial era, for it was considered a pious act (and in some cases a necessary one in order to avoid a charge of heresy) to endow the Church with lands and other properties in one's will. Because these legacies remained in the hands of the Church, its vast properties grew greatly over the years, and inasmuch as Church property was tax exempt, the state was deprived of much revenue. In some countries the Church as a financial institution rivaled the state. Its tax-exempt status, its fueros, and its numerous religious orders evoked the resentment of merchant and commercial interests in the colonies. This sentiment was particularly strong in Paraguay, where the Jesuits constructed an economic empire that surpassed that of the Crown.

On the other hand, the Church was an indispensable institution in many ways, providing many of the services that are today considered responsibilities of the state. It was, for example, the primary educational force. Many of the major universities in existence today were founded and run by religious orders and their curricula reflected it. Lesser schools were almost exclusively Church schools. In Paraguay the Jesuits were schoolmasters to 150,000 Indian charges.

The Church also founded and maintained hospitals, orphanages, and homes for the aged. Monasteries served as inns for those who traveled about the empire.

Ever zealous about the purity of their religion, the Catholic kings and the Church set up agencies to ensure that purity. The two most important devices were the Inquisition and the Index. The Inquisition was a Church tribunal whose primary function was the discovery and punishment of heresy and other offenses against the Church. The Inquisition was also a defensive mechanism of the state. In that capacity, utilizing the Index (a list of books forbidden to the faithful), it sought to prevent the reading and circulation of radical new ideas considered dangerous to the religious and political order of the day. The works of many important theorists were (and still are) on the Index, especially those who questioned the divine right theory or who espoused the doctrine of popular sovereignty. Possession of any of the forbidden literature was considered cause enough to bring an individual before the dreaded Inquisition.

Certainly the Inquisition and the Index helped to keep the Spanish colonists orthodox and loyal citizens by creating an atmosphere of religious and intellectual stultification. They could not, however, entirely prevent the spread of contraband literature, much of which found its way into the libraries of Church dignitaries.[24] In the case of Venezuela and Paraguay, Spain's

[24] Haring, p. 205.

indifference to them made it possible for their citizens to escape the more stringent application of the censor's rule.

The Church and its various religious orders played another vital role in the establishment of Spain's political control over the New World possessions. Everywhere in Spanish America the Church developed into the most important agency of political socialization. The missions in particular functioned as state devices through which Spanish civilization was transmitted to the indigenous population. In addition, missions were expected to teach the Indians the dogmas of the Church and to bring them to a state of development where they could be turned over to the secular arm of the Church as practicing Christians and to civil officials as subjects of the political system.

Venezuela   An excellent evaluation of the mission effort in Venezuela can be found in Mary Watter's book on the Church in Venezuela. She writes:

> The missionaries had been the most effective institution of the state in the colonization of Venezuela; they had accomplished its pacification where the conquerors had failed; in doing so, they had conserved the life of the Indian, so that today he forms the base of the population in the republic. They had opened up the interior; explored the country, leaving in the records of this work valuable geographic, scientific, and historical documents; they established towns and defended the frontier. They had reduced a large part of the Indian population to the mission; within it, they had given the native an introduction at least to Spanish civilization, including industrial training and preparation for civil life. . . . With the abolition of the missions in the revolutionary epoch, the control of the Church over the Indian was lost. He became either hostile because of the hatred of the missionary, or indifferent through failure of the Church to make a permanent impression on his mind. The civilizing effect of the missions disappeared with them.[25]

In Venezuela the Church as a whole suffered from factionalism and decentralization during the colonial years. This was also true of Venezuelan society. There were quarrels between

[25] Watters, p. 29.

the secular and regular clergy and between various religious orders, such as the Capuchins, who were the most numerous in Venezuela, and the Jesuits. Jurisdictional disputes between political and religious officials also occurred frequently. Indeed, the religious hierarchy was motivated by their desire to dominate society and to secure civil control over the country in competition with the political establishment.[26] Many priests, in fact, did hold high political office in Venezuela, as they did elsewhere.

The Church in colonial Venezuela was criticized for its great wealth, its control of valuable lands, its opposition to new ideas, its monopoly of the educational system, its political power, and, as the republican period neared, its continued support of the royal power of Spain. These facts helped to ensure the complete subordination of the Church to the state when revolution severed the ties with Spain and removed the protective influence of the Crown.

On the other hand, the Church, in its numerous rituals both public and private, edified the heart and the eye. It provided, moreover, a channel through which the various levels of Venezuelan society could express their class feelings through such things as devotions, public processions, and the many religious brotherhoods and organizations.[27]

Paraguay   In Paraguay the Church was quite different in the range and effect of its influence. As the Services have observed, the Church was

> never strong politically or influential culturally and it is not to this day. . . . There were no native state religions competing with Catholicism and the Holy Inquisition touched the La Plata people hardly at all. Except for the isolated mission area, neither Church nor state created large planned towns (*reducciones*) of Indians which lasted long enough to be of consequence.[28]

We must take note, however, of the Jesuit mission undertaking in Paraguay.

[26] Watters, pp. 39–40.
[27] Watters, p. 38.
[28] Service and Service, p. 289.

In spite of the amity in which the Indians and the Spaniards lived in Paraguay, there were those among the latter who wished to take more advantage of the natives than the Crown allowed. Many of the humane regulations affecting the Indians were either ignored or ineffective. The Indians found a champion in the Society of Jesus, better known as the Jesuit Order, and for over 160 years the Jesuits were the dominant religious influence in Paraguay. They came in 1588 and, according to the historian Herring, did more to shape the colony than all the governors and Spanish settlers in its history.[29] The native intelligence and adaptability of the Indians, as well as the persistence and energy of the Jesuits, accounted for the success of this militant and disciplined order.

The Jesuit Order became the single largest *encomendero* in Paraguay. Over the years the Jesuits gathered an estimated 150,000 Indians into thirty *reducciones,* or missions, thus effectively removing them from the exploitive designs of civil governors and the landed gentry. The Jesuits instructed the Indians in a variety of new crafts, helped them improve their farming skills, and taught them to raise stock. They demanded and got complete obedience from their charges.

> Jesuits regulated life for all ages and for both sexes. Religious services at morning, noon and evening broke the routine of work, provided opportunities to check on the neophytes and fortified habits of benefit to the Church. . . . A system of cultivation, vaguely resembling communal practices under the Incas of Peru, prevailed. Each family received a plot which would produce the necessary food, while orphans, widows, religious personnel and others . . . were fed from public storehouses. . . .[30]

The Guaraní Indians flourished under this regimen. Heretofore a disorganized society with many warring groups, they responded to this sheltered existence that protected them from their enemies and released them from want, fear, and war. The isolation of the Indians by the Jesuits aroused the ire of those

[29] Herring, p. 672.
[30] Warren, p. 93.

who wished to make use of their labor, and the Jesuits were constantly embroiled in disputes over raids on their missions.

The wealth and success of the missions, their tax-exempt status and their growing commercial empire also created enemies for the Jesuits. Many priests in the secular arm of the Church were hostile to them. These forces and others combined their efforts and finally won the ear of the king. By 1767 the Crown had come to fear the formidable economic and political power of the Jesuits throughout the Spanish American possessions, and it issued an order for their expulsion from the colonies. In countries such as Venezuela, where many other orders were sharing the missionary effort, the expulsion of the Jesuits did not bring undue hardships. The effect of the order's expulsion from Paraguay was to end the disciplined, sheltered Arcadia in which the Indians lived. The entire mission system collapsed in an astonishingly short time. Bereft of the paternal protection of their masters, the Indian population dwindled in the space of forty years to about 45,000. Some returned to the forests, some were absorbed into the main bloodstream of Paraguay, while others were unable to survive in the competitive society into which they were thrown.

The rapid disintegration of the Jesuit mission system after 1767 leads one to speculate on the lasting cultural influences of the order. During their 160 years of control did the Jesuits change the nature and character of their Indian charges in such a way as to affect the political system of today? That question is not easily answered and scholars differ greatly in their evaluation of the Jesuit occupation. On one point at least there is agreement: The Indians did not outwardly change, since the object of the Jesuits was to domesticate and Christianize them while preserving their racial identity. The socializing efforts of the Jesuits were directed to the formation of a society obedient to a *religious* system and to protecting it from what the order regarded as the pernicious effects of the *political* system.

The argument centers around the obedience issue. The severest critics of the Jesuits contend that the requirement of absolute obedience from the Indians introduced and consolidated a character trait that has been largely responsible for the creation of an obedient, passive, and subject society, which, in the political system, has endured the dictates of numerous despots. Unused to thinking for themselves for over a century and a half, the Indians would naturally be ill-prepared to do so when the order was expelled. Thus they would fall victim to demagoguery.

In view of the fact that the number of full-blooded Indians has never been very large in Paraguay since the Jesuit period (about 30,000 survive today and live in the Chaco), it seems more reasonable to accept the point of view of Warren, who writes:

> Had Jesuit Missions controlled most of Paraguay, this judgment might have more weight. Distance more than theocracy generated isolationism; inherent faults of Indian and *mestizo* character, not paternalism, made Paraguay easy prey for ruthless dictators.[31]

As stress on obedience is also a character trait of the Spaniard, and because his values are the ones that have predominated in Paraguay, it seems unfair to lay the whole blame on the Jesuit Order. The tendency among historians today is to minimize the influence of the Jesuits.

Turning to the secular branch of the Church in Paraguay, it may be observed that it never became as wealthy as the other Spanish colonies. Paraguay was a poor country by and large, and the Church remained basically a poor institution. Its relative poverty did not prevent it from interfering in political affairs, however, and there were numerous quarrels between civil and religious jurisdictions.

In both Venezuela and Paraguay the secular and regular branches of the Church hierarchy were powerful socializing forces during the colonial period. Religious attitudes shaped political attitudes and greatly facilitated the continuity of absolutist political doctrines. The existence of specific devices such as the Inquisition and the Index aided the Church in maintaining a fairly high degree of conformity to the prevailing religious and political philosophies of Spain.

The Church was also an instrumentality for political sub-

---

[31] Warren, p. 96.

jugation because part of the rationale for the existence of missions, particularly those on the frontiers, was to reduce the Indians to obedient subjects, amenable to economic exploitation and civil control.

Summary

How might the Venezuelan and Paraguayan man-in-the-street perceive his social and political system at the end of the colonial period? If he were a criollo, he saw Spanish interest in the economic welfare and development of his country directly tied to the measure of monetary return from it. He was continually frustrated by the fact that Spain's neglect, generated from economic causes, did not mean political indifference or neglect. Thus he saw an authoritative administrative structure that, in spite of the indifference of the Crown, prevented him from exercising his growing desires for meaningful self-government. The often venal governmental structure inspired little more than contempt, since not only could the highest officials be bribed, but the criollo himself could purchase from the Crown a seat on the town council. Law he saw as something that could be set aside, modified, or ignored, depending upon the circumstances, the pecuniary interests of officialdom, or the impracticality of the legislation. Respect for the law was thus seriously compromised.

Respect for Spain's officials was also precarious. Not only were they often corrupt, but the officious conduct of the peninsulars antagonized the criollos to such a point that there was a general alienation from a political system that discriminated against them so openly.

The criollo saw, finally, a religious-political partnership that sought to prevent him from broadening his philosophical, economic, and political horizons.

In the case of Venezuela, the criollo's view of his system was complicated by the fact that there were several provinces. The criollo of one province usually felt that his regional culture made him superior to the criollo of another province. Venezuela's task of nation building would be greatly hampered by the persistence of regional views.

If he were a mestizo in Venezuela he saw all of the above things as well as a class society that discriminated against him as a person, exploited him in its extractive economy, regarded him as a disturbing influence, and denied him any participation in the political affairs of his province. Religious, political, social, and economic institutions were allied to keep him in his subservient place. Thus there was little in the prevailing system with which he could identify. The Paraguayan mestizo was far better off, and his judgment of the system would have been less harsh.

In Venezuela, the Indians and Negroes were really not part of the larger political system at all. Their horizons were the boundaries of the hacienda or a mountain village. They were chattels—property—and were treated accordingly.

Paraguayan society was less encumbered with these elements and thus was more homogeneous and unified—a point of strength for the country when it achieved independence. Nation building, in a word, would be easier in Paraguay than in Venezuela.

INDEPENDENCE AND NATIONHOOD

The struggle for freedom and sovereignty: 1810–1821

Unlike the revolt against England that occurred in the North American colonies in the late eighteenth century, the independence movement in Spanish America was a response to international events that were occurring in Europe. In 1808 Napoleon Bonaparte invaded Spain, deposed the Spanish king, and placed his own brother Joseph on the Spanish throne. The incensed Spaniards refused to recognize the authority of the usurper and proceeded to set up *juntas* (governing committees) in various parts of Spain to govern in the name of the deposed Ferdinand VII. A central junta, later established in the unoccupied port of Cadiz, attempted to extend its authority to the colonial possessions. Most of the overseas provinces declared their opposition to the Bonapartes and transferred their allegiance to the central junta. However, when that body ignored them in its composition and found that it could not defend them, the colonies began to assert their own competence. Venezuela and Argentina were the first to claim the right to govern themselves in the absence of a legitimate authority in Spain. It was Argentina's decision to reject the authority of the Cadiz junta and to set up its own government that provoked the Paraguayan independence movement.

Paraguay   Paraguay had in 1776 been placed under the larger jurisdiction of the newly created Viceroyalty of Rio de La Plata with its seat in Buenos Aires, and it was not happy about it. The Buenos Aires cabildo, asserting its right to create a governing junta, expected the provinces subject to the Viceroyalty to accept its authority. Paraguay was not prepared to do this. To compel its allegiance Argentina sent an armed expedition against the rebellious riverside province. The Argentine armed force was decisively beaten by the nationalistic Paraguayan soldiers in two battles early in 1811. These battles ended both Argentine and Spanish control over Paraguay. On May 14, 1811, Paraguay proclaimed the independence it had already won. Its remote and isolated position enabled it to gain its freedom in what was a relatively painless process and within a short time.

Venezuela   Venezuela was not so fortunate. Its struggle for independence lasted eleven years, and during this period of agony and dissension the country lost one-fourth of its people and suffered enormous property damages. Venezuela's revolt began in 1810 with a defiant declaration of support for the deposed king and the Cadiz junta that governed in his name. It was not long, however, before the Venezuelans, claiming as much right to govern as the Cadiz junta, proclaimed their independence from Spain. On July 5, 1811, some of the provinces promulgated a constitution that provided for a federal form of government, thereby recognizing the strong attachments of the Venezuelans to their regional roots. This act provoked considerable dissension among the provinces, which had by this time increased in number from six to ten as Spain had repeatedly responded to separatist tendencies within the original six. The seven eastern provinces signed the constitution; the three western provinces remained aloof. The new republic was almost immediately in difficulty. Not only were the lower classes of mulattos, Negroes, and mestizos, who made up the majority of the population, against the new regime controlled by the despised wealthy criollos, but the white population itself was engulfed by bitter conflicts between royalists and rebels. Even the powerful Church was split into two factions by the severance of ties with Spain. The movement was thus both a revolution and a civil war.

A disastrous earthquake on March 26, 1812, killed nearly 20,000 people in Caracas, the center of rebel activity. It left the loyalist western provinces untouched. The Archbishop of Caracas interpreted this event as a just punishment for a people who had rebelled against a divinely appointed monarch and called upon the people to renounce their rebellion. The attitude of the Archbishop infuriated the rebels and the civil war increased in intensity. The course of the eleven-year struggle was marked by bloody campaigns in which men were slaughtered with no more compunction than if they were cattle.[32] Much of the Venezuelan elite was destroyed during the period, a fact that made it easier for the rude llaneros of the plain to retain the power and leadership they had gained as military leaders. A country with an estimated population of over 700,000 suffered 300,000 casualties during the war. A war to the death against the Spaniard was proclaimed by Simon Bolívar, the great liberator, and who was forced to flee Venezuela and take refuge in Colombia when a fierce fighting force of llaneros under a Spaniard, Boves, attacked in 1814.

The loyalty of another great mestizo llanero, General José Antonio Páez, later made it possible for Bolívar to return to Venezuela and pursue his goal of liberating the country from Spanish control. More than 20,000 llaneros followed General Páez. Their war cry of "death to the wealthy and the whites" indicated that for them the war was a war between classes and a struggle for greater social justice.[33] Although Venezuela was not yet free, Bolívar was proclaimed president of a new Republic of Venezuela under a constitution that had been written by a congress convoked by him in Angostura (now Ciudad Bolívar) in 1819.

Victory over Spain was finally realized in the Battle of Carobobo in 1821. Shortly thereafter a third constitution was announced in which Venezuela, together with Colombia and

---

[32] John A. Crow, *The Epic of Latin America* (New York: Doubleday, 1946), p. 437.

[33] Arturo Uslar Pietri, "No Panacea for Latin America," *Politics of Change in Latin America,* Joseph Maier and Richard Weatherhead, eds. (New York: Praeger, 1964), pp. 76–77.

Ecuador, became the Republic of Gran Colombia. This arrangement lasted until 1830, when General Páez took Venezuela out of the confederation. The constitution proclaimed in that year marks the beginning of the truly independent history of Venezuela.

Independence came to Paraguay quickly and at little cost in property or lives. No great military reputations were made and thus there were almost no ambitious military caudillos who could plague the country in their competition and thirst for power. Paraguay had no warring provinces to contend with, and its population remained cohesive and untouched by civil strife and economic ruin. Venezuela, on the other hand, emerged from an eleven-year struggle, scarred by internecine conflicts, with an impoverished and decimated people, and saddled with a number of generals who would insist on their right to share power in return for their services. They retained or were repaid with control of various regions, which they administered as private estates.

The position of the Church on the matter of independence foreshadowed difficulties between it and the new government of Venezuela. The Church was on the losing side. In Paraguay, its officials, although opposed in principle to independence, were unable to make their influence felt and took no active part in the process that was, in any event, over before the Church had time to react vigorously.

Finally, it should be noted that during the years in which their military energies were being expended in the fight for freedom, the Venezuelan people wrote three different constitutions: in 1811, 1819, and 1821. Like most of the people of Latin America, they were eager to define the nature and limitations of their new form of government. It was also necessary to define the relationships between the component provinces if the new nation was to endure as a unified entity. Paraguay was already a unified entity and thus did not need a constitution to achieve that objective. Indeed, Paraguay did not bother to write a real constitution at all until 1844, some thirty-three years after it had broken ties with Spain. Venezuela, on the other hand, has shown from the beginning a concern for the rule of law, however imperfectly observed. Much of Paraguay's history demonstrates the contrary.

The success of the independence struggle presented the people of Venezuela and Paraguay with a problem common to all the colonies that had freed themselves from Spain—that of establishing a new legitimate authority to take the place of the all-pervasive royal will. The North American colonies emerged from their revolution minus a king, but with most of their institutions of authority basically intact and a long-standing philosophy about the necessity of limited government and inherent individual rights. Latin Americans on the other hand, by terminating the power of the king, ended their one and only source of legitimate authority. Independence did not change much in the social and economic order, but in the political order a legitimacy vacuum existed. Most of the new nations, including those of this study, sought to establish legitimacy by writing constitutions in which power was declared to be from the people. These fragile paper arrangements often gave way to the more powerful forces of family and regional alliances and ambitions of caudillos and military heroes.

The evolution of state and nation: 1821–1870

Paraguay   The first twenty-seven years of Paraguayan independence were so completely and absolutely dominated by one man that his story is the nation's story. Dr. José Gaspar Rodríguez de Francia ruled Paraguay with a despotism unequaled in the history of Latin America. One of the very few educated men in all of Paraguay, he was naturally called upon to participate in the early political decisions that had to be made. He moved rapidly from a position of equality in a two-man consul form of government that had been set up after independence, to the position of first consul, and from there to president for life. In 1816 he was "elected" Consul by plebiscite. Other titles conferred upon him were Dictator, Father of Country, Pontiff, and El Supremo.[34] From that moment until his death in 1840 Paraguay knew only the will of the inscrutable, mystical, tormented, and neurotic tyrant (to use only a few of the many adjectives found in the literature about him). Francia ruled without the limitation of constitution, legislature, or court. There were no elections, no politics, no parties. The bureaucracy was prac-

[34] Crow, p. 560.

tically nonexistent because government and authority were personalized in him.

Aware of the strife and conflict going on in other areas of Latin America, obsessed with the idea of maintaining order, and wishing to preserve Paraguayan nationality, Francia embarked upon a policy of isolation that closed the doors of Paraguay to all international trade and commerce. Paraguayans were not allowed to travel abroad, and only a few foreigners found their way into the country. The ban on trade forced the Paraguayans to become a self-reliant and self-sufficient people. All able-bodied men were forced to work for the good of the state on agricultural stations controlled by the dictator.

The peace and order of a graveyard descended on Paraguay as Francia inexorably wiped out all opposition to his regime. Although of European origin himself, he hated the Spaniards for a real or imaginary slight in his educational career. One of his more vicious regulations decreed that Spaniards might marry only mestizos or Negroes. Many were imprisoned, dispossessed of their property, or otherwise persecuted. His scourging of the small Paraguayan nobility ultimately produced an even more egalitarian society than he had inherited.

His concern with Paraguayan nationalism, his suspicion of foreign influences, and his determination to bend all institutions to his will led Francia to renounce the religious hegemony of Rome and to proclaim himself head of a Paraguayan national church. Church properties were seized, priests were reduced to mere agents of the dictator, and many religious ceremonies were either curtailed or abolished altogether.[35] He was equally harsh on education, which he regarded as a disturbing influence, particularly among the Guaranís. Institutions of education, therefore, were almost nonexistent during the long rule of El Supremo.

Francia sustained himself in power by building a loyal army of Indians and mestizos. The superstition and mystery with which he surrounded himself secured their fearful obedience. In addition to his personal army, the state under Francia consisted of himself, a minister of finance to keep the books, a prefect of police, and a secretary who also served as minister of foreign

[35] J. Lloyd Mecham, *Church and State in Latin America* (Chapel Hill, N.C.: The University of North Carolina Press, 1934), pp. 236–238.

affairs and justice. The country was divided into twenty districts, each of which was commanded by an agent of the security police. All officials were under the tight control of the dictator, and government business depended upon his merest whim. A tiny and intimidated bureaucracy executed his every wish.

In spite of its terrorism, the bizarre rule of El Supremo did have some beneficial effects. Francia's repressive policies brought order to Paraguay, thus permitting it to escape the bloodshed and violence that bedeviled the other countries of Latin America for years after the winning of their freedom. And it made the Paraguayans self-sufficient. The years since his death have softened the harsher aspects of his rule, and today he is honored as the founder of the fatherland.

The death of the dictator in the autumn of 1840 provoked a succession crisis because there was no constitution to legitimatize the transfer of power. Francia's secretary vainly tried to grasp power but he was speedily dealt with by other more powerful figures. Again Paraguay went through a familiar cycle: junta, consulate, and dictatorship. Carlos Antonio López, a mestizo and sometime lawyer-teacher who had managed to survive the Francia regime by retiring to the country, dominated the junta and the consulate and finally emerged as president when a presidential system was decreed by his constitution of 1844. Although El Excelentíssimo (as López preferred to be called) desired to govern under a constitution, he paid no attention to it and was no less absolute than his predecessor had been. He was more benign, however, and did not insist on doing everything himself. During his twenty-two-year tenure (1840–1862) the rudiments of a court system appeared, and several small government departments staffed by loyal bureaucrats were created. The government under López was a nepotic affair and it continued to be so under his son and successor.

López desired to end the isolation imposed upon Paraguay by Francia and took the initiative by reopening Paraguay to international trade and commerce. His efforts were not entirely successful because he had earned the enmity of the Argentine dictator, Juan Manuel Rosas, who proceeded to block river access to Asunción for a time. López reestablished diplomatic relations with some countries, including the United States, and deserves credit for building the first railroad in South America.

In politics there were elections, but only in the sense that an obedient congress several times elected the president to succeed himself. In 1857 it voted him the title of president for life with the right to name his successor. No one was surprised when he named his son, thirty-six-year-old Brigadier General Francisco Solano López. Carlos died in 1862, and his son immediately became president. Under this man Paraguay headed for a disaster from which it has not yet fully recovered: the War of the Triple Alliance.

Francisco Solano had spent two years (1853–1855) in Europe and acquired there a great admiration for Napoleon III, as well as an inflated notion of his own military ability. Upon his return to Paraguay his indulgent father allowed him to recruit and train an army. Two years after he came to power, he used this army to plunge Paraguay into a six-year war with its neighbors. The immediate cause of the conflict was an attempt by Brazil to collect damages from Uruguay for injuries suffered by Brazilian nationals in Uruguay's numerous civil wars. Francisco Solano regarded Brazilian interference in the domestic affairs of Uruguay as a threat to his own country. His goal, never seriously considered feasible by Brazil or Argentina, was to raise Paraguay to the rank of a great power in the Plata Basin. Brazil's refusal to listen to his grievances or to countenance his power pretensions led him to declare war upon that country and later upon Argentina when it refused him the right to send his troops against Brazil through Argentine territory. By 1865, Brazil and Argentina had been joined by Uruguay in an alliance that finally brought the downfall of the Paraguayan dictator.

The savage and brutal war was valiantly fought by the Paraguayan soldier, who was literally, in the final phases, fighting for the very existence of his country. The troops were often under the personal command of Francisco Solano. He met his death in battle in 1870, and the war came to an immediate end. Dependent on and bereft of strong leadership, the Paraguayans capitulated. The havoc wreaked on their country was enormous. More than half of the prewar population was killed. Of the surviving 220,000, only 28,000 were adult men.[36] Towns, farms, businesses, and commerce were obliterated in the long struggle.

[36] Warren, p. 243.

The victors also exacted their settlement price: 55,000 square miles of Paraguayan territory and a huge reparation bill that Paraguay could not and ultimately did not pay. Paraguay also had to suffer the humiliation of a six-year occupation by military forces of Argentina and Brazil.

Thus in their first sixty years of national life, the submissive Paraguayans had been led through a series of absolute dictatorships to catastrophe, from absolute isolation to ruinous involvement in the international affairs of the Plata Basin. They had had no opportunity to participate in the political processes of their country, either because the processes were not open to them or because appropriate channels simply did not exist. The failure of the political leaders of Paraguay to develop even moderately strong and effective political structures, to provide a firm administrative base for the state, and to involve the citizen in the political life of the country resulted in a complete collapse of the state at the end of the war. The tiny, subservient bureaucracy was depopulated as young and old were drawn off to the battlefield. The most important instrument of the state—the army— was obliterated. In 1870 Paraguay had to begin the process of state building all over again—and under the watchful eye of foreign military forces.

Although the state was in shambles, the course of events from 1811 to 1870 had brought about an intensification of the feelings the Paraguayan people had for their country and their culture. The war may have destroyed an appalling number of their countrymen, but those that survived were more nationalistic than ever. The memory of the heroism of their compatriots during the long war lives on to this day. In spite of the disaster and humiliation Paraguay suffered as the result of his policies, Francisco Solano is a national hero, and everywhere there are tangible reminders of him: streets, statues, stations, and a palace (Government House). The war took a terrible toll in terms of lives, property, and state, but a Paraguayan nation lived on in the fullest sense of the word at the end of it.

Venezuela   Paraguay had had over fifteen years of heavy-handed dictatorship under Francia when Venezuela embarked upon its own independent course. The first thing the Venezuelans did then was to write another constitution.

The system of government created by the constitution of 1830 was "centro-federal" and rested upon thirteen provinces with limited powers. Most of the power was assigned to the national government and to the president, but this constitution did not restrain the caudillos that contended for power. Venezuela, like Paraguay, also had its strong man, General Antonio Páez, and its family dynasty, the Monagas.

> General Páez, with conservative support became Venezuela's first president, elected by a clumsy system of electoral colleges. Páez never learned to read with great care and never saw or used a table fork until he was made a brigadier general. When he worked as a peon on a hacienda, after finishing his chores he would return to the mainhouse and wash the overseer's feet in the most servile manner imaginable.[37]

For sixteen years, this military hero controlled the political life of Venezuela either as president or as president maker. Although the constitution of 1830 forbade a president to seek immediate reelection, General Páez filled his intervening terms with pliant men, and thus the practice of *imposición* (the process by which the incumbent president determines his successor and sees to it that he is "elected") began.

Not everyone, of course, was happy with this arrangement and Páez had to suppress at least five major rebellions against his government during the span of his power.

In addition to his military power base, General Páez was supported by what is generally referred to as the conservative oligarchy, composed of what was left of the criollo aristocracy —wealthy merchants and influential professional men—all of whom were interested in protecting property rights.

One of the most pressing needs of General Páez and his administration was to establish confidence in his regime. He sought to do this by creating a loyal administrative apparatus, by reforming the tax structure, by rebuilding the war-torn economy, by stimulating agriculture, and by responsible fiscal policies that would attract foreign capital to Venezuela.

Although the government of Páez was conservatively oriented, its attitude toward the Church—a most conservative in-

[37] Arturo Uslar Pietri, pp. 76–77.

stitution—was more in harmony with liberal anticlerical sentiment. Conflict with this powerful organization was inevitable
as the new government sought to subordinate it to the interests
of the state. The controversy centered around the government's
claim of the right to appoint ecclesiastical personnel and of its
insistence that the hierarchy swear allegiance to the constitution.
After a series of unsuccessful maneuvers, the Church finally
capitulated to the government's demands.[38]

As a whole, the political environment during the period
from 1830 to 1848 was marked by a good deal of freedom and
personal liberty—a striking contrast to the repressive atmosphere in Paraguay at the same time. An opposition Liberal
party, for example, was permitted to organize in 1840 under the
leadership of Antonio Leocadio Guzmán and to oppose the
government in succeeding elections. The Liberals were disgruntled because Páez had not implemented some of the more
liberal provisions of the 1830 constitution. The new party
counted among its members petty merchants, intellectuals desir-
ing reform and some of the landowning class. Among other
things the party platform advocated an end to slavery and capital
punishment and a more clear separation between church and
state. The Liberal party ran candidates in the elections of 1842
and 1846. Their failure to dislodge the conservative oligarchy
sowed the seeds of political cynicism. The Páez administration
was charged with manipulating the election results in such a way
as to secure its own victory. Every succeeding administration
since has heard the same charge, and, until very recently, it was
justified.

Venezuela came under the control of the Monagas family
in 1848 when General José Tadeo Monagas, who had been
elected to the presidency with the blessings of the conservatives
in 1846, declared a dictatorship and exiled General Páez in retaliation for the former president's attempt to unseat him for his
Liberal sympathies. In the manipulated election of 1852, José
maneuvered his brother, Gregorio, into the presidency. The
principal achievement of Gregorio's four-year term was the abolition of slavery.

In 1857 Venezuela had its first taste of constitutional engi-

[38] Mecham, chap. 4.

neering when the fundamental law of the land was subverted to the interests of the ruling powers. The Monagas-controlled congress adopted a new constitution in that year that discarded the quasi-federal system in favor of a unitary, centralized government with some fanciful features. It also abolished the no reelection principle, thus making it possible for the Monagas family to perpetuate itself in office. These and other drastic changes provoked the ire of both the Conservatives and the Liberals, and by their combined efforts they overthrew José Monagas shortly after he became president again under the new constitution.

The federal system was restored in the constitution of 1858, but there was by no means a consensus on the form of government suitable for Venezuela. Conservatives were in favor of a central government, whereas Liberals were supporters of a federal system. The attachment of the latter to the doctrine of federalism was a superficial one. Antonio Guzmán Blanco, son of the Liberal party organizer and shortly to dominate Venezuela, remarked on one occasion, "If our opponents had said 'federalism,' we would have cried 'centralism.' " [39]

In 1858 the partisan political passions that had been simmering for over a decade broke out into a bloody full-scale civil war that lasted until 1864. The Federal War, as it was called, revolved around the issue of federalism, but it was at the same time a war between rival provincial caudillos who wished to consolidate their power. It was however, more than a personal power struggle, being a popular revolution in that its purpose included a program of social reforms. Written at the end of the war, the constitution of 1864 included reforms that eliminated imprisonment for debt and political rights based on monetary wealth. The government created by the new constitution resolved the political dispute in favor of federalism, but was not strong enough to give much meaning to the reform program, and disorders continued to plague the country until Antonio Guzmán Blanco seized power in 1870 and imposed his long-lived dictatorship. During the twelve-year span between 1858 and 1870 there were seven presidents when constitutionally there should

[39] Cited in W. H. Pierson, 'Foreign Influences on Venezuelan Political Thought, 1830–1930," *Hispanic American Historical Review,* 15 (February 1935), 24–25.

have been only three. One of these was General Páez, who had returned from exile to govern dictatorially from 1861 to 1863.

Some important political roots were laid in Venezuela during the first four decades of its national life. A tradition of violence in politics was begun as rival caudillos sought to gain control of the country through force instead of the ballot. Regionalism and personalism in politics was intensified as dissatisfaction grew with the long ascendancy of the llaneros in national life. The importance of the military in the political fortunes of the country and in the political disputes of the day foreshadowed their prominence in government for the next 100 years. (Nine of the presidents between 1830 and 1870 were generals.) The pronounced subordination of the legislative and judicial branches of government to the executive branch reflected a reality in the power pattern that has continued down to the present. The subjection of the constitution to the vagaries of factional politics, begun in 1857, has remained a basic feature of the Venezuelan political system. The imposition of the 1857 constitution by the Monagas caudillos is described by a Venezuelan historian as the initial breach of the constitutional order, introducing into the constitutional fabric of the country an element that would cause the nation to fluctuate for years between anarchical tumult and despotic order.[40] A political dispute between two opposing streams of political thought was initiated during these years, as Conservatives contended with Liberals at first in words then later in arms. At issue in their disagreements were states' rights, curtailed religious power, more individual freedom, and participation in the political process (Liberal); and order, religion, and property (Conservative). The relations of the church and state formed a basic issue in politics that has not been entirely resolved today.

Unlike the Paraguayans, the small element of politically articulate Venezuelans had some opportunity to participate in the political life during these early years of their republic. They might join revolutionary organizations of the various rival caudillos in the most direct assault of all on power—rebellion. They could participate in the drafting of the constitutions (four of them). They could be elected to congress, be appointed to the

[40] Ulises Picón Rivas, *Índice Constitucional de Venezuela* (Caracas: Editorial Elite, 1944), pp. 44–45.

bureaucracy, and organize or join political parties. Indeed, according to the historian Munro, during the first years of Páez's administration "the country enjoyed a more truly republican form of government than it was to know for a century to come. Congress and the press were relatively independent, and the elections were actively contested with comparatively little interference." [41] This did not mean that many people actually voted. In the election of 1846 only 60,000 persons of 1,275,000 met the property qualifications to vote. For the average Venezuelan, participation in the political process of the country meant attaching himself to one or another powerful caudillo and being servile to him. Power remained in the hands of the power elite, principally the military dictators and their private armies.

In terms of state building, Venezuela made some real progress during its first forty years as a republic. The achievements of Páez in that respect have already been mentioned. Venezuela developed a far more extensive and enduring administrative apparatus than did Paraguay because her first president was vitally interested in creating effective machinery of government. It is true that the machinery was buffeted by the civil disturbances after 1848, but it managed to survive the effects of the Federal War. In 1870 Venezuela's governmental apparatus was in good shape, in striking contrast to the pitiful condition in which Paraguay found herself.

While it was able to develop governing institutions and an administrative basis for the state, Venezuela's progress in nation building was a different matter. The formerly independent provinces that comprised the new nation were not happy about the hegemony Caracas sought to exercise over them. Political rivalries and jealousies between different regions of Venezuela and the ambitions of their military leaders and leading families tended to fragment the political culture and to perpetuate divisive tendencies that reduced the attachment of citizens to the central government and reinforce their loyalties to regions. Thus, in 1870, the situations in Paraguay and Venezuela at the end of a war were quite different. Venezuela emerged with the state intact but with the nation lacerated and wounded; Paraguay had a strong national sentiment, but no state.

[41] Dana Gardner Munro, *The Latin American Republics,* 3d ed. (New York: Appleton, 1960), p. 314.

Consolidation of state and nation: 1870–1935

Although the period between 1870 and 1935 is somewhat arbitrary as a historical and political time unit, it does provide a convenient span of time. For Venezuela, 1870 marked the end of the civil strife that had plagued the country since 1858, and the beginning of a series of dictatorships that began with that of Antonio Guzmán Blanco and ended with the twenty-seven-year rule of Juan Vicente Gómez in 1935. For Paraguay, 1870 meant the end of the War of the Triple Alliance, the end of domestic tranquillity, and the beginning of a new phase of political activity that included rebellions, party strife, and confusion, all new phenomena for the republic. In 1935 Paraguay was once more prostrate at the end of another calamitous war: the Chaco conflict with Bolivia.

Venezuela From 1870 to 1935, with the exception of a brief interlude between 1888 and 1899, the political situation in Paraguay and Venezuela was reversed. In Venezuela the turmoil and civil war of the preceding years, the ambitions of the caudillos, and the disruptive dispute between the advocates of federalism and unitary government all ended with the ascendancy of Guzmán Blanco. His eighteen-year rule (1870–1888) brought to Venezuela the order and peace that Dr. Francia and Carlos López had imposed on Paraguay. Guzmán Blanco ruled Venezuela as a fief. Nominally sovereign entities in the federal system, the several states of the United States of Venezuela were entirely subject to the will of Guzmán Blanco. Indeed, the president renamed some of them and in 1881 reduced their number from twenty to nine.

"The Illustrious American" and "The Regenerator of Venezuela," as the dictator liked to be called, tolerated no opposition in party or in government. All branches of the administration were abjectly subservient to him. Although not at all the same type of man as Francia, his fondness for titles, his preoccupation with absolute power, and his harassment of personal enemies are points of similarity. Like Francia, he persecuted the Church and, indeed, even threatened to create a national church in Venezuela if the religious hierarchy persisted in its opposition to him and his regime. He did not take that drastic step, but did close all monasteries and convents, confiscate many properties of the Church, secularize some of the Church buildings, authorize civil marriages (including those of priests), and place cemeteries under the control of the government.[42] These actions were grievous blows to the Church authority and power and destroyed its political power for years to come.

In politics, Guzmán Blanco was nominally a member of the Liberal party. Given his intolerant and dictatorial nature, however, he naturally brooked neither opposition or criticism from the oligarchical forces whom he had defeated in 1870. He did not dispense with elections, but his 1874 requirement that all voters sign and deposit their votes in the presence of his appointed election judges vitiated what little value they may have had.

During the years he controlled Venezuela the state enjoyed relative prosperity. Roads and railroads were built, foreign investment was welcomed, government revenues increased, and some progress in education was made. The president and his family also prospered and were said to have accumulated great fortunes.[43] Guzmán Blanco was not president during all of his eighteen years of power, spending some time in Paris while puppet presidents ruled. Finally, the last one turned on him in 1888 and made his exile permanent. In the political vacuum that followed, president after president followed revolt after revolt. Four more constitutions were written during the next decade. During this ten-year period of hectic politics, a dispute with Great Britain arose over the boundaries of British Guiana. An international arbitration tribunal ruled in favor of Great Britain, and much of the disputed territory was confirmed to that country. Recent Venezuelan administrations have expressed their dissatisfaction over what they consider the injustice of the award, and the issue has once again become a matter of diplomatic negotiation.

In 1899, an event of political importance occurred when power passed from the hands of the llaneros and the forces they had supported to the Andinos (people of the mountain states in the Andes). In that year General Cipriano Castro, the "Lion of

[42] Mecham, chap. 5.
[43] Munro, p. 316.

the Andes," seized power following the death of the incumbent president. For the next fifty-eight years the Andes, and in particular, the state of Táchira, enjoyed an almost unbroken monopoly on the presidency. The illiterate, vain, and corrupt Castro subjected Venezuela to a despotism more thoroughgoing than any of his predecessors. This "Moses of the Republic" distinguished himself by giving Venezuela one of the worst internal administrations it has ever had.[44] His international record was no better; arrogant treatment of foreign powers on matters relating to debts owed them and their property claims against Venezuela led Great Britain, Italy, and Germany to set up a blockade of Venezuelan ports in 1902. Theodore Roosevelt exerted his efforts to bring the affair to an end by arbitration in 1903.

Cipriano Castro made a serious political miscalculation when he awarded the vice-presidency to his trusted military colleague, General Juan Vicente Gómez, another illiterate Andino. Able, astute, ambitious, and opportunistic, Gómez had no intention of remaining in a subordinate position. His chance came when Castro went to Europe for medical attention in 1908. Gómez declared martial law and intimated that the absent president's health might continue to improve were he to remain in Paris indefinitely. In 1909 he prudently amended the constitution to abolish the office of vice-president. Gómez was responsible for seven of the twenty-six constitutions of Venezuela. One, the Provisional Statute of 1914, was in force only two months while his obedient assembly drafted one more to his liking.

Gómez looked upon Venezuela as a personal possession. Rich and choice properties found their way into his hands, so that by the end of his long rule he was one of the richest and largest landowners in Latin America.

El Benemerito ("The Well-Deserving") Gómez had little regard for the political liberties of his fellow countrymen. He retained control over his well-trained army throughout the twenty-seven years of his rule, even when he was not actually in office. His efficient spy system filled the jails with political prisoners who were treated with great cruelty.[45] State legislatures, the national congress, and the courts were meaningless appendages since Gómez regarded their members as personal employ-

[44] Hubert Herring, p. 467.
[45] Herring, p. 468.

ees. The "sovereign" states had no power independent of the will of Gómez. Because political opposition and competition were not permitted, the political parties atrophied and disappeared from public view altogether.

Nevertheless, a future generation of political leaders was born in the closing years of the Gómez regime—the generation of 1928. In that year a number of students at the Central University of Caracas began to agitate for the end of the dictatorship and for more political freedoms. A national student strike was called, and the government responded by closing the universities and by sending the agitators into exile. They returned to Venezuela after the death of Gómez in 1935 and have played leading roles in the political system since that time. Former presidents Betancourt and Raúl Leoni were among the student protestors.

Like Francia, his nineteenth-century counterpart in Paraguay, Gómez brought domestic peace and order to Venezuela, and at about the same price in terms of political liberties. In the field of economic development, however, Gómez turned to international capital for exploitation of the vast deposits of oil newly discovered in his country. His wise oil laws, the inducement of low taxes, and promises of secure property rights attracted foreign oil companies. The oil policy introduced by Gómez has made Venezuela the second largest oil-producing country in the world and the wealthiest country in Latin America.

During the sixty-five years between 1870 and 1935, Venezuela was largely under the control of three men: Guzmán Blanco, Castro, and Gómez (Paraguay it will be remembered was also governed by three men from 1814 to 1870). The early promise of constitutionalism gave way to extreme forms of *personalismo* and caprice in government. The rule of law gave way to the rule of men. Political servility, political cynicism, military domination, and inefficient and corrupt regimes were all characteristics of this period in Venezuelan national life. A major shift of power had occurred: Leadership of the country had passed from the llanos to the Andes, and remained there until 1958.

Paraguay   While Venezuela for the most part enjoyed stability and economic progress between 1870 and 1935, the same years for Paraguay were full of confusion and at times of anarchy. Much of the strife originated in power struggles for the presidency. The powerful office had been created by the constitution of 1870, written under the watchful eye of the occupying forces. Under the terms of the new constitution the Paraguayan president was to be chosen by a small electoral college, a provision that immediately generated a power struggle among the leading families, each anxious to possess the post. The struggle intensified after the Allies of the Triple Alliance withdrew from Paraguay in 1876. Between 1870 and 1935 there were over thirty presidents, about twice the constitutional number. Presidents were jailed, murdered, or exiled, and very few indeed were fortunate enough to be able to complete their constitutional terms of office. Paraguay became the victim of militarism, political strife, and corruption—all of the evils from which Francia had tried to save it.

Much of Paraguay's difficulty can be traced to its political heritage. Bereft of most of its educated male population, politically immature after years of despotism, and having had no opportunity for developing political parties with real roots in society, Paraguay entered upon this phase of its national development at a decided disadvantage.

Paraguay's two leading parties had their origin during this period. The Conservative party (the *Colorado,* or Red) was founded in 1887 by the military hero General Bernardino Caballero. The general contributed to political instability after the departure of the occupation forces by naming and removing presidents at will. He was the dominant political personality until the 1890s. The Liberal party was also organized in 1887, principally to secure the freedom of suffrage set forth in the constitution of 1870. That document established a senate, to be directly elected for a six-year term, and a chamber of deputies similarly elected for a period of four years. All eligible males over eighteen years of age were permitted to vote in the "elections," but the government in power never permitted itself to be defeated at the polls.[46] Indeed, in many of the elections that took place between 1874 and 1936 no opposition candidate

[46] J. Fred Rippy, *Latin America, A Modern History* (Ann Arbor, Mich.: The University of Michigan Press, 1958), pp. 287–288.

presented himself for the office of president, and so a characteristic of the Paraguay political structure in this period of its development was that of *candidato único* (sole candidate). In a
number of the cases the ruling party simply did not permit
opposition. In others, the opposition party refrained from running a candidate in what it regarded as a futile exercise.

This closed political system naturally aroused the wrath of
persons denied access to power through the ballot, and often
they resorted to force and violence to unseat the offending
administration. Over fourteen revolts took place during this
epoch in Paraguayan history, as well as innumerable minor
skirmishes.

By controlling the army and by manipulating the electoral
machinery General Bernardino Caballero and other Colorado
presidents were able to control the presidency for thirty years.
Power was finally wrested from them in 1904 when the Liberal
party overthrew the Colorado administration in what has been
described as the "first popular movement the Republic had
known." [47] For the next thirty-two years Paraguay was governed by the Liberal party.

The victory of the Liberal party, however, did not bring
tranquillity. Rivalries between opposing wings of the new party
and between ambitious families within the same wing of the
party, as well as continuing antagonisms between the two principal parties, kept political tempers at high pitch. Because the
Liberal and Colorado parties had no basic ideological differences at this time, the battle for power was purely a personalistic
one. The parties were collections of the elite of Paraguayan
society. The Colorados were landowners, church officials, and
high-ranking military officers. Many of the Liberals were drawn
from the same echelons of society but were intellectually committed to a greater degree of political freedom and reform, an
efficient but decentralized administration, and, of course, the
separation of church and state, a characteristic of many liberal
parties that developed in Latin America during the nineteenth
century. For the most part, however, Liberals in office were
hardly distinguishable from Colorados in office.

In spite of the political turmoil, a number of solid achieve-

[47] Warren, pp. 264–265.

ments were realized. The National University was founded by the government in 1892, and a public school system was initiated in 1870, the year the war ended. Intellectually, the period has been called the golden age of Paraguayan literature.[48] Politically, after 1900 Paraguayans were allowed more freedom than they had ever experienced. Immigration was encouraged, though with small success, and the Liberal administrations attempted to encourage small farm ownership through their agricultural policies. Foreign investment was invited, and a fairly reliable banking system was created. These achievements were offset by an episode that occurred during the thirty-year Colorado control of the political system (1874–1904) when large portions of the public domain passed into private hands—many of them foreign —in the great land sales of 1886–1904.

The population had begun to recover from the ravages of the War of the Triple Alliance (partly through the early cooperative efforts of the occupying Brazilian soldiers) when Paraguay was again laid low by war, this time with Bolivia in a dispute over ownership of the great Chaco wasteland. The war lasted from 1932 to 1935. When it was over Paraguay had lost 40,000 men and had spent $124 million to retain 20,000 square miles of uninhabited land. Both sides had been spurred on by rumors of oil in the region as well as by painful memories of earlier military defeats. The war was fiercely fought and ended in great economic losses for both countries. In the treaty that concluded the war, landlocked Bolivia obtained the right of river access to the sea through Paraguayan territory. Bolivia's double dependency on Paraguay and Argentina for freedom of riparian navigation remains a potentially dangerous issue in the politics of southern South America.

Summary   Developments in Venezuela and Paraguay during the sixty-five years from 1870 to 1935 indicate that Venezuela enjoyed greater political stability. In gaining this, however, it lost much of its earlier political freedom. Paraguay, on the other hand, enjoyed more political freedom but less stability. It is true that Paraguay had only one constitution during all of this time,

    [48] George Pendle, *Paraguay, a Riverside Nation,* 3d ed. (London: Oxford, 1967), p. 28.

while Venezuela had thirteen, but constitutional changes in Venezuela were purely superficial; the power structure remained the same.

In the area of political party activity, it should be noted that Venezuela's personalistic parties, dating from the Páez administration, were gradually rendered impotent and practically disappeared under the administrations of later dictators. In Paraguay, political parties arose for the first time and their undisciplined rivalries were the cause of much of the political chaos of the time. In both countries political cynicism was the order of the day as fraudulent or meaningless elections succeeded one another. In neither country was there anything remotely resembling mixed or balanced government. The heavy hand of the executive was the ruling force.

The Venezuelan system was completely dominated by the military caudillos, at first from the llanos and then from the Andes. The losses suffered by the Paraguayan army in the War of the Triple Alliance destroyed much of the power of the armed forces in Paraguay. When the influence of General Caballero ceased, politics passed into the hands of the two parties and their civilian leaders.

Both Venezuela and Paraguay had made progress in the economic field, but Venezuela, with its oil reserves, was far better situated. The Chaco War destroyed for Paraguay much of the economic gains that had been made over the years.

Recent political developments: 1935–1970

Venezuela The death of Juan Vicente Gómez in 1935 ushered in a new period of political development. Long committed in theory to the constitutional principles of democratic government, the politically aware Venezuelans at last began to see the application of them in several areas. Progress has been slow and has been interrupted several times by violent and authoritarian regimes, but in 1964, for the first time in 133 years, Venezuela saw a constitutional, freely elected president transfer his power and office to another similarly elected one. Even more auspicious was the inauguration in 1969 of a duly elected president from the opposition. These events are rightfully regarded as two of the most significant achievements in the country's political life and have been hailed with great satisfaction. The road to the realization of such a momentous occurrence was a rocky one, however.

The people had very little to say in the selection of a successor to Gómez. A *gomecista* power elite had grown up around the dictator during his twenty-seven years in power and had no intention of surrendering its influence or privileges. The oligarchy and its subservient congress quickly named as president Gómez's minister of war, General Eleazar López Contreras from the Andean state of Táchira.

Under the new president, the worst aspects of the Gómez tyranny disappeared, but Venezuela remained far from the realization of the democratic ideals that had been faithfully reproduced in the new constitution of 1936. It is true that López Contreras responded to popular discontent and restored some political liberties by freeing political prisoners and lifting censorship of the press and by allowing political parties once more to organize and function. It was during this time that *Acción Democrática* (AD) was organized in 1937 by members of the returning Generation of 1928.[49]

The 1936 constitution stopped short of establishing a process in which the people could have a meaningful vote. The only official of any importance, the president, was indirectly elected by a congress that was chosen by state legislatures and by municipal councils. These provisions made it easy for López Contreras and the gomecista oligarchy to retain control of the power structure and impose their candidate on the Venezuelan people. It did so when it elected López Contreras' minister of war, General Medina Angarita, as the new president at the end of Contreras' term in 1941.

The liberalization that occurred during the early part of the López Contreras administration encouraged the mobilization of leftist and revolutionary political forces. A liberal new labor law guaranteed the workers the right to organize and gave them a weapon heretofore denied them. The oil workers organized in 1936 and felt strong enough to call a general strike late in the year in an attempt to force the oil companies to meet their demands. After a month of agitation, President López Contreras

[49] For a comprehensive study of the origins of *Acción Democrática* see John D. Martz, *Acción Democrática, Evolution of a Modern Political Party in Venezuela* (Princeton, N.J.: Princeton University Press, 1966).

ended the strike by executive fiat and ordered the workers back to their jobs with only a token increase in wages. Repressive executive action soon relieved labor of its new rights.

Political parties fared no better. Suspected of being communists and agitators, party leaders were jailed or exiled, and the parties were progressively dissolved until by 1940 only the administration party remained in legal existence. Late in 1941, however, *Acción Democrática* was legalized and allowed to run candidates in the elections of that year.

The selection of Medina Angarita as president continued the tradition of military executives from the Andes. Medina was López Contreras' personal choice, and few persons expected any major changes in policy or in tactics from him. The new president, however, restored many of the suspended political liberties but retained considerable power to meet threats to his regime. To deal with problems created by World War II, he asked for and received from an obedient congress even more power than had been constitutionally conferred upon him.

Both Presidents López Contreras and Medina Angarita were able to continue the domination of the Táchira military clique, not only because they themselves were military leaders with all the inherent power of that connection, but also because their governments were able to control the electoral machinery and thus ensure an outcome favorable to them. Venezuelans expected them to do so and were not disappointed.

Although the two presidents had labored to improve and diversify the economy of the nation by investing the proceeds of the oil industry in the domestic economy and in various internal improvement programs in agriculture and education, their efforts fell far short of the social and economic needs of the people.

López Contreras had been able to impose Medina on the people in 1941, and in 1945 Medina prepared to engineer the choice of his successor. He organized a new political vehicle, the Venezuela Democratic party, to ensure that state legislatures and municipal councils would elect a congress he could control. Elections to those two bodies in 1944 produced that satisfactory result, and Medina looked forward to the pleasure of naming the next president, who, hopefully, would keep the presidential chair warm until 1949 when he could again legally run for office. This was precisely what López Contreras had planned when he delivered the office to Medina. Medina, however, had other plans, and it was not long before he broke with the former president. When Medina's party failed to nominate López Contreras, the latter's supporters began to talk of using force to regain power. Before that could happen, the power of Medina, López Contreras, and the *táchirense* military oligarchy, together with that of its ally, the landed gentry, was ended in the Revolution of 1945.

Venezuela was ripe for change in 1945. New social and political forces—the result of the exploitation of the oil resources, World War II, and the growing political awareness of the Venezuelan people—had begun to make themselves felt. Political parties were allowed to organize and function. Oil workers were given the right to organize and strike. New social security laws, while not affecting many people, provoked an interest in a more equitable distribution of the oil revenues. World War II had called attention to the abuses under totalitarian and authoritarian governments. *Acción Democrática* also appealed to the urban poor and to the white-collar class and oil workers. Finally, junior officers in the armed forces were coming to view with concern the continued control of Venezuela by senior Andean generals. They decided to cast their lot with AD, the new champion of the people and a vocal exponent of their demands.

Committed to far-reaching economic and social reforms, AD was impatient with the slow progress being made under the conservative administration of Medina. It found a willing ally in the young officers whose career ambitions were being thwarted by older generals whom they regarded as technically backward and unresponsive to the real needs of the people. The Revolution of 1945 thus brought about a new power alignment: an alliance between leftist political leaders with a base in mass popular support and revolutionary young officers.

Following their overthrow of President Medina, the revolutionary forces appointed a seven-man junta composed of four members of *Acción Democrática,* two officers, and one independent civilian. The president of the junta was Rómulo Betancourt. One of the early actions of the new governing body was to try ex-presidents Medina and López Contreras on charges of illegal enrichment. They were convicted and exiled.

The coup of 1945, which claimed an estimated 2500 casualties, ushered in a period of revolutionary democracy that lasted until 1948, when it was terminated by another military coup. During the three-year period, AD continued its mobilization and politicization of the peasants. The number of peasant unions rose from 77 in 1945 to 515 by 1948. AD also organized the Venezuelan Peasant Federation, whose membership grew from 7000 in 1945 to over 43,000 in 1948. The growth of the peasant unions denoted a shift of power from the landowners to peasant union leaders. The number of labor unions also increased during the three-year span. AD was responsible for the establishment of 500 new labor unions and 13 national labor federations.[50]

A principal concern of the new provisional government was the drafting of a new constitution that would end the system of indirect elections and thus make the government more responsive to the people. A very liberal electoral law and a complete restoration of civil and political liberties brought a rash of new parties. Five major parties competed for seats in the constituent assembly that would write the new constitution. *Acción Democrática* won 137 of the 160 seats. The constitution of 1947, therefore, was a reflection of the political, social, and economic philosophy of the party.

In the general elections that followed the promulgation of the new constitution on July 5, 1947, AD was able to retain its control by electing the distinguished Venezuelan novelist Rómulo Gallegos to the presidency and by capturing 38 of the 44 senate seats and 83 of 111 seats in the Chamber of Deputies. President Gallegos was inaugurated on February 15, 1948. His tenure was an exceedingly brief one, even by Venezuelan standards. He was overthrown on November 24, 1948, by the same military faction that had helped bring AD to power in the first place. The *coup d'état* clearly demonstrated that the military machine was still the ruling force in Venezuela and that electoral victories in themselves did not provide an adequate power base for an administration or guarantee continuity in office.

Before its three-year taste of power was ended by violence,

[50] *Venezuela Election Factbook, December 1, 1968* (Washington, D.C.: Institute for the Comparative Study of Political Systems, 1968), p. 9.

AD had managed to institute a number of significant changes and reforms. The oil policy of Venezuela was revised to permit the government to share oil revenues on an equal basis with the foreign producing companies. Moreover, the oil companies were forced to invest a sizable portion of their share of the revenues in projects for the economic betterment of Venezuelan workers. New labor legislation was particularly advantageous to workers in the petroleum industry. The party also began to put into effect its proposals to tax excess income and to bring about agrarian reform. All of these activities constituted a revolution in the broader sense of the word, for they represented a philosophy of genuine change and a threat to the status quo. Many of the measures were thus repugnant to the traditional sectors of society and to AD's disillusioned military partners, who gradually became more and more concerned with the leftist orientation of the government. *Acción Democrática* leaders compounded their error by thinking that their 1947 success at the polls gave them a power base independent of the military forces. They attempted to reduce the armed forces to the status of a subordinate institution under civilian control.

The dissatisfaction of the armed forces with the policies of AD took on a new dimension when President Gallegos and the party began to tamper with the very existence of the armed forces. Not only did Gallegos reduce the number of "independent" (that is, military) officers in his cabinet, but he also advocated a reduction in the size and expenditure of the military machine. Workers and peasant militias were projected to take their place.[51] The military—the most powerful institution in the Venezuelan political system—had no intention of being relegated to a subordinate political role. It countered by demanding that the president not only retain the miliary men in his cabinet, but that he should appoint three more. Given the mood of the party, the president naturally refused and the stage was set for a showdown.

The opportune moment arrived late in November 1948 when a labor organization controlled by the executive committee of AD called a general strike. Charging the AD government with corruption, disruption of the social and economic life of the

[51] Harry Bernstein, *Venezuela and Colombia* (Englewood Cliffs, N.J.: Prentice-Hall, 1964), p. 61.

nation, and incompetence and collusion with subversive forces, the military wing of the 1945 revolutionary partnership seized power. AD's reforms were promptly stopped, the 1947 constitution suspended, congress sent home, and the party itself outlawed. It led an underground existence for the next ten years.

The brief experiment with civilian government had failed partly because the armed forces were not ready to accept a nonpolitical role. From 1948 to 1958 Venezuela was once again under military administration. A three-man junta governed until 1950. In November of that year, Lieutenant Colonel Delgado Chalbaud, president of the junta, was assassinated on the way to his office. He was the first head of state in Venezuelan history to be murdered in office. Chalbaud's place on the junta was taken by a powerless civilian, but the real power had passed into the hands of an ambitious young military officer from Táchira, Major Marcos Pérez Jiménez, and the junta finally called for elections to be held in 1952 to elect members to a constitutional assembly. All political parties except AD and the Communist party were permitted to run candidates. Pérez Jiménez had persuaded himself, or had been persuaded, that the people would send delegates to the convention who would support him, and he allowed a free election. Early election returns were alarming in that they revealed strong trends against the dictator. In the midst of the counting he suspended the whole process, dissolved the junta, held hurried conferences with other military leaders and finally declared himself provisional president. The count was then resumed and the unfavorable trend was quickly reversed to produce a victory for Pérez Jiménez.[52] The constituent assembly that convened in January 1953 was ready and willing to do the bidding of the provisional president. It wrote a constitution in three months and to no one's surprise elected Marcos Pérez Jiménez for a five-year term as Venezuela's next constitutional president. It completed its labors by naming the members of all the state legislatures and the municipal councils in the republic. It also selected the membership of the new national congress. A "republic" was in business again.

Not much was accomplished during the next five years

[52] For a detailed account of the 1952 elections, see my article, "The 1952 Venezuelan Elections; A Lesson for 1957," *The Western Political Quarterly,* 10 (September 1957), 451–458.

for the people as a whole, although general prosperity prevailed. Showy projects were the order of the day: expensive superhighways from Caracas to the coast, skyscrapers, and mountaintop hotels. Much of the government revenue found its way into the pockets of administrative officials, including the president.[53]

By 1957 Pérez Jiménez had succeeded in alienating almost all sectors of Venezuelan society. The growing social conscience of the long quiescent Church was disturbed by the regime's venality, corruption, and disregard for pressing social and economic issues. It began to voice its concern in pastoral letters and in other Church publications. University students, always a volatile element in Latin American politics, were incensed over the closing of the Central University in Caracas and by the regime's attempt to convert it into an agent of the government.

Pérez Jiménez's harsh treatment of political parties earned him the enmity of most of the politicians. *Acción Democrática* had been outlawed, as had been the Communist party. Relentless harassment by government security police caused other parties to go underground.

The dictator's preoccupation with grandiose improvement projects in the capital city and his lack of concern for the economic plight of the rural masses caused them to turn against him. The middle classes were disgruntled because the economic policies of Pérez Jiménez offended their sense of nationalism by favoring foreign enterprises. They also resented the heavy favoritism shown to the military officer class. Even within the armed forces there was considerable dissatisfaction with the government. The notoriety and harshness of the Pérez Jiménez administration was bringing discredit to the military institution as a whole.

By 1957 the dictator was in an uncomfortable position. Enjoying what appeared to be complete control of the country, he had no desire to relinquish either office or power; yet his own constitution forbade a second term for him. He could, of course, resort to a device familiar to Latin American executives and amend the constitution to delete the proscription. But most of the population was against him, and he would surely lose an election if he permitted an uncontrolled one. His solution was

[53] Edwin Lieuwen, *Venezuela,* 2d ed. (London: Oxford, 1965), p. 98.

the unconstitutional device of a plebiscite. He called the people of Venezuela to the polls in December 1957 to vote *yes* or *no* on the question of continuing him and his administration in office for another five years. The voters also had the choice of accepting or rejecting a single list of legislators. The outcome of the controlled plebiscite gave him the majority he sought, and he prepared to settle down for another five years. His victory was short-lived, however. A month later he was out of office and in exile. A general strike and a series of popular anti-government demonstrations supported by some elements of the armed forces and the business community ended the military dictatorship in January 1958.

Within a short time a new military junta headed by Admiral Wolfgang Larrázabel (Venezuela's first naval chief executive) announced that general elections would be held in December 1958 for the purpose of filling the presidency and all other elective offices under the 1953 constitution. All political parties who wished to do so and who could meet the modest legal requirements were allowed to participate. AD and the Communist party emerged from the underground, were legalized, and ran candidates. Two other major parties entered the contest: the nationalistic Democratic Republican Union (URD) and the religious-based Social Christian party (COPEI) (see Chapter Five for a discussion of the parties and their programs). Three presidential candidates competed for office: Rómulo Betancourt (AD), Wolfgang Larrázabel (URD and the Communist party), and Rafael Caldera (COPEI and two minor parties).

The integrity of the Larrázabel administration was demonstrated when fair and honest elections were permitted and Larrázabel accepted his own defeat at the polls. The victor was Rómulo Betancourt who won the presidency with 49 percent of the popular vote. AD also captured both houses of the congress. The new administration took office on February 13, 1959. Hoping to keep alive the embryonic spirit of national unity, President Betancourt kept his campaign promise and invited URD and COPEI to participate in his government. Both parties accepted, although URD withdrew from the coalition in 1960. COPEI remained a partner of AD throughout the administration of Betancourt. Indeed, its support became vital to AD as that party suffered serious membership defections in 1960 and

1962. Dissident members of the party were protesting the moderate approach of the majority wing to some of the basic problems of Venezeula as well as the continued control of the party by the seasoned veterans. The 1960 defectors were pro-Castro and called themselves the Movement of the Revolutionary Left (MIR).

In 1961 a new constitution similar in content to that of 1947 was promulgated. In addition to restating the basic philosophies of the ruling party, the constitution decreed that a president could not seek a second term until the elapse of ten years from the end of his term.

The new administration initiated some far-reaching programs whose objectives are still priorities. President Betancourt attacked with varying degrees of success the problems of illiteracy, dependence on oil, lack of housing, unemployment, and agrarian reform.

The political climate in Venezuela during the Betancourt term of office was troubled. The major threat to stability was the Communist party and the supporters of Fidel Castro. During 1962, members of these two groups organized the Armed Forces for National Liberation (FALN) and embarked upon a destructive program of terrorism and sabotage against the government and foreign enterprises. To combat these illegal activities President Betancourt suspended constitutional guarantees of civil liberties. They were curtailed during most of his five years in office. He also suspended MIR and the Communist party and prohibited their participation in the election of 1963.

As that election approached, FALN intensified its harassment. Its objective was to create such disorder as to bring about the cancellation of the election in the hope that such a move by the government would provoke a situation favorable to communist takeover.

President Betancourt, however, managed to survive the numerous attacks on his regime (and one attempt to assassinate him) and to carry out the election on schedule.

The election of 1963 demonstrated that although AD was still Venezuela's strongest party, it had lost some of its appeal. Raúl Leoni, AD candidate, won with only 33 percent of the vote as compared with Betancourt's 1958 victory with 49 percent. AD lost control of both houses of the legislature, and thus coalition became an absolute necessity. When COPEI, now the country's second largest party, supplanting URD, refused to continue as a coalition partner, President Leoni sought cooperation elsewhere. Long negotiations with URD and the National Democratic Front (FND), a newcomer to the political scene, finally produced a workable coalition.

A government crisis was created in March 1966, when internal party revolts forced URD and FND cabinet members to resign their posts. URD eventually reentered the cabinet, but FND declined to do so. Its three posts were accepted by representatives of independent groups in congress. Enough FND members agreed to continue to vote with the coalition to give President Leoni's government a very shaky majority.

Under the Leoni administration Venezuela continued to prosper, industrialize, and diversify its economy. The government claimed that great strides had been taken in building schools, roads, hospitals, and sanitation facilities. Distribution of land under the agrarian reform program was accelerated, and the administration undertook the creation of new jobs to reduce the chronic unemployment.

The election of 1968   The establishment of democratic government and constitutional stability took another step forward in Venezuela as the result of the December 1968 election. The 4 million eligible electors (25 percent of whom were illiterate) went to the polls to elect a president, the congress, state legislatures, and municipal councils. Interest centered almost entirely on the presidential race. After ten years in power, *Acción Democrática* lost control of the government. Its position vis-à-vis its political opponents was greatly weakened by a new split in the party. Because he was denied his party's presidential nomination, Luis Beltrán Prieto Figueroa bolted and organized the People's Electoral Movement, thus adding another personalistic party to the Venezuelan potpourri. Had the party remained united behind the official candidate, Gonzalo Barrios, the presidency would probably have remained in its hands. The two factions together polled about 45 percent of the popular vote. As it was, however, Rafael Caldera, nominee of the Social Christian party, was elected with barely 30 percent of the 4 million votes cast and only a few thousand more votes than Barrios. Because of Caldera's razor-thin victory, coalition government continues to be a feature of the Venezuelan political system.

Eighteen political parties and several other minor groups were active in the campaign. Only six presidential candidates presented themselves, however. Many of the minor parties supported one or another of the leading contenders.

An interesting feature of the 1968 election was the reentry into politics of former president Marcos Pérez Jiménez who had spent the previous five years in prison upon an embezzlement conviction. Although he was in Spain, his National Civic Crusade attracted enough support among those alarmed at the growing rate of crime to send him and three supporters to the Senate and twenty-one followers to the Chamber of Deputies. The Venezuelan courts, however, ruled that the former dictator was not entitled to his seat because he was in Madrid during the December elections. The constitution forbids the election of anyone who did not vote in the election.

The Caldera administration took office in March 1969. The new president was immediately plunged into difficulties, not the least of which was forming a stable coalition. With the help of independents, the National Civic Crusade, and a splinter party of AD, he got his government off the ground. AD grew increasingly obstructionist during the remainder of the year, and the president was hard-pressed on a variety of fronts involving political and domestic issues. The record of his first year in office is discussed more fully in the following chapters.

Paraguay We have seen how events and forces have operated to change the political system of Venezuela in the direction of greater democracy. The political evolution of Paraguay from 1935 to 1970 has been characterized by a decrease in effective popular participation in the political process and a reversion to a more authoritarian mode of government. Although there were a number of very short-term presidents, the government of Paraguay has been under the control of two different generals during much of the thirty-five-year period.

Military involvement in politics, somewhat reduced between Paraguay's two wars, began in earnest following the end of the Chaco War. That three-year conflict unleashed considerable social unrest and produced a new element in the power structure

—a generation of war veterans who began to demand a voice in the affairs of the nation and who were eager to demonstrate the efficiency of government along totalitarian lines.

These forces entered active politics and ended the thirty-two-year Liberal domination of government when military units under the command of Colonel Rafael Franco overthrew President Ayala on February 17, 1936. The *Febrerista* regime, as it was known, was openly contemptuous of the democratic process and dedicated itself to the creation of a "new Paraguay." In a manifesto to the people, the Febreristas declared that their "Liberating Revolution is of the same character as the totalitarian transformation occurring in contemporary Europe in the sense that the Liberating Revolution and the State are now one and the same thing." [54] Implementing that philosophy, Franco prohibited all political activities and suppressed the parties.

The Febreristas were unable to hold onto power for long. They were driven from office in August 1937 in another military coup encouraged by the displaced Liberals. A period of *confusionismo* ended in 1939 with the election of the Liberal party candidate. General Estigarribia, a hero of the Chaco War. Numerous disorders early in his term caused him to assume dictatorial powers until a constitution more clearly in tune with Paraguayan political realities could be written and adopted.

Such a document was ratified by the people of Paraguay in 1940. Paraguay's third constitution, it concentrated great powers in the executive and made no pretense that the legislative or judicial branch of the government were coequal with the former. In its social and economic philosophy it gave expression to some of the Febrerista proposals for the establishment of a system of state socialism to which Estigarribia was sympathetic.

General Estigarribia was killed in an airplane accident three weeks after his constitution went into effect. His power passed to his minister of war, General Higinio Morínigo, who had been selected by the rest of the cabinet on a purely provisional basis.

General Morínigo was of a different persuasion and soon made it clear that he did not intend to be a figurehead at the

[54] Cited in Pendle, p. 33.

beck and call of the cabinet that had elevated him to his high post, and he gave every indication that he intended to be far more than a temporary president. He dealt quickly with various uprisings against him and replaced the Liberal members of his cabinet with military men. Indeed, he shortly assumed "the total responsibility of political power," dissolved the legislature, curtailed party activity by exiling the Febrerista leaders, and suppressed the Liberal party altogether. With political opposition crushed, he proceeded to have himself elected president, allegedly at the request of "military friends." In the unopposed presidential election of 1943, in which Paraguayans were compelled by law to vote, Morínigo naturally won an overwhelming victory. The election was a typical one for Paraguay in that there was only one presidential candidate.

General Morínigo consolidated his position with the military machine by allocating to it about 50 percent of the national budget. With military support, the president ruled Paraguay in an extremely authoritarian manner. He dismissed the democratic process in a few well-chosen words:

> An exclusively electoral democracy for a people not yet educated to vote conscientiously and freely is a farce. It does not assure government by the people, but only for dictators and demagogues . . . we reject liberalism, a product of the nineteenth century, because it does not admit of the positive intervention of the state in satisfying human needs . . . We propose interventionist methods, above all in the field of economics and especially in the relations between capital and labor in order to rectify social injustices. The inertia of the liberal state must give way to the dynamism of the state as protector and leader.[55]

In line with this philosophy, labor unions were speedily brought under control, and full censorship of the press and radio were imposed. Government supervision was extended to all social organizations, student groups, and the entertainment field. Political prisons awaited those who openly opposed the general, and many students and professors were incarcerated.

General Morínigo was in power during World War II, and

[55] Cited in Warren, pp. 338–339.

his sympathies were pro-Axis. He allowed groups and individuals who supported Hitler and Mussolini a considerable amount of freedom. He received aid from pro-Axis Argentina and also was able to cultivate and profit materially from the friendship of the United States. Only when the outcome of the war was no longer in doubt did he declare war on the Axis (February 1945) and associate himself with the Allies in signing the United Nations Charter.

In July 1946, in an abrupt about-face in the domestic political arena, Morínigo lifted his ban on parties and gave them the right to criticize his regime; he even invited the Colorado party (out of office since 1904) and the Febreristas to join in a new cabinet. Colonel Franco returned from exile, and even the communists were permitted to engage in politics. The long ban on political party activity, coupled with the dissolution of the Liberal party in 1942, however, had created a political vacuum that ended only when General Morínigo openly embraced the Colorado party as his electoral vehicle. Not all the Colorados were overjoyed by this alliance, and Morínigo's action caused a party split that endures to this day.

These moves toward democracy were all too late; no one apparently believed in the dictator's conversion. An uprising against him in December 1946 caused his coalition cabinet to resign, and shortly afterward Morínigo again formed an all-military cabinet. Genuine civil war broke out in March and it did not end until Colonel Franco went into exile again in August.

Employing the technique of *imposición,* President Morínigo prevailed upon Juan Natalicio Gonzalez of the Colorado party to be a candidate for the presidency in 1948. As that party was the only one to offer a candidate in 1948, it elected the president and the entire membership of the legislature.

Discontented military leaders felt strong enough to move against Morínigo, and a group of them soon forced him into exile. His eight years in power were years of strong dictatorship, sometimes cruel, sometimes benevolent. He kept order at the price of liberty. He pacified the army with matériel obtained through gifts and loans from the United States. He encouraged immigration and brought in foreigners with badly needed skills. He made moves in the direction of agricultural colonies. Under the impetus of World War II, Paraguayan foreign commerce was expanded.

The dictator's removal from the political scene initiated another period of *confusionismo* as five presidents came and went in an eighteen-month period. Power was finally stabilized in the hands of Federico Chaves in 1949. He became constitutional president in 1953 for a five-year term, but served only one year of it. General Alfredo Stroessner unseated Chaves in 1954, and since that time Paraguay has been governed by the general. His regime is a military dictatorship based upon the support of the Colorado party, which he had managed to take over.

General Stroessner ran for the presidency in 1958 and again in 1963, despite the fact that the constitution forbade more than two terms. Stroessner's argument, accepted by his legislature, was that his first four years in office completed the unexpired term of ex-president Chaves and thus he was entitled to two full terms in his own right. In 1958 Stroessner had no opposition. In 1963, apparently sensitive about foreign public opinion concerning his one-party state, he prevailed upon a newly formed splinter group of the Liberal party, called *Renovación,* to run a candidate against him. In return for this gesture, the group received twenty of the sixty seats in the Chamber of Deputies, and the defeated presidential candidate was appointed ambassador to Great Britain.

A constitutional convention was called in 1967 to revise the 1940 constitution in order to permit General Stroessner to continue in office. By 1965 the president had felt sufficiently secure to permit his opponents to enter candidates for elective municipal offices. And he actively sought their participation in the constitutional assembly. When the convention met in May 1967, it had a membership of 120 delegates, 80 of whom were Colorados. *Renovación* elected 29 and the Liberal party itself returned 8. Even the Febreristas were represented by 3 members.

The new constitution retained the two-term limitation on the presidency but declared that terms served under the 1940 constitution would not be counted. Thus President Stroessner may look forward to another ten years in power provided he can retain the loyalty of the armed forces. He promptly accepted the nomination of the Colorado party for a new term. He won the election and was inaugurated in August 1968. The constitution also abolished the one-house Chamber of Deputies and provided for a bicameral legislature. These reforms were purely artificial for they made no real change in the nature of power or in the political system as a whole. The manipulation of the constitutional system by Stroessner is a good example of *continuismo* (manipulation of the constitutional system by the president in order to prolong his tenure in office beyond his legal term).

SUMMARY

The political history of Paraguay since 1935 demonstrates anew the fact that most of the population has little realistic alternative to submission to the administrations of strong men. This does not mean that Paraguayans are supine. About one-third to one-half of the total number of Paraguayans are said to be living in exile—voluntary or forced—rather than endure the dictates of the present regime. Many others have participated in unsuccessful revolts. Militarism has been a predominant feature of the political system since 1935. The emergence of the Colorado party as the political vehicle for the elite and its partnership with the military has made Paraguay essentially a one-party state despite recent involvements of other political parties in the political process.

At this point in Paraguay's history one may say of it what has been said of France: The more things change, the more they stay the same.

Several conclusions may be drawn from the events and developments of 1935–1970 in Venezuela. Violence as a mode of political expression has been an ever-present characteristic, but as a successful technique for acquiring power it has been in abeyance since 1958. The overthrow of the military dictatorship in that year seems to have ended the military's open preoccupation with politics and political power. The honesty and regularity of elections since 1958 are encouraging signs that the political process is responding to the demands of society and that constitutional government is becoming more and more a way of life. The revolution of 1945, far from being a change in the palace guard and in spite of its interruption by ten years of dictatorship, has made significant changes in the economic, political, and social life of the people. Therefore, it deserves to be rated as a watershed in the political history of Venezuela.

In this long chapter we have endeavored to trace the influence of the religious, political, social, and economic institutions implanted by Spain during its 300-year hegemony on the evolution of Venezuela and Paraguay as independent states. The lack of a true standard of legitimacy has plagued the two countries throughout most of their history. They inherited contradictory principles that have been in conflict with each other ever since. They inherited authoritarian institutions as well as enormous respect for the dignity of man. They inherited a high regard for the spiritual and cultural attainments of man but access to them has been limited to an aristocratic few. They glorified power and authority in the person of military caudillos but sought to contain them with paper constitutions. They sought the ideal and were often confronted with hard realities when theory and practice collided. Wars over both principle and politics convulsed the two nations, inflicting hard penalties in terms of wasted resources and lives. Military rivalries and personal ambitions hindered the development of national allegiant societies. Intolerance of opposing views, normative absolutism in politics, and resort to force for conflict resolution are deeply ingrained traditions that have persisted up to the present in varying degrees in the two republics.

TWO
AUTHORITARIANS, INNOVATORS, AND RESISTORS

POLITICAL SOCIALIZATION, RECRUITMENT, AND PARTICIPATION

The generalization was made in the introductory chapter that the political systems of Paraguay and Venezuela are populated to a greater degree by political subjects than by political participants. In the preceding sections some historical and social explanations for this situation were suggested. Now we turn our attention to contemporary Venezuelans and Paraguayans and to the institutions that condition and influence the formation of their political beliefs, their attitudes toward those in power and toward the exercise of power, their identity with the political system, and their acceptance or rejection of the political ethic under which they are governed. We are interested, too, in the processes and channels through which these people are inducted into the political system to carry out the roles necessary to the functioning of the system: the formation of a political class. These processes we refer to as political socialization and political recruitment. They are the means by which one generation passes on to the next its mores and myths.

The thesis of this chapter is that because of the nature of their social systems, which emphasize elite, traditional, and ideal patterns and values derived from their Spanish colonial experience, Venezuela and Paraguay lean more toward authoritarianism in their political systems than toward democracy. Wagley cites Lenten's definition of an ideal pattern as a "consensus of opinion on the part of a society's members as to how people should behave in particular situations" and adds to it the notion that such patterns would reflect attitudes about how an institution ought to be structured and how it should function.[1] An ideal pattern thus includes both the way society thinks an institution (family, church, school) should be organized and how an actor (father, priest, professor) ought to behave in his particular role. The value patterns are *elite* in the sense that they represent the dominant cultural system of the small upper class. They are *traditional* in the sense that they are derived from sixteenth- and seventeenth-century Iberian customs, usages, and social organization.

It is true that in Venezuela a strong current is presently running for democracy and for the implementation of constitutional provisions that provide for it, and that recent developments offer signs that the political system is moving gradually in the direction of freer participation by more citizens in the political life of the nation. Venezuelan society is clearly in a transitional stage in which social change is taking place, and as it generates political expectations, it creates conflict between the innovators and the resistors—the members of the traditional upper echelons of society, the military caste, and others who do not want their way of life disturbed.

Nevertheless, the values of the aristocratic class in Venezuela and Paraguay form the dominant values of the social system and determine the behavior of the individual who aspires to rise in it. Wagley and others assert that the elite value pattern has filtered into all societal sectors with the exception perhaps of the most isolated Indian communities.[2] To the extent that upward social mobility is possible, it means the acceptance by the lower classes of the norms and standards of the upper class and the acquisition of its status symbols. In spite of constitutions

[1] Charles Wagley, *The Latin American Tradition* (New York: Columbia University Press, 1968), pp. 2–3. Wagley argues (p. 7) that "any set of ideal patterns derived from historical experience and institutionalized in religion, family structure, the relations of socio-economic classes and in the educational system of a society will affect the behavior of future generations, even after such patterns have become outmoded."

[2] Wagley, p. 3.

in both countries that stress democratic values and political processes, the traditional aristocratic mentality persists, even in the face of rapid social and economic change in the great metropolitan centers.[3] In the small interior towns and villages this mentality has undergone practically no change in the last 300 years. This situation obtains particularly in Paraguay, where communications and transportation facilities are primitive indeed.

Basically authoritarian in their outlook and values, the traditional social structures—the family, the Church, the armed forces, the educational system, and the upper classes—socialize their young in values and modes of conduct that conflict with the democratic and egalitarian values embedded in their constitutions. Authoritarian institutions in a predominantly democratic society may have their influences diluted by the democratic socializers. But when they function within a sympathetic environment, they tend to reinforce the values of the other similarly inclined institutions. The same would be true of democratic institutions in an authoritarian environment.

The social structures operate in such a way as to produce individuals who see natural order and merit in hierarchy, privileged status, obedience, inequality, absolutism, and deference. Even in the agricultural sector the influence is at work. The hacienda complex with its *patrón-peón* (landlord-worker) relationship has always been an isolating factor and a conservative influence that stands in the way of effective political integration of citizens into the larger political community of the nation.

The political effects of the socialization process among these agents are: intolerance of opposing viewpoints and policy alternatives; unwillingness to compromise views, desires and goals; a decided tendency toward nepotism and *continuismo;* personal rather than institutional authority; a tendency to look to persons in any position of influence or authority to make the necessary decisions; an abdication of personal responsibility for events; and finally, an acceptance of privilege and inequality as a natural state of affairs.

In Venezuela, as has been observed, there is evidence that this situation is changing. New social demands and changing

[3] Wagley, p. 6.

attitudes within certain elite sectors—the Church and armed forces for instance—are beginning to have moderating effects upon the old system of values. Greater observance of the constitution is also having its beneficial effects. In Paraguay, however, things remain much as they have for decades.

The principal socializing agents

The family   The principal and foremost transmitter of political and social values is, of course, the family. If it is true, as has been argued, that the aristocracy sets the cultural standards in Latin America, then it becomes important to examine the upper-class family unit in some detail.

The Hispanic-American family in the elite sector is usually a large, paternalistic one that seeks to maintain its solidarity and strength in elaborate kinship ties. It particularly emphasizes solidarity. For a great many years the family was the recreation center, the charitable institution that cared for all its members during their lifetime; in more remote colonial times, it was often a miniature state within a state. The family-owned estates were often distant from government seats and thus were able to develop a considerable degree of autonomy and self-sufficiency. This situation still persists in many rural areas of Latin America. Metropolitan families, however, are beginning to show the effects of their contacts with non-Hispanic cultural patterns, notably those of the United States and France.

The Hispanic aristocratic family has always set great store in social status and class, intellectual and artistic achievements, cultural advancement, formal social relations, and showy displays in religion. It has exalted the status of the male and promoted a sexual double-standard.[4] It has regarded with disdain occupations involving manual labor, which it considers socially and economically degrading. Until recently it conditioned its sons to expect careers in the Church, in the military establishment, in high-level politics, and in the prestige professions. Now other opportunities are opening up.

A familial set of values such as these tends to produce a society that stresses *who* one is more rather than *what* one is or has become. Working one's way through college, for example,

[4] Wagley, pp. 3–4.

or being a self-made man are achievements not so highly regarded in Latin America as they are in North America. Of all of the "who people," says Madariaga, the Spaniards are the "who-ist." [5] Family connections and a good name are vital assets and usually rank ahead of accomplishment.

It may be said of the Latin American family, as of all others, that many of the patterns of action, beliefs, and values of the people in their political activity are the natural results of the conditioning influences of the family. One of the most important lessons a child in Latin America learns in his early development relates to the authority of the father and mother. Children are taught to respect the opinions and judgment of the father and to fulfill his commands with unquestioned obedience, seeking his approbation in all things. The father is thus naturally highly influential in all important decisions affecting the collective life of the family and the individual actions of his children. The process of reducing a child to a quiet, obedient, helpful, and respectful individual in Paraguay is called "taming." It begins at about age five.

The authority pattern of the Spanish family derives from the Roman tradition of *pater familias,* that is to say, it is a family unit organized around the absolute authority of the father. The Roman patriarch could dispose of his children as he saw fit in certain circumstances, and there are instances in the colonial period where Latin American fathers put their children to death for offenses against their authority. Although the state long ago withdrew that power from the heads of households, the absolutist concept of parental authority has been transmitted down to the present. There is a Latin American saying that a man of fifty is like a child of four in the presence of his parents. Filial obligation is a feature of many other cultures, of course, notably the Oriental. In Latin America it has persisted as a cultural trait and is far more deeply rooted than it is in North American society.

Accustomed to respecting the authority of the father, the Latin American does not find it difficult to understand the prevalence of dictatorial and authoritarian leaders. These individuals

[5] Salvador de Madariaga, *Latin America Between the Eagle and the Bear* (New York: Praeger, 1966), p. 55.

are understandable as visible extensions into the political system of power of the father. The state is, in fact, a larger version of the family.

Cultural patterns also place the wife in a submissive and obedient role, one that encompasses such functions as homemaker and cultural, religious, and moral preceptor. In the latter role she is the direct ally of the Church. Although the wife is theoretically subject to the husband's authority in the hierarchical arrangements of the family, in fact she occupies an equal position with him in many of them. In most Latin American families, the wife is the disciplinarian (Latin American men are softhearted and tend to spoil their children). Her power as a disciplinarian, however, rests ultimately on the power of appealing to the father's authority. Physical punishment—if matters proceed that far—is administered by the father.

In the nuclear family unit (father, mother, children) power and status are accorded the children in direct relationship to their birth and sex. The eldest son and his brothers take precedence over the female progeny. Within this immediate hierarchy sons are entitled to special privileges, education, travel, associations, and sexual freedom denied to the carefully chaperoned daughters of the family. In the nuclear family the children soon learn that they have both superiors and inferiors among their siblings, and that basic inequality in rights and status is a way of life. In their study of Tobatí, the Services found a decided inequality in the treatment of the sexes within the family in Paraguay. Parents from all walks of life were disposed to favor the boys over the girls and to show their concern and preference even more as their sons matured.[6] A child's inferior position in his family vis-à-vis others, however, in no way lessens his loyalty and attachment to the family, for it is his shelter, his comfort, and his security.

Even though sons have privileges and opportunities not available to their sisters, they are also indoctrinated with an abiding sense of family responsibility and identity. The family interest and integrity must be protected and furthered at all times. A son or father in politics is expected to provide some-

---

[6] Elman R. Service and Helen S. Service, *Tobatí: A Paraguayan Town* (Chicago: The University of Chicago Press, 1954), p. 221.

how for the unemployed members of his family within limitations of the job resources and competing claims of other families. Nepotism has been an integral part of the established framework of expectations in the Latin American family for a great many years.

We have been speaking thus far of the simple family unit of husband, wife, and children. But there is also a much larger aggregation of relatives that must be considered in the typical upper-class aristocratic family in Latin America. The *extended* family consists of a number of nuclear units bound together by marriage, blood relationship, or the institution of *compadrazgo* (godparenthood). In this larger universe, each individual occupies an acknowledged place and feels secure in it. As nuclear families become associated with and bound to others by strong kinship ties, marriage, and economic undertakings, family responsibilities also increase. Thus it is possible to speak of the 400 families of Chile and the 40 families of Panama.

One device by which powerful and important families (and indeed families in all strata of society) are linked together in social and economic alliances is that of *compadrazgo*. A godparent in the Latin American tradition must pay more than formal lip service to his solemn promises. He is expected, for example, to remember birthdays and feast days of his godchild and to provide educational and financial assistance and political and social advancement for him as the need arises and as opportunities present themselves. The godchild in turn is taught to respect and honor his godparents (*co-madres* and *co-padres*), particularly if they are from the same social class.

While the normal practice is to seek godparents from one's own social level, it is by no means uncommon for a family in one station of life to seek to better its position by securing godparents for its children from a higher social class. They are successful more often than not because it is considered an honor to be asked to sponsor a child.

The extended nuclear families in the traditional social structure have been generally conservative influences that seek to preserve old ways of life and inherited patterns of authority and social relationships. This is particularly true among the great landowning families in Venezuela. In such families, an attachment to the land, a high regard for the hacienda and its environs, and a love of the region is a part of a child's upbringing. Thus the rural-based family is a powerful socializer in a particularistic sense. A child learns to identify with a regional and particular set of values and interests—the llanos, or the Andes, for example. These regional sets of interests have not always been compatible in Venezuela and in the volatile political atmosphere of the country the result until the last decade has been political turmoil or political dictatorship.

The extended family is much more common in Venezuela than it is in Paraguay, the hacienda complex being a more conspicuous feature in Venezuela during colonial days. The attentions of Francia and the ravages of the War of the Triple Alliance depleted the ranks of the great landholders in Paraguay. During the war, many of them left Paraguay never to return. Occupation, confusion, and disintegration of much of the state apparatus clouded land titles, and the landlords have never regained the foothold they had prior to 1870.

In the traditional aristocratic family of Venezuela the elders are entitled to great respect. Like the English monarch, they have the right to be consulted, to warn, to advise, and to encourage. The family is tight-knit and presents a united front to the society external to it. It is not an uncommon practice for a patriarch in Venezuela to build an apartment building to house his children and their families so that all may live under the same roof. In Paraguay, where there is less of an aristocratic, patriarchal family, this practically never happens. Indeed, the older generation prefers to live apart from its children and to remain independent of them. Bonds of parental authority are naturally looser where offspring are encouraged to go their own way and where the parents have no practical means of maintaining their authority. The typical Paraguayan parent has little to pass on to his son or daughters. Small landholdings are the rule, and sons often secure their own little private plots independently of the parent merely by squatting on public and private land. Thus, parental authority over children is diminished in the rural sections of Paraguay by the landowning and occupying pattern.

Although no studies have been made of the impact of Paraguay's two wars on family structure and behavior, it seems reasonable to conclude that the heavy male losses in them (344,000) must have had a debilitating effect. One result al-

most certainly was that the surviving men became the pampered
subjects of competition among the women. The scarcity of men
in the periods following the two wars enabled them to pick and
chose their women and to abandon them at will. The frequency
with which they did this tended to center family authority and
responsibility in the hands of the women. The Services found
that in Tobatí less than one-half of the 301 families living there
were complete households.[7] One hundred and thirteen households
were headed by women who had been deserted by their common-
law mates. Although the authority of the Paraguayan male in a
complete household is generally respected, it is only nominally
exercised, for it is the woman who rules. In the upper-class complete household of the cities, one finds a closer adherence to the
idealized pattern of Spanish life. A growing number of important
families in Asunción are of non-Spanish origin, however, and
thus observe their own cultural patterns.

A significant difference between Paraguay and Venezuela
lies in the fact that in Paraguay the women were the chief trans-
mitters of values and culture for long periods of time. They in-
stilled Paraguayan nationalism as they passed on to their children details of Paraguayan heroism and sacrifice in the wars of
their country. While they played an influential role in keeping
alive the spirit of Paraguayan identity, they were not, nor sought
to be, influential in the choice of leaders. Only in 1963 were
women permitted to vote for the president. Before that date
their participation had been confined to voting in municipal
elections.

The family in Latin America is often the spawning ground
of politics. The Latin American male is above all a political
animal. Only those who are completely out of touch with political developments and currents (as are many of the rural
peasants in Paraguay and Venezuela) show little interest in or
concern for national politics. Although the Venezuelan and
Paraguayan urban male satisfies his appetites for political dis-
course in his clubs and social organizations, politics is inevitably
a subject of family discussion. The views of the father are at-
tentively listened to, and sons often follow in their father's foot-
steps. (To cite only two examples, consider the political orienta-

[7] Service and Service, pp. 150–152.

tions of Carlos López and Francisco Solano López of Paraguay and Antonio Leocadio Guzmán and his son, Antonio Guzmán Blanco of Venezuela.) The masculine authority pattern of the family facilitates the father's ability to influence his children in the matters of his prejudices and preferences. Children learn at an early age in Paraguay to which of the two traditional parties, Colorado or Liberal, they belong. Almost all Paraguayans outside the capital city identify themselves with one or another,[8] despite the fact that Paraguay has been a one-party state on the national level for years, under the nominal control of the Colorado party. On the basis of the foregoing observations, it seems reasonable to argue that it is the woman who is the primary agent in transmitting political values, including party preferences. The role of the Venezuelan family as a socializer for party membership is less clear because there have been a great many parties in Venezuela, particularly in recent years. Many of these have been ephemeral and highly personalistic. It seems reasonable to conclude, however, taking into consideration the nature of family organization and values, that whatever the party of the father is at a given time is also generally the party of the entire family. There are, of course, instances of sons rejecting the political affiliations and status of the father and pursuing their own political inclinations. One of the terrorist guerrillas killed in Venezuela not long ago was the son of a governor of one of the states in Venezuela.

If all the children of the elite obediently followed their fathers' political persuasions, and if most of the important families were linked by common concerns and interests, it would seem that political stability would be the result so long as the masses remained passive.

As a matter of fact, however, Latin Americans in general are highly individualistic, often governed by emotion (and politics generates a great deal of it) and persuaded that their view of politics and constitutional organization is the correct one. Given their orientations, it is an easy step for them to rebel against established authority in an effort to place themselves in the seats of power. Thus we see a society that stresses obedience

[8] Frederick Hicks, "Politics, Power and the Role of the Village Priest in Paraguay," *Journal of Inter-American Studies,* 6 (April 1967), 276.

to authority in most of its basic institutions, engaging in frequent attempts to overthrow that authority and substitute another. In the case of Paraguay from 1870 to 1935, competition between families of the elite caused most of the political turmoil. The Latin American family, then, is both an agent of social unity and of political discord.

The Church   A second major socializing agent is the Roman Catholic Church. There are other religious organizations in both countries, but their membership is very small (Venezuela, 26,000; Paraguay, 30,000) and their socializing influence of little consequence in the overall Catholic environment.

The close identity of the women of Venezuela and Paraguay with the Church and their active participation in religious activities gives the Church a channel into the family circle. By securing the affections of the women, who are custodians of the children and the morals of the family, the Church has an effective means of maintaining its role as ultimate guardian of the family and individual morals. The Church has had less success with the men, who generally give up going to church and adopt anticlerical views.[9] In spite of their defection, their Catholic values stay with them or such astute observers as F. Garcia Calderón would be totally in error about their own countrymen.

As a religious and economic force, the Church in Paraguay is also a relatively weak institution. It owns little property, and the lower ranks of the priesthood, at least, live on a very reduced scale. The Services observed that priest and population alike are poorly educated in religious matters.[10] Mecham made a similar observation with respect to the Venezuelan clergy.[11] The people are given little training in the fundamentals of Catholic theology and traditions. Local superstitions and beliefs are often as important as religious dogma that may be imperfectly understood.

Although the Church may perform less than adequately in a religious and spiritual capacity, it functions in both countries as an important social institution. In Paraguay the celebration

[9] Peter Merkl, *Modern Comparative Politics* (New York: Holt, Rinehart and Winston, Inc., 1970), p. 114.

[10] Service and Service, chap. 13.

[11] J. Lloyd Mecham, *Church and State in Latin America* (Chapel Hill, N.C.: The University of North Carolina Press, 1934), chap. 4.

of religious events and anniversaries, particularly local patron saints' days, brings together all social classes on a basis of equality and attracts villagers from tiny hamlets. The *fiestas* are organized by societies (*sociedades*) whose primary function is to provide amusement and entertainment on religious occasions for the town and country residents. The ardent interest and participation of the people in these fairly frequent Church activities reinforce their identity with the manifest symbols of their religions, for the fiestas feature parades of religious symbols and ornate images. To the extent that townsmen and villagers attend celebrations in other communities, as they often do, the Church can be considered an integrative force bringing people together from diverse regions and localities for a common purpose.

In Paraguay the open participation of the military personnel in religious festivals links the two institutions. In the fiesta of María Auxiliadora in Tobatí, the Services noted the music was provided by a band of army musicians, and that the commander of the army engineer corps gave a speech. An armed guard of soldiers also took part in Good Friday observances.

Everyone is expected to contribute according to his means to pay for these celebrations. In poverty-stricken Paraguay this expectation can work a real hardship, yet funds generally seem to be forthcoming. Church festivals and celebrations in Paraguay are among the principal sources of amusement and entertainment and are subscribed to willingly enough.[12]

Many of the same observations may be made about the Church in Venezuela, although the Venezuelan Church is perhaps better off economically and financially than is the Paraguayan Church.[13]

Because the religious significance and meaning of the numerous celebrations are subordinated to their entertainment value, a certain formalism has come to characterize the ceremonies of the Church in Latin America as a whole. Observances of the forms and ceremonies, parades and fiestas, the regard for images and icons instead of substance have led some scholars to

[12] The author has relied heavily on the Services' study of Tobatí for most of the material dealing with the Church and the rural social structure in Paraguay. See Chapter 13 of their book.

[13] See Mecham, chap. 4, and Watters, throughout.

assert that it is the gloss and color of religious ceremonies that attract participation, not the content of the religion.

Perhaps the most powerful agency of the Church in inculcating its values and furthering its interests is its educational arm. Although the number of schools operated by the Church has decreased in proportion to those operated by the state in both Venezuela and Paraguay, still a significant number of schools and universities are under the aegis of the Church. In Paraguay, most of the primary school children (grades 1–6) were in public schools, but 11 percent of the primary schools, 45 percent of the secondary schools and one of the two universities are Catholic. Fifty-six percent of the total general secondary school enrollment in 1965 (as distinct from the enrollment in technical and vocational schools) was in Church institutions. Thirty-one percent of university enrollment is in the Catholic University. In Venezuela in 1964, 7 percent of the primary schools, 45 percent of the secondary schools and two of the then seven universities were Catholic. Enrollment figures indicate that 18 percent of the primary students, 45 percent of the nontechnical, nonvocational secondary schools and 20 percent of the university students were studying in Church schools.[14]

The *raison d'etre* of Church schools is to indoctrinate the young people in the values and aims and beliefs of the Church as well as to give them an education consistent with those values. The Statute of the Catholic University in Paraguay declares it to be the purpose of the University to preserve, transmit, and enhance the spiritual heritage of the human race in its moral, scientific, and technical dimensions, both in the natural and supernatural order; to provide a sound religious education in conformity with the doctrines and precepts of the Catholic Church: and to provide training for the proper exercise of liberal and technical professions. Similar provisions may be found in the articles incorporating the Catholic universities in Venezuela. Church schools may accomplish these purposes by prohibiting the teaching of certain doctrines (evolution, for example), forbidding the study of certain authors and philosophies (The

[14] These figures were compiled from data extracted from the *Statistical Yearbook of Latin America* (1966) and the *5th Annual Report of the Social Progress Trust Fund* (1965).

Index); by presenting materials in ways favorable to the Church, and, of course, by giving religious instruction. Although the basic curriculum content of all schools in both countries is set by the National Ministry of Education, Church schools may add others.

The Statute of the Catholic University of Paraguay places supreme authority in the hands of the Grand Chancellor, who is the Archbishop of Asunción. He has far-reaching powers in matters of faculty appointments and subject matter of the disciplines. He is specifically directed to preserve the orthodoxy of the whole university in faith and customs and to receive professions of faith from the rector and staff. Discipline, therefore, is an ever-present feature in the Church schools—and in most public schools for the matter. One authority argues that in its education activity the Church has been a restrictive force in the sense that it provides moral, doctrinal and disciplinary checks on human intelligence and activity.[15]

The Church may also influence the faithful through the media of publications, periodicals, labor organizations, layman associations, *sociedades,* pastoral letters, and student groups. The Venezuelan Church publishes four daily newspapers with a total circulation of 31,000: *La Religión* (Caracas); *La Columna* (Maracaibo); *El Vigilante* (Mérida); and *El Diario Católico* (San Cristóbal). The Church does not publish an official daily paper in Paraguay at present, but has published the weekly *Comunidad* off and on since 1958.

In both countries, widely held feelings of anticlericalism tend to bind much of the male population together. The role of the Church in colonial development and in the fight for independence, its ownership of large amounts of land (at least in Venezuela), its insistence upon the retention of special privileges and exemptions, its association with unpopular regimes or its opposition to popular ones and, until recently, its resistance to democratic trends are in part responsible for the indifferent or hostile attitudes toward religious institutions and personnel in Latin America as a whole. In some countries, during the nineteenth and twentieth centuries, anticlerical sentiments resulted in the

[15] Jorge Mañach, "Religion and Freedom in Latin America," a paper prepared for the Latin American Conference on Responsible Freedoms in the Americas, 1954, p. 4.

formation of radical and sometimes liberal parties dedicated, among other things, to the idea that the Church should play no political role in the system. The effects of anticlericalism, at least in Venezuela, have been traced in Chapter One.

The public educational system   A third important agency of political socialization is the educational system. The public and private schools of Venezuela and Paraguay during most of their existence have reflected the interests and the values of the elite sector of the traditional social structure. These were derived from the colonial epoch, an age when the educational institutions were dedicated to teaching and maintaining the elite echelon of society. Education in that far-off time was considered to be essentially a right of the upper class and had as its objective the creation of a man of culture. The lower classes had neither money nor leisure to acquire any formal education, nor were they expected to aspire to it ("We need peons, not diplomas and degrees."). A university education that trained one for a profession was, of course, totally out of the question for the vast majority of people, who thus remained illiterate and ignorant.

Matters changed very little in Venezuela for many years after the achievement of independence. Priorities other than that of establishing an extensive educational system took precedence. Then too, geographical, social, and economic factors tended to perpetuate the elite notion of education by making it almost impossible for anyone but the wealthy aristocrats to send their sons to the schools in the larger urban centers or to foreign universities. Only since World War II has Venezuela vigorously attacked the basic ills in its public education system. Its illiteracy rate, formerly about 30 percent of the population, is now down to about 11 percent of the population over the age of ten. (Thirty percent of Paraguayans are illiterate.) In Paraguay, public and private education under Francia was nonexistent and remained so under the two Lópezes. Not until after the War of the Triple Alliance did the government, under the prodding of the occupying powers, begin to create a public school system.

Such public educational institutions as presently exist in Venezuela and Paraguay are directly under the control of the Ministry of Education of the national government. The minister is charged with the responsibility of implementing the constitutional provisions concerning education. The frequency with which this office has changed hands in both countries in the varying fortunes of politics has meant not only frequent disruptions and disorders in the educational system, but also periodic uncertainty until the educational philosophies of the new minister are made public.

The guidelines for such philosophies are expressly laid down in their respective constitutions. The 1967 Paraguayan constitution guarantees to every inhabitant the right to an education that shall develop his spiritual and physical abilities, his civic and moral conscience, and prepare him for the struggle for existence (Art. 89). Stressing concepts of liberty and equality, the constitution also assigns to the state the responsibility of promoting national culture in all of its manifestations. It is specifically expected to promote and protect the Guaraní Indian heritage, of which the Paraguayans are inordinately proud (Art. 92). Primary education is compulsory and free from age seven to fourteen, but since facilities are nonexistent in many areas, large numbers of school-age children cannot and do not attend.

Venezuela's constitution of 1961 contains a similar broad statement of the goals of the country's educational system. Educational objectives there stress the full development of the personality, the training of citizens adapted to life and democracy (an overt expression of the obligation of the state to engage in political socialization), the promotion of culture and the development of a spirit of human solidarity (Art. 80). All Venezuelans have the right to an education at state expense through all phases, although the government reserves the right to charge a fee to those able to afford university education (Art. 78). Their educational philosophies at present thus commit both Venezuela and Paraguay to the development of a system of universal education, at least through the secondary level.

The educational structure in the two countries is organized on a similar pattern: six years of primary schooling, six years of secondary education (five years in Venezuela), followed by the university for those fortunate enough to be able to qualify in the examinations. At the secondary stage there are also various vocational schools as well as normal schools, but these facilities are not adequate to fill the needs of either country for middle-level technicians.

For the rural child in each country, education is an off-again-on-again affair. Poverty (uniforms are usually required), indifferent parental attitudes, inadequate school facilities (particularly notorious in Paraguay), teacher shortages, and a curriculum irrelevant to the rural way of life cut down considerably upon school attendance where schools exist at all. The dropout rate among those who begin an education is high in Paraguay, despite the fact that Paraguayans value education as a status symbol. In 1963, only 31.8 percent of the children who had entered the first grade enrolled in the second grade. Of those who had begun the six-year primary phase in 1958, only 15.5 percent completed the cycle. About one-half of these sixth-grade graduates matriculated in the six-year secondary phase. Less than one-third of the students who entered the secondary school cycle completed the full six years. Many dropped out at the end of the third year and entered one of the vocational schools.

Venezuelan figures are better, but they too show significant dropout tendencies. Twenty-eight percent of the primary students who entered the first grade in 1958 were still enrolled at the end of six years. Thirteen percent of these children went on into the secondary system, and of this number, a little over a third completed the secondary phase.[16] One reason for the dropouts in both countries may be the fact that although education is free, the students must buy their own books. For many lower-income families this is simply not possible. Also, vocational and technical schools claimed many of the dropouts from the general educational system.

The curriculum is established by the national government in both countries, and it includes heavy doses of national history and culture. The Paraguayan curriculum is one that promotes extremely nationalistic sentiments as well as cultural chauvinism.[17] Besides reading and writing, the first- and second-year students learn about national holidays and their significance. In Paraguay these celebrations usually center about the achieve-

[16] *Fifth Annual Report,* Social Progress Trust Fund (Washington, D.C.: Inter-American Development Bank, 1966), pp. 495 and 580.

[17] Service and Service, p. 227.

ments of past dictators and the commemoration of military and religious events. Third-graders are introduced to national symbols and biographies of Paraguay's heroes: Francia, Carlos and Francisco López, and other leaders. In grades 3 and 4, the students are subjected to a nationalistic treatment of Paraguayan history up to the beginning of the regime of Francisco Solano López (1862). The Paraguayan text describes Paraguay at this point in time as being in a "state of grandeur." [18]

The Paraguay secondary cycle is in two phases. The first three-year course of study is compulsory for all who enter. After three years a student may decide to terminate his formal education, and many do. Those that choose to go on have several options open to them: preparation for the university, teacher training, and commercial and vocational education. General secondary education in Paraguay has as its primary objective the preparation of students for the university, but only one-fourth actually go on to the higher educational level. Education at the secondary level consists of instruction in ten to fourteen sciences, as well as continued instruction in the cultural, military, and economic history of the nation. Much of this part of the curriculum stresses the greatness and bravery of the Paraguayan people during their wars.[19] The Paraguayan's emotional attachment to his folk anthropology (the Guaraní heritage) is heightened by the intellectual's efforts to prove the uniqueness and superiority of the Guaraní people, and therefore of the Paraguayan people. Schoolteachers stress the valor and beauty of Paraguayan women and cite the fearlessness and ferocity of the Paraguayan male in battle—traits they believe came to them from their Guaraní ancestors. The Paraguayan curriculum indicates that in the secondary and primary levels a rather significant amount of time is devoted to patriotic themes designed to evoke nationalistic feelings and identity.

The Venezuelan student's training in his country's literature, language, history, and social, moral, and civic training also emphasizes nationalistic themes, although to a lesser degree than in Paraguay. Historic and patriotic themes are much in evidence in Venezuela, and deeds of arms and valor in the

[18] Service and Service, p. 231.
[19] Service and Service, pp. 233 ff.

various epochs of the republic receive detailed treatment, particularly the roles, careers, and achievements of the military heroes, such as Simón Bolívar.

Within all the lower levels of schools in Venezuela and Paraguay, discipline and obedience to the teacher are stressed; lessons are often learned by rote, texts memorized, lessons recited in unison, and until recently the sexes were segregated and each given a different kind of education. Teachers are expected to use the textbooks selected by the Ministry of Education or one of its agencies. However, in a 1957 study of secondary education in Latin America made by the Pan American Union, Paraguay and Venezuela indicated that the same texts were not uniformly used in all of the schools. Paraguayan teachers could make recommendations concerning the texts they wished to use; Venezuelan teachers, according to the survey, were listed as having freedom to select the texts. In Venezuela, but not in Paraguay, a list of officially approved texts was published.[20] In Paraguay, teachers were subject to periodic visits by ministry personnel who observe their teaching techniques and had to conform to prescribed curriculum and lesson plans.[21] It must be observed, however, that teachers in the two republics have little control over the curriculum and over course content. Control of the educational system by the national government in both cases facilitates its utilization for whatever propaganda purpose the regime sees fit.

In a society that values and respects the educated, cultured, and professional man, and in which education is a mark of status and prestige, the university assumes great importance. Latin Americans have inherited a bureaucratic cultural pattern [22] in which status positions are restricted to the professions, with those of doctor and lawyer heading the list.

The universities naturally provide the main recruiting ground for all of the professions, including that of politician.

---

[20] *Estado actual de la Educación Secundario en la America Latina,* 2d ed. (Washington, D.C.: Division de Educación, Union Panamericana, 1957), p. 135.

[21] Service and Service, p. 229.

[22] C. H. Haring, "The Universities in Latin American Life and Culture," a paper prepared for the Latin American Conference on Responsible Freedoms in the Americas, 1954, p. 5.

Entrance into any of the desirable careers has been generally dependent upon a university education, which in turn depended upon the satisfactory completion of secondary schooling and the successful passing of a rigid entrance examination. The overriding importance of a university degree has led students to conform to the dictates of the professorial class in order to secure the credentials for their chosen career. This has often meant the memorization of the professor's lecture notes and their regurgitation at examination time. Most young people aspire to the prestige professions, for to be forced into manual or physical labor is to be demoted to an inferior social level. Very few upper-class, or aspiring middle-class, women, for example, enter the nursing profession, which, although a humanitarian occupation, is considered to have certain degrading physical aspects. Students will go to great lengths to acquire professional credentials and therefore will submit to the academic discipline and formality of the classroom, The style is mainly expository with little give-and-take between student and professor. There is, moreover, a certain air of cynicism about the educational process in the higher institutions of learning. Many professors are only part-time teachers, pursuing more lucrative careers elsewhere. The possession of a university chair is often sought because of the social prestige it carries, but few seek it as a full-time occupation. Only 10 of the 574 Paraguayan professors in 1965 devoted full time to their teaching professions. Venezuelan and Paraguayan students quickly learn that their professor may put his other occupational concerns above his university obligations and that classes are as likely to be cancelled as not.

In the area of higher education, the experiences of Venezuela and Paraguay have been somewhat similar, although the Venezuelan university dates far back into the colonial period, while that of Paraguay is just 100 years old. In each case, the university is basically a collection of independent professional faculties that introduce the student immediately to the required courses of his chosen profession. The liberal arts preparation of the North American student is not generally considered to be the function of the university except in the faculty of arts and science.

The educational systems in Venezuela and Paraguay thus

appear, at the pre-university level, as institutions designed to create devoted, nationalistic, and obedient citizens along the lines valued by the dominant institutions. At the university level, however, the students are often a source of annoyance to the government because they rebel against the ordered and closed society of their country and university and seek other solutions to social and economic problems. When they become political leaders, they often find that other important and powerful institutions have an equal stake in society and are opposed to their liberalizing tendencies. The early political liberalism of politicians often has to give way to the realities of the social and political structure.

The hacienda Another major political and economic socializing agent in Latin America is the great agricultural unit called the hacienda. It is in many ways similar to the pre-Civil War plantation of the American South. Landownership in most of the Latin American republics has been characteristically polarized between the large landholdings (*latifundios*) and small landholdings (*minifundios*). In Venezuela 2 percent of the people are *hacendados* (owners of haciendas) and own about 75 percent of the arable land in the country. Most of the people own no land at all. In 1945 there were about 345,000 propertyless peasants in the countryside. Peasants who do own land are usually *minifundistas,* with only a few acres in their possession. In spite of progress under the agrarian reform program, the bulk of the land in Venezuela is still in the hands of the hacendados.

A hacienda usually embraces a considerable expanse of land. It is home to the hacendado and his family when they choose to visit it, to his retainers, and to numerous peon tenants who make up his labor force. These latter have been born on the hacienda in families that for generations have been connected with the hacendado's family in a menial capacity. They identify with it, take pride in its fortunes, and are loyal subjects for the most part. Indeed, there is often a close bond between patrón and peon, a relationship sometimes cemented by *compadrazgo,* with the patrón serving as godfather to numerous peon children. Most of the peons could not leave the hacienda even if they wanted to, since most are in debt to the hacendado for purchases made in the hacienda store. The vast majority of them cannot hope to rid themselves of debt incurred in the high-priced stores and debts may be passed on from generation to generation.

As an economic unit, the hacienda seeks to achieve and maintain self-sufficiency. It prefers to buy as little as possible and to manufacture all the necessary articles of daily life and to raise its own food. The peons would not buy in the open market anyway, for most are paid in hacienda scrip, redeemable only in the hacienda store. Although taxes on land are low, they are often not paid. A study of taxation of land in underdeveloped countries indicates that 53 percent of such taxes in Paraguay were unpaid at the end of one year; 34 percent at the end of six years; 14 percent at the end of eleven years; and 8 percent at the end of twenty-one years. The most frequent delinquents were the large property owners.[23] In Venezuela there is still no effective land tax because of the opposition of the landowners. Many of the hacendados are content with a minimal return on their land and have not shown much interest in modern agricultural techniques that would greatly raise the level of their production. Then, too, large acreages are allowed to lie fallow.

Tannenbaum describes the hacienda as a cultural, social, and economic institution.[24] The center of activity on the hacienda is in the complex surrounding the residence of the patrón. Here there is often a chapel, a school of sorts, granaries, storehouses, repair shops, and the hacienda store. All roads on the hacienda lead to this nerve center. There may be several small hamlets on the hacienda where workers live, but there is little communication between them. The peons meet at the "great house" when they meet at all. They come to observe the fiestas, religious holidays, births, deaths, and other social occasions, many of which are connected with the patrón's family rather than with their own. The hacienda way of life tends to produce an individual who looks inward on the hacienda and not outward

[23] Haskell P. Wald, *Taxation of Agricultural Land in Underdeveloped Economies* (Cambridge, Mass.: Harvard University Press, 1959), p. 53.

[24] Frank Tannenbaum, *Ten Keys to Latin America* (New York: Knopf, 1963), p. 85.

on the world; who identifies with the locality, the region, and its dominant family or families. He cherishes local customs and values that may set him apart from the national culture.

The hacienda also is a closed political system in its own right. There is an inner hierarchy of authority (patrón, manager, peon), which to the peon is often more important than the national or provincial official hierarchy. In terms of political socialization, the hacienda produces a servile relationship between landlord and tenant. Three hundred years of exploitation and class stratification have caused the latter to look up to his betters and to seek their advice and follow it. In return for this he expected a measure of social security in his old age. In this essentially inegalitarian society, the peon became an obedient individual who existed to carry out the economic and political wishes of the patrón. The patrón decides whether the peon would vote or not and for whom he would vote. The traditional hacienda, in short, was not only an economic unit, but an authoritarian political structure in which subservient farmers did as they were told. In this type of social and economic organization the individual had little opportunity for developing self-reliance and for participating responsibly in the affairs of his community.

Even the rural peasant in Venezuela who does not live on a hacienda is affected by the preponderant influence of the great haciendas that surround him. The village in which he lives is usually politically and economically dominated by the nearest hacienda. A peasant or villager may be as deferential in his attitudes to the neighborhood hacendados as are peons who live on his land. The success of *Acción Democrática* in organizing the peasants of Venezuela and in winning much of the rural vote in recent elections, however, indicates that the traditional hold of the landlord over the peasants has deteriorated significantly. Land reform programs of the government will make further inroads.

It is Tannenbaum's thesis that the political effects of the hacienda system have been manifested in other ways. In the troubled year followed independence in Venezuela, compadrazgo and the loyalty of the extended family combined to produce a political power base for an hacendado. In his political capacity he was known as a *cacique* or caudillo. Because local interests and family concerns were often predominant over national ones in the rural areas, local and regional arrangements evolved to combat what was regarded as the pernicious power of greedy national politicians. The local cacique was usually an influential hacendado, linked by blood to other landowners in the area. His power was for many years enhanced by the relative weakness of national institutions and government. In this environment the hacienda had "a strength that was genuine. The hacienda community's fealty gave the hacendado a power that was immediate and direct. And a group of hacendados, related and interdependent, controlled a region." [25] Such a situation inevitably produced instability as one region challenged the interests of another in the quest for national power. This was the case in Venezuela, where rivalry existed between caciques in the llanos and those in the Andes until the professionalization of the army brought into existence an institution with effective national power to curb such rivalry.

The rural, conservative hacienda has been an agent of particularistic socialization; it has created and perpetuated a parochial servile class of peasant. It has been an impediment to effective political integration and the creation of a sense of national loyalty. The cacique-hacendado-peón relationship has also encouraged and reinforced the tendency of the masses to follow a leader—to identify with a person, to see authority as personal, not institutional. The hacienda complex thus must share with other institutions the responsibility for producing in Venezuela a rural society and a political system in which *personalismo* is a primary fact of life.

These observations are more relevant to Venezuela than to Paraguay, partly because the hacienda as an economic device and a way of life was never a particularly vigorous institution in Paraguay, and partly because there are fewer regions to compete with one another for national power. Rural existence in Paraguay is essentially a peasant one; there are practically no farmers in the North American sense. The majority of the peasants live on plots of land called *chacras,* which they usually do not own. The peasant seems to prefer a more solitary existence to hamlet or town life. In striking contrast to Venezuela, with its large agricultural haciendas, in Paraguay about

[25] Tannenbaum, p. 87.

the only large landholdings are those of cattlemen and are generally not suitable for farming. The overwhelming majority of the rural Paraguayan population is economically independent in the sense that they are not peons or tenants dependent upon the benevolence of an hacendado. Although the hacienda is not an important Paraguayan institution today in the sense that it involves large numbers of peasants, "to a very large degree the contemporary Paraguayan lives with the psychological vestiges of this pattern which is based on general conviction that life depends solely upon the forces above: God, State, and Patron." [26] The relative absence of the restrictive hacienda in Paraguay has helped to produce a culturally integrated and nationalistic people.

Peer groups   The influence of numerous peer groups in Venezuela and Paraguay on the socialization process may be only guessed because their numbers and roles have been inadequately studied. In both societies, however, there are many religious associations that recruit members from specific social strata. In Paraguayan towns, the *sociedad,* or better class of people, join clubs and groups quite distinct from those formed by the *gente,* or common folk. Sociedad groups seek to preserve their superior status by exclusive membership policies and by this means reinforce their common social and political interests. The gente in turn are socialized to accept their more lowly position in the social order of things.

Other socializing forces   Urban labor unions, peasant organizations, and student and teacher associations (particularly those on the university level) are active participants in the political system and help to shape the values and affections of their members. Political parties are also important socializers. Their effectiveness in this role is in direct proportion to their longevity and nationalistic spirit. These forces will be more fully discussed in Chapters Five and Six.

In the sense that political socialization involves the effective orientation of the individual toward his political system, the

[26] Byron Nichols, "Paraguay—A Future Democracy?" *SAIS Review* (Summer 1968), 26.

constitution is both a positive and a negative conditioning instrument in Venezuela and Paraguay. To the extent that its broad social, economic, and political philosophies raise the level of expectations in the people, it is an important value conditioner. To the degree that these philosophies and their attendent expectations are ignored by the power structures, they serve as agents of disaffection and alienation.

Finally, ideologies—political, military, and religious—help to socialize those elements of society able to read and comprehend them. The number of those who can do so has always been small, but they have often controlled the destinies of the two countries. Both political systems are controlled by a small elite with powerful interests. In a conversation with an American journalist, a cabinet minister in the Pérez Jiménez regime remarked that Venezuelans had to be governed by an elite . . . "And of course," said he, "we are the elite." [27]

Summary The thesis of this chapter so far has been that the dominant socializing forces in Venezuela and Paraguay have predisposed the average citizen to tolerate authoritarianism in politics. The emphasis on such values as obedience, deference, discipline, family loyalty, hierarchy of status, class distinctions, and military achievement and deeds has resulted in a political society that has acquiesced in absolutist concepts, paternalism, intolerance of opposition (thus breeding violence as a political technique), nepotism, and inequality among citizens. At the same time, one must note that the attachment to democratic ideals, at least among the intellectuals, placed alongside the values mentioned earlier, has produced a dualism in conceptions of authority that has made the process of governing a difficult one. In the environment that has been described, politics has been the province of the elite sectors—military, religious, educational, and societal. The point was made in the Introduction that the majority of Venezuelans and Paraguayans must be regarded as subjects in their political systems, rather than as participants. This observation is more true of Paraguay than of Venezuela. Casting a vote in an election is, of course, one indication that the citizen functions as a participant, but

[27] Tad Szulc, *Latin America* (New York: Atheneum, 1966), p. 24.

the circumstances under which he does so and the effectiveness of his vote need to be analyzed to determine the real degree of his participation. This we will do later in this chapter.

The social institutions that have shaped the political attitudes of Latin America have their roots deep in their Iberian heritage. They have developed and flourished in geographic environments that have encouraged isolation, regional particularism, and political rivalries. In short, Venezuelan and Paraguayan society is the product of history, geography, and social influences, as are all societies.

Before we leave this section, we must stress the fact once again that while the cultural forces in general have produced aristocratic concepts of society and politics, a strong ideological affinity for the egalitarian concepts of democracy exist in both Paraguay and Venezuela. These concepts are expressed in their constitutions, in the writings of political theorists, in the platforms of leading political parties, and in the communication media when freed of censorship.

We have, therefore, opposing conceptions of authority in both countries: practical authoritarianism and visionary democracy seen as a desirable, idealistic objective. Authoritarianism has always prevailed in Paraguay, and it prevailed in Venezuela until the death of Gómez in 1936 and has triumphed sporadically off and on since then. The discrepancy between the actual authoritarian organization and operation of government and society in the two countries and the popular democratic ideals espoused by government leaders and often ignored by them have produced attitudes of alienation and hostility toward the leader and toward government in general.

Political recruitment

If political cultures and political systems are to maintain and adapt themselves—to survive as political entities—they must be continuously involved in the transmission of political values, attitudes, beliefs, myths, and emotions from one generation to the next. Reinforcement of the dominant concepts governing the political activity by and through such agents as those discussed in the preceding section help to join the individual with his political system by creating both a feeling of loyalty and nationalism. But political systems need more than just people who share political values. They need actors—men and women who will fill the various roles of the system—such as legislators, judges, executives, and party leaders. If there is to be an organized government, some citizens must be induced to discharge specific political roles, to become members of officialdom. We refer to this function of the political system as *political recruitment*.

The more advanced systems have generally added to their ascriptive norms such universalistic criteria as elections and examinations, by which all those who are interested may compete for political posts. Less modern societies rely more upon ascriptive and particularistic criteria for the selection of political personnel: school ties, personal friendships, family connections, regional connections, and so on.[28]

The role of regions and the military   The historical experience of Venezuela and Paraguay demonstrates that militarists from particular regions have monopolized top positions in the political structure for most of the time since independence was won from Spain. In Venezuela from 1830 to 1899 the government was dominated by generals who hailed from the desolate, rough plain, the llanos. The llanos produced a tough breed of men, born to the saddle and willing and able to take great risks to achieve their aims. Two sons of the llanos, Generals Páez and Monagas both rose to prominence because of their military records during the war of independence. Later llanero generals, such as the self-appointed Antonio Guzmán Blanco, saw military activity only in the turbulence of the domestic scene. The supremacy of the llanero caudillos came to an end in 1899 when insurgents from the Andean state of Táchira overran Caracas and seized control of the government and army garrisons. Táchira monopolized the presidency for the next sixty years as five of its military sons occupied the office: Cipriano Castro (1899–1908), Juán Vicente Gómez (1908–1935), Eleazar López Contreras (1935–1941), Isaías Medina Angarita (1941–1945), and Marcos Pérez Jiménez (1950–1958). The interval between Medina Angarita and Marcos Pérez Jiménez

[28] Gabriel A. Almond and G. Bingham Powell, Jr., *Comparative Politics* (Boston: Little, Brown, 1966), pp. 47–48.

was a revolutionary and turbulent period in which power was not overtly exercised by the *táchirense* oligarchy.

One salient fact thus emerges from the history of Venezuela: the predominance of the military establishment in the political system. The record clearly shows that a military career conferred great rewards on the successful contenders. Even if one had to create his own army, recruit his own personnel, and design his own uniform, military rank came to be regarded as the principal avenue to power and to the ultimate prize, the presidency. Lesser political figures also came from the military sector of society. In the 1873 congress of Venezuela, for example, 19 of the 32 senators and 51 of the 70 deputies were generals. Before the professionalization and the nationalization of the armed forces took place, many of these men came from the private armies of the caudillos. After professionalization was achieved, military men did not seek the lesser posts in government, but continued to demand cabinet posts and other influential positions. Today, military men appear to have moderated their political ambitions and for the time being, at least, seem willing to accept a nonpolitical role.

The importance of such outlying regions of Venezuela as the Andes and the llanos in the recruitment process has diminished as governments with a power base in a national electorate have become a reality. Caracas has become the dominant region and supplies most of the political contenders and government personnel. Although they may have been born elsewhere, almost all influential men live in Caracas, center of culture and seat of the national government.

In Paraguay there is basically only one important region: the fan-shaped nuclear heartland that radiates from Asunción eastward for about 120 miles, containing most of the nation's population. Asunción, the only large city in Paraguay, dominates the political life of the republic and has always done so. Most of the Paraguayan presidents and power contenders have come either from the capital city or from nearby areas. No other urban area offers comparable opportunities for political power, for cultural enrichment, and for educational advancement. The central military garrison is also located in the capital city. In terms of power and politics, Asunción *is* Paraguay.

The involvement of the military establishment in Paraguay

between 1870 and 1936 took the form of harassing and over-throwing the political leaders in numerous civil revolts and coups. Over thirty presidents came and went during this turbulent era. Beginning in 1936 with the successful conclusion of the Chaco War, the armed forces moved into direct and open control of the country. With brief interludes of civilian leadership, Paraguay has been ruled since 1936 by military men who are either products of metropolitan professional military schools or heroes of the Chaco War, or both. Not only have presidents been generals, but other important members of their cabinets have held that rank. President Stroessner's cabinets have always included at least three generals.

The educated classes in the recruitment process As we have seen, during most of its independent existence Venezuela has been dominated by strong military presidents. Many of them had little or no education. General Páez began life as an illiterate peon and never really learned to read well. Generals Castro and Gómez were semiliterates with more native cunning and physical stamina than education. General López Contreras was a notch higher; he graduated from high school.

The same situation obtained in Paraguay with the exception of Dr. Francia, who as one of the few men in all Paraguay with a doctorate enjoyed great prestige. The two Lópezes who followed him were uneducated for the most part since Francia was opposed to education for his people.

Although their presidents from 1830 to 1945 were not men of great intellect, the Venezuelan people have traditionally held the intellectual, university-educated class in high regard. When they have had an opportunity to do so, they have always given them their support in their pursuit of political careers. In 1948, for example, in what is regarded as the first truly honest election in Venezuelan history, the people elected to the presidency their illustrious novelist and man of letters Rómulo Gallegos.

Presidents may have come from the uneducated classes, but cabinets and congresses will ordinarily reflect a high preponderance of well-educated men. In the 1953–1958 congress of General Marcos Pérez Jiménez, 64 percent of the senators and 55 percent of the deputies held doctorates. During the same five-year period, 25 percent of *all* state legislators and

10 percent of the 1113 individuals appointed to the municipal councils throughout the republic also held doctorates.[29] Figures on the legislative personnel for Paraguay are not available, but the Paraguayan admiration for education and the preeminence of the educated man in the social structure probably have produced an equally high ratio of academic men in the legislature.

A study of President Stroessner's cabinets since 1954 clearly reveals the overriding importance of the academic elite sector and the military establishment as sources of governmental personnel. Paraguayan cabinets have been remarkably stable since Stroessner took office, although there has been some reshuffling of offices. About thirty men have served in the ten cabinet positions since 1954. Of these, ten have held doctorates and five have been generals. The eight without titles of any kind have been loyal Colorado party members with some expertise and education. They are also members of the elite echelons of metropolitan society. Stroessner himself is the son of a German immigrant, however. He was commissioned in 1932 and rose to the rank of general by 1951.

Politics in Venezuela and Paraguay attract the intellectuals because they are interested in ideology and philosophy, and there is a great deal of both in party politics. In the Latin American countries, an academic person is considered admirably suited to discuss and pronounce on the nuances of politics, and the Latin Americans have come to expect him to do so.

Many of the prominent Venezuelan leaders of today have had a student revolutionary background and are part of the Generation of 1928. Several of Venezuela's leading parties in the last two decades were founded by members of this group. *Acción Democrática* was organized by Rómulo Betancourt and Raúl Leoni, both of whom became presidents of Venezuela. In 1968, two other founders of AD were unsuccessful presidential candidates of opposing wings of the now badly split party. The Democratic Republican Union, for a number of years Venezuela's second party, was organized in 1945 by Jovito Villalba. Gustavo Machado organized the Communist party. Admiral Wolfgang Larrázabel, who participated in the overthrow of Marcos Pérez Jiménez, was provisional president (1958–1959)

[29] *Gaceta Oficial de la Republica de Venezuela,* No. 373 *Extraordinario* (April 17, 1953).

and a presidential candidate in 1959. He organized and was the leader and presidential nominee of a new party in 1963, the Popular Democratic Force.

Competition for political office in the 1968 election was largely confined to the middle and upper classes. The roster of the leading personalities in the election indicates that the following professions were represented: lawyer, law professor, historian, editor, diplomat, writer, admiral, general, and labor union officials. Many of these were from well-to-do families and held academic degrees. Several, however, were of more humble origin. The leading intellectual, Dr. Arturo Uslar Pietri, for example, is the son of a German immigrant. Former President Rómulo Betancourt came from a Corsican lower-middle-class immigrant family. Still another leader is the son of a coal miner. Regardless of their origins, all of them today are men of reputation, substance, and education.

The evidence presented so far supports the conclusion that policy makers, officials, and bureaucrats have historically come from the well-to-do educated elite, from certain regions, and from the military establishment. The ordinary citizen— common man—has had little opportunity to secure political office in either country. While this observation is still basically true in both republics, the situation may be expected to change in Venezuela because of the education, social, and economic advances being made there.

Political participation

Political participation may take a variety of forms: running for political office, casting a vote, contributing to campaign coffers and working for a party, or engaging in such activities as strikes, demonstrations, terrorist raids, guerrilla warfare, and open rebellion. Only a tiny fraction of the population is normally involved in the race for office. A much greater percent, of course, can and does participate in the other types of activity.

In both Venezuela and Paraguay the law requires all persons (with a few exceptions) between the ages of 18 and 65 to vote, regardless of sex or literacy. Over 40 percent of both populations fall in this age category. The sanctions are such, however, that they do not realistically affect the lower classes. Nevertheless one might expect that because of these laws voter turnout would be rather high, and that proves to be the case. In the last three elections in Venezuela (1958, 1963, and 1968) more than 90 percent of the registered voters fulfilled their obligation to vote. This was true in both urban and rural areas. In spite of severe penalties (not easily enforced) 10 percent of the registered voters stayed home. The 1968 election in Paraguay brought out the largest number in Paraguayan history, some 897,000, or about 95 percent of the electorate. The large number of people who cast votes can perhaps be attributed to the fact that four candidates were campaigning for the presidency— an almost unheard-of event for this essentially one-candidate country. Then, too, the electorate had been greatly expanded since President Stroessner took office. With illiterates and women voting, the 1968 suffrage base was twenty-two times larger than it was in 1953, when only 40,000 persons voted.

The bulk of the voting population in Paraguay is concentrated in the heartland around Asunción. In Venezuela, the electorate is distributed unevenly throughout the several regions of the country. The Guayana-llanos region contains 22.4 percent of the voting population; Maracaibo and the coastal regions (which includes Caracas and the Federal District), 66 percent; and the Andean region, 12.6 percent.

In terms of the ratio of voting individuals to the total population, Paraguay in 1968 ranked ahead of Venezuela, with 41 percent of its population voting as compared with 36 percent of Venezuela's. One must note, too, that an estimated 600,000 Paraguayans are living outside their country in protest against the regime or for economic reasons. Their return and involvement in politics would alter these figures considerably.

The political participation of the majority of the adult population of both countries is largely limited to casting a vote in the periodic elections. The present liberal trend in Venezuela makes voting a more meaningful exercise than it is in Paraguay despite greater party freedom there. Also, during most of Paraguay's history the political climate has been such that parties opposing the government were either denied legal existence or were unwilling to run candidates for office in the face of sure defeat.

From 1954 to 1962 the only legal party in Paraguay was the Colorado party, which had been adopted by Stroessner as his electoral vehicle. The outlawed parties—the Liberals and the Febreristas, continually conspired to overthrow the dictator and engaged in various acts of violence. In 1962 Stroessner, partly to placate international democratic opinion, began to relax his policy about the other parties. In that year he recognized a few dissidents of the Liberal party as the authentic party with the realized expectation that they would shadowbox with the dominant party in the 1963 election. By 1967 the Febreristas, the Christian Democrats, and the Radical Liberals (the authentic Liberal party) had all been granted legal status and the right to participate in the 1968 elections.

In spite of this relaxation in the political atmosphere, voting is still largely a meaningless activity for most Paraguayans. Elections in Paraguay do not have to be rigged because the number of registered voters is carefully controlled by the government months ahead of time.[30] The number of opposition party voters who are permitted to register is kept well below the critical number that would spell defeat for the Colorado party. Then, too, all elective officers of the national government must run at large and the majority party (the Colorado) is entitled to two-thirds of the seats in both houses of the national legislature. Few of the illiterate voters in the rural towns and hamlets know anything about the individuals who are seeking office. The almost permanent state of siege is lifted only on election day itself, thus permitting the government to regulate all preelectoral political activity. For reasons of its own, the government does not often announce the location of the polling booths until the day before the election. Opposition parties are often denied permission to hold public meetings; their leaders are detained for varying periods of time, and their party newspapers are victims of censorship or suspension. Critics of the regime argue that such tactics greatly minimize the influence of whatever opposition exists in Paraguay. When the voters go to the polls they are presented with colored ballots printed by the participating parties. A voter selects one of the ballots, places it in an unofficial envelope, deposits it in the electoral urn, and discards the rest. He is given a receipt that must later be produced for a variety of services and privileges. In the

[30] Nichols, p. 31.

controlled political environment of Paraguay it is usually wiser and safer to choose the Colorado ballot.[31] Votes cast for the opposition parties are perhaps wasted votes because the Colorado party, the majority party at present, is constitutionally assured enough seats in the congress to control the legislature.

It can be seen, therefore, that the political party in Paraguay is not only a very important agency for political recruitment, but is also the main channel for participation in the political process. Politics is dominated by the spoils system, and political office is sought for the patronage power it confers upon the winner. Since the national government is controlled by the Colorado party, all appointive offices are held by Colorados, both on the national and provincial level. Hicks describes local party activity in the following passage:

> On the local level, the political activity of party members is coordinated by units called *comités* in the case of the Liberals and *seccionals* in the case of the Colorados. Each such unit is composed of a president, a series of minor officials, and a dozen or so members at large, chosen in regular intervals in elections supervised by the party leadership in Asunción. These local officials are expected to look after the welfare of party members within their area, and this includes seeing to it that as large a share as possible of the relatively scarce economic opportunities are used so as to benefit fellow party members, especially those that are most loyal. Since it is the Colorado party that is in power, the president of the *seccional* is aided and encouraged in his efforts by the national government, and he is therefore likely to be a very powerful figure. The Liberal leader is at a definite disadvantage; but by virtue of their numbers, the Liberals can, if organized as a bloc, exert a certain amount of economic and political pressure.
>
> The president of the *seccional* shares in the municipal government with the *intendente,* or mayor, and the *comisario,* or police chief, both appointive offices (that of *intendente* was made elective in late 1965). Although the *intendente* is theoretically the chief municipal officer, he is likely to be overshadowed in actual power by the president of the *seccional.*[32]

[31] Harry Kantor, *Patterns of Politics and Political Systems in Latin America* (Skokie, Ill.: Rand McNally, 1969), p. 707.

[32] Hicks, p. 277. Reprinted by permission of *The Journal of Inter-American Studies.*

This is particularly true when an overwhelmingly Liberal town manages by some miraculous intervention to elect a Liberal to the office of *intendente*. The national government in this case will deal almost entirely with the local party chief.

Political advancement, political office, and effective political power in Paraguay have for many years depended upon affiliation with the ruling Colorado party. Party loyalty was usually rewarded by a position in the government (the Liberal party has called Stroessner's 50,000-man bureaucracy the cancer of the regime, charging that many of this labor force were superfluous).[33] Nichols observes, however, that today it is becoming indispensable to have Stroessner's personal favor to obtain or retain government jobs. Stroessner has gained so much control of the party apparatus that it is now necessary to pay constant personal homage to him. His high-handed tactics with the party have created some discontent and there are those in the party who would be delighted to drop him as the nominee of the party in 1973 if that could be done.[34]

The situation is more complicated in Venezuela because the country functions under a genuine competitive multiparty system. It is becoming rare for any party to win enough seats in the congress to control it, and therefore power and influence must be shared by the president's party with those which can be induced to join a coalition with a governing majority. COPEI won the presidency in 1968 but succeeded in winning only 16 of the 42 senator seats and 59 of the 197 deputy seats. In situations such as this some assignments to cabinet posts and positions of authority in the congress naturally go to the parties of the coalition. They are negotiated by their leaders on the basis of seniority and loyalty, as well as on expertise.

Political office in Venezuela is not confined to the national level, although power is concentrated in the national government and administration. Venezuela is technically a federal system composed of twenty states with little power and little to do except apply federal directives and laws. The state governor is both an appointee and an agent of the president of the

[33] *Hispanic American Report,* 16 (August 1963), 620.
[34] Nichols, p. 29.

republic. In past days, all governors were loyal party members (when there was a party at all) or were military men or henchmen of the chief executive. With the advent of coalition government, governorships are no longer the sole province of one party. Coalition partners expect to, but do not always receive, a proportionate share of the posts, and the matter is one of negotiation prior to joining the coalition. President Rafael Caldera was severely criticized for awarding sixteen of the twenty state governorships to members of his own party.

Multiparty competition is also reflected in the membership of the twenty state legislatures. State lawmakers are directly elected on the basis of proportional representation. Since all elections, national and state, are held on the same day, a party's strength in the presidential vote is likely to be repeated in contests for national and state legislative seats. Although definite data are not available, it seems probable that the three Andean states of Táchira, Mérida, and Trujillo (which in 1963 cast 50.4 percent, 57.6 percent, and 43.3 percent of their respective presidential vote for the Christian Socialist party and elected five of their six senators and fourteen of their twenty-two deputies from the same party) showed similar party preferences for state legislative seats.

Because the national government has over the years largely preempted the lion's share of power (and totally absorbed the taxing power), the unicameral state legislatures are virtually impotent and therefore play an insignificant role in Venezuelan politics. They do pretty much what they are told to do by their governors, who in turn receive their instructions from Caracas. No one expects much of the state legislatures. It may be, however, in view of the success of the Christian Socialist party in electing a president of Venezuela, that the members of that party in the Andean state legislatures might conceivably have a little more influence and prestige than would those of other parties.

Citizens participate in the political process in ways other than voting or holding office. Whenever they attempt to determine the outcome of an election through campaign activities, they are sharing in the ultimate decision as to who shall exercise power. Let us consider the elections held in Venezuela on November 30, 1952, to select delegates to a constitutional convention that would write a new charter and launch Venezuela once more into legitimate government.[35] One of the duties of the convention was to name a provisional president until a constitutional executive could be chosen. A widespread movement in support of junta member, Marcos Pérez Jiménez, for the post began to develop as election day neared. The movement was at first distinct from political party activity. Committees were established in many states and in the Federal District to coordinate the "spontaneous movements" designed to catapult Pérez Jiménez into the presidency. It steadily gained impetus during the last few weeks of the campaign. The president of the Federal District committee announced on November 5 that over 1,600,000 persons (or one-half of the *total* registered voters) had signed pledges of support for Pérez Jiménez. Capital newspapers began to refer to the movement as the "National Movement." Oil workers and other groups also set up their own independent committees for adherence to the "glorious Armed Institution" and to demonstrate patriotic support for Pérez Jiménez. In the state of Lara, for example, thirty-seven masculine and fifteen feminine committees canvassed all the districts, towns, and villages of the state in quest of signatures. The teaching profession of the state was complimented by national leaders for its unqualified support and vigorous participation in obtaining the signatures. On November 28, the Venezuelan Teachers Federation announced its unanimous support of Pérez Jiménez in a full-page advertisement in *El Universal,* one of Caracas' leading newspapers. Another full page photograph in *El Universal* on November 26 proclaimed in its caption that more than 60,000 persons had shown their allegiance to Pérez Jiménez and to the armed forces by participating in a massive public meeting held in his honor.

By identifying themselves with the regime in power and by proclaiming in advance their unreserved support for the dictator, all of these persons, regardless of their sincerity, were participating in the political process by making their views known either by their signatures or by their presence at rallies.

[35] See Leo B. Lott, "The 1952 Venezuelan Elections: A Lesson for 1957," *The Western Political Quarterly,* 10 (September 1957), 541–558. Quoted and paraphrased by permission.

Finally, citizens are active participants, although alienated ones, when they seek to bring about changes in policy, in leadership, or in the nature of the system itself by organized violence or by mob activity. Violence has been used so frequently in Venezuela and Paraguay that one can characterize its use as an institutional method involving both political participation and political communication.

While violence as it is ordinarily employed in Latin America is little more than an organized attempt of thwarted politicians or military officers and their followers or both to seize power, it by no means always has that objective as its chief goal. Often the primary objective is that of forcing the government to act in ways favorable to those protesting. Indeed, those who resort to violence feel that they have no other effective access to the channels of authority. Thus, citizens communicate their dissatisfaction with the system or some aspect of it, such as their opposition to the personnel and policy of the regime in power through the media of protest marches, uprisings, guerrilla warfare, and terrorism.

When violence results in a basic change in direction for the system as a whole or in a realignment of the power forces, it takes on the character of a genuine revolution. The upheavals of 1945 in Venezuela initiated such a change. Paraguay has yet to experience anything that approaches a genuine revolution.

Elections now appear to have supplanted violent techniques as a legitimate means of acquiring and maintaining power, but violence as a political expression has by no means disappeared. Armed peasants who occupy a landlord's land, students who revolt on the campuses and occupy buildings (a frequent occurrence in Venezuela and in Latin America generally), labor unions that call for a general strike, and terrorists who harass villages and cities are all communicating in the most effective way open to them: direct action.

Violence brought Marcos Pérez Jiménez to power and it unseated him. Since his time Venezuela has been plagued with activities of terrorists who seek to bring an end to what they regard as the power domination of the conservative elite. Even the establishment of a genuine constitutional government under President Betancourt did not diminish the incidence of violent activity; indeed, it may be said to have increased it. During his administration Betancourt successfully quashed several military plots against his regime and survived several assassination attempts. His most implacable foes were a pro-Castro splinter group from his own *Acción Democrática* party that called itself the Movement of the Revolutionary Left (MIR), and the Communist party. Together these two forces harassed him throughout his term, and he was forced to suspend constitutional guarantees to deal with them. Some members of the two parties and other dissidents banded together under the name of the Armed Forces of National Liberation (FALN).

The antiregime activities of this group became particularly virulent in 1963 as the December presidential elections neared. Its members resented the policies of the Betancourt administration. They were convinced, correctly as it turned out, that the electorate would return another *Acción Democrática* government to office. FALN's dislike of the regime was exacerbated when the government outlawed both the Communist party and MIR and denied them the right to participate in the forthcoming election. It was determined, therefore, to prevent the election at all costs. FALN threatened to kill any Venezuelan who had the temerity to cast a vote on election day. The harassment and threats failed. Venezuelans turned out in large numbers to vote for the continuation of constitutional government.

The failure to prevent the election of a new government and the orderly transfer of power did not discourage the terrorists. During President Leoni's administration, public officials were kidnapped and murdered; vital oil lines, power lines, and bridges were blown up; foreign properties were burned; and art treasures were stolen. The intention of a good deal of the sporadic violence in Venezuela now seems to be more in the hope of attracting attention to the dissidents and their goals than in proving a popular overthrow of the government. Earlier they were clearly undertaken to provoke the government into such repressive measures that the number of insurgents would increase in protest and the military would intervene. A military take-over would, FALN hoped, precipitate a crisis from which the Communists and the MIR could profit.

The government of Venezuela responded to such activities by the devices hoped for by the dissident elements: renewed suppression, armed retaliation, capture, trial, imprisonment, and exile for those apprehended. In an effort to bring peace to the country and end the violence, President Caldera made conciliatory measures. He legalized the Communist party and attempted through an emissary to initiate a dialogue between the government and the insurgents. In July 1969 his government claimed a victory for his pacification policy when FALN commander in chief, former naval captain Pedro Medina Silva, surrendered to the government. FALN, however, claimed that it recognized a different man as its sole commander in chief.

Every president of Paraguay since 1870 has had to deal with armed rebellions, most of them unsuccessfully. President Alfredo Stroessner came to power through a violent power play and was faced with at least two major revolts a year during his first ten years in power. Such activities have decreased in recent years as the president consolidated his hold upon the system and permitted freer political expression. Rebellion and insurrection, however, have always been the principal means of protest and power acquisition in Paraguay, and there is simply no evidence to suggest that the predisposition of the people has changed significantly merely because of the existence of a prolonged period of dictatorship. If rebellion is the Paraguayan cure of tenacious governments and self-perpetuation,[36] as has been suggested, then the country is ripe for a violent change of power.

SUMMARY

In this chapter we have tried to show that the political history and the social, economic, religious, military, and educational institutions of Paraguay and Venezuela have been instrumental in predisposing the citizenry to accept authoritarian patterns of government and politics for long periods of time. Early effects of the Hispanic-oriented socializing agents, geographical regionalism, and military intervention in the political process have kept

[36] Warren, p. 339.

the populations primarily subjects of the political process rather than participants in it. To say this does not mean that the people in either country have been abjectly supine or passive in the face of tyranny. The numerous political disturbances that have plagued both nations during their political evolution give evidence to the contrary. One must remember, for example, that about 600,000 Paraguayans are living in countries other than their own because of the dictatorial nature of the regime. (Some of these are exiles rather than voluntary expatriates.)

Increased education opportunities, moderating attitudes on the part of the military establishment and the Church, economic reforms, and three genuinely successful elections are all indicators that Venezuela is breaking away from her past, that she is no longer a status quo country bound irrevocably to conservative cultural and social patterns.

An astute student of Latin American politics remarked in 1967 that "the distance Venezuela has traveled since the overthrow of the unstable dictatorship in January 1958 is in fact one of the most phenomenal demonstrations of growth the Western Hemisphere has ever seen." [37] The remarkably peaceful election of 1968 lends weight to this evaluation. Certainly the events of the past ten years seem to justify the conclusion that elections are preempting the place of violence as a means of access to the power structures and that there is a "deepening consensus over democratic and constitutional institutions." [38] Venezuela in 1970 is a vigorous, healthy country engaged in the absorbing process of modernizing its economic and political structure.

Similar influences may be at work in Paraguay, but they are not immediately apparent. There is no doubt that the political environment is more repressive now than it was in 1963. Paraguay is still for all practical purposes an isolated praetorian state with an archaic social and economic structure. It has not yet been able to shake off the debilitating effects of its eighteenth- and nineteenth-century experiences.

A firsthand observer of recent developments in Paraguay, however, asserts that Paraguay is in the midst of a major change

[37] Philip B. Taylor, Jr., "Progress in Venezuela," 53 *Current History* (November 1967), 308.

[38] Taylor, p. 270.

that will involve a diminution of the power position of both the army and the Colorado party. For this transition it needs the firm hand of Stroessner. Paraguay apparently now has peace and order; but is that enough? Paraguayans claim they want democracy. If at the end of the transition period they have achieved it, it will be a "uniquely Paraguayan democracy with a traditional and ascriptive political culture that still seeks a patron." [39]

[39] Nichols, p. 33.

THREE
VARIATIONS
ON THEMES
OF HISPANIC
HERITAGE

Ingredients of the political cultures

Political culture is the pattern of individual attitudes and orientations toward politics among the members of a political system. It is the subjective realm that underlies and gives meaning to political actions. It includes knowledge, emotion, reactions, judgments, and opinions about political objects.[1]

Venezuelan and Paraguayan politics operate within an environment conditioned in great part by their Hispanic heritage and value system. Foreign influences, of course, have found their way into the political systems of the two countries, particularly that of Venezuela. While control of the two systems long ago passed from the hands of the aristocratic Spanish elements into the hands of the mestizos, the dominant political characteristics are still those inherited from Spain. These characteristics have been reinforced to a degree by some of the cultural components of the original civilizations encountered by the Spanish explorers in their conquest and settlement of the New World.

[1] Gabriel A. Almond and G. Bingham Powell, Jr., *Comparative Politics* (Boston: Little, Brown, 1966), p. 50.

POLITICAL MAN:
SPANISH VIEWS AND VALUES

Since the Spanish heritage is so indelibly imprinted upon the culture of Latin America as a whole—except in Haiti and Brazil —an analysis of the Spanish mentality will shed some light upon political practices, attitudes, and institutions of contemporary Venezuela and Paraguay.

The Spaniard is an ardent idealist who seeks perfection in all things.[2] His idealism has affected his political views and the political process in important ways. It has, for example, produced a person who has an innate distrust of government, unless, of course, he happens to be a part of it. This distrust is founded upon his idealization of liberty, for which he constantly strives. But government, by its very nature, must deprive a citizen of some of his liberties in order that all citizens may enjoy some. When restrictions are imposed, the Spaniard resents them as intrusions into the sacred realm of his individual rights. Above all, the Spaniard is an intense individualist, a volatile atom, a man of passion who protests and resists any restriction imposed upon him by collective life.[3] He is not, nor does he want to be, a responsible pillar of society or a member of service-oriented organizations. His preferences lean toward intellectual, scholarly societies or toward those which encompass highly valued principles, notably honor (army) and religion (the Church). It was no accident that for a great many years military and church careers were the chief prestige professions of the Spaniard. If the Spaniard is willing to compromise his individuality in any way, it is in pursuit of principle.

Resistance to collective restrictions plagued the Spanish government during the colonial period. Laws that displeased the Spanish settlers were simply disobeyed in many cases. Offensive royal decrees met with the classic formula, "obedezco pero no cumplo"—"I obey, but do not comply."

Yet the Spaniard, recognizing that government was a necessity, sought the ideal form. But his ideal did not originally

---

[2] Cecil Jane, *Liberty and Despotism in Spanish America* (Oxford: Clarendon Press, 1929), pp. 24–25.

[3] Samuel Ramos, *Profile of Man and Culture in Mexico,* trans. by Peter G. Earle (Austin, Tex.: University of Texas Press, 1962), pp. 29–30.

include Anglo-Saxon ideals: separation of power, civil rights, and restraints upon government. These concepts came later in the colonial period and then they were borrowed from the constitutional experience of such countries as England, France, and the United States. The search for an ideal form of government reveals itself in the numerous constitutions that have been written in Latin America.

Because he idolized the ideal, the Spaniard has sought the best of all possible worlds: the highest degree of efficiency in government and the maximum of individual liberty in his role as citizen. In his inaugural address as constitutional president, Pérez Jiménez of Venezuela declared that his government would adhere to the principle of governing with the utmost efficiency in the orderly execution of the state's mission. Since it is impossible to achieve both of these goals at the same time the Spaniard has often been frustrated by the political process. Cecil Jane argues that the political experience of the Spaniard in Spain and in Latin America has demonstrated that in his search for perfection he has swung from one political extreme to another: from liberty to despotism.[4]

To be meaningful to the Spaniard, authority must be personal and immediate. The individual holding power is more important than the power itself, for his character and personality often determine how his power will be used. Although the Spaniard regards government in general with distrust and wants little to do with it, he nevertheless expects the man in power to rule "fully, absolutely, exerting his authority without restraint and upon all in every relationship of life. He must be a despot or nothing, for if he be less than despot, he is forthwith imperfect, mediocre." [5] The strong virile caudillo has always been the idealized type of ruler. The list of such individuals in the histories of the Latin American republics is impressive indeed. In Venezuela they include such figures as José Antonio Páez, Antonio Guzmán Blanco, Juan Vicente Gómez, and Marcos Pérez Jiménez. Paraguay's roster features Francia, the two Lópezes, and Generals Higinio Morínigo and Alfredo Stroessner.

Intensely individualistic himself, the Spaniard has always admired a virtuoso display of individualism in another and

[4] Jane, p. 27.
[5] Jane, p. 26.

this had led him to submit to despotism over and over again as such dictators as those just listed have displayed their talents. From considerations such as these has arisen a conception of authority that accepts and respects the caudillo man on horseback, the powerful charismatic leader able to reduce the anarchy implicit in the Spaniard's predilection for absolute liberty to order.

A regard for the vigorous exercise of power, while usually resented, leads the Spaniard to expect his government to make far-reaching decisions within a paternalistic framework. He is noted for his lack of strong civic pride and sense of personal responsibility. Even in such matters as relations between the sexes, the Spaniard expects his will power to be provided by other people rather than by personal inhibition,[6] hence the chaperone system. The governmental systems of both Venezuela and Paraguay have been highly paternalistic throughout most of their independent existence. Venezuela is now moving toward more participatory democracy, while Paraguay retains its paternalistic stance.

Attitudes toward power and authority in Latin America were also conditioned by Spain's experience during the long battle with the Moors, a battle that emphasized regional abilities and bred in the Spaniard a strong spirit of local independence. Indeed, localities often were rewarded with political privileges in return for heroic services against the Moors. The innate separateness of the Spaniard, which led him to value a highly restricted circle peopled by family, friends, and neighbors, also caused him to view with distrust institutions and areas outside his immediate area. Thus the Spaniard was able to extend his concept of liberty outward to include the local area in which he lived, but not much farther. The central government was an abstract, impersonal, and distant entity that evoked little warmth or affection in the citizen. He recognized, of course, the legitimacy of the royal regime, but preferred to administer the affairs of his locality without too much interference from the capital. Indeed, "it has been the unending task of every ruler to discover some solution for the problem presented by the intense localism of the people by their reluctance to subordinate their personal

[6] Edwin T. Hall, *The Silent Language* (Greenwich, Conn.: Fawcett, 1959), pp. 49–50.

and individual freedom even to the highest considerations of the general good." [7]

Regionalism has always been an important force in Venezuela and is by no means dead. There is a depth of attachment to localities, modes of dress and speech, and way of life in both Paraguay and Venezuela. Mention has been made in Chapter Two of the historical roots of such attachments. Cultural, intellectual, and political rivalry mark the relations between important regions in Venezuela, as the Andean cities and Caracas, or between the llanos and Caracas. Part of the rivalry is due, of course, to the isolation of the regions and the lack of contact between them, but it also stems from the Spanish desire to be left alone. It reveals itself in voting patterns and political preferences, as we shall see later on.

A particularly important characteristic of the Spaniard is his reluctance or inability to compromise. This trait comes from his obsession with perfection, as well as from the absolutist nature of his political philosophy and religion. To compromise with false doctrine and fallacious ideas would be absurd, and in matters of religion, heretical. One should not stress this tendency too much, but it seems reasonable to argue that absolutism in religion can have a cultural effect in politics when that religion occupies a preferred place in the society. Compromise and concession have long been considered signs of weakness. Such an attitude can lead to violence in politics as the "outs" seek to oust the "ins" in the only way open to them.

The Spaniard has been described as being congenitally pessimistic and fatalistic. Because life and fate in his opinion are unjust, he expects the worst to happen. Yet there is undoubtedly a countervailing force at work in his personality. Who but an optimist could search the forbidding jungles, deserts, and mountains of the vast new continent in often fruitless quests for gold and silver? The dichotomy is revealed further in the fact that the Spaniard often is seized by impractical, visionary undertakings while his language and philosophy are full of proverbs that reflect a basic pragmatic approach

[7] Jane, pp. 22–23.

to life. Yet it was this "least utilitarian of Europeans" who performed such heroic deeds in taming a new continent.

Fatalism covers a multitude of sins. *Que será será.* What will be will be. Calamities, tragedies, political disorders, tyrants are accepted and endured as visitations of an inscrutable fate—up to a point. In politics passivity in the face of fate—if fate persists too long—gives way to violent action as formerly servile citizens rise up in arms. A popular uprising unseated Marcos Pérez Jiménez after he had been in power some eight years. Persons plotting against the government are playing for high stakes indeed and the risks are correspondingly high. If fate is kind they will succeed in their efforts to achieve power; if not, *que será será.*

The Spanish value system also affects attitudes toward occupations and work. The true Spaniard abhors physical labor, and indeed, all labor. The mark of a true gentleman is the absence of any visible means of support. Work is eschewed as something demeaning and undignified. Manual labor is reserved for the lower classes. Thus the upper-class Venezuelans and Paraguayans seek the prestige professions: doctor, professor, military officer, author, or priest. Technical occupations rank below these. One of the most authoritative figures in the eyes of the people has been—after the priest—the lawyer.[8] This attitude derives from the colonial period when theology, philosophy, and law were the main focuses of intellectual endeavor. A society that places a premium upon intellectual and professional occupations and dislikes manual or physical labor finds itself in a situation where all aspire to free themselves of work. Attitudes toward work help to perpetuate sharp class cleavages that will sooner or later make themselves felt in the political arena.

Other Spanish characteristics affect the day-to-day conduct of politics in Venezuela and Paraguay. The concept of personal dignity, deeply rooted in Hispanic civilization, results in a rather high degree of personal respect. Officials will go to great lengths to avoid offending persons calling on them. Courteous inquiries into the state of affairs of one's family and conversation

[8] Ramos, p. 48.

on a variety of other topics will ordinarily precede a discussion of the business that brings official and citizen together. A North American official has little patience with this sort of thing and finds it difficult to understand why he is kept waiting by a Latin American executive who seems to be passing the time of day with a client. Business and political discussions are conducted in a leisurely fashion that often tries the patience of North Americans.

Part of this custom may be attributed to the Spanish attitude toward time. Time in Latin America is something to be enjoyed and savored. Most Latin Americans simply do not understand the North American's concern with time. Latin Americans enjoy life at a leisurely pace. The *"mañana complex"* makes it very easy for them to postpone action until tomorrow or some indefinite future. Indeed, it is tempting to blame on this tendency to postpone matters for later consideration some of the lack of progress made by Venezuela and Paraguay during the first 150 years of their statehood. Latin Americans rarely find matters so pressing that an immediate solution is necessary. More often than not the attitude is one of *no importa*—it is not important. North American preoccupation with immediate action does not strike a similar chord in the Latin American. Too much activity might very well prompt a typical Spanish remark: "All that, in order to become a dead man." [9]

Concepts of personal dignity and respect for one's individuality do not necessarily lead to egalitarian practices. Their Spanish heritage, historical evolution, and the composition of their social structures predispose the Venezuelans and Paraguayans to attitudes of deference bordering on servility toward those in authority over them. The ordinary citizen is extremely deferential in dealing with any government official who is, in turn, most considerate of the wishes of his superior. Officials at all levels expect deference in their relations with the citizenry and enjoy the exercise of their power. The tendency to exalt the ruler is manifest in such flowery titles (often self-conferred) as *El Supremo, El Benemérito, El Ilustre Americano, El Excelentísimo, El Pacificador,* and *El Regenerador.* Consider also the words of a congressman referring to the dictator Gómez:

[9] Salvador de Madariaga, *Latin America Between the Eagle and the Bear* (New York: Praeger, 1962), p. 52.

From the bosom of the people there always surges a superior man, a light who illumines the path to the promised land, a Moses who, with his magical wand can cause not only the water to gush from rock, but also the spirit of love and fraternity to spring from the human heart. This man of robust complexion, of soul as lofty as the clouds of his native Andes, is for us, Juan Vicente Gómez.[10]

POLITICS AND THEOLOGY:
THE CATHOLIC INFLUENCE

Politics takes place within an environment profoundly conditioned not only by the Spanish mind, but also by the teachings and principles of the Roman Catholic Church, an absolute value-oriented institution that has enjoyed an almost total monopoly on the religious life of the people.

The seminal influence of the Church and its political role during the long colonial period and the formative years of nationhood have been discussed in Chapter Two. The Church in Venezuela and Paraguay has gradually lost much of its former political power, but is by no means moribund as a political force.

Following independence the Church found itself in conflict with the new political leadership. Even though it encouraged (and still does) submission to authority and acceptance of status, its attempts to remain independent of secular authority inevitably caused it to clash with governments that viewed it as a dangerous rival. Then, too, its absolutist notions were antagonistic to the liberalism, freedom, and democratic philosophies espoused—but not practiced—by those in power. Political authoritarians sought respectability by attacking religious authoritarians. The argument over the proper role of the Church in society, and its relations to the state in particular, were issues that divided the traditional liberal and conservative parties when they appeared.

Although the Church today is a relatively weak political power, its importance in the political culture should not be underestimated. In the first place, its teachings about authority and power have long been and still are in harmony with the

[10] Cited in Ernesto Wolf, *Tratado de Derecho Constitucional Venezolano,* Vol. I (Caracas: Tipografía Americana, 1945), p. 348.

realities of the political environment in Paraguay. It shares and reinforces the values of the other basic traditional institutions such as the family. As a cultural agent, the Church has made an unmistakable imprint on the arts, customs, and politics of the people, penetrating to the very ethos of the culture. Latin America, it is argued, is what it is because Catholicism is what it is.[11] To the extent that they affect political activity, the teachings of the Church and its attitudes toward the individual, society, politics, and economics have been important ingredients of the political culture of the two countries.

The power and influence of the Church in this area have long been noted by scholars. F. García Calderón, an eminent Latin American authority writing on his own culture, argued that the intolerance of divergent religious views, learned in the Church, carried over into Latin American politics. Instead of being willing to compromise, the "dominant party preferred to annihilate its adversaries, to realize the complete unanimity of the nation; the hatred of one's opponents is the first duty of the politician." [12]

Compromise appears to be essential to the democratic process and the notion that man in society can and ought to make his own decisions is basic to it. The Church in Latin America has been indicted because it has usurped the citizen's right to settle public issues for himself.[13]

While often bringing it into conflict with political authorities, the willingness of the Church to accept this important role reinforces the lessons learned in the family, where each member looks to the father or eldest surviving member to advise him on all important decisions. Obedience, a cardinal principle of familial organization, is also a major feature of Catholicism, and for that matter, of most religions. One need only recall the recent controversy over the position of the Pope on the problem of birth control to realize that the faithful are expected to obey without

[11] Richard Pattee, *Catholicism in Latin America* (Washington, D.C.: National Catholic Welfare Conference, Part I, 1945). See pages 7–9.

[12] F. García Calderón, *Latin America, Its Rise and Progress* (London: T. Fisher Unwin, Ltd., 1913), p. 369.

[13] Kingsley Davis, "Political Ambivalence in Latin America," *Journal of Legal and Political Sociology* (October 1942), 143–144.

question the dictates of the hierarchy in matters of Church doctrine and observance of ritual. That they do not always obey is
a matter of growing concern to Church authorities. Nevertheless,
obedience and submission to just authority are working principles of the Church. The stress is on the *lawful and just* concept
of authority. But who is to decide whether a particular government is entitled to power or is exercising just and lawful authority? Might not the criterion be whether or not the interests of the
Church are being harmed or furthered by a given regime? Consider, for example, the pronouncement of the Archbishop of
Brazil on the matter of legalizing divorce in that country.
"Should any Brazilian government dare to institute divorce in
Brazil, the people would have a right to oppose by armed resistance this attempt to undermine the foundation of Christian
family life." [14] A clear justification for such an assertion lies in
the attempt of the Church to identify its interests with the stability and integrity of the State. Pope Leo XIII declared:

> If the laws of the state are manifestly at variance with the
> divine law, containing enactments injurious to the Church . . .
> then truly to resist becomes a positive duty, to obey, a crime;
> a crime, moreover, combined with misdemeanor against the
> State itself, inasmuch as every offence leveled against religion
> is also a wrong against the State.[15]

The same pontiff claimed a political role for the Church when
he argued in another encyclical that to exclude the Church from
the affairs of life, from the power of making laws, from the
training of youth, from domestic society, would be a fatal error.
A state from which religion was banished, he said, could never
be well regulated.[16]

When authority has been judged just and lawful, however,
Latin American Catholics (and indeed, Catholics everywhere)
are exhorted to obey it and to accept their station and lot in life.
Until very recently, when the Church began to adopt more enlightened views about social issues in Latin America, discontent

---

[14] *The New York Times,* August 18, 1953.

[15] Cited in Francis J. Powers, *Papal Pronouncements on the Political
Order* (Westminister, Md.: The Newman Press, 1957), p. 30.

[16] Powers, p. 119.

or rebellion against the established traditional order was regarded as heresy because "lawful authority is from God and whosoever resisteth authority resisteth the ordinance of God." In the sense that such an argument could be advanced to uphold dictatorial regimes in which the interests of the Church were protected, the Church position clearly is an attempt to socialize in political matters.

The foregoing remarks must be tempered by the fact that perhaps no more than 20 percent of the population in either country understands and applies Catholic religious doctrine or dogma. In Venezuela perhaps about 3 percent of the rural population attend weekly Church services.[17]

IDEOLOGIES AND POLITICS:
AUTHORITARIANISM AND DEMOCRACY

Attitudes such as those described above denote the lofty position of the president in the political culture of Venezuela and Paraguay. Indeed, in Venezuela a philosophical basis to justify such a position can be found in the doctrine of the democratic caesar, made popular during the regime of Juan Vicente Gómez (1908–1935). It had been, however, an important principle of politics from the beginning of the republic, combining as it did elements of both militarism and authoritarianism. Its most overt expression is contained in a greeting made to General Páez, first president of the Venezuelan nation: "General, you are the fatherland."

Cesarísmo democrático

As a philosophy *cesarísmo democrático* was an apology for the dictatorial nature of the Gómez regime. Vallanilla Lanz, author of the idea (and book), declared that dictatorship was an ideal and appropriate form of government for his country, rather than a necessary evil. He saw Venezuelan society as composed of mixed and primitive persons who desired vigorous, wise, and

[17] François Hautart and Emile Pen, *The Church and the Latin American Revolution,* trans. by Gilbert Barth (New York: Sheed and Ward, 1965), p. 152.

effective leadership unimpeded by conflicts and struggles inherent in the democratic system. In his elaborately constructed theory all men were democratically harmonized and equal under a common powerful superior—the democratic caesar. Vallanilla Lanz rejected the premise that Venezuelans in his time were capable of democracy. Another apologist argued that democracy was a mystic doctrine that was crumbling in the face of a national desire to make the country "great by utilizing all its forces, organized to function harmoniously through the control which can be exercised only by a Supreme Director." [18] Ideas such as these were enthusiastically adopted by Marcos Pérez Jiménez between 1952–1958 and the Lanz book had a comeback. Many intellectuals subscribed to the ideas outlined in *cesarísmo democrático* and as a political philosophy it has had some importance in Venezuela. It may be revived, in view of the fact that Pérez Jiménez's supporters control the city council of Caracas, and twenty of his followers are representatives in congress.

Democracia solidarista (solidary democracy)   Paraguay has had less intellectual discussion about the nature of government and its proper organization and less tampering with its constitutional system than has Venezuela. Francia and the Lópezes did not take kindly to treatises except those that exalted them personally. One modern political theorist, however, attracted considerable attention, particularly that of the *Febreristas,* in the volatile political climate which followed the end of the Chaco War. Dr. Juan Stefanich preached the need for a New Democracy, which he labeled *democracia solidarista.* His system emphasized a solidarity of interest and a natural sequence of interdependency among men. His philosophy attempts to extract the best that "individualistic democracy, fascism, nazism, and communism" have to offer and to reconcile them all in one philosophy that he hoped would be valid for the needs of Latin America. When President Estigarribia came to power he utilized the doctrine of *democracia solidarista* to justify his vigorous exercise of power. He denounced individualist democracy for

[18] Pedro Manuel Arcaya, *The Gómez Regime in Venezuela* (Washington, D.C.: Sun Printing Press, 1936), p. 59.

a state which actively intervenes in all spheres and problems. Only thus could a strong national state be created in which all persons would subordinate their interests to the collective good.[19] To achieve this utopia, however, it would be necessary to replace the 1870 constitution with one that would reflect the new thought. That was accomplished in the constitutional revision of 1940, which reduced the legislature to nothing more than a sounding board for executive initiatives.

Both *cesarísmo democrático* and *democracia solidarista* seek to reconcile democracy with authoritarianism. They are thus philosophical manifestations of the long-standing clash between aspirations and fact, between the hard political realities of executive dictatorship and the democratic desires of the people. The two doctrines are essentially paternalistic and are in harmony with the paternalistic environments of Venezuela and Paraguay. They attempt to supply a positive theory about the aims and values of man and a logical, organic, and doctrinaire system of political organization. That appeals to the intellectual tradition in society.

The doctrine of *cesarísmo democrático* runs counter to the genuine attachment of the Venezuelan to real democracy, an attachment expressed over and over again in the numerous constitutions of the country, in their bills of rights, and in the writings of the intellectuals. All politicians pay lip service to the ideals of democracy and all argue that their activities are in the best interests of the people. Democracy means different things to different people, however. In the electoral campaign of 1952 one newspaper carried a column that asked: what is democracy? and it answered, democracy is order. President López Contreras saw democracy as a system in which the lowly could rise to heights of eminence. "In my youth," said he, "I also wore the *alpargata* (shoe) of the worker and I am not ashamed of it. Today I am the President of the Republic. What greater democracy could one wish for." [20] He later admitted that he had never had the opportunity to vote!

[19] See Harris Gaylord Warren, *Paraguay, An Informal History* (Norman, Okla.: University of Oklahoma Press, 1949), pp. 325–327.
[20] Eduardo Picón Lares, *Ideológica Bolivariana* (Caracas: Editorial Crisol, C.A., 1944), p. 8.

Although there are many excellent treatises that explore the philosophical foundations of democracy and explain the French Declaration of the Rights, a precise definition of democracy in Latin America is difficult to come by. Latin Americans tend to express it in more flowery or mystical terms than do North Americans. Consider the following comment on democracy: "Democracy consists of the following: in opening the door to all aspirations, in making the gifts of God common, insofar as that is possible without harm; in not falsifying one's work or wishing to level the cedar or the reed . . ." [21] Rafael Caldera, now president of Venezuela, looked upon democracy as the opportunity to confront realities, to reorganize and vitalize the nation's forces in order to bring about more effective solutions to problems and thus restore to the people the consciousness of its dignity.[22] Former president Medina Angarita considered the essence of democracy to be a dialogue with an adversary, a clash of ideas in which one has to defend his position.

In the final analysis, many Latin Americans view democracy in terms of social justice, which emphasizes the indivisibility of the legal and social rights of man. Every person has a right to political liberty, to economic security, and to individual progress. But he is obligated also to serve the community and the nation in a useful and self-denying way.

However defined, democracy is a goal in Venezuela and all the constitutions attest to it. Having been embattled first with a rightist dictator and then with leftist terrorists, Venezuelans today are passionately democratic, with the fervor of men who fight hard for their political tenets. Even the more authoritarian constitutions of Paraguay emphasize the essentially democratic nature of their political organization and goals. The political environment in both countries is charged with democratic aspirations and the irresponsible exercise of power must conform to them more and more.

However little it has been observed in practice, an enduring

---

[21] Cecilio Acosta, *Pensamientos,* p. 31.

[22] *Report of the Second Inter-American Conference for Democracy and Freedom* (New York: Inter-American Association for Democracy and Freedom, 1961), p. 27.

feature of the political system in Venezuela has been the attachment to the federal form of government. Historical reasons for this attachment were suggested in Chapters One and Two. Federalistic sentiment, in addition to social and economic motivations, was responsible for the bloody Federal War of the mid-ninetenth century. The preference for federalism reflects the intellectual influence of the dominant politicians. Psychological roots for regional autonomy in a federation are of course found in *localismo,* attachment to haciendas and regions, but Antonio Guzmán Blanco asserted that federalism in Venezuela was more a result of political opportunism than it was of strong affinity for it. Venezuelans, said he, did not even know the meaning of the word and Siso asserts that most of the soldiers who fought in the war died without understanding what they were fighting for. Guzmán Blanco claimed credit for introducing the cry of federalism into the political struggle of the mid-nineteenth century and then proceeded to indoctrinate the Venezuelans with his own meaning of the word. He said federalism was the answer to all their problems and he even went so far as to link the concept of God. The federalist motto became "God and Federation." A dying soldier described federalism as a "thing so great that it ranks after God." [23] A deputy in the 1864 constitutional convention, which adopted the federal structure that has prevailed since, exhorted his colleagues: "Let us realize Federation; Federation is not anarchy; Federation is peace, because it is the harmony of all tendencies and of all forces for man and society." [24] Later political theorists did, of course, expound more realistically upon the theoretical aspects of federalism and came close to the ideas expressed in the *Federalist Papers,* but not many Venezuelans were educated enough to understand them.

The persistence of the federal form of government in the face of the actual unitary organization of the republic indicates the depth of the Venezuelan's commitment to federalism in his conception of authority and purpose.

[23] Carlos Siso, *La Formación del Pueblo Venezolano,* Vol. II (Madrid: Ed. Garcia Enciso, 1951), p. 280.

[24] Venezuela, *Diario de Debates de 1864,* p. 16.

POLITICS OF CONSENT AND COMMAND:
ELECTIONS AND FORCE

Ex-president López Contreras (1936–1941) of Venezuela speaking to an organization in Colombia said

> It is not easy to judge from the outside the difficulties we encounter in Venezuela in trying to arrive at representative democracy. In Colombia you people have had elections. That is part of your civil tradition. But to us they are unknown. When I was President, at a cabinet meeting where all the men were older than myself, I asked the question: which of you have ever voted in a popular election? Not one of them had done so. Not a single living Venezuelan had had this experience. Now we have to start with what to everybody in other countries is the ABC of political life. . . .[25]

It is clear from this statement that the electoral process in Venezuela was not a significant part of the political process nor deeply grounded in the political culture until the death of Gómez in 1935. Power was acquired through force and lost through violence. Elections held in Venezuela during the time of López Contreras and Medina Angarita were not free elections because the government in power always won. The 1947 election that brought AD to power was generally considered to be relatively fair and free, but the 1953 election was full of fraud. Venezuelans could fairly argue that an election was a process, the results of which were known before the votes were cast. With three democratic elections behind them since 1958 the Venezuelans are coming to reassess more favorably the electoral method of coming to power. In short, elections are becoming a viable part of the Venezuelan political culture and are considered by the responsible politicians to be the only legitimate source of authority.

In Paraguay no such development has taken place. Paraguay has never had a free, popular election. Presidents are never unseated by the electorate at the polls; they lose power in civil strife. General Higinio Morínigo scornfully rejected electoral

[25] Quoted in German Arciniegas, *The State of Latin America,* trans. by Harriet de Onis (New York: Knopf, 1952), pp. 98–99.

democracy as a farce. Paraguayans, he asserted, were not educated enough to vote properly and consequently would be victims of dictators and demagogues. Whether that assertion is true or not, Paraguayans do not know what a free election is. For them it has ordinarily been a sterile process in which only one party backs a presidential candidate and legislative slate.

Yet, even in Paraguay, an election serves several useful purposes. First, it serves to demonstrate the attachment of the regime to the liberal-democratic notion that the electoral process is the proper way of organizing and transmitting power. A periodic election thus seems a sure way to placate public opinion in the powerful United States and other democratically inclined countries. Second, an election gives the government in power (which does not intend to lose) an opportunity to present its material achievements to the people and through the controlled press to persuade them that the official candidate is indispensable. An election that produces an overwhelming majority—as Paraguayan elections do—can be cited as evidence of massive popular support. If 55 percent of the electorate vote favorably, is not 75 or even 90 percent better? Third, to the opposition groups an election can be used in providing the moral justification for revolt because it gives them an opportunity to compile a new list of violations and abuses. There is a distinct tendency in Venezuela and Paraguay for an opposition party that either loses or does not participate in an election to regard the election as dishonest. That being the case, there is a disposition to conspire against the regime in power rather than to seek majority support itself.

Venezuela views its electoral successes as evidence that the battle for democracy has been solidly won at home. As a result it now feels it is better able to lend its moral authority and experience to aid democratic processes in the rest of Latin America.

One must not, however, discount the persistence of the tendency to resort to force in the whole area of conflict resolution. Violence has been endemic in the political culture of both Venezuela and Paraguay throughout their histories. It has been intimately associated with another salient feature of politics: militarism. A number of factors contribute to the tendency to use violent methods to achieve political power or bring about change: the intransigency of the status quo elite; the importance of physical prowess and rude strength in establishing grass roots power in isolated localities; the rivalry between regional caudillos inspired by a belief in the need to redeem or save the country through the "sacred right of insurrection"; [26] the absence of an effective national government to combat regional animosities; the inability of the electoral method to produce leaders with enough power to keep the caudillos and militarists in check; the uncompromising attitude of those in power, which caused despair among groups seeking to come to power legally; and finally, a disposition to seek a quick and decisive solution to political struggles.

Not all of these factors apply to Paraguay. Regional rivalries, for example, have not been important. Then too, there were periods in its history when no one dared so much as voice an opinion let alone conspire to overthrow the dictatorship. The regimes of Francia and the two Lópezes are cases in point. Since 1870, however, Paraguay has been beset by civil disturbances and revolts against the government. In one *cuartelazo* (barracks revolt) after another the game of musical presidential chairs had been played out. The presidency changed hands almost yearly and sometimes much oftener: twice in 1894, 1902, and 1911, and three times in 1912. Five presidents succeeded one another between 1949 and 1954. In 1949 Felípe Molas López invited most of the members of the government of General Raimundo Rolón to his home for dinner. At dinner, having taken the precaution of having his home surrounded by his supporters, he announced to the company, "Gentlemen, the jig is up." [27] Indeed, it seems no exaggeration to say that revolution is an inalienable right of Paraguayans and is often used. As a part of their national life, it is a disease that flares without warning and then subsides for a time.[28] It is, to be frank, the only realistic way to unseat an administration.

[26] Pedro Manuel Arcaya, pp. 31–32.
[27] William S. Stokes, "Violence as a Power Factor in Latin American Politics," *The Western Political Quarterly,* 5 (September 1952), 459.
[28] Warren, p. 266.

From 1830 to 1900 Venezuela was disturbed fifty-two times by revolts, twelve of which resulted in changes of government. Since the death of Gómez in 1935 more than thirty-five reported incidents of revolt and conspiracy to unseat the government have occurred. Four of these brought about the collapse of the government. The success of elections in Venezuela since 1959 as a means of changing or transferring power are hopeful signs that the popular vote will be the sole source of legitimate government in the future.

Violence was used so many times in both countries by groups ambitious to come to power and successful often enough that the technique was institutionalized to the degree that, in the minds of some, power through revolution was legitimate. There were many in Venezuela and Paraguay who could wholeheartedly subscribe to the doctrine enunciated by the Supreme Command of the Armed Forces in Brazil, following their takeover of power in that country in 1964. Said the officers in the preamble to their Institutional Act, which laid the foundations of their government:

> A victorious revolution is invested with the exercise of the constituent power. The constituent power is expressed through either a popular election or a revolution. Revolution is the most expressive and radical form of the constituent power. Thus, the victorious revolution, as also the constituent power, is endowed with legitimacy in its own right. It deposes the preceding government and has the capacity with which to constitute the new government. The leaders of the victorious revolution, thanks to the action of the Armed Forces and to the unequivocal support of the nation, represent the people and in their name exercise the constituent power, of which the people are the sole owners.[29]

One should note the use of the word "victorious." A victorious revolution is a legitimate source of power. An unsuccessful one is an act of treason against the government. A victorious general in a coup becomes president; a defeated one, an exile.

[29] *Brazilian Embassy Information Bulletin,* 69 (April 10, 1964).

THE POLITICS OF MILITARISM:
THE PRAETORIAN GUARD

Whenever the armed forces or a section of them interfere in the political and constitutional life of their country, both their members and society at large are in effect socialized in their attitudes. Officers will reaffirm their moral obligation to set things right, to resist communism, to cast out political criminals, to set the political and moral tone of their nation. The element of society that sympathizes with army interference, for whatever reason, is confirmed in its view that such a move was necessary and that the military establishment was the proper instrument for rescuing the country from the grave evils threatening it. Thus they identify with the military regime and accept its political philosophy. For those who regard military intervention as a blow to the orderly evolution of stable political institutions and effective popular government, views antagonistic to the military institutions are reinforced and political cynicism is increased. In each case, the authoritarian and democratic elements of society see their conception of the officer class borne out by deeds.

It must be pointed out, however, that many Latin Americans do not regard military interference in the political life of the nation as an evil in itself.

The tendency in Hispanic-American cultures to glorify deeds of arms and valor dates back at least as far as the struggle in Spain to dislodge the Moors. That took about 700 years to accomplish. The energies released by the Spanish success in Granada in 1492 were channeled into the exciting exploration ventures in the New World as military and religious thrusts.

Military careers for those born in the New World became a realistic possibility in the eighteenth century when royal reforms permitted the recruitment of a colonial militia from the aristocratic criollo class. An officer class soon grew up that identified itself with aristocratic interests of land, Church, and Crown. Military personnel were exempt from the jurisdiction of civil courts, which tended to create a privileged class above the law and exempt from public liability and civil responsibility.

The war for independence naturally accelerated the growth of a military class in Latin America. It did so in Venezuela, although in Paraguay it was restrained under the personalistic rule of Francia. The political role of the military in Venezuela stems from the fact that the military caudillos (some were mestizos and plainsmen) were identified with the success of the independence movement and accorded the distinction of national heroes. Successful in war, the generals were able to provide leadership in the awkward period of nation formation. They also caused instability as their fanatic supporters tried to gain control of the government. The Venezuelan Ernesto Wolf assigned another cause to the development of militarism in Latin America. He argued that a caudillo, in order to protect himself against that element of the "illustrious few who had been excluded from power," had to support an armed force and thus Latin American government assumed a military character. The chief of state had to show capacities of a military strategy before a talent for good government if he were to remain in office.[30]

In many areas of Latin America, direct rule by the military began to give way by 1860 to indirect rule under civilian fronts. That did not happen in Venezuela until almost 100 years later. In Paraguay, militarism blossomed in 1860 with Francisco Solano López. The military heroes created by the War of the Triple Alliance became president makers and were actively influential in politics. So great was the decimation of its forces, however, that the power of the army as a whole was weak in Paraguay for many years thereafter. The great war did stimulate nationalism, and in its observance today, the military glories of the Paraguayan leader and his people are emphasized with pride.

The growing professional character of the armed forces in most countries has helped to create a belief in their infallibility, a belief naturally encouraged by the high command and the officer class. Such an attitude was reflected clearly in the *pronunciamiento* (statement of purpose, goals, or justification for a course of action) of the Independent Electoral Front (FEI), a collection of political groups who were advocating the elevation of Colonel Marcos Pérez Jiménez to the presidency in 1952. The pronunciamiento read in part:

> Whereas the unity of the National Armed Forces, its institutional spirit, and its growing technical perfection are guar-

[30] Wolf, Vol. II, p. 13.

antees for stability and democratic progress in our public life; whereas, the people of the Federal District, organized in blocks of FEI, have held ward assemblies and have instructed the convention to public recognition of the patriotic attitude of the Armed Forces as factors of prosperity and order which the Venezuelan people enjoy today; whereas Colonel Marcos Pérez Jiménez is the most outstanding representative of the Armed Forces and is the individual to whose efforts is owed the high level of morale and of progress in the Armed Forces, the party resolves: to express publicly its adherence to the National Armed Forces, basic institution guaranteeing stability and progress in our public life, in the person of Marcos Pérez Jiménez, who is recognized as Chief and Supreme Head of our democratic movement.[31]

The armed forces socialize, condition, and influence the members of the political system not only by their active and open participation in the affairs of government, but also by what they say about their *right* to do so. Each successful military take-over in Venezuela, and in the rest of Latin America for that matter, usually is accompanied by a pronunciamiento. In a speech to the Venezuelan people on the occasion of the first anniversary of the overthrow of constitutional government by his Military Junta in 1948, Colonel Delgado Chalbaud, Junta president, reviewed the causes that impelled the military usurpation. It is a classic example of military thinking. Chalbaud said:

> The occasion is again favorable to reaffirm not only the motives that induced the National Armed Forces to assume control of the Republic, but also the principles which the Provisional Government imposed on itself as justification of its primary task of preparing the nation for an institutional life dedicated to order, work and freedom.
>
> The political life is undergoing a "de facto" period. We officers of the armed forces find ourselves heading the government. This was imposed on us by a situation which threatened the very existence of the nation, and which compromised the possibilities of a normal, economic, social and political development. The procedures by which the former government originated are susceptible to different viewpoints. But the rea-

[31] *El Universal* (Caracas), November 24, 1952.

son for the November 1948 movement is not exactly a denial
of the legal or political legitimacy of the government which
preceded us. The fact is that the former single-party regime,
overwhelming the Chief of State, revealed itself against the
supreme interest of the country, the basic foundations of national life and the future of the Republic, when it destroyed the
abilities of the State to attend to pressing national problems;
when it threatened the institutional independence of the armed
forces and when it converted the labor movement into an instrument of a totalitarian hierarchy which affected the activity
of the workers in the national economy. . . . The life and
integrity of the nation were in danger, as well as its ability for
national defense.

We had to do our duty. But we did not come to substitute
that totalitarian policy for another one. We came to reestablish
the prestige of the law and public office by energetic and serene
leadership. We came to correct evils and to practice sincere
principles of public morals. We came to accomplish plain objectives adjusted to the national reality and to respect the
liberal spirit of our traditions, even during the "de facto"
period. . . .

No provocation has made us deviate from the course
which has been charted. We know that our work has followed
fundamental principles of national interest. We know that we
are proceeding according to the principles of law and justice,
under the extraordinary circumstances of a "de facto" state.
We act with frankness without pretense or change of purpose.
We make cautious use of the extraordinary authority with
which we are entrusted, always respecting the democratic feelings of the Venezuelan people, but without disguising its exercise with demagogic formulas or promises.

. . . As a result of this policy and the great spirit of the
Venezuelan people, the nation has passed the serious crisis in
which it found itself. We have peace, regular employment, a
friendly life and a unity of spirit which are essential to national
existence. Among the nations of the world, we are able to
present a picture of social and economic life with appropriate
guarantees, and a political system which insures the security of
all individuals.

These objectives made the Junta form a nonpartisan government. Under normal conditions, political parties constitute
a natural element of a democratic life. At a time of readjust-
ment in national security, it is dangerous and self-defeating to

entrust them with the cure of wrongs caused by distorted use of political activities. Nevertheless, this circumstantial judgment has not made the government underrate the contributions to the political future of the nation by those free from totalitarian aspirations, and who dedicate themselves to the task of building the political future of the nation in keeping with the trends of the modern world and in an atmosphere such as ours which has been so overrun with individualistic habits. . . .

The National Armed Forces is composed of men who come from the social heart of the nation; to her they belong; to her alone they serve. We, because of this and because of the feelings of the generation to which we belong, cannot lend ourselves to egotistical aspirations which are contrary to social progress and justice that characterize Venezuelan history. . . . The Junta retained all the improvements worthy of being maintained. They are, specifically, those that do not have a label or a proper name, nor those that sprouted from a whim of a group of people or a governor. We have not resorted to the vast resources that power places in our hands to stir the national atmosphere or create prejudices that could affect our national capacity for work and the ability of the government to function.

It is within the general framework outlined here that the political measures which today have been decreed are explained and justified. At this very moment, it pleased the Provisional Government to announce that there is not one Venezuelan in any correctional or penal institution who is being deprived of his liberty for reasons of a political nature. . . .

The most recent experience shows us that unpreparedness and blunders have helped the enemies of democracy to frame a whole system of invectives against the possibilities of democracy and its very existence. It cannot be denied that the administrative inability of demagogues in the government has helped all men and groups of dictatorial minds. The political aims which we pursue, directed towards national harmony and the existence of Venezuelan democracy on a stable basis, must follow a firm and active pattern to prove that progressive governments are able to organize and carry out necessary activities.

The structure of Venezuela itself increases the responsibilities of the government. Politicians, not understanding this, placed their interests above national interests; made many promises all over the country; made an improvised inventory of the nation's problems and their solution. Their loud and scattered actions caused many Venezuelans to lose faith in the earnestness of the Government.

The Junta considers that maintenance of a social and political atmosphere of unity and labor for a greater development of our petroleum wealth and mining resources, which will soon be intensified, constitutes a valuable contribution to the defense, stability and progress of western civilization.

The positive results of the official tasks at which we preside confirm our purpose of being here on a provisional basis. We have observed the great disposition of the Venezuelans, influenced by the government for public welfare. Our success would not have been possible without the cooperation of the Venezuelan people and all the interest, enthusiasm and effort of the public officials in charge. This intensifies our faith in the destinies of this nation, and our responsibilities to clearly show the country the goal that our government pursues. Our actions indicate where we are going. We are going to conquer the existing emergency with integration of constitutional power, elected in a democratic way without official intervention. Those so elected will decide patriotically how the Venezuelan democracy will function, based on the ideals of our Liberators and with the best of our experience.

The armed forces represent the supreme guarantee of these aspirations. Their attitude, maintained with the limits of specified functions, merits the respect that has been paid them by the entire nation, especially by those political groups which patriotically inspired have not attempted, against their integrity, to turn them into instruments for their personal designs.

VENEZUELANS: The ideas and facts that we present on this occasion, as they describe the situation which we found, and as they reveal the success of our efforts in remedying it, do contain a severe criticism of the work of those to whom the government was entrusted in 1945, and constitute ample justification for the rectifying actions imposed upon ourselves on November 24, 1948, in response to a national clamor. On both occasions, the National Armed Forces acted in good faith with exceptional disinterest and a profound feeling of patriotic responsibility. Those of us on both occasions have fulfilled our duties as Venezuelans and as military men. The guarantees that we give the country are that we are headed for the fulfilment of the national democratic aspirations, which are the practice of freedom and equality, in an atmosphere of sincerity and mutual respect.[32]

A year later, shortly before his assassination, Colonel Chalbaud again referred to his conception of the role of the armed forces in the national life of Venezuela. It was, he said, the primary task of his government to assure the harmonious development of national life. Claiming that the support given to his regime by the people had enabled it to "lead the forces that determine social equilibrium and political stability," the leader asserted his determination to prepare the country for democratic life. The rest of his speech is instructive as a statement of social and political philosophy of a controlling authoritarian institution:

> The success of the government might induce the belief that to satisfy the highest desire of the nation, an honest and efficient administration would be sufficient, and that therefore the best government would be that whose work is the most productive. From the material standpoint, to govern would then be only overseeing valuable property, and the rulers would satisfy public clamor by the use of limited administrative ability. Our country, however, hardened by the sacrifices of our liberators—who served an ideal—and consolidated throughout the vicissitudes of the Republic, imposes upon us the duty to obtain by serious discussion and collaboration the answer to the problem of man in society. In Venezuela, this consists of harmonizing the free and dignified life of the citizens with social discipline, to prevent not only excessive individual passions which lead to anarchy, but also to prevent the sectarian despotic exercise of authority which results in tyranny and absolutism. To earnestly meet this, is to govern. The good use of our monetary resources for the material improvement of the country cannot be an end in itself. It is only one of the component elements for welfare environment in which the citizen must act with dignity and freedom.
>   . . . The government has decided . . . to abide by the postulates of a policy destined to recuperate our democratic

[32] Embassy of Venezuela, *Venezuela Up-to-date* (December 1949).

institutions and assure a full social life, without favoritism to any class or political affiliations. . . .[33]

In a vein characterized more by rhetorical sentimentalism and idealism than by realism, he then urged Venezuelans to heed the experience of their forefathers.

> . . . We of the present generation must take advantage of historical teachings and note that perfection of the Venezuelan's life cannot be achieved without the practice of the virtues of our fathers, of the founders and leaders of the nation. They were frugal and led a simple life. They were brave and courageous. Their lot was not an easy one. They did not promote dissolving forces within the community. . . . In the government, in private business, in the fields, in the factories, and in the shops, all Venezuelans must work conscientiously and responsibly, without overlooking an opportunity to consolidate the basis of our greatness. In this regard the main task falls upon those of us who perform public functions; to those who because of their background and intelligence or their position in the national economy, are considered representative men and women; and to students to whom the Republic will entrust tomorrow the responsibility of her destiny.[34]

The nationalization and professionalization of the armed forces has resulted in the end of regional, caudillo-led insurgency. To the extent that violence now figures in the transfer of political power, it must be assigned to the power struggles within the armed forces. No civilian government in Latin America can be said to be irrevocably immune to military intervention. If the military establishment feels its existence threatened by civilian forces, it will use its power to strike them down and, in the last extremity, to remove those responsible.

The fathers of the 1961 Venezuelan constitution sought to reduce the armed forces to a nonpolitical, nondeliberate, and obedient institution. As an entity organized by the state it is charged with the defense of the nation, the stability of democratic institutions and the respect for the constitution. The constitution declares the armed forces to be exclusively in the

[33] *Venezuela Up-to-date* (January 1950).
[34] *Venezuela Up-to-date* (January 1950).

service of the state and in no case to serve any person or political party. There is, of course, absolutely no way to guarantee that the military establishment will obligingly accept that role. Its record since 1958 has been very satisfactory. In 1968 President Leoni praised it for its defense of "institutional democracy" that protects the freedom and dignity of every citizen. Its conduct, said he, was an "example of efficiency and excellence for the entire continent."

The Paraguayan constitution says only that the armed forces is an institution that has the responsibility for the defense of the sovereignty and the maintenance of the republic's territorial integrity. There are no restraints on it other than those imposed by political expediency or circumstances. The absence of restrictions suggests the strength of the armed forces in the political arena.

THE POLITICS OF POWER AND RESTRAINT: CONSTITUTIONAL TRADITIONS

The constitution in Venezuela and Paraguay both affects and is affected by the prevailing political culture in each. The purpose of writing a constitution, to the Anglo-Saxon mind at least, is to provide an effective framework within which the political system can operate. The Latin Americans also write constitutions for this basic purpose, but they tend to take a somewhat broader view of them and make a somewhat different application than does the United States, for example.

If a nation writes a constitution that sets up authoritarian institutions for a society controlled by small aristocratic elites, it has the merit of being in tune with the political facts of life. If, on the other hand, the same society establishes a constitution that creates an institutional and structural framework for democracy, the constitution is likely to suffer. Because Venezuela and Paraguay have often written democratic constitutions, constitutionalism has been precarious there.

Constitutionalism—that is, limited government—occurs when the powers, procedures, and restraints embedded in the constitution or sanctioned by a framework of established expectations are effectively and meaningfully observed by those in power and by those who hope to be. It means creating and guaranteeing political conditions that permit the constitution to be put into practice.

The preceding sections of this chapter have examined forces that have affected the constitutional systems of the two countries. Before discussing the role of the constitution in the independent life of the two countries, it is necessary to make several background observations. As was that of the United States, the early constitutions of most Latin American countries were written to fill the vacuum created by the termination of the power of the mother country. The political environment in which they were conceived was different from that which existed in the North American colonies. The constitution of the United States was a product of compromise molded by the political demands of the time and created out of the wisdom of collective experience. It stood on a solid basis of accumulated values, morals, beliefs, and practices. This is not, however, to minimize the regional differences that beset the American colonies.

The Spanish colonies, on the other hand, possessed few of the elements that have contributed to the stability and success of the American constitutional system. That in itself might not have been a serious flaw except that the principles and doctrines of the American, French, and other constitutions were the very ones so ardently admired by the Latin Americans: self-government, civil liberties, representative government, separation of powers, and many others. Three hundred years of Spanish autocracy had left the people of Latin America with little practical experience in any of these areas. Paraguay and Venezuela conform to this generalization although they had had some genuine contact with self-government.

For some years after its freedom from Spain these shortcomings did not matter much in Paraguay. There the dictator, Dr. Francia, promptly instituted an authoritarian government without parallel in Latin America. He was the author of the constitution of 1813, but speedily forgot its existence. Paraguayans, therefore, had no opportunity to develop a sense of constitutionalism until 1844, thirty-three years after their independence was achieved. Even in 1844 very few Paraguayans had anything to say about their basic document, which was in any case, little more than a piece of paper.

The Venezuelans were more sensitive to the limitations of their colonial political experience and were determined to express the ideas of limited, responsible government in their constitution.

Foreign influences in the constitution

It should not be surprising that the Venezuelan (and later Paraguayan) constitutions derived their inspirations from foreign sources. The United States Constitution and the French Declaration of the Rights of Man had a particular appeal. The deliberate imitation and borrowing of institutions and practices resulted in wordy documents that were distinguished more by frequent digressions into moral and political philosophy than they were by political realism. They were in fact productions of a mechanical labor of adaptation, not the expression of any tendency in national life.[35]

Simón Bolívar, an admirer of Montesquieu, pleaded with the countries of Latin America to make their constitutions conform to the political habits and abilities of their people and even to reflect the influence of soil and climate. His advice was ignored. They drafted lengthy sections dealing with rights and equality of men for a society that had been stratified and riddled with rank, privilege, and inequality. Indeed, the founding fathers included in their constitution all the institutions and principles that they considered would insure good government. The tragedy was that many of their innovations had no practical basis in the authoritarian society and culture of their coun-

---

[35] Thus Pedro Manuel Arcaya describes the 1857 constitution. His words could be applied as well to most of the other Venezuelan constitutions. See his *Gómez Regime in Venezuela,* p. 49. A Colombian's description of his country's constitution is illuminating and could be descriptive of the Venezuelan documents of earlier years. "Our innumerable constitutions, regarded as portraits of society since 1810, have a close symbolic resemblance to the gift which one of our presidents received, bearing the following legend:

> Portrait of the Honorable President of the Republic, by John Doe, painted without his having studied art, or having seen a photograph of, or having the pleasure of meeting his Excellency.

Quoted in Vernon Fluharty, *Dance of the Millions* (Pittsburgh, Pa.: University of Pittsburgh Press, 1957), p. 224.

try. The introduction of federalism was perhaps one of the more realistic measures as it reflected provincial jealousies and aspirations.

The first Republic of Venezuela, established in 1811, endured ten months. It was disdainfully referred to as *patria boba,* "silly fatherland," because its originators wanted to govern through a federal system when conditions called for strong measures and a centralized government to combat reactionary forces seeking to reestablish ties with Spain. After the fall of the republic, Bolívar complained in his 1812 Manifesto from Cartagena that his compatriots were not yet capable of exercising their legal rights because they were lacking "in those virtues which distinguish the true republican." Moreover, he asked, "what country on earth can afford a weak and intricate system of government such as a federation of states, where different factions quarrel within and war threatens from without?"

The desires of the early constitutionalists in Venezuela to produce a system of government in harmony with the liberal concepts of the enlightenment were thwarted not only by the undemocratic nature of their society, but also by the unwillingness of the new military leaders to abide by the restrictions contained in the constitutions.

It would be a mistake, however, to attribute too much of the blame for the constitutional instability that has plagued Latin America for years to the practice of imitating foreign models or to the deficiencies of colonial experience. Perhaps some of the responsibility may be traced to the temperament and political predilection of the Spaniard, whose character presents a dichotomy striving for the maximum of both individual liberty *and* governmental order and efficiency. Translated into opposing conceptions of authority, these two differing principles and ideals have thus far divided the politically articulate populations of Latin America into battling elements whose contests have precipitated a good many constitutional crises.

The discrepancy between the actual pattern of power and its exercise (the real constitution) and the paper provisions (the nominal constitution)[36] has been a glaring one in Vene-

---

[36] J. L. Mecham, "Latin American Constitutions, Nominal and Real," *Journal of Politics,* 21 (May 1959), 258–275.

zuela. The call for a democratic, federal republic in which the rights of individuals were secure from government oppression simply could not be realized in the face of ambitious military caudillos who had no intention of honoring paper restrictions. A hundred years were to elapse before the first enduring elements of responsible and limited government were to appear. The numerous violations of the constitution in Venezuela over the years, as well as the frequent changes in the document itself, have produced in the Venezuelans a decidedly cynical attitude about the efficacy of constitutional arrangements. The Venezuelan scholar Ernesto Wolf reflected the prevailing view about constitutions in his country when he referred to the constitution as a "little yellow book which is made every year and broken every day." [37] The Venezuelans have come to expect a new constitution with every major change of government direction. They have not often been disappointed.

The Paraguayans have historically been far less preoccupied with constitutionalism than the Venezuelans. The reasons for this have been set forth in earlier sections. Here we need only say that the first three presidents of Paraguay possessed extra-constitutional powers of such magnitude that a constitution was meaningless. Indeed, most citizens did not know one existed. The 1844 constitution of Carlos López was a totally ineffectual restraint and it conferred upon him little power that he did not already possess. In this case the adoption of the constitution merely acknowledged a political reality: the existence of another supreme caudillo.

The Paraguayan constitution of 1870, adopted after the end of the War of the Triple Alliance, introduced into Paraguay the foreign governmental forms and concepts of democratic government that Venezuela had been experimenting with since 1811. Although this constitution endured for seventy years (an amazing span for Latin America), it was in trouble almost from the beginning. Concepts of democratic participation and self-government were blunted by the fact that the country was reeling from the demise of half of its population and most of its male leadership. Then, too, the critical economic problems and social dislocation brought on by the war demanded vigorous

[37] Wolf, Vol. I, p. 315.

executive action. Long accustomed to executive domination, the Paraguayans were not surprised to see their new legislature speedily reduced to a secondary position in the structure of government. Nevertheless, the political atmosphere was considerably more liberal and the regimes far less repressive than had been the case before 1870. Party politics was possible in this more relaxed period of Paraguayan history and two major parties were organized to compete for power. While the new constitution did not prevent frequent violence and civil strife that resulted from such competition, it was an instrument of power for succeeding administrations in their battle to establish a viable economy.

The symbolic significance of the constitution

The question might naturally arise: If the above observations are true, why do Latin Americans have constitutions at all if they conform so little to reality? [38] One answer has already been given: Latin Americans were motivated to make their new political systems responsive to the enlightened political attitudes prevailing when they achieved independence and they have never lost their faith in the legitimacy seemingly conferred by them.

A second answer may be found in the value of a constitution as a symbol and as an instrument of political socialization. While admitting many faults with their basic law, Venezuelans and Paraguayans will defend it as the embodiment of their hopes and ideals. It has been argued that the advanced social, political, and economic aspirations woven into the constitutions of the two countries, although not immediately within reach, are by their mere presence subtly influencing the action of the political

---

[38] James Busey argues persuasively that perhaps too much of the environment of Latin America has found its way into the constitutions, rather than too little. By their various provisions the framers of the innumerable charters have opened the door to caudillismo, personalismo, executive domination, weak legislatures, and a weak rule of law, all of which reflect political realities rather than theory. See his "Observations of Latin American Constitutionalism," *The Americas,* Vol. 24, No. 1 (July 1967) 60. The discrepancy between theory and reality arises mainly in the areas of social and economic philosophy and civil liberties.

leaders and are conditioning the action of future governments.[39] They may even allay popular discontent by promises of good things to come. However reasonable that argument may be, another result may, and indeed has, occurred. Constant manipulation of the constitution for political or personal reasons, disregard of the restraints embedded in it, and the inability or unwillingness of officialdom to implement its social and economic provisions have produced deep feelings of frustration and cynicism among the people. Attitudes such as these may well stand in the way of the development of the genuinely allegiant participating society considered necessary for a true constitutional democratic system. In spite of the cynicism about the fundamental charter that may be found in Venezuela and Paraguay, it seems generally agreed among Latin American observers that constitutions do point the way to a better life for the people and as a guide for the future perform a useful and necessary function in legitimatizing the goals of government.

The constitution as a panacea

Venezuela's continual tinkering with its constitutional system reflects a widespread belief among the articulate and politically active population that by merely writing a new constitution or by amending the old, the major ills of society can be eliminated. Cecilio Acosta, grand old man of Venezuelan letters, observed that his countrymen had the pernicious habit of looking for the real constitution between the covers of a book instead of searching for it in custom.

> We write beautiful phrases, precious guarantees and sacred principles and we judge that by so doing we have done all that is necessary. The people are now rich; the ignorant are wise; the farmer is president. Gold flows, industries flourish, commerce prospers and credit is opened. . . . To be always

[39] Alfred B. Thomas, "The Caudillo in the Caribbean," *The Caribbean: Its Political Problems,* A. Curtis Wilgus, ed. (Jacksonville, Fla.: The University of Florida Press, 1958), p. 189. Compare K. H. Silvert, "Political Change in Latin America," *The United States and Latin America,* Herbert Matthew, ed. (New York: The American Assembly, Columbia University, December 1959), p. 67.

drafting law is a fatal symptom in people, for the result is that they have none nor respect none.[40]

One result of such a belief is that constitutions have been ephemeral, because they are in part experimental in nature (see, for example, the Venezuelan constitutions of 1857, 1858, 1874, 1936, 1947, and 1958). Innovations in these documents dealt either with the form of government or with the economic system. Often the constitutions have had the character of legislation rather than of fundamental laws—as is the case with the 1947 *Acción Democrática* constitution of Venezuela and the 1940 constitution of Paraguay. In societies where there is no consensus upon the social and economic objectives of government and where it is believed that such problems are capable of solution by constitutional engineering, one cannot expect constitutional stability.

The constitution as a vehicle for personalismo [41]

Venezuela's large number of constitutions (twenty-six) can be attributed in part to the use of violence to bring about political change. The constitutions of 1858, 1864, 1901, 1947, and 1953 were produced by constitutional assemblies convoked by the winners following the successful outcome of a revolt. The remaining number, and even those mentioned above, were motivated to some extent by the personal wishes of the strong man in government. Indeed, one of Venezuela's eminent historians declared that the principal weakness of the Venezuelan constitutions lay in the fact that they were nothing more than responses to the whim of *el presidente*.[42] Gómez's seven constitutional changes, for example, involved little more than tampering with the vice-presidency. He had used the vice-presidency as a springboard to power when he usurped the

[40] Cited in Wolf, Vol. I, p. 335.

[41] The material in this section has appeared in substantially the same form in my article "Executive Power in Venezuela," *The American Political Science Review,* 50 (June 1956) and is reprinted and paraphrased with permission.

[42] José Gil Fortoul, *Filosofía Constitucional,* 3d ed. (Caracas: Ed. "Cecilio Acosta," 1940), p. 12.

office of president while the incumbent was in Europe. As chief executive, Gómez took immediate action to ensure that no other ambitious politician would have the same opportunity. The office was abolished in 1909. Later, however, possessed by dynastic ambitions and feeling secure in power, he instructed his docile 1922 Congress to restore the dual vice-presidency that had existed for several years prior to 1909. His brother and one of his many sons were elected by Congress to fill the posts. After his brother had been assassinated and his son disgraced, he again abolished the offices. The vice-presidency has never been reestablished.

Another example of *gomecista* manipulation of the constitutional system occurred in 1914. Gómez wished to take to the field against regional insurgents who were challenging his power and it was inconvenient for him to be in Caracas as the constitution required. Also troubling him was an awkward provision in the 1909 constitution that forbade his reelection. To surmount these difficulties he convoked a congress of "plenipotentiary deputies," and ignoring the amending provisions of the document in force at the time, presented them with the Provisional Constitutional Statute. It was promptly and obediently adopted.

The Provisional Statute varied only slightly from the constitution it superseded. The important innovations dealt with the executive branch of government. The Statute called for a provisional president, but took away his military powers and lodged them in a separate officer, a commander in chief of the national armed forces. Gómez was elected to this office and a puppet to that of provisional president. The purpose of this wily maneuver became clear when the deputies proclaimed a new constitution two months later in which the no-reelection clause was removed. Congress was then free to elect Gómez for a new term. Appended to the new constitution was a transitory provision that revealed a more subtle purpose of the Provisional Statute. The provisional president would continue in office until the constitutional president entered into his duties. The commander in chief would remain at his post until the constitutional president assumed offices. Meanwhile, the provisional president would exercise the powers of the presidency in the consultation with the commander in chief.

Under these provisions, Gómez, who had been elected commander in chief under the Provisional Statute and constitutional president under the 1914 constitution, was free to choose which office he cared to exercise! Instead of assuming the presidency immediately, he retained his military post and set about consolidating his control of the country. During the next seven years, therefore, Venezuela had the unique experience of having a provisional president performing the functions of a constitutional president-elect who, although he did not occupy the office, nevertheless exercised all of its powers. Gómez resumed open control of the destinies of his country in 1922 under a new constitution that combined once more the offices of president and commander in chief.[43]

Presidentially inspired changes are abundant in the Gómez constitution of 1925. They range from such minor ones as removing a clause that forbade the president to be absent from Caracas for more than twenty-five days (Gómez preferred to live in Maracay) to changes affecting the nature of the federal system. Gómez desired to find a formula for appointing the governors of the "autonomous" states without destroying the form of the federal system. He had been appointing them for years but now wanted a legal basis. The 1925 constitution supplied that basis. The president was authorized to exercise those state powers that the states in their several constitutions might delegate to him. Since the subservient states knew the purpose behind this provision they promptly and obediently signed away their executive rights and conferred upon Gómez the right to appoint their governors. In spite of several attempts since then, the states have not recovered the prerogative of electing their own executives.

Personalismo in the constitutional development of Venezuela is not limited by any means to the seven constitutions of Gómez. President José Tadeo Monagas initiated the custom of legalizing usurpation of power through the simple device of revising the constitution. Under his tutelage the 1830 prohibition against presidential reelection was eliminated and the

---

[43] See Leo B. Lott, "Executive Power in Venezuela," *The American Political Science Review,* 50 (June 1956), 422–441.

presidential term extended from four to six years—Venezuela's first experience with *continuismo*.[44]

President Guzmán Blanco was responsible for some curious innovations that did not survive him. In 1874 he introduced open and direct voting in which the voter was required to sign his ballot in the presence of electoral judges; changed the names of seven states—two to his own name; and reduced the term of president from four to two years. In 1881 he reduced the number of states from twenty to nine. The Congress of Plenipotentiaries agreeing to this change was composed of the governors of the twenty states! He also created a Federal Council after the Swiss model. One of the functions of the Federal Council was to select from its own membership the president of the republic. Guzmán Blanco was elected despite the fact that he was not a member of the Council.

The most recent example of presidential influence in bringing about constitutional change can be found in the drafting of the 1953 document. The only draft brought before the Constitutional Assembly was that written by the leading members of the provisional president's party in cooperation with the executive branch of the government. This party, the Independent Electoral Front, and its affiliates dominated the Assembly and were instrumental in strengthening the powers both of the president and of the central government. One result of the labors of the Assembly was to end once and for all the fiction that the states possessed the right to elect their own executives, a right that passed unconditionally to the national executive. Powers of the state legislatures and municipal councils were curtailed and their sources of revenue drastically reduced.

This recitation of examples of presidential influence in Venezuela's constitutional development does not exhaust the list by any means, but is long enough to lend support to the thesis that many of the changes have had their origin in nothing more than the individual will of the president.

The absence of regional interests and divisive partisan influences in Paraguay up to 1870, and the firm control of the

[44] Ulises Picon Rivas, *Índice Constitucional de Venezuela* (Caracas: Ed. Elite, 1944), pp. 45–46.

government for long periods after that date by one or the other of the two major parties in effect reduced the number of occasions on which constitutional changes could be engineered. In any event, Paraguayan executives have tampered far less with their constitutions than have the Venezuelan leaders. Yet two strong-minded executives have been instrumental in bringing about constitutional innovations.

The Paraguayan generation that came to power after the Chaco War looked upon the 1870 constitution as an obsolete document out of tune with the new demands of society. In his preliminary arguments for a new charter, President Estigarribia told the people that the procedures permitted by the 1870 constitution were simply too slow for a modernizing nation. Paraguay could no longer afford the luxury of endless discussion in two different houses of the national legislature (which was in theory a coequal partner with the executive) during prolonged periods of national stress. He therefore called for a new distribution of power that would endow the president with sweeping new authority in the social and economic field and that would take from the legislature its status of equality. The president asserted that all administrative power must be concentrated in the hands of the executive and that the legislature's future function would be to legitimatize his proposals by collaborating fully with him. These ideas and others were incorporated in the 1940 constitution, which was adopted by plebiscite. This document, says George Pendle, was a "deliberate adaptation of past and contemporary foreign theories and practices of government to the peculiar circumstances of Paraguay." [45] As such it is a far less alien form of government than was the 1881 Swiss-oriented constitution of Venezuela, for example. The constitution of 1940 and its successor, that of 1967, are perhaps the most realistic constitutions of Latin America, for their provisions clearly legalize the authoritarianism that has always existed. The 1940 document was revised and amended in 1967 by a constitutional assembly elected upon the initiative of President Alfredo Stroessner, who found his desire to continue beyond two terms as president specifically forbidden

[45] George Pendle, *Paraguay, a Riverside Nation,* 3d ed. (London: Oxford, 1967), p. 35.

by the constitution. As other presidents in other countries before him, he simply had the limitation removed while overhauling the document in general.

The two examples given above represent the extent of executive interference in the constitutional framework of the government since 1870.

The constitution as a political instrument

New constitutions serve a political function when they clarify the political atmosphere or legitimatize a revolutionary regime. Latin American presidents much prefer to be known as *el presidente constitucional* rather than as *el presidente provisional*. Marcos Pérez Jiménez, revolutionary leader and provisional president of Venezuela from 1950 to 1953, legalized his regime in his own opinion by convoking a constitutional assembly and having it change his status from provisional to constitutional. Within ten minutes after his election by the constituent body it was possible to buy a newspaper at the door of the capitol proclaiming in banner headlines his elevation to the status of constitutional president. The word "constitutional" became a permanent part of his title in all subsequent official public references.

Then, too, a regime that comes to power through revolt espousing new ideals, elevated political morals, and social and economic reform feels the need to write its own philosophy into the constitution and to disassociate itself from the discredited predecessor. The Venezuelan constitutions of 1947, 1953, and 1961 are in this category.

The constitution fulfills a political role when it becomes a backdrop against which the drama of politics may be played. A favorite cry of revolutionaries in Latin America is that the possessors of power have violated the constitution in any number of different ways. Such an accusation is both an excuse for and a prelude to violence to eliminate those guilty. The government naturally regards this activity as treason and responds by suspending the constitutional guarantees and labeling the rebels traitors to the fatherland (quite forgetting in some cases that it came to power in exactly the same way). The constitution and its guarantees are thus caught up in the interplay of political passions and forces concerned not so much with the legal exercise of power as with the acquisition of power by any means. The resulting influence of the constitutional system in both Venezuela and Paraguay has been detrimental to the development of a genuine consensus.

The constitution as a symbol of restraint

One of the important characteristics of a genuine constitutional system is the effectiveness of its restraints upon the exercise of power of those in official positions. In the case of Paraguay and Venezuela, the constitution more often than not has failed as an effectual curb on the powers of the governing elite, or to be more specific, on the president. This state of affairs results from two factors: the extraconstitutional power position of the president (derived from his stature as a political boss or military man) and the prevalence of societal attitudes that condone and even encourage strong executive action. There is a fairly deeply held feeling that an executive, once in power, should be given an almost entirely free hand, interference from the legislature and the court being the exception and not the rule. Some writers argue that the Spanish race, while devoted to the concept of liberty, always is ready to admire and submit to despotism.

So great has been the personal influence and extraconstitutional power of the presidents of Venezuela and Paraguay that many of the constitutions of the two countries have been only what the chief executives have chosen to recognize as such.

Paper restraints are to be found in every constitution, although they differ from country to country. In the Venezuelan constitution the sum total of power delegated to government by the "sovereign" people is separated into the customary functional elements of legislature, judiciary, and executive. A system of checks and balances is erected among them. Presidents may be impeached, their vetoes overridden, their regulations, edicts, and decrees require the counter-signature of an appropriate minister, and they are ineligible for immediate re-election. The president theoretically is restricted in the exercise of his power by the congressional power of the purse, the right of congress to approve nominations and to initiate laws. Congress also has a special watchdog committee to keep track of the president during its recesses.

Another element of theoretical restraint is found in the

court's power of judicial review of both legislative acts and executive decrees and administrative law.

All branches of government are forbidden by the 1961 constitution to violate its provisions and the extensive bill of rights that forms such an important part of the document. Indeed, the constitution goes even further. It proclaims itself to be inviolable. Article 250 asserts that the constitution will not lose its effect even if its observance is interrupted by force or is repealed by means other than those provided for in the amending clauses. Should that happen it enjoins upon every citizen, whether he is invested with authority or not, the duty of cooperating in efforts to reestablish it.

Elaborate precautions of this nature have not, in the past, prevented extensive abuse of power nor the concentration of it in the hands of the executive. The doctrine of separation of powers in Venezeula has been meaningless until fairly recently. So, too, have most of the other restrictions in the face of a constitutional grant of power to the president to declare a state of emergency (*estado de sitio,* or state of siege). During such an emergency he may suspend the operation of parts of the constitution and rule by decree. Considering the unsettled nature of Venezuelan politics, it has not proved difficult for a president to find an excuse to invoke the power. Determined administrations have used it many times to deal with obnoxious and outspoken opposition groups, as well as to expose plots against the government and to crush revolts. The 1961 constitution requires the president to get the approval of his cabinet and submit the suspension within ten days to Congress if it is in session, or to the watchdog Delegated Committee of Congress if it is not. Such stipulations have not ordinarily meant much, since past presidents have controlled both their cabinets and the legislature. In the new environment of today the requirements are more restrictive. Nevertheless, the Betancourt and Leoni administrations have often resorted to emergency powers to combat the terrorism of leftist forces.

The Paraguayan constitution of 1967 is more realistic about the true nature of governmental power. It places few restraints upon its president. The bicameral legislature is expected to approve the president's legislative proposals in the legislative session during which they are introduced. Article 156 declares that if Congress does not have time to take them up they will be considered approved. This provision, given the one-party nature of Paraguayan politics, means that it is the president who legislates, not the legislature—a state of affairs desired by the 1940 constitutional fathers and continued in the new charter. The legislature does not even possess the right to impeach the executive, nor would it make much sense for it to have the power. Like most Latin American presidents, the Paraguayan executive has the power to suspend the guarantees of the constitution when he deems an emergency has arisen. In Paraguay they have been suspended in whole or in part for most of the time since 1945. It is quite clear, therefore, that the Paraguayan government is not restricted by the bill of rights.

It would be a mistake to conclude that the power-elite of the Venezuelan and Paraguayan political systems are callous about individual rights, however. Modern executives are very sensitive about the repercussions stemming from their suspensions and would prefer to govern without resort to the state of siege. Much of couse depends upon the attitude of the president and the acquiescence of the opposition. Mecham remarks that "rights are null and void, declarations are mere words if means are not provided to make them effective; these means are the penal code, responsibilities of authorities, inflexible punishment of all attacks on rights. This and nothing else constitutes the guarantees." [46] Many Venezuelan and Paraguayan presidents have been willing to play the game only when it did not inconvenience them.

The constitution as an instrument of power

In spite of the fact that most Latin American executives prefer to live with a constitution (Castro of Cuba is an exception) and covet the legitimacy it confers on their regimes, it must nevertheless be stated that many could govern just as effectively without one if public opinion would permit it. President Stroessner of Paraguay does not in fact need a constitution. He can rule with nothing more than the support of the army and the acquiescence of the Colorado party. Many presidents of Paraguay have been strong and effective because they have

[46] Mecham, p. 267.

had a power base in other than constitutional sources. They have been able to exercise the powers of the presidency to the fullest (and indeed to expand them considerably) precisely because they brought their power with them into the government.

The same has been true of most of the Venezuelan presidents, excluding the puppets of the dictators. Of course, it was a comfort to the dictatorially inclined presidents to find specific and generous grants of executive power in the constitution, but one must also remember that because of their extraconstitutional bases of power (army, land, and so on) they were usually in a position to dictate such grants to the constitutional conventions. They, too, could have ruled without a constitution had not the political ethic of the nation demanded such a document, however defective it might be. This observation reflects Venezuela's experience before 1948. The three elected presidents since then have had no outside bases of power other than in the electorate. They have, therefore, had to rely upon the constitution for power to carry out their executive functions and to put their programs into effect. Such reliance has not produced exceptionally strong presidents. Nowadays the executive is strong in direct proportion to the willingness of the military forces to lend him their support, or at least not to interfere with him in the pursuit of his proper duties and to his ability to persuade opposition parties to cooperate with him and his party.

The constitutions now in force in Venezuela and Paraguay are those of 1961 and 1967 respectively. The scope of power conferred upon the government by them is impressive indeed. The government of Paraguay may exercise and utilize those powers as vigorously as it desires, limited only by its economic resources. The government of Venezuela must utilize the powers within the more limited context of party competition and coalition government. With this observation in mind let us look at some of the more unusual provisions of the two constitutions, both restraints and powers.

The Venezuelan constitution provides that no one may be sentenced to death or to perpetual or infamous punishment. Penal servitude is limited to thirty years (Art. 60). Sanitary inspections of homes may be made only in conformity with the law undertaken only after prior notice from the officials who order them or who are to make them (Art. 62). With respect to the exercise of freedom of expression, no one has a right to anonymity (Art. 66). The state shall protect the family as the fundamental nucleus of society and shall see to the betterment of its moral and economic position (Art. 73). Motherhood shall be protected, regardless of the civil status of the mother, and the state undertakes to ensure full protection of a child from his conception to maturity, without discrimination of any kind, under favorable material and moral conditions. It also assumes an obligation to help a child know his rightful parents. The state shall share with the parent the responsibility of rearing the children, with due regard to the resources of the parents (Art. 75). Everyone is guaranteed the right of protection of health (Art. 76). The state shall strive to improve the living conditions of the rural population (Art. 77). Education shall be entrusted to persons of recognized morality and proven fitness for teaching, according to the law. Education has the following objectives: the full development of personality, the training of citizens adapted to life and for the practice of democracy, the promotion of culture, and the development of a spirit of human solidarity (Art. 80). The state shall promote culture in its diverse forms (Art. 82), and it guarantees to everyone the right to work. Indeed, labor shall be the object of special protection: the government promises to provide whatever is necessary to find jobs, and to improve the material, moral, and intellectual conditions of the workers (Arts. 84 and 85).

Chapter V of the constitution declares that the economic system shall be based on the principles of social justice (which is not defined). The state has the obligation to restrict usury and to suppress nongovernmental monopolies except under unusual circumstances. It is empowered to protect private initiative, to engage in business, and to promote industry. It may expropriate but not confiscate property and it declares the great landed estates system contrary to the public interest.

In the area of social and economic concerns the 1967 constitution of Paraguay assigns to the state the obligation of preventing private interests from taking precedence over the national interest (Art. 123); to prevent the exploitation of man by man (Art. 104); and to create opportunities so that every

Paraguayan may earn his living by legitimate work and may live in a house on his own property (Arts. 126 and 83). The family is explicitly recognized as the basic unit of society and the state is charged with promoting and maintaining it. Maternity is specifically promised assistance. Declaring that every Paraguayan has a right to the full development of his health, the constitution entails upon all members of society the duty to submit to sanitary measures designed to protect the health of all. Although the right of private property is protected, the state may regulate the economic life of the country, outlaw monopolies, regulate labor unions, dispose of the subsoil minerals and oils, and carry out an extensive agrarian reform program (Arts. 94, 95).

All Paraguayans are obligated to defend their country and the constitution (Art. 125); they must refrain from preaching hate and class warfare and from advocating crime and violence. No one may take the law into his own hands (Art. 71). The state may not impose the death penalty for political offenses (Art. 65).

It can be seen from this recital that the Venezuelans and Paraguayans are specifically provided with far more state attention than are citizens of the United States. The important fact to remember is that the realization of state goals and obligations of the state vis-à-vis the citizens of Paraguay and Venezuela depends in large part upon the willingness and ability of those in power to implement them.

In terms of actual constitutional experience, Venezuela and Paraguay have not been very far apart despite the fact that Venezuela is credited with twenty-one more constitutions than Paraguay. The disparity arises from the Venezuelan custom of promulgating a new constitution each time an amendment, however minor, takes place. A new document therefore ordinarily differs from its predecessor only in the deletion or addition of certain sections or perhaps in new wording. It is far more accurate to say that Venezuela has in fact had no more than six basically different constitutions. These have differed fundamentally from each other on the issue of the form of government or upon the distribution of power within the system. The centralized unitary concept of the 1830 document was discarded permanently in the federal constitution of 1864. The actual organization of the republic continued to be unitary, however, under the administrations of powerful executives. The 1925 constitution represented an explicit move toward centralization. The 1947 document was largely programmatic in character, reflecting as it did the basic philosophy of the leftist party, *Acción Democrática.* All of that was done away with in 1953 in the brief, authoritarian charter of Marcos Pérez Jiménez. The 1961 constitution, written after the overthrow of Pérez Jiménez, restores most of the civil, social, and economic provisions of the 1947 law and is more honest in its federal features than those that preceded it. It asserts that the Republic of Venezuela is a federal state *within the terms* affirmed by the basic law. The terms are limited indeed.

The constitutions of Venezuela and Paraguay have rarely been the product of compromise between relatively balanced forces in society. They represent far more often the victory of one force over another. Society is stratified, basically conservative and dominated by authoritarian institutions of the family, Church, and army. There is, however, in Venezuelan society a group of intellectuals, enlightened aristocrats, and ardent reformers, all demonstrating considerable attachment to liberal democratic ideals and institutions. The battle is joined between these two major elements, each of which recognizes a different conception of authority. This split produces a lack of consensus about the fundamental aims and objectives of government and society. The liberals are at a disadvantage because they cannot remake society or even reform it greatly without resorting to violence and dictatorship, and so the advanced humanitarian, democratic constitutions are in varying degrees inoperative. Society is dominated by institutions that are not democratic and no constitution will alter this state of affairs significantly until society itself changes.

It would be unfair to conclude on such a pessimistic note. There is no doubt that the framers of the liberal constitutions are aware that their constitutions are not fully in harmony with the prevailing institutions and patterns of power in society. They are aware, too, that respect for the rule of law, fair play, tolerance, compromise, majority rule, and minority rights are things that cannot be imposed either by legislation or by constitution. Nevertheless, every successful application of democratic principles, every fair election, every peaceful transfer of power adds significantly to the growing democratic sentiment in Venezuela. The citizens of Venezuela were understandably pleased when these goals were realized in the elections of 1958, 1963, and 1968.

The Paraguayans have yet to experience any of these things in a meaningful way.

SUMMARY

The purpose of this chapter was to analyze the basic ingredients that both comprise and influence the political culture of Venezuela and Paraguay. Some of the ingredients tend to reinforce each other, such as violence and militarism, caudillism and militarism, caudillism and regionalism. Others have more unfortunate connections—violence and the role of elections, for example.

The political culture described in the foregoing pages represents an intimate connection with the past. It is characterized by dualism, contradictions, and inconsistencies in the area of political authority. A powerful executive is both expected to exercise his powers to the limit and even to exceed the constitution while at the same time honoring the constitution in its entirety. A president who does the former can be both applauded and censured by public opinion, according to whether his critic is first a Spaniard or a constitutionalist. A legislature is the representative of the sovereign will of the people, yet it is expected to subjugate itself to the executive. A militarist responsible for overthrowing the constitutional authorities will cite love of democracy and constitutional reasons for so doing.

The topics discussed in this chapter have by no means exhausted the list of ingredients of political culture, but hopefully they have indicated the broad outlines.

FOUR
NATIONAL, STATE, AND LOCAL GOVERNMENT
Federal and unitary systems

Most countries in Latin America have adopted a unitary form of government instead of a federal form. Paraguay has been governed throughout its national history under unitary structures. Venezuela, on the other hand, is one of the four countries that have consistently shown a preference for a federal system. Some historical and economic reasons for Venezuela's preference were set forth in earlier chapters. The other three countries with federal systems are Argentina, Mexico, and Brazil. While all four federal republics show strong unitary characteristics, Venezuela, perhaps, goes farthest in that direction.

A careful examination of the distribution of power in the two systems under study will reveal that in spite of constitutional differences relating to unitary and federal forms of government, both republics are in fact governed as unitary states.

FEDERALISM IN VENEZUELA: IDEAL AND REALITY
Constitutional organization

The federal Republic of Venezuela—known until 1961 as the United States of Venezuela—is governed under a constitution adopted unanimously in that year by the legislatures of the twenty states that compose it. In addition to the states there are seventy-two federal dependencies—mostly islands; two federal territories and the Federal District (Caracas). The states are Anzoátegui, Apure, Aragua, Barinas, Bolívar, Carabobo, Cojedes, Falcón, Guárico, Lara, Mérida, Miranda, Monagas, Nueva Esparta, Portuguesa, Sucre, Táchira, Trujillo, Yaracuy, and Zulia.

In terms of population, the units range in size from the Federal District with 1,300,000 people to about 850 persons in the island dependencies. The four states with the largest populations are Zulia, 919,863; Miranda, 493,000; Lara, 490,000; and Sucre, 400,000. The smallest state, Cojedes, has a population of 73,000.

Politically and administratively, all of the twenty states are organized on the following lines. The chief executive office is the governor (sometimes called president), who is the direct agent of the president of the republic. The governor is assisted by an official called the secretary-general of government and by an attorney general, who is named by the state legislature. The attorney general, of course, represents the state in all judicial proceedings involving the state as a legal entity. The secretary-general is appointed by the governor and countersigns all his official acts. He also serves as the latter's representative before the state legislature and often delivers to it the governor's annual message. Under the secretary-general there are such officials (appointed by the governor) as the director of administrative affairs, the director of public works, and the director of political affairs. The latter is responsible for supervision of state and municipal security forces. The governor also appoints for each of the districts of the state a prefect who will be his agent in all civil affairs, particularly in matters of police authority. The prefect is under the office of the director of political affairs.

For all practical purposes the Federal District is treated as a state. It has a governor appointed by the president and is entitled to elect senators and representatives to the national congress. It does not have a legislature that would correspond to the state assemblies, but has a large municipal council.

Legislative power rests with a unicameral state legislative assembly that is elected on the basis of proportional representation. It has little to do other than approve the budget submitted by the governor and to approve his yearly report on the conduct of his administration. State government in Venezuela at present is concerned almost entirely with the management of state property and the organization of urban and rural police within the state. The national government takes care of almost all other important services, such as health and educational facilities and social welfare activities.

The national constitution declares the states to be autonomous and equal entities and requires them to give full faith and credit to the official acts emanating from the national government, the other states, and the municipalities.

The Venezuelan states are divided into administrative districts or municipalities similar to the North American counties. The largest populated center in each district will be the administrative capital and seat of government. There are at present 170 such municipalities in Venezuela. The civil authority in each is in the hands of a municipal council chosen by direct popular vote on a proportional-representation basis every five years. The municipal council of the Federal District (Caracas) has twenty-two members. Each council elects one of its members to be its presiding officer who thus becomes mayor, in effect. He has little power, however. Each council also has a secretary on whom much of the administrative responsibility falls. It is with this official and the local police constable that the citizen usually deals. The average Venezuelan rarely sees a national government official except during political campaigns, as such men are based and prefer to live in metropolitan centers. The larger towns and cities in the district are divided into wards or precincts variously called *barrios* or *parroquias*. Each has a *jefe* (chief) and a *juez* (judge), who officiate at weddings, validate papers, and so on.

The municipal council is the smallest elected body in Venezuela. Below it are *juntas comunales,* or community boards, whose members are appointed by the municipal council to administer the civil affairs in each of the other organized communities in the district. In 1969 there were 636 boards. The areas under the jurisdiction of juntas *comunales* would correspond roughly to the small towns and communities of the North American county. They are often referred to as *municipios*.

At the very bottom of the scale in some rural areas are tiny collections of houses and people called a *caserío*.[1] It has almost no political organization other than a constable who represents the *junta comunal*.

Maintenance of public order and the supervision of police are the responsibilities of district prefects, named by the state governor.

States have had no independent judicial structures since 1950 when the judicial system was nationalized.

The role of the states in the federal system

One important aspect of autonomy is the right of the unit to maintain its territorial integrity. The Venezuelan states have not been able to do so. Many changes have taken place in the number and size of the states of Venezuela since it gained its independence. States have been abolished, created, combined, and separated at least eight times since 1819 on the initiative of the national congress acting on orders from the president. All of the changes in territorial status were unanimously ratified by the pliant state legislatures, even by those which were being legislated out of existence. In most of the alterations, the states were not consulted in advance.

An autonomous entity in a federal system might be expected to possess the indispensable power of taxation. The Venezuelan states no longer have that power. They cannot levy taxes on imports, exports, consumer goods before they enter their territory, livestock or any of its products or by-products. They are also forbidden to tax any item taxed by the national government or by the municipal governments. These prohibitions effectively deprive the states of tax revenue bases and thus the states are almost totally dependent on federal funds for their administration. Their one remaining source of income apart from federal money comes from investments and state properties. Former sources of revenue, now preempted by the national government, were sales from salt, public lands, official papers for legal documents, lotteries, and taxes on fishing. Surrender

[1] Thomas McKorkle, *Fajardo's People: Cultural Adjustment in Venezuela* (Caracas: Editorial Sucre, 1965), p. 12.

of these important fiscal powers has been described as an admission by the states of their incapacity to manage their own interests.[2]

Even before they lost most of the revenue bases, the states were deriving about 93 percent of their funds from the national treasury in the form of a subsidy called the *situado constitucional.* The *situado* is now a mandatory item in the national budget. Fifteen percent of the total ordinary revenue of the national government is earmarked for distribution to the states. The money presently is allocated on the basis of the following formula: 30 percent in equal amounts and 70 percent divided among the states in proportion to their population.

A United Nations report on the Venezuelan fiscal system concluded that beneficial results flowed from these arrangements in that duplication of revenue collection was eliminated and states were deprived of the power to interfere in the application of a coordinated federal policy.

Although technically the states are free to spend their subsidies as they see fit, this principle has never been observed in practice. For one thing, they are obligated to distribute a portion of their situado to their municipalities on terms laid down in Caracas. Then too, the constitution provides that the central government may lay down guidelines for the expenditure and investment of the funds it contributes. The annual meetings of the state governors in Caracas and the Ministry of the Interior are opportunities through which the national government coordinates state expenditures with administrative plans emanating from the Federal District. In 1945, for example, the governors were told by the minister of interior that the coordination of their budgets with that of the national government was a preliminary step toward the much broader task of planning the wise investment of the situado. To this end the governors were instructed to submit to him detailed plans for the use of the money.

Another move in the direction of achieving uniformity in state budgeting was a 1949 decree that announced that the fiscal year of the states would henceforth coincide with that of

[2] M. Marques Rivero, *Relaciones entre el Gobierno general y los Gobiernos locales* (Caracas: Imprente Bolívar, 1904), p. 34.

the national government. The 1949 governors conference approved a uniform fiscal law for the states and recommended that they adopt it as soon as possible. The law had the basic objective of unifying all fiscal legislation of the country, coordinating the state budgeting systems, bookkeeping, and statistics with those of the national government. By 1952, all of the state budgets had been coordinated with the national, and there now exists centralization of budget control and fiscal accounting. During the three *de facto* regimes since 1945, governors were empowered by the national executive to draft and promulgate the state budgets. Unilateral action by the governor is standard practice during abnormal political situations when the states are without legislative bodies.

The national government does not limit its grants to the situado. From time to time the states receive direct emergency subsidies as the need arises. A common type of aid is that applied to the construction and maintenance of secondary roads. An example of such aid is contained in a decree of 1952 in which the national government committed itself to supply 50 percent of the costs, the remainder to be borne by the state government and individuals. The decree required the governor, after consultation with municipal authorities, to advise the minister of agriculture of the need for such a road, its proposed location and cost, and the sums that would be contributed by the state. The minister of agriculture and the minister of public works then examined the information submitted by the governor, determined its feasibility, and had the appropriate sum deposited to the official account of the governor for disbursement if they approved. Control followed the bolívar, for the governors were required to accept the findings of the federal officials with respect to the building and repairing of roads. The national government could withdraw its share of the money if the work were not carried out in conformity with its plans and programs. To ensure that it was, the governor was required to submit detailed progress reports.

National aid to the states also extends to the construction of hotels through the agency of the Ministry of Development (*Fomento*), as well as to the construction of state government buildings. The federal government helps to maintain public health services in the states under the technical and administrative direction of the Ministry of Health and Social Welfare. It participates in construction programs for hospitals under special arrangements whereby the states pass their administration to the Ministry of Health and Social Welfare. National grants for less fundamental purposes are exemplified in subsidies to state governments to enable them to make year-end bonuses to their employees.

Not only have the states lost control of their fiscal powers, but over the course of the years they have had to yield to the national government almost all of their other important prerogatives. In 1881 they ceded jurisdiction to the national government over martitime and coastal matters; in 1901, secondary education; in 1914, posts, telephones, telegraph; and health in 1922. A wholesale transfer of power took place in 1925 when the federal government was empowered to legislate on banks, credit, social welfare, conservation, natural resources, labor, expropriation, and public registry. The judicial system was nationalized in 1945, and legislation relating to hotels, recreation, tourism, and lotteries was declared to be exclusively national in the constitution of 1953.

What powers then remain with the states? The list is brief. They may merge with the approval of the national senate. They may preserve or change their names, write their constitutions and organize their political structures so long as they conform to the national constitution or national law. They may use public credit, subject to national laws. They may legislate on the organization of municipalities, urban and rural police, and may administer state property and expend the funds derived from the national government—the so-called constitutional allotment. Finally, they may legislate on any matter not assigned to the national or municipal governments.

Almost everything falls within the domain of either the municipality or national government. The national constitution, not that of the state, defines the area of municipal jurisdiction, and it declares the municipality to be autonomous. As an autonomous unit the municipality may freely elect its city council, create, collect, and spend its revenues. Municipal monies are derived from excise taxes, property taxes on urban real estate, proceeds from municipally owned properties and communally owned lands, fines, certain licenses, and from their share of the state *situado*.

The subordinate nature of the states' position in the Venezuelan federal system is exemplified further by the national government's control of their executive branches.

The states definitively lost their power to choose their own governors in 1925; in the Gómez constitution of that year, the president was authorized to exercise any powers that the state constitutions might delegate to him. The states immediately and obediently bestowed upon Gómez the faculty of appointing their governors, a power he already possessed. Since then, the states have been managed by governors who "in their own sphere have had an omnipotence that in certain respects is a continuation of local *caudillismo* which is basically the historical reason for the creation of the so-called states." [3] In effect, however, their omnipotence was an extension of the president who appointed them.

Evidence that the states were not entirely satisfied with presidential appointment of their governors and regarded the prerogative as recoverable can be seen in an *acuerdo* (resolution) sent early in 1936 by all twenty state legislatures to President López Contreras, who had assumed the presidency on the death of Gómez. In that *acuerdo* the states extended to the president the authority to continue to appoint their executives until December 1939, a clear indication that they considered the extension to be temporary. A new constitution was adopted in 1936 that reiterated the Gómez formula, however. State attempts to regain the right to elect the governors have been thwarted not only by the executive but also by the Supreme Court. In 1937, for example, the Court ruled invalid the election of the governor of Portuguesa by its legislature on the grounds that such action conflicted with the national constitution. The present constitution contains a seed of hope. Under it the congress is authorized to pass a law dealing with the manner of election of state executives. It has not yet done so, nor is it likely to do so, and therefore the president continues to appoint them.

[3] Ernesto Wolf, *Tratado de Derecho Constitucional Venezolano,* Vol. I (Caracas: Tipografía Americana, 1945), p. 104.

The state governor is in an ambiguous position in that as the direct agent of the president he is responsible for the enforcement of all national laws and executive decrees, while as chief executive of the state he is charged by its constitution with preserving state autonomy against all encroachments. In the latter obligation he is less than effective, for he is first and foremost an officer of the national government.

No adequate study is immediately available that deals with the power and influence of the governor vis-à-vis the state legislature, but the whole nature of Venezuelan government points to the fact that the state legislative body is almost completely at the command of the governor. The legislature, in theory, has the power to call the governor to account and by a two-thirds vote to bring about his immediate removal. This does not happen. An example of the attitude of one governor toward the legislature is to be found in the response of the governor of Zulia to his legislature after it had approved his account of his administration. Two representatives dissented from the approval. The governor said, "The public can now see that there has been no executive intimidation of the legislature—a vicious practice of past regimes—for it has deliberated with all the autonomy which the law grants it." Speaking directly to the two dissenters he declared:

> I have noted your disagreement with the account of the achievements of my government. Let me assure you that you have nothing to fear since I am not accustomed to making reprisals against those who unfavorably judge my conduct as governor. It pleases me to assure you that you will not be molested as a consequence of having dissented from the approval.[4]

The office of the state governor has been in the past and continues to be more a political office than an administrative office. So few matters are left to state governments to administer that the governor has little state business to occupy him. His duties lie with the national government. The governor is expected to exert his efforts to deliver the state to the party in

[4] Estado Zulia, *El Presidente del Estado Zulia, censurado en la Legislatura* (Maracaibo: Tipografía "El Debate," 1941), p. 8.

power when elections are held. In the aftermath of the farcical election of 1952, although he had publicly affirmed his confidence in all of the state governors, Pérez Jiménez replaced the governors of all states where the combined strength of the opposition exceeded that of his supporters. Since the overthrow of the dictator, proliferation of parties, proportional representation properly applied, and fairer elections have made it difficult for the governors to ensure victory for their party. In 1968, for example, with party governors in fifteen states, *Acción Democrática* failed to capture a majority of the vote in any state and it lost the presidency to COPEI. Still, governors are in a position to exert influence in the electoral process.

In what sense can the state governor affect state elections? Part of the answer appears in a message sent by the governor of Zulia to the legislature in 1948 in which he criticized the election activities of the previous administration. He accused his predecessor of organizing forced parades of eminent citizens to support the candidacy of Medina Angarita and of instructing his secretary-general to ignore opposition groups in the composition of the electoral boards of the state. The electoral boards were instructed to ignore the credentials issued to members of opposition parties entitling them to be observers at the polls.[5] No doubt, too, the governor had access to funds that helped to ensure victory of his party.

The removal of governors supports the allegation that the state apparatus is little more than a political instrument inherited from the dictators and that governors are chosen, not for their administrative ability, but for their ability to direct elections and for their loyalty to the president. Whether this is true or not, governors have come and gone with astonishing rapidity. Many hardly have time to familiarize themselves with the routine of office before they are replaced. During the relatively calm years between 1936 and 1945 there were 141 governors, an average of seven per state. During the next seven and one-half years, which were abnormal ones in that two revolutions took place and two constitutions were written, 121 men served as governors. Considering the fact that 207 of the total 262 men who were

---

[5] Estado Zulia, *Mensaje que el Gobernador del Estado Zulia presenta a la Asamblea Legislativa del Estado Zulia, sesiones extraordinarias de 1948* (Maracaibo: Imprente del Estado Zulia, 1948), pp. 4–5.

governors in these 17 years were in office for less than 15 months and that 106 held power for less than 6 months, questions might be raised about presidential motives and the incentives for the choice of the governors. Data are not readily available on tenure of governors since 1958.

It does not seem unreasonable to suggest that presidents of Venezuela have used the office of the governor to discharge political debts, or to remove unwanted but important men from the capital city by assigning them to interior regions. On at least seven occasions during the period mentioned above, cabinet ministers were appointed to governorships. Since this can only be considered a demotion, it can be assumed that the president had a political reason for wanting the men out of the capital.

The attractiveness of the office to politicians might lie in several other considerations. We can dismiss one immediately. As a steppingstone to higher and better things in the national government the record is dismal. Again, in the same seventeen-year period only four men rose from governor to cabinet rank. Perhaps a more adequate explanation for the willingness of men to accept posts in the interior away from the excitement and glamor of the capital city is that the office presents an opportunity for personal enrichment. Certainly this factor cannot be discounted. The Venezuelans have adopted an extremely cynical attitude about graft at all levels in government. It is the governor who prepares the state budget, and it is he that has overall supervision of state funds. Various federal monies are deposited in his official account for subsidizing activities in the state. From this account he has the power to increase specific budget allocations when deficits appear—as they often do—and his office contracts for the construction of state public works, one of the most notorious sources of graft and corruption throughout Latin America. Such powers as these provide the unscrupulous man with ample opportunity to net himself a rich profit. Speculation and graft cannot be documented, but Venezuelans have insisted for a long time that men have grown rich in the governor's office.[6]

[6] See for example, R. F. Seijas, *El Presidente* (Madrid: Imp. y Lit. Terceno, 1891), pp. 27–29.

Undoubtedly some honor and prestige attaches to the office, and the salary is relatively attractive. Perhaps a partial explanation lies in the possibility that governors enjoy power even when it does not emanate from them per se. In the political system of contemporary Venezuela, governors exercise power in direct ratio to the strength of their personal relations with the president. It would not be unreasonable, therefore, to assume that the brother of ex-president Pérez Jiménez was a powerful governor during his short term as the executive of the state of Táchira. Informed Venezuelans insist that in those instances in which the governor does not appear to have much power, there is always another person close to the president, either in an official capacity or as a private citizen who wields the real power in the state. Obviously, such an allegation would be difficult to ascertain and document.

In recent years it has become customary for the president to appoint natives of the state to be governors. Party affiliation is, of course, an important determinant for appointment, and presidents will ordinary appoint as many governors of their own party as the traffic will bear. President Leoni appointed members of his *Acción Democrática* party to fifteen governorships, an action that disgruntled COPEI. In 1969 President Caldera, head of COPEI, appointed sixteen *Copeyanos* to be governors, evoking criticism from his coalition parties.

Concentration of power in the hands of the national executive has been furthered through the agency of the now annual governor's convention that meets in Caracas under the chairmanship of the president or the minister of interior relations. The announced purpose of the conventions is to bring about an ever-increasing coordination of state activities with those of the national government. In view of the fact that the governors are completely dependent on the president for their offices, it would be reasonable to assume that in these annual meetings personal relations with him are strengthened, errant governors are warned, and all are indoctrinated with the programs and policies of the national government.

The meetings of the governors began on a regular basis in 1947. Topics on the agenda for the convention have included the condition of the state treasuries, state public works, plans for carrying out projects by means of combined national and state resources, and legislative modification of state administration techniques.

The major emphasis on recommendations that come from the governors' conferences has been on more uniformity in state activities and stricter collaboration with the ministries of the national government. With this objective in mind, the minister of the interior requires monthly reports from the governors on all activities of a political-administrative character.

The trend toward greater state and national government coordination has been a consistent feature of political development in Venezuela for the past several decades. The latest manifestation of it occurred in 1969 when the national government superimposed eight large administrative zones upon the twenty states. The zones were based more on geographical considerations than on political factors, with the result that some states are divided between several zones. The purpose behind the creation of the zones was a desire by the national government to bring about a more consistent, orderly, and harmonious economic development in the various regions of Venezuela.

The national government will supervise all development activities in the eight zones through branch officers of the national Office of Coordinating and Planning. These regional offices will in turn be assisted by regional coordinating committees made up of state and national officials and by a National Development Council. State governors will play an important role in the regional councils.

In the other federal states of Latin America—Mexico, Argentina, and Brazil—the president has the right under certain conditions to intervene in state government, dismiss the legislature and elected governor and rule through an *intervenor*. The Venezuelan executive does not have this authority, nor does he need it. Governors are already his appointees, and through the state-of-siege powers he can intervene in state affairs.

The place of the municipality in the federal system

The division of power in Venezuela seems to be more between the 170 districts and municipalities and the national government than between the national government and the states. A closer examination of the facts, however, will reveal that this is not really the case. The city or municipal councils, it is true, have the legal power to legislate on all matters pertaining to local life that have not been preempted by the national government. They have, for example, the power to raise some of their own revenue. Municipalities may collect monies from such sources as licenses and franchises, car registrations, fees for public services, fines, public entertainment, some real estate and commercial taxes, and from the use of their communally owned lands (*ejidos*). In the collection of these funds, however, they are enjoined from taxing anything that is subject to taxation or has been taxed by the national government. Revenues derived from these sources are entirely inadequate to meet the administrative and improvement costs of the municipality, and it is therefore necessary for municipalities to rely heavily on the state situado for a substantial portion of their funds. The state situado is allocated among the municipalities on a proportional basis.

The obligations and powers of the city council include such things as the maintenance of cemeteries, slaughterhouses, water and sewer installations, marketplaces, and urban beautification. The organization of all of these services is subject to national laws and regulations, not to state laws.

Despite the apparent desires of the constitutionalists in 1961 to restore to the municipalities some of their earlier powers, they are still to a large degree greatly influenced by the state governor and his prefect. The dependency of the unit on funds from the state and the absorption of most of its jurisdiction by the national government have reduced the city council to an administrative adjunct of both state and national government with few unencumbered powers.

Municipal autonomy has rarely been respected in the matter of police organization and administration. Prior to 1953 the municipalities had the legal power to organize their own forces of law and order. The police codes of the state, however, declared that the municipal forces were a part of the state police force, and that as such they were subject to the exclusive authority of the state governor in such matters as organization, discipline, and control. The constitution of 1953 nationalized the police forces. Although the 1961 law restores to the states the authority to organize their urban and rural police forces and to determine what branches of these services will be under municipal jurisdiction, matters have not changed significantly. For all practical purposes, the police forces of Venezuela remain nationalized.

Municipal government is almost as unimportant in the policy process as are state governments. A basic fact of Venezuela political life is that most decisions are made in Caracas by national officials.

Other factors that influence the power and effectiveness of the city councils and the mayors are such obvious things as the size of the town, the degree of its advancement, the nature of its problems, and the party affiliation not only of its membership, but also that of the majority of the community. Although there is no objective evidence, it seems reasonable to assert that towns and cities that have elected councils composed of members of parties that are hostile to the party of the president will fare less well than those composed of members of his party. This may be true today of councils dominated by members of *Acción Democrática*. Since 1969 AD has been unrelentingly hostile to President Caldera and his government and has harassed him at every opportunity.

In addition to the officials, there are local notables in most communities who exert considerable influence in their restricted geographical areas. Since many Venezuelans are *campesinos* (peasants) and live on land owned by others, they are often subject more directly to the political power of their landlords than they are to the elected officials in the nearby town. The ability of the landlord to exercise *de facto* power has always been related to distance from the capital, friendship with state and national officials, and to his own inclinations and abilities. Rural *caudillismo* is by no means dead in Venezuela.

A strong feeling of *localismo* (attachment to a region or locality) still pervades most small rural communities. Many campesinos simply are unable to identify themselves meaningfully with national structures or urban concepts. Those who have been affected by agrarian reform, new roads, and schools are naturally more affectively oriented to the national government. For many years the countryside in Venezuela was only slightly affected by the distribution of goods and services at the disposal of state and national government. Little was done for those who lived in the interior, and little was expected of them beyond payment of taxes, military service, or loyalty to the local caudillo. To leave the urban centers and to go into the interior where most small towns are found was to go backward from one century to another. This is still true in the more remote centers.

Left largely to their own devices, the rural communities fashioned their own power structures, which might or might not include elected or appointed officials. The local notables— members of leading families, a highly regarded wiseman (*culto*), persons of superior physical powers, and the local priest were often the men who really counted in the decision-making process. Now, however, the national government is penetrating more and more into the rural regions, and a higher degree of centralization is taking place as programs of rural development expand. Thus, the national bureaucracy is coming to play a more important role in Venezuelan rural life.

The problems of the rural community and countryside are considerably different from those of the major populated areas. Rural regions need secondary roads to make transport of their agricultural surpluses to the markets easier. The problem of subsistence farming has been an acute one. The smaller rural communities usually are almost totally deficient in water, sewage, and electrical facilities. Issues confronting city policy makers concern adequate housing, job opportunities for increasing numbers of young people and persons who migrate from the country-side, law and order, transportation facilities, and so on. Substandard living conditions, particularly in Caracas, present the government with a severe challenge.

The judicial structure and inter-governmental relations

One feature of a federal system is the power of the central government to counteract official actions of the states when they conflict with national law or the national constitution. The national government of Venezuela has that power and exercises it through the Venezuelan Supreme Court.

Since states are little more than administrative units of the national government, it seems reasonable to suppose that their legislative activity would occasion little need for court scrutiny. This has been the case. One cannot help but be struck by the similarity, not only in the uniformity of state constitutions, but in the number and content of their laws—about ten major ones. Such uniformity is not accidental, but responds to pressures from the national administration. Because that is the case, litigation between the states and the national government does not often arise.

There have been occasions when such litigation did arise. In former years, when indirect election to both state and national legislatures was the rule, the Supreme Court on a number of occasions, when asked to do so by the national authorities, nullified the election of deputies and state representatives accused of being communists. State legislatures and municipal councils, said the Court, were obligated not to select legislators whose political affiliations placed them within the category of persons with subversive designs on the social and political order, and were not guaranteed the protection of the constitution.

Attempts by the states to limit the president's appointment powers have also been struck down. The Court invalidated certain articles of the constitution of Táchira that required the state's secretary-general be a native-born citizen of the state and that prefects be state residents at least three months prior to their appointment. In the opinion of the Court, no state could elaborate on the national constitution, wherein it was specified that in all matters relating to elections and suffrage, it was enough to be a Venezuelan. In 1941 the Court held that certain provisions of the constitution of the state of Aragua were invalid. The articles in question had converted the city councils into constituent bodies by giving them the power of requesting and ratifying amendments and additions to the state constitution. The Court decided this delegation was illegal in that it granted to city councils—considered economic and administrative bodies—a share in the legislative process of the state. The unitary structure of the state would thus be transformed into a species of federation of districts. The record of the Court in cases dealing with state legislation and constitutions clearly indicates that the states can hope for no aid in stemming the encroachment of the federal government or in recovering any of their powers.

Summary

From the foregoing discussion, it can be seen that Venezuela is a centralized democratic republic in which the dominant voice is the executive branch of the national government.

As McKorkle notes:

> The system operates under the theory that local people should vote for a centrally located authority that will operate paternalistically. It is felt that this system allows more adequate planning and educated Latin Americans are likely to believe that local people are too inexperienced and ignorant to manipulate democratic local institutions. . . .
>
> The centralized system is more in accordance with the Hispanic tradition than is the federal one. Under this system constitutional control is not so regular in practice as in theory and it is possible for a relatively small group to control or seize control of the whole system. . . .[7]

For the reasons cited in this section, Venezuela has more characteristics of a unitary repubilc than it does of a federal republic.

THE UNITARY SYSTEM OF PARAGUAY

A unitary system of government prevails when the central government has exclusive power to legislate for the entire country. Unlike Venezuela, Paraguay is and always has been a unitary state. Indeed, until the adoption of the 1967 constitution, units subordinate to the national government were not mentioned at all in the constitution. The 1967 document explicitly confers upon the national government a power it has always exercised: that of creating and rearranging administrative districts in the national territory.

Constitutional organization

Today Paraguay is divided into sixteen departments, twelve of which are governed by presidentially appointed prefects called *delegados,* all of whom are members of the ruling Colorado

[7] McKorkle, pp. 137–138.

party. The almost uninhabited departments in the Chaco do not have prefects or any municipal organization. Officials are sent directly from Asunción by the minister of the interior when the need arises. Asunción in theory is governed by its city council. In fact, however, its policies and programs are determined by the national government. The departments correspond to the Venezuelan states. Each is divided into a number of districts— presently there are 143 in Paraguay—which in turn are divided into smaller units called *compañías*. The Paraguayan department is the counterpart of the Venezuelan district and the *compañía* of the Venezuelan *municipio*. *Compañías* are sometimes made up of *colonias,* the smallest subdivision in the administrative pattern.

The chief population center of each district is the seat of the district government, composed of an *intendente* (mayor), a *comisario* (police chief), and a municipal council. Prior to 1965 all of these officials, as well as the local tax collector, telegraph operator, and justice of the peace were appointed by officials in Asunción. In 1965 the districts were given the right to elect their own *intendente* and their city council, but for all practical purposes these men are still dependent upon the president for their positions. Political office, even on the lowest level is eagerly sought because of the patronage opportunities it confers upon the occupant. In the present environment, politicians must be members of the Colorado party if they expect to obtain national and local government posts.[8] Of all of these officials, perhaps the most powerful one is the police chief, supported by his squad.[9]

The role of the municipality

In the actual decision-making process in the Paraguayan communities where municipal councils now exist, the mayor is likely to find himself overshadowed by the chief officer of the Colorado party, the president of the party's *seccional* (local party organization). Of course, the mayor may himself be the

[8] Frederick Hicks, "Politics, Power and the Role of the Village Priest in Paraguay," *Journal of Inter-American Studies,* 6 (April 1967), 275.

[9] Harry Kantor, *Patterns of Politics and Political Systems in Latin America* (Skokie, Ill.: Rand McNally, 1969), p. 714.

seccional president; in that case his position of authority is undisputed. The seccional president functions as a caudillo who is regarded by other party members as being responsible for the welfare of all party members in the area. One of his most important obligations is to see to it that his party receives the lion's share of whatever economic benefits come to the community. Since the population of many Paraguayan communities is about evenly divided between partisans of the two traditional parties, the Liberal and the Colorado, the politically neutral local priest may function as an important and influential figure in mediating disputes between the two rivals. Such conflicts arise over distribution of available jobs, expenditures of funds collected by civic improvement groups and over the nature and type of such improvements: roads, schools, beautification, and so on.[10]

Perhaps one may draw some conclusion as to the unimportance of official local government machinery in Paraguay from the dearth of information on it. Practically nothing exists either in English or in Spanish. Certainly another indication is the fact that municipal elections were held in 1965 for the first time in forty years.

In theory the Paraguayan municipal councils have about the same powers as those attributed to the Venezuelan, but they are considerably more restricted in the exercise of them. The president of Paraguay may intervene in the affairs of the districts and towns when the councils request him to do so; when they are unable to discharge their duties; when a budget deficit occurs in the district for two consecutive years; or when "grave irregularities exist." These powers together with the state-of-siege power give the president unlimited authority to impose his will on the most elementary of local government structures. He has often employed these powers. Since 1963, when the state of siege was lifted in all but four departments, the departments and their subdivisions had been under almost continuous emergency regulations since 1940. The situation is not much improved today.

The Paraguayan constitution does not mention the sources of municipal revenue. Considering the backward state of the

[10] Hicks, pp. 278–279.

Paraguayan economy, particularly in the rural areas, independent funds must be meager indeed. The administrative units in the Paraguayan system are dependent upon the national government for money to carry on their day-to-day activities.

The high degree of executive control, the dominance and penetration of the Colorado party, the lack of independent sources of money, and the long period of local government inactivity means that effective local government structures have not developed. Government is likely to be on an *ad hoc* personal basis in the small villages and towns of Paraguay.

Summary

All available evidence on local government structures in Paraguay and Venezuela point to the conclusion that this element of the political system is either poorly developed, obscure, and ignored (Paraguay) or consists of bodies with a clearly defined constitutional position yet unable to take courses of action independently of the national government (Venezuela). Compared to the Paraguayan *delegado,* the Venezuelan state governor has more to say about the affairs of the territories under his jurisdiction because the states are in theory autonomous. Both the Venezuelan governor and Paraguayan *delegado,* however, are *national* officers and continue in office solely at the pleasure of the president. All important matters are arranged and decided in the national capital. In spite of constitutional dissimilarities, the real distribution of official power in federal Venezuela and unitary Paraguay is almost identical.

THE COMMUNICATION RESOURCES

Official media

The governments of both countries communicate with their citizens by means of daily editions of the *Gaceta Oficial,* in which all official acts are promulgated. Only a tiny fraction of the people ever see the *Gaceta,* however, since it is not widely distributed. The only copy in rural areas is likely to be in the hands of the prefects, the *delegados,* or the municipal councils. The result is that few citizens are well informed about the official acts of their government except in those cases where the government makes a sustained effort to educate the people. Such a controlled effort took place in Venezuela in November 1952, when the *Junta de Gobierno* launched a massive newspaper campaign to bring to the Venezuelan people an awareness of the material accomplishments of the government over a period of four years. The success of such efforts is easier in communities that have newspapers and citizens who can read them. Despite the fact that illiteracy is rapidly decreasing in Venezuela, 11 percent of the population still cannot read. Many, indeed most, of the small towns and villages have no newspapers at all.

Press, radio, and television

Venezuela has 36 newspapers with a total circulation of 630,000 copies, a ratio of 78 per 1000 people. Paraguay is worse off by far. It has only 8 newspapers with a circulation of 90,000 or 45 copies per 1000 people. Circulation in Paraguay is limited almost entirely to Asunción and several minor cities. The rural regions are hardly touched. One-third of all Paraguayans can neither read nor write. Effective communication is severely compromised.

The population of the two countries is more easily reached by radio and television. Here again Venezuela is far more advanced than Paraguay. In the former, one government and three commercial radio networks broadcast through 170 station outlets. There are 200 radios for every 1000 persons. Venezuela also has one government-owned and three commercial television networks. Television programs reach about 75 percent of the population through 650,000 sets. The prevalence of urban television is credited with helping Arturo Uslar Pietri, a popular urban presidential candidate in 1963, to carry the capital city.

By way of comparison, Paraguay has only 19 radio stations and 90 radios per 1000 population. Television, introduced in 1966, is still out of the reach of all but the most affluent members of society. Paraguay has only one television station and about 1000 television sets.

The effectiveness of the various communication media naturally depends upon the number of the persons they are able to reach, as well as the extent of their freedom to express their views. Both countries have endured severe restrictions in the freedom to disseminate information. During the Pérez Jiménez regime in Venezuela, the communication facilities were permitted to publish only laudatory, or at best, inoffensive, accounts of government activities. Nor was much favorable publicity permitted about groups that opposed the government. The press and radio reports, therefore, were sterile and misleading. The tendency of the literate population in this situation was to discount much of what they read and heard. People were more likely to accept word-of-mouth reports.

Despite the fact that constitutional guarantees relating to freedom of expression have been suspended on several occasions since the fall of Pérez Jiménez in 1958, the Venezuela press, and indeed the whole area of mass communication, has been relatively free from governmental interference.

Within the context of the political environment, labor unions, student groups, and professional associations issue manifestos outlining their goals, purposes, and demands. Associations run full-page advertisements in leading newspapers proclaiming their political intent and political loyalty. The Church hierarchy circulates pastoral letters, delivers political sermons, and pronounces excommunication if necessary. Military forces explain their motivations and justify their interference in the political system in *pronunciamientos*.

Since the state siege is a near normal state of affairs for Paraguay, censorship of the press and government interference in the broadcasting media are almost continuously in operation. The Inter-American Press Association frequently called attention to the repressive acts of the Stroessner regime during his first fourteen years in power. Many times during those years newspapers were either suppressed altogether or had their editions confiscated because of the publication of criticism adverse to the government. Publishers were denied newsprint or their facilities were physically occupied by government security forces. In October 1968 the IAPA removed Paraguay from its blacklist of nations, because it appeared that the government was permitting greater freedom for the press. The move was premature. Encouraged by the relaxation of censorship, opposition forces intensified their criticism of the tactics and policies of the government. President Stroessner therefore reestablished strict government control over news and broadcasts.

Within the framework of the restrictions imposed by the government, newspapers and periodicals can play an important role in political communication. Two Venezuelan newspapers, *El Mundo* and *Ultimas Noticias* and a periodical, *Elite,* all owned by a prominent family, consistently voiced opposition to the policies of the Betancourt and Leoni administrations. *El Universal,* the leading conservative newspaper of Caracas, also has been generally critical of left-of-center governments. *La República* and *El Nacional,* on the other hand, have supported AD policies in their editorials. Indeed, the editor of *El Nacional* was President Betancourt's executive secretary from 1953 to 1963. The Venezuelan parties ordinarily do not have official party newspapers. The Caracas dailies adopt parties and give them such publicity as their policies dictate. The Church in Venezuela publishes four papers with a total circulation of about 31,000 copies. Its Caracas voice is *La Religión.* Church periodicals support the Social Christian party of President Caldera.

Paraguayan parties can be more clearly and consistently identified with newspapers and publications than can the Venezuelan. There are far fewer parties in Paraguay, and they have had a much longer existence as organized entities. The Colorado party speaks through its paper *Patria.* A splinter faction of the old Liberal party airs its views in *La Libertad,* while the Febreristas speak through *El Pueblo.* Only the Colorado party organ has remained untouched over the years. The others have all been closed at one time or another on charges of subversion. The most widely read daily newspaper with independent inclinations is *La Tribuna.* It has a circulation of about 30,000. The voice of the Church in Paraguay is the weekly *Comunidad.*

In a recent survey in Paraguay,[11] respondents were asked to choose from a list of eight sources, the two that they would give the most weight in seeking information on important national problems. Fifty percent of the members of the governing Colorado party said they would give more attention to the independent dailies such as *La Tribuna* than to any other source, including their party paper. Opposition party members

[11] Byron A. Nichols, "Las Espectativas de los Partidos Políticos en el Paraguay," *Revista Paraguaya de Sociología,* 5 (Diciembre 1968), 22–61.

were far less willing to accept information published in the daily papers and placed their faith instead in their party papers. Thirty-four percent of the Radical Liberals, 37.3 percent of the Febreristas, but only 1.6 percent of the Christian Democrats said they would look to their party papers for information. *Comunidad* was chosen by 20 percent of the Colorados, 38.3 percent of the Radical Liberals, 50.7 percent of the Febreristas, and 94.9 percent of the Christian Democrats as a reliable source of information on national issues.

Face-to-face contacts

Person to person communications take place at all levels of the political system. Individual peons who complain to the local priest are communicating to the political structure when the priest is one of the most important local political figures. This is true in the Venezuelan Andes, a stronghold of conservative Catholicism. Face-to-face contacts with the village priest in Paraguay are particularly important because of the moderating role he may play in the political and economic systems. A household servant in the city who passes along observations to her mistress, who happens to be the wife of a political party leader or member of the government, is articulating some of the grievances of her class. A follower of a local caudillo and a peon talking to his patron may be voicing their concerns. All of this is not to say that the face-to-face contacts always produce results, but at least those in positions of influence or power are made aware of issues about which they might otherwise be ignorant.

Political party leaders, of course, are often in daily contact with members of their party, particularly with other notables. Parties are more formally structured in Venezuela and Paraguay than they are in the United States. Political passions run particularly high in election years and there is a great deal of frenetic campaign activity, oratory, and mass meetings. Face-to-face contact between minor party officials and party members is both important and frequent in Paraguay where local rewards and opportunities .depend upon such relationships. Television, particularly in Venezuela, is reducing the number of personal contacts, but it is greatly increasing the overall exposure of party leaders, politicians, and government officials.

Violence as communications

The role of violence in the political culture has already been discussed. Violence is, of course, a method of citizen communication with the policy structure. Where excessively employed, it usually reflects a system in which parties and interest groups have proved to be ineffective channels of communication. This has always been the case in Paraguay and, until the last decade, in Venezuela. Direct-action politics has normally been the only effective method by which the ordinary citizen in the two countries could have an impact on the official structure.

Demonstrations are very much a part of the Latin American political culture. The demonstrations may or may not have anything to do with politics; often they are primarily of religious significance. Students are particularly given to demonstrations, marches, and parades as well as to other more vigorous forms of expression. Some demonstrations are in support of rather than against a particular policy or decision.

If one may discount the natural disposition of the Latin American male to engage in volatile political behavior, one might reasonably conclude that as the party system evolves into an effective channel of political expression, resort to violence or threats of violence will gradually diminish in both countries.

Summary

Neither Venezuela nor Paraguay is a particularly advanced country with respect to its communication structure. In this category Paraguay is one of the most deficient countries in South America. Communication facilities are largely restricted to the capital city and to two or three other populated centers. The bulk of the population, however, lives in rural hamlets or on tiny plots of land, has little access to papers or radios, and is thus little affected by the information released in the capital city. Rural residents depend upon the local party organization to inform them of government policies that affect them. The press as a whole is highly partisan, and the radio and television networks are completely under the control of government censors.

Venezuela has moved decisively away from the restrictions of the dictatorial period. While press, radio, and television are almost completely free at present to inform the public as they see fit, Venezuela, too, is handicapped by the lack of a penetrative communication system. In both countries, significantly large parts of the population are uninformed on day-to-day developments.

FIVE
THE PARTY
SYSTEM

Multiparty coalition democracy and status quo one-party rule

HISTORICAL PERSPECTIVES

Venezuela

Venezuelan historians seem to be in agreement that the political forces contending for power during the ninetenth century were not distinguished by doctrinal differences. Venezuela did not, of course, escape the social cleavages between conservatives and liberal elements following the war for independence, but the political expression of the cleavage was artificial, because the aristocratic class provided the bulk of both currents of political thought. There was little else for an educated man to do but enter politics, Church, or army.

For the first eighteen years of its national existence, Venezuela was dominated by the Conservative oligarchy, principally large landowners and the wealthy commercial class. It was permeated with ideas concerning the privileged status of the aristocracy, the Church, traditionalisms in society and politics, and the need for strong government. Indeed, it sought to maintain the colonial economic and social structure, but with political power in the hands of the Venezuelan criollos.[1]

There was, of course, opposition to this philosophy. Through his newspaper, *El Venezolano,* the influential intellectual Antonio Leocadio Guzmán became the articulate spokes-

---

[1] Edwin Lieuwin, *Venezuela,* 2d ed. (London: Oxford, 1965), p. 35.

man for those persons who wished to see society, government, and the economic order liberalized. Under his leadership the Liberal party was organized in 1840. It drew its support not only from the intellectuals, but also from small farmers and modest commercial interests. Insofar as they were aware of it, the masses were attracted to the Liberal program. Specifically, the Liberals sought the abolition of the death penalty, lower interest rates, emancipation of the slaves, and a broadening of suffrage. In the election of 1846 only 5 percent of the population could vote. For attacking this system, Leocadio Guzmán was sentenced to death. He was later reprieved by the Monagas administration.

Although much of what the party advocated found its way into the statute books under the Monagas brothers, the Liberal party did not triumph over the Conservative oligarchy until Leocadio's son, Guzmán Blanco, seized power in 1870. Guzmán Blanco was hardly a liberal in any sense of the word. He ruled Venezuela more autocratically than had any of his conservative predecessors. His political philosophy was grounded in order and *personalismo,* not in liberalism.

Thus the early political associations of Venezuela tended to coalesce as much around personalities as around the economic and political issues of the day. Little more than coalitions of caudillos, they were motivated in their struggles for power less by a theory of government than by a consuming desire to govern. During the Conservative oligarchy, persons of Liberal persuasion often were included in the cabinets. Once in power, they conveniently forgot the contradictions that separated them from the Conservatives while in opposition.[2]

The period between Guzmán Blanco and Juan Vicente Gómez was marked more by regional and personal power struggles than by genuine party activity. Such party organization as did exist was ended by Gómez. He did allow one of his own to function—the *Causa Rehabilidora,* but it could hardly be called a party. Partisan politics ended under the oppression of *El Brujo* (the sorcerer, as Gómez was sometimes called).

[2] José Gil Fortoul, *El Hombre y la Historia* (Madrid: Editorial America, 1916), pp. 84–85.

The death of Gómez in 1935 ended an era. Political activity during the next ten years increased greatly in the freer environment. Deserting the old two-party lineup, the Venezuelans now fragmented into many different groups. Some were based on ideology, such as the Communists and *Acción Democrática,* and some on personalities such as the Venezuelan Democratic party, whose members were called *medinistas* (followers of Medina).

In the election of 1946 to the constitutional assembly, fourteen parties participated. Most of these distintegrated after the convention was over. Only *Acción Democrática,* COPEI, and the Communist party still were organized to take part in the presidential election of 1947. A new one had appeared: *Unión Republicana Democrática* (URD). In the 1952 constitutional assembly election a new party list included *Frente Electoral Independiente, Frente Electoral, Unión Nacional,* and *Organizaciones Independientes,* all of which supported Pérez Jiménez for the office of constitutional president. Other new parties legalized by the government were the Venezuelan Socialist party, the Socialist Workers party, and the Independent Revolutionary Front. Gone from the scene were the Communist party and *Acción Democrática,* both of which had been outlawed, and all of the others that had made their appearance after the 1945 revolution.

In 1958 there were eight party slates of candidates; in 1963, thirteen; and in 1969, over twenty. Only the major parties continued under the same names. In general the existence of minor political parties has tended to be extremely brief. The present party system, therefore, is characterized by a high degree of factionalism. Parties are ephemeral as groups coalesce, separate, and merge. Each of the principal parties has its groups of dissidents and malcontents who often organize splinter groups to challenge the control of party stalwarts.

Paraguay

Let us now turn to the development of parties in Paraguay. Before 1870 there were no parties at all, as the three dictators who had dominated the scene were unsympathetic. After the War of the Triple Alliance the present party system gradually began to take shape. In 1887 both the Colorado party (The

National Republican Association) and the Liberal party were organized (some authorities give the year 1874 as the date of the founding of the Colorado party). A striking feature of Paraguayan politics since that time has been the persistence of a basically two-party system in the face of one-party government. Until the advent of the Febrerista party in 1936, politics was monopolized by the two historical parties. The principal matter that separated them, beyond sterile paper declarations of programs, was the determination of each to keep the other from the seats of power. Thus the Colorados kept the Liberals from office from 1870 to 1904. The Liberals then held power until 1936. The rivalry between the two groups filled the years with civil disturbances and innumerable acts of violence and intrigue. The Liberal party was outlawed in 1942 by Morínigo, and the Colorado party was more or less in limbo during much of his eight-year span of power. The Colorado party triumphed in 1947, however, when the dictator adopted it as his political vehicle. Although the party has since become a captive of President Stroessner, it technically has been in power since 1947.

Paraguay is, therefore, and has always been, a one-party state. In most of the elections since 1880, only one party has offered a slate of candidates to the electorate. Opposition groups, convinced that the electoral system was rigged and that the party in power did not intend to lose the election, simply abstained. One-partyism has by no means lessened with the appearance in 1959 of the Christian Democratic party, the reemergence of the Febrerista and the old-line Liberal parties and the splintering of the latter. The chief victim of the trend has been the Liberal party.

THE CONTEMPORARY LEGAL AND POLITICAL MILIEU

The legal life of the political parties in both countries now is embedded in the constitution itself. The Paraguayan parties are recognized for the first time in a brand new section of the 1967 law. Its provisions are basically as follows.

All Paraguayans who are eligible to vote have the right to organize political parties in order that they may participate "through democratic methods in the selection of government authorities and in the determination of national policy." Congress is authorized to pass a law that will guarantee the democratic nature of the parties and their equality before it. No political party will be allowed to organize or function that has as its purpose the destruction of the representative, democratic, and republican character of the government and the multiparty system. They may not subordinate or ally themselves with foreign parties having that character, nor receive subsidies or directives from them. This means, of course, that the Communist party is constitutionally barred from Paraguay. Legally recognized parties may not encourage nonparticipation in the election process. The legal nature of the party cannot be cancelled or suspended except by judicial decision following a violation of the law.

The Venezuelan constitution says much the same thing; indeed, the Paraguayan seems to be a replica of it. The Venezuelan constitution, however, makes no mention of subversive parties or foreign connections. At present the Communist party is a legal entity in the party system.

Under the terms of the constitution, then, political parties are conceded to have a role to play in the political system: the election of public officials and a share in the determination of public policy. The proliferation of parties in Venezuela since 1961 indicates not only that the citizens are availing themselves enthusiastically of this right and that the government is not interfering, but also that Marcos Pérez Jiménez was wrong when he observed that Venezuelans were not inclined to political parties.

The functioning of the party system in Paraguay depends upon the mood of President Stroessner. He is not unduly bothered by his constitution and has ample power to dissolve political parties (if they are undemocratic or foster hate and class strife), despite the constitutional guarantees, to harass them in a variety of ways, to prevent them from achieving any meaningful electoral success, and, above all, to keep from them a share in the patronage system. Opposition parties in Paraguay know from long experience that not only do they not win, but that they can expect unwelcome attention from the government during campaign periods.

Until 1963 opposition political groups were simply not

permitted to function freely in Paraguay. Many of the vocal leaders of the Liberal and Febrerista parties found it wise to take up residence in Argentina or Uruguay, bases from which they continually plotted against the Stroessner regime.

In 1959 the exiled leaders of the Liberal party and the Febreristas joined together in the *Unión Nacional Paraguaya* pact, agreeing to work together to bring about the downfall of the Stroessner regime and the restoration of their constitutional liberties to participate in Paraguayan politics. Specifically, they asked for an end to the state of siege and an amnesty for all political exiles. Stroessner rejected their petition and countered with the charge that the parties themselves were responsible for their repression because of their "irresponsible and subversive behavior."

Several developments ended the pact. For one thing, Stroessner began to relax the more stringent controls in order to clear the environment for the 1963 presidential elections in which he proposed to run for a third term. Although the 1947 constitution forbade him to do so, he had his pliant Congress declare that he had served only one full term, his first merely rounding out that of his deposed predecessor. To achieve the illusion of broad popular support among the Paraguayan people, he then encouraged opposition parties to present candidates. The Liberals and the Febreristas refused to do so, claiming that nothing had changed in Paraguay. A number of more cooperative Liberals in Paraguay, under the leadership of Carlos A. Levi Ruffelini, organized the *Directorio Revolucionario del Partido Liberal,* also known as *Renovación* and *"levirales,"* and asked for legal status. In December 1962 this group was recognized by the Central Electoral Board and accorded the exclusive right to use the Liberal party label and the party's blue color. *Renovación,* of course, was vigorously denounced by the traditional Liberals in exile, but the splinter group ran a slate of candidates, knowing full well that its presidential candidate would lose. The party was, however, awarded twenty of the sixty legislative seats in the then unicameral legislature. In 1963, therefore, for the first time in thirty-five years an opposition party was seated in the legislature.

The Febrerista party broke the agreement when it decided to run a slate of candidates in the municipal elections of 1965, the first such held in Paraguay in forty years. In 1967 the old line Liberals, now known as the Radical Liberals, decided to end their boycott and were permitted to participate in the election of delegates to the 1967 constitutional assembly. Of the 120 delegates to the convention they elected 20; *Renovación,* 8; and the Febreristas, 3. The willingness of these parties to take part in the election was an indication that they thought a freer political climate existed and that perhaps they had a chance of exerting some influence in the deliberations of the assembly.

The 1968 election provided no surprises for anyone, least of all for the Colorados. "We know exactly what the political sympathies are of every voter in every community in the nation," declared Stroessner's campaign manager.[3] During the campaign, the Colorado party monopolized the broadcasting system and the government withheld from the opposition parties the necessary police permits to hold rallies in the cities and towns. Then, too, the Colorado government officials supervised, counted, and reported the electoral results. The opposing parties had legitimate grounds for their complaint that conditions after all had not really changed much.

The role of opposition parties in the formation of national policy is insignificant. Lacking power in the new legislature where together they have only one-third of the seats in each house, they are virtually ignored by President Stroessner and the Colorado party.

Despite the fact that the Colorado party has been in control of the government for thirty-two years and that the Liberal party was illegal from 1942 to 1967 with its leaders in exile, the people of Paraguay are still almost evenly divided between the Liberals and the Colorados, each of which claims about 400,000 members.[4]

It seems clear that in spite of long periods of party rule, party membership in one or the other of the two traditional parties is important to the average Paraguayan citizen. His affiliation with his party is not a rational one, but one that he inherits. Most party members are recruited from families whose allegiance has for years been given to the party. Political attach-

[3] *The New York Times,* February 18, 1968, p. 5.

[4] Byron A. Nichols, "Paraguay—A Future Democracy?" *SAIS* Review (Summer 1968), 27.

ments therefore divide the Paraguayans into two political camps, and third parties find the going difficult. The Christian Democrats and the Febreristas have so far managed to attract only about 10,000 members each. Those who have joined them expect them to function like the traditional parties.[5]

What are the two parties like and how do they function? In a recent study of the party system of Paraguay, the author asserts that the two major parties are outgrowths of friendships among benevolent rulers of large estates. The patrón was absolute boss in his region. Because the peons naturally accepted his party affiliation, the parties gradually assumed the character of large families, oriented not to a political philosophy or program, but to the acquisition of power by the powerful patrón. The patrón has gradually disappeared as a political force, and his functions have been assumed by the parties.

> It is not surprising, therefore, that the major functions of political parties in Paraguay are primarily social for the majority of their members; the parties provide medical and legal assistance, employment and social events. Most Paraguayans feel that their political party is *obligated* to perform these services for them and leaders of both parties readily acknowledge that their organizations have more social responsibilities than political ones.[6]

Paraguayan peasants are excluded from village and town groups, and one result of this is that they are not much interested in politics. Townsmen, on the other hand, are intensely factional and politically minded. In the towns, open and complete identification with one of the major parties is absolutely indispensable. A man's commitment must be made known,

> because one cannot deal normally with a person without knowing what his commitment is. One doesn't know how to interpret what he says, or how his own statements will be interpreted. Paraguayans are very adept at seeing the functional relations between politics and other aspects of their culture, and practically everything has its political significance. Neutrality is socially impossible. If someone were to try to maintain an

[5] Nichols, p. 27.
[6] Nichols, p. 26.

attitude of neutrality or aloofness, it could only mean that he
had something to hide, and he would be viewed with suspicion.
He might be a spy, or an informer, or a "communist"—that is,
someone who works secretly toward vaguely evil ends . . .
Once an individual's commitment is known, then, even if he
belongs to the opposition, one can deal with him in a normal
friendly manner.[7]

Despite the importance attached to ideology by many
Paraguayans, the traditional parties are nonideological in nature
and over the years have taken on the character of mutual aid
societies, which look out for the separate interests of their
individuals and factions. These interests take the form of competition for the limited job opportunities, government contracts,
and allocation of community funds. In his study of the town
of Capiatá and its surrounding district, Frederick Hicks found
that in this community of 2000 persons the main source of
employment was an Uruguayan factory that processed vegetable
and animal products and employed between 250 and 600
workers, depending on the season. Distribution of the jobs in this
one-industry town becomes a sensitive operation as political
leaders seek to satisfy the claims of their loyal followers. In
this task party leaders turned to the village priest, seeing in
him a neutral, nonpolitical mediator between their competing
claims.

The villagers and the managers of the company prefer to
bring their disputes to the priest rather than to involve the
national government, particularly because there is a widespread
belief that the national government will generally ignore community interests in favor of national ones. Thus Hicks argues
that the social and political structure of the countryside accounts
for the prominent position of the village priest and not the super-
stitious nature of the Paraguayan or even the outstanding personal qualifications of the priests.[8] His article suggests an
important political role for the grass-roots priest as a vital cog
in conflict resolution. The priest's mediation efforts are often

[7] Frederick Hicks, "Politics, Power and the Role of the Village
Priest in Paraguay," *Journal of Inter-American Studies,* 9 (April 1967),
276. Reprinted by permission.
[8] Hicks, pp. 273–282.

successful because he has come to be regarded as a politically neutral agent, and he is expected to maintain that position. His success in adjudicating claims in his immediate jurisdiction reinforces the village belief that he is the proper agent to undertake conflict resolution in economic matters, at least. Thus the character and functioning of the party system gives the lower hierarchy of the Church a measure of influence in community affairs it might not otherwise have.

THE POLITICAL PARTY SPECTRUM

Paraguay

The game of politics in Paraguay is played out in an atmosphere that is basically conservative because it has always been dominated by two essentially conservative political groupings. Clear and concise statements of party principles and objectives are difficult to come by and difficult to understand, as they are usually couched in abstract and ornate language. Parties seem to prefer to harass their opponents through metaphysical abstractions rather than to compete with them by offering reasoned programs of action.

The Colorado party, as the government party and the chief input party structure, is primarily concerned with staying in power and maintaining order, with refuting charges that it runs a brutal police state, and with justifying its actions. The Colorado party has been in power so long that it has come to identify itself with the state and therefore to regard the attempts of other parties to unseat it as both pernicious and bordering on treason. Pictures of President Stroessner posted in public places carry the slogan *"Un presidente colorado para todos los Paraguayos."*

The party has been described as a "nationalistic, aggressive, economically progressive" group.[9] The designation could be equally well applied to the Liberal party, particularly if it were in power. The Colorados regard their doctrine of the interventionist, positive state as being in harmony with Paraguayan

[9] Paul E. Hadley, "Paraguay," *Political Forces in Latin America: Dimension of the Quest for Stability,* Ben G. Burnett and Kenneth F. Johnson, eds. (Belmont, Calif.: Wadsworth, 1968), p. 380.

realities. It emphasizes the interests of both individual and the collectivity in the political, economic, and social systems. The individual, however, has often been on the losing side. Although the party subscribes to the principle of liberty and equal opportunity for all Paraguayans, it is clear that the *Colorados* occupy a preferred position in Paraguay. A key concept of the Colorado party is that of *"co-religionario,"* which means "a preferential form of relationship among the members of the organization." [10]

The goals of the Colorados are "spiritual pacification of the country," reorganization of the economy, and order and progress. It has perhaps achieved more order—through a strong police state—than progress, yet undeniably some advances have been made in the fields of transportation, communication, health, and welfare.

Technically in control of the destinies of Paraguay, the Colorado party today responds to the wishes of General Stroessner, who dominates both it and the army. Prior to 1953, Stroessner had had no contact with the party. On coming to power he chose to collaborate with it rather than to throw out the entire bureaucracy that was composed of Colorados. He intended to bring it under his control, however. He soon appointed a general to the sensitive post of party treasurer. Government employees are required to contribute part of their earnings to the party coffers and its members in Congress return a portion of their salary to it also. Having secured control of the fiscal apparatus of the party, he began to ignore the party leaders in the matters of government appointments. Indeed, he has gone so far as to appoint nonparty members to the party's executive council! His influence in the party has progressed to such a point that today the Colorado party is a personalist organization, dominated by *"Stroessneristas."* [11]

Like most other Latin American parties, the Colorado had been split by factionalism. The party has a radical wing in exile, the *Movimiento Popular Colorado*. It is chiefly preoccupied with supplanting the present administration. Within the party in Paraguay there are two factions. The liberal group seeks to end the more vicious aspects of the police state and

[10] Hadley, p. 380.
[11] Nichols, pp. 28–29.

bring about a general relaxation in the whole political atmosphere. The majority wing, the *Stroessneristas,* argue that Paraguay has precisely the kind of government that she needs.

The Liberal party has been out of power since the end of the Chaco War. It was illegal from 1942 to 1967. During those years its primary concern was to regain legal status, end Colorado domination, and end the dictatorship. Consequently, the party has tended more to criticism of the techniques and strategies of the Colorado party than to the development of a concrete, well-rounded program to present as a reasonable alternative to the material achievements of their opponents. The Liberals claim a passionate attachment to a "state of law" in contrast to the police state they say exists under Stroessner. The Colorados have countered with the charge that the state of law desired by the Liberals is a police state itself, because law is coercive, obligatory, and punitive, and is "indifferent to misery and wealth, alien to justice and injustice. . . ." [12]

Although the Liberal party is controlled by an aristocratic-professional elite, it claims to be the principal party of reform. During the period 1904–1936 when it was in power, the party did not unduly demonstrate that this is the case. There was possibly greater personal freedom under it, but the party did little to improve the lot of the lower classes of society.

The Liberal party is split between those who wish to continue the fight against the Colorados and Stroessner (the Radical Liberals) and a minority wing that has been willing to cooperate with the regime. In 1967 the Radical Liberals were legalized and ran candidates for the constitutional convention. In the general election of 1968 they seated sixteen deputies and nine senators. The cooperative minority wing seated three deputies and one senator.

Despite the fact that politics in Paraguay has been the almost exclusive domain of the two major parties, two newer ones have arisen. The first of these appeared after the end of the Chaco War. Led by Colonel Rafael Franco, war veterans and disgruntled students began to agitate for some basic reforms via the totalitarian model. These forces came to power through a coup d'etat in February 1936. The Febreristas, as they were

[12] Hadley, p. 380.

called, soon proved they were more adept at creating an ideology than they were at governing. Many of Franco's military supporters, fearing the leftist tendencies of his government, unseated him in August 1937.

Ideologically, the Febreristas are a part of the populist *Aprista* party family of South America, to which category *Acción Democrática* of Venezuela also belongs. The party seeks the "uplifting of individual liberalism as a plan for solution for our national problems; . . . the liberation of the oppressed, the dignification of the working masses, the farmers, and the middle class in a harmonious consolidation of ideals and united action, all for a national renascence . . ." [13] It adheres to the doctrine that political parties are the natural organs of democracy.

The Febrerista party has an elaborate structure, but it cannot afford the luxury of a full-time staff to make it work. Its dedicated workers are for the most part highly motivated minor politicians. Denied any share in disposing government patronage—a fate they share with all opposition parties—the Febreristas have little to offer their membership but an organization with inadequate funds and personnel to make it an effective political force. The party organs do function, but they do little more than educate and socialize their membership.[14] The Febrerista party is not a united body; its two wings presently represent a split between political activists and idealistic intellectuals.[15]

The second new organization is the Christian Democratic party. Organized in 1959 under the name of *Movimiento Social demócrata Cristiano,* it is a part of a movement of the same name in Latin America. As such it is ideologically akin to the Christian Democrats of Chile and the Social Christians (COPEI) of Venezuela. In the one-party atmosphere of 1959, the Christian Democrats became the nucleus of the opposition to Stroess-

[13] Hadley, p. 382.

[14] For a detailed and incisive description of the Febrerista party see Paul H. Lewis, "Leadership and Conflict within the Febrerista Party of Paraguay," *Journal of Inter-American Studies,* 9 (April 1967), 283–295. See also his more comprehensive study, *The Politics of Exile: Paraguay's Febrerista Party* (Chapel Hill, N.C.: University of North Carolina Press, 1968).

[15] Hadley, p. 381.

ner. It has been a vehicle for the concerns of intellectuals, progressive Catholics, agrarian reformers, and laborers who are offended by what they regard as the self-seeking ends of the Colorados. Its 10,000 members, 7000 of whom are affiliated in agrarian leagues, subscribe to a long-range program that calls for genuine agrarian reform as well as for labor unions freed from government control, and an end to the state of siege. Like the Febreristas, the Christian Democrats hope to be the party instrumentality through which the oppressed people of Paraguay may be liberated. In the view of the Christian Democrats, the political problem is the most acute problem facing Paraguay. The solution of economic and social problems, pressing as they are, is contingent upon the solution of the political crisis.[16] The Christian Democrats decry the present power base of Paraguay and declare that God, not man, is the foundation of power and that only God has absolute power. "The liberty of man supersedes the excesses of human power. . . ."[17]

In its approach to politics, the party advocates intelligent planning to remedy the economic and social ills of society. The political crisis will have been solved if the Christian Democrats are ever in a position to put their program into effect. Complete secular education is renounced because all education possesses spiritual, moral, and religious content. Party doctrine calls for professionalization of the armed forces and the demilitarization of politics. The military establishment should be nonpartisan. The Christian Democrats have been involved in recent demands for reform within Paraguay's two universities. In international affairs it is strongly anticommunist and nationalistic.

The Christian Democrats abstained from the municipal elections in 1965, the constitutional assembly elections in 1967, and the presidential and legislative elections in 1968. This is in keeping with their inclination to passive resistance as a mode of

[16] "Movimiento Social Demócrata Cristiano del Paraguay," *Mensaje del Movimiento Social Demócrata Cristiano al Pueblo del Paraguay,* cited in Edward Williams, *Latin American Christian Democratic Parties* (Knoxville, Tenn.: University of Tennessee Press, 1967), p. 81.
[17] Movimiento Social Demócrata Cristiano del Paraguay, *Acta Fundamental y Declaración de Principios,* cited in Williams, p. 64.

expression. Despite the abstentions and their continued attacks on his government and party, President Stroessner has allowed the party to function. This tolerance may well be an indication that the president does not regard the party as a serious threat to his government.

The Christian Democratic party is perhaps stronger in rural areas than in urban, and much of its political activity is concentrated there. Since 1965 it has organized some twenty-two Agrarian Leagues with a total membership of 45,000 farmers.[18]

At the far left of the political party spectrum is the Communist party. It is split into pro-Peking and pro-Moscow factions. Founded in 1928, the party has long been illegal. Most of its membership is in exile; those who remain are in constant danger of apprehension by government security forces. In the 1940s the party claimed a membership of about 8000. Perhaps about 1000 are presently in Paraguay. In the authoritarian environment of the country, the Communist party has never been an important force in national politics.[19]

Venezuela

Venezuela is presently untroubled by a major party of the extreme right. The group lying farthest in that direction is the Nationalist Civic Crusade (CCN), a personalistic movement generated in 1968 by followers of former president Marcos Pérez Jiménez. Its most spectacular success was the election to the Senate of the former absentee dictator, an election that the Supreme Court speedily ruled invalid. CCN elected three senators in addition to Marcos Pérez Jiménez, twenty-one deputies, and a working majority of the Caracas municipal council, through which the federal government carries out its programs in the capital city. CCN's strength is primarily in metropolitan areas such as the populous Federal District and Maracaibo, capital city of Zulia. These two areas accounted for 70 percent of CCN's total vote. Its program calling for restora-

[18] Hadley, p. 383.
[19] Rollie Poppini, *International Communism in Latin America: A History of the Movement 1917–1963* (New York: The Free Press, 1964), p. 83.

tion of a government strong enough to deal with terrorism and sabotage had a certain appeal for the strife-torn cities. Nationwide, however, CCN polled only 1.1 percent of the total vote.

In spite of its relatively weak electoral showing, CCN is not without influence in the present government. In 1969 it held the key to the organization of the two houses of congress, for example. Since no party held a majority of seats in either house, it was necessary for COPEI to bargain. The decisive votes that enabled the houses to elect their officers were cast by CCN members on orders from Pérez Jiménez in Lima. For their willingness to accept these votes of the former enemy, COPEI was accused by URD of casting Pérez Jiménez and his followers in the role of umpires.

Today the executive branch of government is in the hands of COPEI. The legislative branch is in the hands of opposition groups led by *Acción Democrática*. Not until early in 1970 was President Caldera able to put together a working majority in congress. *Acción Democrática* finally decided to cooperate with Caldera and COPEI.

COPEI is the fastest growing political party in Venezuela and the second largest Christian Democratic party in Latin America. Its leader, Rafael Caldera, is second only to Eduardo Frei of Chile in prestige and influence in the hemispheric movement. In 1958 COPEI polled 423,000 presidential votes, or 16 percent of the total, to place third below AD and URD. In 1963 it moved to second place, increasing its vote to 589,000, or 21 percent of the total. In 1968 it forged ahead of AD (partly because the latter had serious party difficulties during the year) to poll 1,083,000 votes, representing 29 percent of the total votes cast. Under the proportional representation system of elections for Congress, however, AD elected 63 deputies to COPEI's 59, and 19 senators to COPEI's 16.

COPEI had its roots in the pro-Catholic National Student Union established in 1946. The leaders of this group, headed by Rafael Caldera, organized the Committee for Independent Electoral Organization (hence the initials COPEI) to vocalize its opposition to AD, which had come to power in that year. Since that time COPEI has had a change of mind and, to some degree, of membership. The party's original supporters were mainly the conservative Catholic Andean oligarchs. Landowners flocked to its banners as AD, in its first brief span of power, began to tamper with the agrarian system. COPEI moved to the right during this period of social ferment. Its direction shifted, however, as it experienced, along with AD and URD, the displeasure of Pérez Jiménez. During the years of clandestine political activity under Pérez Jiménez, COPEI gradually lost its conservative membership, moved to the left, and began to advocate social reforms. COPEI's views were sufficiently congruous with those of AD by 1958 that it was able to join with AD in a coalition that lasted five years. This colloboration was possible because COPEI had traveled leftward and AD toward the center.[20]

Today, COPEI finds its principal bases of support in the rural Andean states of Mérida, Táchira, and Trujillo, where it outdrew AD by almost 100,000 votes. It also led AD—and all other parties—in the four other more or less rural states. Peasant groups, attracted by the agrarian planks, contribute significantly to COPEI's strength. The military has also been partial to it; indeed, they both share the Andes as their power and recruiting bases.

The Catholic Church in Venezuela has been able to accept the leftward movement of COPEI precisely because it, too, has developed progressive attitudes toward the revolutionary trends going on in Venezuela and elsewhere. The Venezuelan Church, which helped to unseat Pérez Jiménez in 1958, can no longer be regarded as a monolithic reactionary force. It has a vocal and liberal wing that finds a channel of communication in COPEI.

COPEI as a leading Christian Democratic party in Latin America founds its program and ideology on the basic tenets of Christianity. It is by no means an exclusively Catholic group. Christian duty is stressed, not the truth of a specific Christian religion. Christianity is regarded as the integrating element of the nationality and a source of obligation of social justice, of human actions, and of public service.[21]

COPEI is an active and founding member of the *Organización Demócrata Cristiana de America* (ODCA), an inter-

[20] Williams, p. 205.
[21] Williams, p. 72.

national association of Christian Democratic parties. ODCA has held seven international congresses since its establishment in 1947. It is a charter member of the World Union of Christian Democracy, founded in Caracas in 1964.

COPEI also helps support the international *Instituto de Formación Demócrata Cristiana.* Located in Caracas, the Institute trains party leaders from all over the continent.[22]

In addition to its international affiliations, COPEI maintains close connections with various interest groups and organizations within Caracas.

President Rafael Caldera announced in his inaugural address of March 1969 the basic objectives of his government to be political and social peace, the promotion of man, and economic development. The speech was strongly colored by Social Christian philosophy. The president, for example, reiterated several times his determination to seek "the promotion of man." Venezuela's principal wealth, he declared, was its human wealth, much of which was being wasted through lack of employment opportunities. The promotion of man therefore required an economy that would be at the service of man, and an intensification of the nation's efforts in education, so that all might learn. Said the president

> In the promotion of man, freedom is the main condition for human improvement. Freedom is the motive power for every individual to better his position in life. And I consider youth the strongest potential capable of being used for the finest enterprises and the most ambitious work. Because of this, the new Administration will offer youth better opportunities for education, work, recreation, sports, and culture.[23]

The latter will prove to be a difficult task because the population is growing at a far faster pace than are the job opportunities. President Caldera invited the labor forces to continue their defense of "constitutional policies" and told them it would be necessary to "open ways for the participation of labor in the creation and distribution of wealth." Inasmuch as economic matters are inseparable from social matters, the government pro-

[22] Williams, p. 86.

[23] Embassy of Venezuela, *Venezuela Up-to-date,* 12 (Spring 1969), 5.

grams would have as an objective the creation of a just and equitable social order in which all have the right to work, health, free expression, a share in the affairs of the community, social security, and fair housing.

Investment of foreign and domestic capital would be encouraged in reproductive (as distinct from extractive) enterprises. Respecting the all-important petroleum industry that supplies about 92 percent of Venezuela's income, the president said he would continue negotiations for service contracts in new areas and would encourage public discussion to find the most practical way to replace the concession system before concessions began to mature in 1973. The country's dependence on oil revenues must be overcome by rational diversification of the economy. The 1963 platform of the party had called for nationalization of the oil and mining resources.

The agricultural policy of COPEI stresses continued distribution of lands among the rural peasantry, but with more atttention to a "rational and just distribution" of the lands available.

Finally, said the president, democratic institutions would be strengthened under his regime and integrity and efficiency would be the prime qualifications for holding government office.

COPEI's platform encouraged the legislature to think of itself as an effective power in the process of governing. It shows every intention of heeding his advice.

Words such as these have been heard before in Venezuela. Indeed, they are remarkably similar to AD's declarations. Whether or not they will materialize into something more than rhetoric will depend in large part on how Caldera gets along with a coalition and with Congress as a whole. The party's willingness to enter coalitions—absolutely necessary in this case —is indicative that despite its ideological foundation, it is pragmatic in outlook. COPEI looked upon collaboration with AD as a realistic way of bringing about social and economic progress. It was COPEI that broke off the partnership in 1963, preferring to be free to criticize AD's administration and to develop an independent program to offer the people of Venezuela in future election contests.

Acción Democrática is one of the major forces with which the administration of President Caldera has to deal. It is one of the principal "national revolutionary" parties of Latin America, along with APRA of Peru, the Febrerista party of Paraguay, and the *Movimiento Nacionalista Revolucionaria* of Bolivia. In harmony with the conditions in their own country, each of the parties seeks to bring about democratic transformation by means of agrarian reform and nationalist economic measures. Each is concerned about the establishment of a genuine political democracy.[24]

After governing the nation for ten years, AD was displaced by COPEI in 1969 as the administration party. Nevertheless, it has more seats in Congress than any other party. AD and COPEI both occupy a position slightly to the left of center, and both advocate policies of economic and social reform. Ecclesiastical issues and political considerations and methods tend to keep the former coalition partners apart, rather than fundamental disagreement about the basic needs of Venezuela. COPEI, for example, was critical of AD's handling of the political crises that arose during its ten years in power, its invocation of the state of siege, and its banning of MIR and the Communist parties.

A careful reading of the platforms of the two principal parties will reveal a remarkable similarity in basic objectives. As a developing country, Venezuela is faced with a number of challenging problems that test the ingenuity and resourcefulness of the contending parties. Both AD and COPEI call for an end to the violence that has racked Venezuela for years, the establishment of a just, legal, and democratic political order, efficient and orderly government, and economic progress. Their statements on the pressing problems of the day such as housing, employment, education, labor, agrarian reform, industrialization, oil and mining, and others, indicate positions not far apart. Both promise to do everything in their power to achieve maximum results. This author, at least, gets the distinct feeling of "me tooism" from the campaign promises of the two parties.

After a number of years of clandestine activity, *Acción Democrática* was legalized in 1941. It is an indigenous party

[24] Robert Alexander, "The Emergence of Modern Political Parties in Latin America," *Politics of Change in Latin America,* Joseph Maier and Richard W. Weatherhead, eds. (New York: Praeger, 1964), p. 116.

that cuts across class lines. As the first major social reform party in Venezuela, it has appealed and continues to appeal to peasants, laborers, the middle class, and to intellectuals who were challenged by the enormous task of converting Venezuela into a modern democratic industrial state. AD is socialist and populist in orientation and like all the national revolutionary parties with which it has ideological ties, it is concerned with the underprivileged classes and a more equitable distribution of the wealth. To effect this goal it relies heavily upon the state as an instrument of planning and control.

Venezuela's power structure was such that AD's liberal, humanitarian, social policies could not be immediately realized once the party came to power through the revolution of 1945. Between that date and 1948 it tried to implement them by means of a crash program that brought about its own downfall at the hands of an alarmed military group. In power once again between 1958–1969, the party was much more moderate in its approach to problems. The moderation was tempered by both pragmatism and a clearer sense of the political realities of the day. It could not afford, for example, to antagonize the military establishment, which had already shown its basic antagonism to AD objectives and methods. Then, too, because it did not command a majority in congress, it had to rely upon cooperation from the other parties. Moderation brought factionalism. Dissatisfaction with the moderate pace of the administration caused the younger, more extreme members of the party to challenge the leadership and eventually to leave the party. Its tendency to split over issues and personalities probably cost AD the election in 1968. When the party convention nominated Gonzalo Barrios as its presidential nominee, the followers of Luis B. Prieto Figueroa, who had been led to expect the nomination and who felt entitled to it, bolted the party to form the People's Electoral Movement (MEP). The splinter wing of the party won 19.33 percent of the vote and seated five senators and twenty-five deputies. Had these votes been in the AD column, that party would have had 47.58 percent of the popular vote and a considerably stronger membership in Congress. So far MEP has cooperated with COPEI in the legislature and in Caldera's cabinet.

The party splits have been reflected in factional struggles for the control of various labor, peasant, and student organizations that are affiliated with *Acción Democrática*.

Perhaps the most significant political reform accomplished by *Acción Democrática* during its tenure in office was the establishment of direct, universal, proportional, and secret suffrage—a democratic goal to which it had long been committed as the only legal way to reduce the hold of the conservative elite. Electoral reform, however, brought with it a decided proliferation of political parties, a development that has undoubtedly contributed to the decrease in AD's own electoral strength.

The Democratic Republican Union (URD), formerly Venezuela's second most important party, has gradually lost its appeal to the Venezuelan voter. An opportunistic, nationalist, personal vehicle for the ambitions of perennial candidate Jovita Villalba, it has seen its vote decline from a high of 800,000 votes (32 percent of the total) in 1958 to 551,000 (17.5 percent) in 1963. Supplanted by COPEI as the leading contender for power in 1968, URD entered into a centrist electoral coalition called the Victory Front. The Front was made up of the Democratic National Front (FND), an outgrowth of the 1963 personalist party of intellectual Arturo Uslar Pietri, and the Democratic Popular Force (FDP), the vehicle of retired Vice Admiral Wolfgang Larrazábal, who was provisional president from January 1958 to January 1959. The coalition named as its presidential candidate Miguel A. Burelli Rivas; he received 829,000 votes, or 22 percent of the total cast. The coalition partners offered individual slates for the legislature and other elective bodies. URD seated two senators and twenty deputies; FND, 1 senator and four deputies; and FDP, two senators and ten deputies. The appeal of these parties was primarily due to the personalities that headed them rather than to distinguishing ideological or doctrinal characteristics.

As the principal party of the electoral coalition, URD declared that it sought a government working for the nation and not one that sought only to perpetuate itself in power. Economic development must not result merely in the rich becoming richer and the poor becoming poorer, but must benefit all Venezuelans. Arguing that agrarian reform as carried out under AD was "incomplete and demagogic," Villalba promised to carry out a "serious and consistent policy" of land distribution.

In other planks, he advocated state control of the steel, iron, oil, and aluminum industries. His party stressed "nationalistic and democratic government that would institute a program of good for all Venezuelans and the liberation and growth of the nation." [25]

The 1968 election was notable for the large number of parties and confusing coalitions that it generated. In addition to those named above, there was the Revolutionary Party of National Integration (PRIN) composed of left-wing dissidents from AD and URD. PRIN in turn allied itself with another AD splinter, the Popular Electoral Movement, to support the candidacy of Luis B. Prieto Figueroa. The election also featured the Democratic Socialist party and ten minor parties with such names as the Independent National Union Bloc, the Independent Democratic Union, the Liberal party, the Popular Alliance, the Popular National Vanguard, and the Union for Progress, the last being the legal arm of the then outlawed Communist party. Members of most of the groups were dissidents from the three principal parties and were *ad hoc* personalist associations.

At the far left of the political spectrum were two banned parties: the Movement of the Revolutionary Left, a radical 1962 splinter of AD, and the Communist party. The program of each of these parties called for a revolutionary approach to the problems of Venezuela.

The Communist party was organized in 1931 and has spent much of the time since then underground. Unable to come to power by constitutional means, the party has engaged in and encouraged violence as a means of disrupting the constitutional order. Together with the MIR and a guerrilla group known as FALN (Armed Forces for National Liberation), it has been responsible for much of the terrorism in the political system since 1958. The party was legalized in 1969 by the Caldera administration, and it promptly declared a policy of total opposition to the government. As is the case with most of the other

[25] *The Venezuelan Elections of December 1, 1963, Part II, Candidate Biographies and Candidate and Party Platforms* (Washington, D.C.: Institute for the Comparative Study of Political Systems, 1964), p. 34.

Venezuelan parties, it is not a completely united force. Its 30,000 members (making it the fourth largest Communist party in Latin America) are split between pro-Moscow and pro-Peking forces.

PARTY STRUCTURES AND CAMPAIGN TECHNIQUES

Venezuela

Both COPEI and AD have developed, over the course of the years, a permanent national organization, an identifiable program, and a nationally based electorate—all characteristics of a modern political party.[26] Each is characterized by a pyramidal power structure with power concentrated in the hands of the leadership group. COPEI's structure is more or less typical of Venezuelan party organization. It stresses internal party democracy but insists upon obedience to party doctrine and policy once it has been decided. Its members can neither accept public office without party permission, nor refuse to accept it if the party so directs. *Copeyanos* are expected to return 20 percent of their salaries to the party treasury. Persons must be sponsored by two members before being accepted into the ranks and they may be expelled—as some have been—for a variety of reasons.[27] At the apex of the party structure is the National Committee, followed by a larger, advisory body called the National Executive Council. The National Committee has the power to dissolve all regional and district organizations and take over direct control of them. An important adjunct of the party is its tribunal, which is its disciplinary arm. The tribunal expelled party members in 1953 for collaborating with Pérez Jiménez.

At the grass-roots level are the local units that elect members to the district convention. State delegates are chosen by the district conventions and national delegates by the state conventions. Yearly party conventions meet in Caracas to review the state of the party and consider future strategy and policies.

Acción Democrática is organized and functions along

[26] John D. Martz, "Venezuela," in Burnett and Johnson, pp. 208–209.

[27] Williams, pp. 81–93.

similar lines. During election years its organization goes into high gear with the appointment of an electoral commission whose head is, in effect, the party's campaign manager. He operates through the party secretariats of organization, propaganda, and press. He takes control of the campaign, supervises the plans of the regional organizations, coordinates their efforts, plans the itinerary of the presidential candidate, checks voter sentiment, and oversees the training of party members to serve at the voting tables.[28] COPEI follows similar procedures.

Posters, motorcades, airborne literature, occasional debates, mass rallies, and increasing use of TV and radio facilities as well as extensive travel of the candidates mark the progress of the campaign. As in the United States, campaign tactics call for the maximum exposure of the leading candidates to the electorate. Personal contact is considered very important. All the parties adopt a color and a design that are featured on the *tarjeta,* or ballot.

Paraguay

The Paraguayan parties are organized along similar lines, each with national executive committees and various offices of party control. The Febrerista party elects a president of the party, two vice presidents, a secretary-general, and a secretary of organization, all of whom serve on the party's national executive committee. As in the Venezuelan parties, the lower bodies elect delegates to the higher bodies, culminating in the national convention, which elects the national executive committee. Most of the high posts of the party have gone to members associated with the original organizing forces. A supreme electoral tribunal reviews challenges to party member credentials. Elaborate structural organization, however, does little to enhance the party's chances in the controlled election process of Paraguay.

Grass-roots organization, at least in the Liberal and

[28] John D. Martz, *The Venezuelan Elections of December 1, 1963, Part I, An Analysis* (Washington, D.C.: Institute for the Comparative Study of Political Systems, 1964), pp. 29–30. For a definitive and incisive study of Acción Democrática, see John D. Martz, *Acción Democrática: Evolution of a Modern Political Party in Venezuela* (Princeton, N.J.: Princeton University Press, 1966).

Colorado parties, is governed by *comités* (Liberals) and *seccionales* (Colorados). These groups are made up of an executive, several lesser officials, and about a dozen members chosen in a local election supervised by party leaders from Asunción.[29] Party matters are directed from the capital where the party's national offices are. The president of the *Colorado seccional* is often the most important person in the community.

A recent survey of Paraguayan attitudes toward their political parties revealed some interesting data.[30] On the question of whether or not the parties educated their members and the public on national issues, party members interviewed responded affirmatively along the following lines: Colorados, 42 percent; Radical Liberals, 43; Febreristas, 53; and Christian Democrats, 13. Asked to say by what manner a political party could best increase its membership, a surprisingly large percent in all parties stressed the need for a comprehensive ideology. In doing so, the Paraguayans rejected as relatively unimportant a party's function of representing social classes and groups and its identity with historical traditions. Seventy-seven percent of the Colorados, 80 percent of the Radical Liberals, 83 percent of the Febreristas, and 89 percent of the Christian Democrats emphasized the desirability of ideology.

In response to the question on how one would judge the conduct of the governing party, 68.5 percent of the Colorados stressed maintenance of internal peace as the principal criterion for evaluation of success, followed by domestic development (61 percent), efficiency (52 percent), and honesty (40 percent). Each of the opposition parties placed a high value on honesty (65, 62, and 72 percent) and two placed a low value on internal peace (39 and 22 percent). All parties would judge the governing party to some degree on how much progress it had made in developing the country's resources. Seventeen percent of the Colorados, 2 percent of the Radical Liberals, and 3 percent of the Febreristas said they would be influenced in their evaluation of the governing party by their membership in it.

[29] Hicks, p. 277.·
[30] Byron A. Nichols, "Las Espectativas de los Partidos Políticos en el Paraguay," *Revista Paraguaya Sociología,* 5 (Diciembre 1968), pp. 22–61.

Another question asked respondents concerned the degree of success they thought opposition parties had in influencing decisions taken by the government. Combining the responses of "much success" and "some success," almost 60 percent of the Colorados thought opposition parties could have some influence on government policy. Only 34 percent of the Radical Liberals, 23.3 percent of the Febreristas, and 42 percent of the Christian Democrats thought their parties could influence the government, even if only modestly.

Asked how opposition parties could best influence government policy, 55 percent of the Colorados thought they could best do so by participating in congressional debates. Forty-three percent of the Radical Liberals, 28.3 percent of the Febreristas, and 23.7 percent of the Christian Democrats felt congressional activity was important. Members of these parties, however, indicated that press, radio, and television declarations were about as productive as congressional debate. The poll also revealed that Paraguayans in general thought opposition party leaders sought to influence government policy because of their convictions that their ideas were superior to those of the government.

A high percent of the respondents cited superior party programs as their reasons for associating with a political party, and a low percent names family affiliation as a reason. Nevertheless, membership in the two traditional parties has been strongly inclined to follow their parents' party preferences.[31]

Summary

Party organization is of more recent vintage in Venezuela than in Paraguay, with party politics dating not much farther back than 1940. Party organization in both countries is oligarchical, with considerable power conferred upon party leaders by the party statutes. In addition to the statutory powers, important leaders have tremendous influence that stems from *personalismo*. In almost all cases they are able to impose their ideas upon the rank and file of the party, and this seems consonant with the deferential attitudes transmitted by the Hispanic culture. This

[31] Nichols, "Las Espectativas," pp. 57–61.

is particularly true of those parties that are clearly little more than *personalista* associations, as is the case with most of the minor parties in Venezuela.

If one applies the criteria of clearly defined programs and objectives, consistent support of a sizable percent of the national electorate over a fairly long period of time, and a permanent organization as characteristics of a modern party, then few of the parties discussed in this chapter would qualify. Most would fall into such categories as *ad hoc, personalista,* and particularistic. The two traditional parties of Paraguay have permanent organizations, have attracted large followings during the last eighty years, but neither has a program of action that transcends the desire for power. The Febrerista and Christian Democratic parties have organization and program, but relatively little national support, and that only fairly recently.

In Venezuela only two parties at present can be really considered as modern parties. They are *Acción Democrática* and COPEI. Both have permanent organizations, roots in various regions of the country, sustained but varying support in the electorate over a sufficiently long period of time, and fairly well-defined programs and theories of government. Both seek to take responsible control of the government. The Democratic Republican Union is a personal vehicle for its leader, has consistently lost electoral support in recent years, is not widely based in the electorate, and seems on its way to complete decline.

Party membership is largely ascriptive in Paraguay, with children often following the party of their parents. Since the two traditional parties lack ideological content (despite the value seemingly attached to it by party members), partisans look to parties for social, economic, and medical services rather than for a share in the political power.

Because the present parties of Venezuela do not have deep historical roots, membership in them can be attributed more to doctrinal preferences, *personalista* considerations, and family connections than to historical associations. Membership in one or another of the parties is also often determined for fairly large numbers by the leadership of interest groups and associations. Peasants, for example, have been organized by AD leaders, as have labor unions. Oil workers and educational personnel will often go the way of their leaders. This sometimes causes difficulties when there are splits between factions of the leadership.

Finally, in both countries, parties are constitutionally endowed with the power to help shape public policy and to compete with one another for political power. The competition, however, must be carried out within the confines of the "democratic" system as it is understood and applied in each. The atmosphere in Paraguay is oppressive, in Venezuela, liberal.

Government in Venezuela is taking on the characteristics of party government (as distinguished from personal government) and more particularly, multiparty coalition government that has social and economic reform at the core of its program. The effect of this development has yet to be gauged, as it is now in troubled waters under the administration of President Caldera.

In Paraguay, the government continues to be the domain of one party and of one man, as it has since the 1880s. The ruling party is dominated by a military figure that has usurped control of it. Paraguay in 1970 is governed by a man who emphasizes continuity in power over social reform and development.

THE ELECTORAL PROCESS

Venezuela

Venezuelan law creates a Supreme Electoral Council (CSE) to supervise the uniform application of the national election law. Its members are appointed by the congress, and care is taken to ensure the equitable representation on the Council for all the major groups participating in the election. Electoral divisions follow the organization of the political divisons. Thus there are twenty-three principal election boards that oversee the elections in the states, the Federal District, and the two Federal Territories. Under them are district boards, municipal boards, and electoral tables for each 300 voters in a municipality. In the election of 1968 there were 15,315 polling places.

The CSE has the authority to set the date for the election. Normally a day early in December is chosen. The registration of voters usually begins in late June or early July and continues for sixty days. CSE has discretionary power to extend the period for an additional thirty days. In each of the elections since 1952 such an extension has been necessary, as the Venezuelans are slow to comply with their duty. In addition to its other tasks, the CSE validates the candidacies of the contenders and legalizes the use of party symbols and colors. The CSE's decision in 1952 to allow a coalition of parties supporting the government to use a round ballot card (*tarjeta*) instead of the rectangular ones authorized for all other parties led to charges of favoritism and executive intervention. In 1963 the CSE was involved in a dispute between opposing factions of *Acción Democrática,* each of which sought to use the official white color. Both sides eventually agreed to relinquish the color for the 1963 election with the understanding that the victorious wing would be entitled to its use in the future. Under this arrangement, the majority old-line *adecos* (members of *Acción Democrática*) regained the right.

These matters are more important than one might suppose, because the electorate has come to associate both color and symbol with the more enduring parties such as AD, COPE1, and URD. Continuity in color and symbol is therefore considered essential, and parties will strive vigorously to retain the colors and symbols. Illiterates, in particular, depend upon colored ballots at election time. The CSE prepares the ballots and distributes them to the polling places. The *tarjeta pequeña* (small card) does not contain the names of any of the candidates who are running for office, merely the party designation. Party lists are widely distributed, however, so that the informed voter knows who his party's candidates are. Because a modified system of proportional representation is used in Venezuelan congressional elections, each party prepares lists of candidates equal to the number of deputies and senators to which a state is entitled. It also submits names of two alternates for each principal candidate.

Each state is entitled to two senators and a number of deputies in the proportion of one for every 50,000 inhabitants. The minimum number of deputies for the Republic is arrived at by dividing the estimated population of the Republic by 50,000. In 1968 Venezuelan authorities estimated the population to be 9.85 million. Thus 197 deputies were to be chosen. The number of deputies in each state ranged from 37 in the Federal District, 25 in Zulia, 13 in Miranda, to 2 in Cojedes, and 1 each in the

Federal Territories. Additional deputies and senators were awarded the contending parties on the basis of a national quotient that was arrived at by dividing the total valid votes cast for Congress by the fixed number of deputies. In 1968 the valid vote was 3,646,610 which, divided by 197, yielded a quotient of 18,538. To determine whether or not a party would win additional seats, the total national vote cast for the party was divided by the quotient. Where the result was more than the seats already won by the party, additional seats up to the result obtained were added. The application of the quotient resulted in the addition of seventeen deputies and nine senators. Some parties that had been unable to elect any members to Congress profited by the quotient.

With few exceptions, all Venezuelans 18 years of age and over are required to vote. Far more persons register than actually vote, however. In 1968, for example, more than 4 million registered, but only 3,646,610 voted (see Tables 5–1 and 5–2). The polls open at six A.M. on voting day—always a Sunday —and remain open as long as voters appear. Fairly large numbers are present at that early hour to cast their votes. Traffic is restricted everywhere, drinking is prohibited, and cars are not allowed to park in the vicinity of the polling places. Soldiers are detailed to keep the peace. Before casting his colored ballot, a voter is required to show his registration card to the election officials and to the witnesses of the participating parties. When they are satisfied as to the voter's identity, he is handed an envelope and the *tarjetas* of the contending parties. Two different kinds of *tarjetas* are used. A *tarjeta grande* (large card) is cast for the president. A *tarjeta pequeña* is cast for the legislators (see Fig. 4). The voter takes his cards into a closed booth and selects the cards of the party of his choice, places them in the envelope, and seals it. The unused ballots are deposited in a locked box in the voting booth. The voter then returns to the election table and there personally deposits his sealed envelope in the official locked urn. The fact that he has complied with his legal duty of voting is noted in his *cédula,* or identification booklet, carried by all residents. The final step is the dyeing of the little finger with an indelible, long-lasting ink, a precaution that makes it impossible for a voter to vote twice. When the polls close the ballot boxes are opened and the ballots counted

Figure 4 **Ballots for the 1952 Venezuela Elections**

DEMOCRATIC REPUBLICAN UNION
(white and black on yellow)

VENEZUELIAN SOCIALIST PARTY
(white and black on blue)

INDEPENDENT ELECTORAL FRONT
(white and black on yellow and purple)

SOCIALIST WORKERS PARTY
(white on orange)

ELECCIONES 1952

ASAMBLEA CONSTITUYENTE
DE LOS
ESTADOS UNIDOS DE VENEZUELA

CONSEJO SUPREMO ELECTORAL

SOCIAL CHRISTIAN PARTY
(white on green)

Table 5–1 Official results of the 1968 electoral census—Venezuela [a]

Entity	Regis. voters	Percent of voters	Illiterates	Rural voters	Urban voters	Male voters	Female voters	No. of polls
VENEZUELA	4,068,481	100	1,123,918	1,028,040	3,040,441	2,071,486	1,996,995	15,315
Distrito Federal	693,684	17.05	50,193	6,451	687,233	359,259	334,425	2,391
Anzoátegui	192,628	4.73	62,027	53,782	138,846	96,140	96,488	714
Apure	60,330	1.48	27,327	31,311	29,019	30,925	29,405	242
Aragua	194,661	4.78	43,205	23,437	171,224	101,302	93,359	695
Barinas	80,025	1.97	32,183	43,117	36,908	42,741	37,284	352
Bolívar	146,455	3.60	25,431	30,873	115,583	78,412	68,043	586
Carabobo	238,292	5.85	55,526	27,380	210,912	122,959	115,333	848
Cojedes	37,757	0.92	18,916	18,674	19,083	19,751	18,006	172
Falcón	164,614	4.05	58,425	68,529	96,085	77,039	87,575	701
Guárico	128,310	3.15	54,578	51,208	77,102	67,876	60,434	503
Lara	257,510	6.58	102,378	83,008	185,502	129,475	138,035	970
Mérida	144,462	3.55	60,728	79,642	64,820	74,138	70,324	556
Miranda	308,719	7.59	62,733	51,278	257,441	154,761	153,958	1,191
Monagas	120,677	2.96	16,946	51,480	69,197	62,173	58,504	480
Nueva Esparta	51,796	1.27	17,282	13,117	38,619	22,013	29,783	188
Portuguesa	116,690	2.87	55,996	45,043	71,647	64,215	52,475	456
Sucre	192,947	4.75	80,392	90,492	102,455	96,300	96,647	742
Táchira	166,838	4.10	53,725	68,871	97,967	83,803	83,035	646
Trujillo	162,429	3.99	77,139	78,778	83,651	79,103	83,326	676
Yaracuy	90,311	2.22	41,595	32,918	37,395	46,691	43,620	355
Zulia	482,924	11.87	118,689	62,104	420,820	247,981	234,943	1,737
T. Amazonas	8,317	0.22	4,624	4,174	4,143	4,312	4,005	34
T. Delta Amacuro	18,103	0.44	3,884	12,313	5,792	10,117	7,988	80

[a] *Source:* Supreme Electoral Council of Venezuela.

Table 5–2   The 1968 Venezuelan elections: final voting results by state

Entity	AD	COPEI	URD	FND	FDP	PRIN	MENI	PSD
VENEZUELA	939,759	883,814	339,799	96,027	194,739	85,694	13,635	29,849
Fed. District	105,637	98,098	44,291	18,863	47,006	13,300	2,583	3,567
Anzoátegui	50,387	26,706	28,229	4,079	6,707	8,005	357	903
Apure	20,001	11,810	3,903	1,267	2,694	903	*****	393
Aragua	30,217	37,055	18,754	6,121	17,185	3,236	1,248	1,787
Barinas	21,705	25,574	7,346	2,271	1,197	1,486	194	676
Bolívar	41,220	18,676	10,607	3,776	8,474	6,057	677	1,211
Carabobo	48,949	47,460	17,190	5,363	20,300	2,903	1,549	2,224
Cojedes	12,872	8,332	5,474	789	1,716	1,310	86	213
Falcón	43,564	38,202	24,275	2,773	4,621	4,487	747	1,296
Guárico	36,581	23,998	15,936	2,239	6,784	2,988	286	1,120
Lara	72,858	89,906	10,906	3,937	6,448	4,529	665	2,262
Mérida	28,389	68,677	4,497	2,164	1,467	1,363	191	1,256
Miranda	65,307	60,292	27,616	11,024	15,896	6,556	1,042	2,495
Monagas	51,700	16,134	9,751	3,716	1,880	4,211	291	475
Nueva Esparta	12,564	1,587	14,514	688	384	548	*****	1,146
Portuguesa	34,854	32,310	8,128	3,405	2,425	1,625	264	1,637
Sucre	69,414	19,298	25,945	2,723	8,975	3,866	342	817
Táchira	39,656	66,194	4,881	3,492	926	1,074	433	693
Trujillo	39,755	60,573	11,214	4,043	3,495	1,654	351	1,485
Yaracuy	27,992	26,206	8,300	1,018	2,624	5,386	763	595
Zulia	78,798	103,174	33,570	11,804	32,292	9,926	1,484	4,468
Amazonas	2,203	1,581	1,817	107	98	37	13	*****
D. Amacuro	5,136	1,971	2,655	364	1,145	244	69	129

Total votes cast in elections of 1958: 2,565,552
Total votes cast in elections of 1963: 2,917,896
Total votes cast in elections of 1968: 3,646,610

Source: Supreme Electoral Council of Venezuela.

in the presence of the electoral judges and official witnesses. The results are forwarded to offices maintained by the CSE, which issues periodic bulletins during the progress of the vote. The 1968 election was noted for prolonged delay in tabulating and reporting the vote. After more than 125 hours of continual counting, many outlying districts had still not reported results to Caracas. Planes sent out to obtain vote totals from districts not heard from returned empty-handed because election judges and party witnesses could not agree on the final totals. The more charitable citizens were willing to see the problem as one of antiquated procedures and partisan collecting methods. Others read more ominous meanings into the delay, speculating that the

and party

OPINA	MAN	MEP	MDI	API	AIR	OPIR	PRIVO	CCN	UPA	TOTALES
7,238	24,190	475,909	18,276	17,833	8,577	2,365	5,445	400,093	103,368	3,646,610
1,388	10,203	68,055	3,198	3,215	2,074	1,171	1,560	168,083	39,542	631,834
170	321	34,434	1,135	724	368	*****	254	6,871	4,260	173,932
54	*****	4,440	257	*****	*****	*****	*****	1,366	474	47,562
546	1039	29,394	1,066	1,240	561	609	823	22,064	6,160	179,105
72	*****	7,013	340	*****	182	*****	*****	3,751	*****	71,807
432	306	21,882	489	759	648	*****	317	12,338	4,332	132,201
315	1,009	18,948	829	1,552	658	*****	661	30,721	6,868	207,621
41	76	3,249	239	255	68	*****	*****	661	*****	35,381
529	2,754	20,335	951	*****	*****	*****	*****	2,865	2,515	149,973
246	281	13,169	897	843	120	*****	228	5,510	1,206	112,432
658	980	25,153	1,375	1,261	633	*****	324	10,777	7,358	240,045
164	279	10,720	302	*****	*****	*****	*****	8,521	1,083	129,073
751	3,740	20,917	1,636	2,084	969	421	670	44,691	8,231	274,336
107	126	18,136	*****	349	*****	*****	198	1,743	2,584	111,401
72	*****	15,772	972	*****	*****	*****	*****	517	1,061	48,825
163	186	10,584	659	511	224	*****	*****	3,882	1,780	102,641
226	*****	35,189	640	1,004	240	*****	204	2,644	3,082	174,631
130	313	6,631	341	*****	368	*****	204	20,503	*****	145,845
194	360	14,140	845	764	*****	*****	*****	4,366	1,187	144,443
96	144	5,342	425	*****	195	*****	*****	2,280	1,253	82,671
823	2,051	86,567	1,641	3,194	1,216	*****	*****	45,939	10,357	427,305
16	*****	1,315	39	*****	*****	*****	*****	*****	35	7,262
45	*****	4,524	*****	*****	*****	*****	*****	*****	*****	16,282

government party (AD) was either attempting or planning to steal enough votes to win the election.[32]

Paraguay

Paraguay entrusts electoral matters to a Central Board. In view of the fact that the Colorado party has been in power so long, it should come as no surprise that present legal arrangements allot it four of the six central board seats. The board has the same type of duties and powers as the Venezuela CSE, but operates in a more arbitrary and partisan fashion. Its apparent function is to ensure the victory of the president's party. It is

[32] *The Christian Science Monitor,* December 10, 1968, p. 5.

able to do this partly because the law requires all elective officers of the national government to run at large in the Republic and partly by carefully controlling the registration process. In a country whose population is about evenly divided between Colorados and old-time Liberals, only 180,000 Liberals succeeded in registering in 1963 compared with 350,000 Colorados. The party that wins a plurality of the national vote is constitutionally awarded two-thirds of the seats in both houses of the national legislature.

Few of the illiterates in the rural towns and hamlets know anything about the individuals who are seeking office on the large national lists. The almost permanent state of siege is lifted only on election days in those departments where it still exists, thus permitting the government to regulate all preelectoral activity. For reasons of its own, the government sometimes does not announce the location of the polling booths until the day before the election. Opposition parties are often denied the right to hold public meetings; their leaders are detained for varying periods of time and their party newspapers are victims of censorship and intimidation. Critics of the regime argue that such tactics greatly minimize the influence of whatever opposition groups exist in Paraguay. Colorado officials in 1968 responded to complaints about irregularities by answering, "We run things here." [33]

When the voter goes to the polls, he is presented with colored ballots prepared by the participating parties. After he has made his choice in the voting booth and has deposited his ballot in the official urn, he is given a receipt that must later be produced for a variety of services and privileges. In 1968, 95 percent of the registered electorate voted.

Breakdowns of the 1968 election results for Paraguay are not available. The 1963 election, in which women voted for the first time, attracted 463,568 of the total 710,000 who registered. More than 22,000 individuals cast blank ballots. Half of the registered voters were women. In 1968, 895,000 votes were cast. President Stroessner claimed 77 percent of them, and the Colorado party won a sizable victory, enabling it to retain its hold on the legislature.

[33] Nichols, "Paraguay—Future Democracy," p. 32.

Summary

As a device that permits popular consultation and control, the electoral process operates far more efficently in Venezuela than it does in Paraguay. Although charges of corruption, fraud, and inefficiency are heard after every election, there can be little doubt that since 1958 Venezuelans have gone to the polls with the expectation that their votes will be counted, the results honored, and power transferred or retained according to the wishes of the electorate.

In Paraguay, a controlled and manipulated electoral mechanism always produces the expected result: an overwhelming majority of votes for the incumbent executive and governing party. Elections do not serve as a method of popular consultation on either policy or personnel, but rather serve as a method of ratifying existing power relationships. Paraguayans have no historical reason to expect any significant change from an election.

In Venezuela it now seems possible for the electorate to turn a government and a party out of office through the vote; in Paraguay it may only confirm those in office.

SIX
OLIGARCHICAL AND INSTITUTIONAL PLURALISM: INTEREST GROUPS

The number of people actively involved in the input process of the political system in Venezuela and Paraguay is relatively small. Economic elites in both the agricultural and industrial segments control the flow of demands to the policy makers in the government. The working classes, particularly those in the rural areas, have not ordinarily been effective parts of the political process until their interests and demands impinge upon those of the elite or until they have been taken up by one of the political parties, such as *Acción Democrática*.

Perhaps only one-third of the people in both countries under study "understand the national political process as a comprehensible area of personal involvement and are capable of political activities and responses appropriate to the western style of politics." [1] Even among those organized to voice demands, paternalism characterizes the relations between the leaders and the rank and file. All groups, of course, compete for access to and favors from the policy makers.

Unable to achieve satisfactory political action through parties and legislatures, most interest groups turned to direct action politics, in which they make their representations directly to those with decision-making powers. Requests are often very specific, and there is a

[1] Charles W. Anderson, *Politics and Economic Change in Latin America* (Princeon, N.J.: D. Van Nostrand, 1967), p. 128.

250

distinct inclination for Latin American pressure groups to see themselves as petitioners after the fact for the redress of government decisions that adversely affect them, rather than as bargainers over policies before they are formulated. Accent is on protest and on the reversal of a ruling, or on the exception of a given group from its application.[2]

Failure of political officials to respond positively to such demands may either result in threats of strikes or the withholding of goods or services from the market, or both. If groups come to feel that the executive branch of the government is unresponsive to their concerns, they may resort to violence to bring their issues before the decision makers. Such is the case with the Armed Forces for National Liberation (FALN), an extreme, terrorist group in Venezuela.

The captivity of the legislature in Paraguay, and in Venezuela up to 1958, discouraged interest groups from regarding it as an institution with which they could realistically deal.

Although both countries have numerous organized groups, many of them are unable to press their claims because they lack the facilities such as research staffs, legal advisers, and communication channels between the leaders and the ranks.[3]

MEN OF THE CLOTH:
THE CATHOLIC CHURCH IN POLITICS

Religious leaders of Venezuela and Paraguay are involved in political affairs in ways other than interpreting the dogma of the Church in a light favorable to the political structure. In both countries the government exercises the right of ecclesiastical patronage, through which it has a decisive vote in the appointment of prelates. Both governments subsidize the Church with financial support. Each of these circumstances would help to explain why the hierarchy has often upheld politically distasteful regimes.

Historically, caudillo presidents have expected the prelates

---

[2] Robert H. Dix, "Oppositions and Development in Latin America," a paper prepared for delivery at the 1967 Annual Meeting of the American Political Science Association, p. 18.

[3] Anderson, p. 129.

to lend their prestige and presence to ceremonies honoring political achievement, anniversaries, military and national holidays. The hope was that the overt identity of the religious establishment with the political structure would consolidate popular support behind the regime and lend legitimacy to it. It also had the effect of discrediting the Church among liberal groups and increasing anticlerical sentiment if the regime was particularly notorious.

There have been occasions in both Venezuela and Paraguay where the Church has taken a stand antagonistic to the political leadership. The difficulties of the Church with the state during the Páez administration in Venezuela and the Francia period in Paraguay have been discussed in Chapter One. In 1870 the Archbishop of Caracas, in a long-standing controversy with President Antonio Guzmán Blanco, refused to celebrate a *Te Deum* mass in honor of the dictator's victory over rebellious forces. Guzmán Blanco responded by exiling the bishop, and closing convents, seminaries, and some churches. Most of the anticlerical legislation on the law books of Venezuela dates from this stormy period. Not until the Pérez Jiménez period did the Church in Venezuela begin to assume an active political stance. Between 1948 and 1967 the Church was discreet. Beginning in 1957, however, it became increasingly concerned about charges of corruption, vice, unemployment, and rumors of torture. It voiced its concern in a number of Church periodical articles. In January of 1958 the Church took the unusual step of denouncing Pérez Jiménez, who had arrested five priests on charges of agitation. For this action the president was condemned by the Vatican. Without attributing an undue causal relationship, it might be pointed out here that Pérez Jiménez fell from power shortly afterward.

In 1963 the primate of Venezuela, Cardinal José Humberto Quintero, assumed an open role in politics when he declared that the pacification of Venezuela was one of the main objectives of his life. He proposed to interview leaders of all parties in an effort to achieve his goal of peace. His effort failed. In 1969 the prelate again headed a team of mediators to try to bring about a cease-fire with the guerrilla forces. His mission was unsuccessful at the time of this writing.

The Church naturally could not be expected to sit idly by

while the government undermines its foundations and threatens its existence, as the history of the Venezuela Church shows. In the reformist environment that has characterized Venezuela since the overthrow of Pérez Jiménez, the Church has been relatively untouched by such economic measures as agrarian reform. It does not own much land and the government, in any event, has been distributing publicly owned land. The growing influence of the Social Christian party and the decreasing strength of *Acción Democrática* will probably result in an even closer relationship between the government and the Church on social and economic matters.

Several Catholic organizations function in Venezuela: *Opus Dei,* the *Movimiento Familiar Cristiano,* and *Caritás,* an association that distributes food received from a Catholic charity in the United States. All three in the opinion of AD are partisan (that is, COPEI) groups.[4]

The more progressive members of the Venezuelan hierarchy are accommodating themselves to the social, economic, and political changes going on in their country. Since 1945 the Church has developed a strong interest in social action and has, by its identification with the expectations of the people, strengthened its moral and spiritual influence.[5]

The identification of the higher clergy in Paraguay with the Stroessner government has undergone some modification. The lower clergy has always been more antiregime than the prelates. In 1959 the former sent a letter to the Archbishop of Asunción urging him to take a stand on police brutality. There is no record that he did so. And in 1962 that prelate joined with President Stroessner in a year-end celebration in which the dictator spoke of progress and the Christian idea. The archbishop addressed himself to fraternal cooperation, peace, and charity.[6] In 1963, in his dual role as head of the Paraguayan Church and President of the Paraguayan Episcopal Conference, the Archbishop commended the government for its collaboration

[4] *Venezuela Election Factbook, December 1, 1968* (Washington, D.C.: Institute for the Comparative Study of Political Systems, 1968), p. 25.

[5] Edwin Lieuwin, *Venezuela,* 2d ed. (London: Oxford University Press, 1965), p. 160.

[6] *Hispanic American Report,* 15 (February 1963), 1160.

in aiding the Church in its work for the moral and spiritual welfare of the people. In the same year, however, a pastoral letter called attention to press censorship and criticized the administration for spending so much money on President Stroessner's inauguration. The Church pleaded for a program of "heroic austerity" for government and people.

It does not seem coincidental that *Comunidad* (Roman Catholic Weekly) ceased in 1963 to publish political, social, and civic news, confining itself to articles of religious content. Two reasons for the benign view of the ranking prelates was a government decree permitting the Church to collect donations and inherit properties without paying taxes on them, and on the inclusion in the national budget of funds to aid the Church in its charitable work.

By 1967, however, the eleven bishops of the Paraguayan Roman Catholic Church had become sufficiently concerned with the dictatorial practices of Stroessner that they expressed it in a pastoral letter, in which they stated their opposition to the new constitution on the grounds that it continued the concept of the "dictatorial president."

The Church leaders particularly resented the presidential use of the state-of-siege emergency powers by which the president is authorized to make arrests at will.[7] By 1967 *Comunidad* has reverted to its pre-1963 policy of publishing critical political articles and editorials. It was temporarily closed by the government in 1968 for its outspoken criticism of the Stroessner administration. Since then, increasingly larger numbers of the priesthood in Paraguay are becoming alienated from the 16-year-old dictatorship. Its harsh treatment of priests active in progressive movements is earning it the enmity of the hierarchy. Catholic students and members of the faculty have participated in strikes and protests against the heavy-handed regime. The government, in retaliation, has expelled a liberal Spanish Jesuit priest whom it regarded as a trouble maker. With priests now advancing social and economic reforms in their sermons, police have allegedly begun to tap Church telephones.[8] In the growing conflict between Church and state, the hierarchy has now united

[7] *The Christian Science Monitor,* February 14, 1968, p. 4.

[8] Center for Latin American Studies, Arizona State University, *Latin American Digest,* 3 (May 1969), 8.

behind the priests and denounced the "flagrant abuses of human rights" in Paraguay.[9] The Archbishop of Paraguay has excommunicated officials whom he regarded as responsible for the physical indignities suffered by priests. His most dramatic move came when he forbade the annual pilgrimage to the sanctuary of the Virgin of Caacupe in December 1969, a move said to be of a "solemnity rather greater than a suspension of Christmas in England." [10] In the intensifying struggle between the Church and the state, President Stroessner early in 1970 discontinued certain funds for Church use and ordered the Church to cease all of its welfare activities in the country.

The Church is a poor institution, and while it is dependent upon national subsidies, it cannot seriously hope to overthrow the dictatorship. Activist priests and laymen in the interior are building up peasant leagues in anticipation of the time when the *campesinos* will have something to say about political affairs in the country. The chief contribution of the Church at present lies in its calling public attention to the excesses of the present administration. Its moral voice is now challenging a regime that has silenced all other voices.

One critic of the Church in Latin America, writing in 1954, argued that the Church over the years had shown an inclination to support order and authority (goals and values of the upper class) and to oppose freedom (the goal of the lower classes).[11] In view of recent developments in the two countries under study and in several other Latin American countries, that generalization may be losing some of its validity. The Church is now calling for social justice and is identifying with forces that advocate it, such as the Confederation of Latin American Christian Trade Unions. Social Christian doctrine has inspired some trade union groups in a number of countries. In Venezuela they constitute a fairly sizable group within existing labor organizations.[12] Paraguayan labor forces are organized under a

[9] *The New York Times,* May 11, 1969, p. 22.

[10] *Latin America,* January 2, 1970, p. 6.

[11] Jorge Mañach, "Religion and Freedom in Latin America," a paper prepared for the Latin American Conference on Responsible Freedoms in the Americas, 1954, p. 14.

[12] Jorge Barria, "The Trade Union Movement," *Latin America and the Caribbean, a Handbook,* Claudio Velez, ed. (New York: Praeger, 1968), pp. 736–742.

government-controlled confederation, and the Church is forbidden to play any part in them.

In the area of political parties, the Church has a party it can identify with in Venezuela: The Christian Socialist party. In Paraguay, the Christian Democratic party has, until recently, given progressive members of the Church and intellectuals from all groups an alternative to the two traditional parties. The Christian Democratic party as a political force, however, seems now on the way to oblivion. One of its leaders is in exile and the party is controlled by a faction that is willing to cooperate with Stroessner.[13]

MEN ON HORSEBACK: THE MILITARY ESTABLISHMENT

One of the major political realities of politics in Latin America is the presence of a powerful military establishment that in general has not usually been willing to confine itself to a nonpolitical role. The military forces in Latin America have been important political forces since the days of independence. Indeed, it might be said that the political role of the military is of greater consequence than its role as a defense institution. Only rarely in Latin American history has a nation's armed forces been called upon to defend the territorial integrity of the country. Paraguay's armed forces have done this. Venezuelan militarists have been challenged only by domestic events and disturbances.

Militarism has been a feature of all of the Latin American republics at one time or another during their history and remains important in a number of them today, including Paraguay and Venezuela. Militarism is seen in the tendency to regard military efficiency as a desirable goal of the state, to exalt the interests of the armed forces, to maintain large standing armies. It involves attitudes of the members of the armed forces about their role in society and politics, and involves attitudes of the ordinary citizen toward the military institution and its conception of its role.

In Venezuela the armed forces number about 37,000 men,

---

[13] *Latin America,* May 8, 1970, p. 148.

of whom 10,000 are members of the National Guard. Venezuela annually spends on military maintenance about 1.8 percent of its GNP, or 10 percent of its budget. Paraguay has about 12,000 men under arms and spends 1.7 percent of its GNP, or 22 percent of its national budget, to maintain them. In both countries, the officer class lives handsomely in comparison with the rest of the population, particularly in Venezuela where Marcos Pérez Jiménez built lavish living and recreation quarters for them in an attempt to keep them loyal to him. In Paraguay, the million dollar Ministry of Defense building is the most imposing of the departmental edifices.

The Paraguayan armed forces have little reason to complain. They do not pay any license fees for their cars; they have a good deal of influence in getting friends and relations on the public payroll; and they may—and do—augment their income through various concessions to import goods duty free. Loyalty of the military men to Stroessner is guaranteed not only through such devices, but also through thorough checks by the political police on the backgrounds of all of the members of the officer class.[14]

The national armies of Venezuela and Paraguay were formerly staffed by officers who came from the elite elements of society and saw the preservation of their status quo and privileges as the primary obligation of the state. This no longer appears to be true in Venezuela, at least. The rank and file army is raised through selective conscription, while the officer class, many of whom come from humble origins in the Andes, compete for careers through examinations in the military schools. They tend to identify economically with the growing middle class and to accept, or at least to acquiesce to, social, economic, and agrarian reform. Nevertheless, their long participation in the political life of Venezuela and elsewhere has caused military men to assume that they have an inherent right to govern in certain circumstances; for example, when they have concluded that constitutional government is in danger or that Communist elements are about to take over the political system. In situations such as these, military leaders have generally cast them-

[14] *Latin America,* January 2, 1970, p. 6.

selves in the role of saviours of society and polity, redeemers, pacifiers, men with missions, preservers of constitutional government, and so on.

Having consolidated and legitimatized his military regime by giving it a constitutional underpinning, Marcos Pérez Jiménez in 1953 sought to depoliticize the armed forces while at the same time relying upon them for his primary power base. In his personal constitution of 1953 it was specifically declared that the military establishment was an impersonal, professional, apolitical servant of the nation. Its members were denied the right to vote or to join political groups while they remained in service. The fundamental duty of the armed forces was to maintain internal stability and ensure the compliance of the constitution and the laws. We have seen in Chapter One how he himself observed those precepts before he was driven from office in 1958.

The 1961 constitution, an expression of a more democratic, civilian element, reacted to the intrusion of military forces into the political life of the nation, and to Pérez Jiménez's manipulation of them for personal power, by declaring in Article 132 that they formed a

> non-political, obedient and non-deliberative institution, organized by the State to ensure the national defense, the stability of democratic institutions and respect for the constitutional and the laws, the observance of which shall always be above any other obligation. The National Armed Forces shall be in the service of the Republic and in no case that of any person or political partisanship.

The fine hand of the military may be seen in this article, nevertheless, for the institution still has a political role to play in its obligation to ensure the observance of the constitutional system. Despite the constitutional restrictions contained in this article and the relative passivity of the armed forces in Venezuela since 1959, one can conclude that the power and influence of the military establishment has not been seriously compromised. What does seem to be the case is that the civilian government has been intelligent enough to realize that it cannot tamper with the "institutional independence" of the armed forces (as it was accused of doing in 1948 with disastrous results) without running the risk of being replaced. History in Venezuela demonstrates that civilian control of the government is possible to the degree that the government recognizes this basic fact of life.

Civilian administrations in Venezuela do not feel completely confident about the loyalty of its military men and often use special occasions to remind them of their obligations. Thus President Leoni, reflecting upon the role and mission of the armed forces in Venezuelan political life, told the graduating class of the Venezuelan Military School and the Officers Training School of the Armed Forces of Cooperation in 1966:

> At no time must you be indifferent to the nation's problems, but your position must be well balanced and must show absolute respect for the Constitution and the Laws. You must be ever ready to preserve the functions of our democratic representative government and become a retaining wall against every totalitarian uprising, regardless of its source.
>
> You must remember that every time an autocratic regime has been shamefully forced upon the nation, the Armed Forces of the Republic have been the main sufferers. They have borne the stigma of the consequences, either because excesses, inequities and arbitrary actions have been committed in their name or because they have been unfairly blamed for policy blunders, while those holding power—men or gangs of voracious exploiters—have enjoyed their privileges and claimed for themselves all credit for any positive accomplishment.
>
> Never keep aloof and lose contact with your own people. Because your moral and technical training, your responsibility toward society is greater. Without forgetting your military condition, you must play an active role among the people, applying to your actions the standards of discipline and military ethics you were taught.
>
> We have felt in our country the treacherous blows of terrorism. Places of work, and national and private businesses have been destroyed, and what is worse, we have paid a heavy toll in human lives. Fellow officers, school teachers, workers, farmers, have fallen victims of traitorous ambushes by those who, following instructions from alien elements, try to overthrow our fundamental institutions.
>
> While our Armed Forces carry out civic programs in cities, towns and villages; while they build roads, schools and churches, lend medical assistance to the poor, and teach ways to a better life, subversive henchmen, obeying orders from

abroad, try to poison the minds of our youths and sow death and destruction in the Venezuelan countryside. This is their vicious plan to weaken the Armed Forces and establish in our country a regime similar to that suffered in Cuba.

The mission of our Armed Forces is to prevent extremism to reach in Venezuela the proportions gained in other countries. There is among us a firm resolve to oppose the inroads of communism, which is nothing but a personalist tyranny disguised as socialism. But communism is not the only danger threatening our institutions. Reactionary sectors and individuals who miss old and lost privileges also try to undermine the foundations of political stability.

At times by cajoling and at other times by offering fantastic pictures of hardships, they attempt to sap the solid convictions of military professionals and induce them to take upon themselves the solution of problems that the Constitution and the Laws entrust to the civil power.

We must rebuke these people as well as the advocates of communist doctrines, for the real objectives of the Armed Forces are the security of national institutions, the development of our wealth and the strengthening of the invulnerable unit of our organization to build a great nation.[15]

And in 1968, near the end of his term, he congratulated the armed forces for their adherence to his advice:

Democratic stability in the country, achieved with the support of all citizens and the Armed Forces, has made it possible to defeat all threats of disturbances. . . . All Venezuelans, except the small extremist groups are in agreement on one fundamental point: the need to maintain an institutional democracy that will protect the freedom and dignity of every citizen. In defense of this we have the firm support and loyalty of the Armed Forces, who have given their sweat and blood to defend national honor and the will of the people, to enjoy their freedom and their rights. We are proud of their conduct, which is an example of efficiency and excellence for the entire continent.[16]

President Caldera, however, has not had such smooth sailing. In September 1969, after six months in office, he announced

[15] *Venezuela Up-to-date,* 12 (Winter 1965–1966), 4.
[16] *Venezuela Up-to-date,* 12 (Winter 1968–1969), 8.

the arrests of two generals and a colonel on charges of insubordination. The men were said to have opposed the president's guerrilla pacification policies. In former days such an action by a civilian president would have been dangerous, if not unthinkable. The acquiescence of the armed forces in this event should not be taken as a reliable guide to their future attitudes and actions. As the most powerful institution in the Venezuelan political system, it is still in a position to alter democratic trends of the past ten years.

Civilian control of the government has been a rare phenomenon in Paraguay during the past 110 years. Militarism has been a feature of the Paraguayan system since the days of Francisco Solano López. For many years after the War of the Triple Alliance, surviving generals were either dominant in politics or were disruptive influences as they sought to achieve the presidency. Between 1880 and the Chaco War (1932) there were many military insurrections that brought about changes in political personnel without changing the real pattern of power. The Chaco War gave a new impetus to the involvement of military men in politics. Colonel Rafael Franco and Generals Higinio Morínigo and José Felix Estigarribia became presidents on the basis of military reputations earned in the war with Bolivia. The seizure of power by General Stroessner in 1954 and his continuation in office to the present time means that Paraguay has been under almost continuous control of the army since 1936, and is in effect a praetorian state. General Stroessner, celebrating his tenth year in power in 1964, was flanked by two generals who had served in his cabinet during that entire time. Stroessner claimed success for his administration and attributed it to the unity of the armed forces, the collaboration of the Colorado party and "all good Paraguayans," his anticommunist policy, his respect for Paraguay's social and political institutions, and, modestly, to his own personal dedication to presidential responsibilities.

Stroessner's handling of the armed forces does not reflect an absolute confidence in them on his part. Not long after he became president in 1954, a number of generals with staunch Colorado loyalties were retired. Stroessner replaced them with younger men loyal to him alone. High-ranking military commanders are geographically separated and thus their ability to plot against the president—if they are so inclined—is reduced considerably. President Stroessner also reserves solely to himself all matériel matters.[17] A commander without equipment can hardly be a serious threat. In Stroessner's Paraguay of 1970, the armed forces seem less of a potential menace than they do in Venezuela. They are more a manipulated and controlled power base for the dictator than an active political influence.

THE MEN AT THE DESKS: THE BUREAUCRACY

As a group, the bureaucracy in Latin America is an institution of considerable importance in the policy process, particularly in the application of official decisions. It may have little voice in the initiation of policy or in the final selection between alternative courses of action, but by its very nature it monopolizes the output function of government. Government programs have to be administered and edicts applied; even the most conscientious and hard-working dictator could not possibly do all the work.

Nevertheless, the bureaucracy in Paraguay and Venezuela has been a relatively weak pressure group. Under the spoils system concept it provides each new regime with ample means to reward the faithful. This generalization is far more true today in Paraguay than in Venezuela. President Stroessner confers jobs upon loyal followers with the result that the Colorado party monopolizes the entire government structure. Entirely dependent as they are upon him, the bureaucrats do not engage in activities that might bring an early end to their employment. Public servants are grateful for their jobs and in general are not anxious to upset the applecart.

The Paraguayan bureaucracy has no central organization for recruitment and supervision. Each ministry has its own personnel officer appointed by the president and directly responsible to him. Enemies of the regime charge that this state of affairs is a calculated attempt on the part of the president to keep the bureaucracy divided and thus make difficult any efforts on its part to challenge the powers of the president. A bureau-

[17] Byron A. Nichols, "Paraguay—A Future Democracy?" *SAIS Review* (Summer 1968), 29.

cratic revolt is nothing short of fantasy. Public service is highly regarded as a desirable profession and a great many people aspire to it. Compared to other occupations, working conditions are relatively good. Bureaucrats have liberal pensions (93 percent of their salary after thirty years of service) vacations, and sick leave. All of these benefits have been conferred upon them by a paternal government.

The 50,000-member bureaucracy has some power and authority, of course. Those in responsible positions are constantly being confronted with situations in which they must decide whether to apply the law or not, and, if so, to what extent. "Fulano es amigo" ("Fulano is a friend") is an important consideration, not only in securing a job, but also in having one's affairs with the government dealt with favorably and quickly. The nearer an individual is to the president, the more likely he is to possess correspondingly greater powers and discretionary authority. Bureaucrats can prevent the work of government from going on effectively. They can, for example, delay the completion of public works by prolonging contract negotiations and by holding up plans and funds. Unqualified individuals whose only asset is their friendship with someone in power may seriously affect the administration of the judicial and educational systems, both under the control of political officials. The evidence seems to point to a status quo public service in an authoritarian state.

The Venezuelan bureaucracy—public servants in a much richer and more complex governmental structure—is not much larger than that of Paraguay, a fact that speaks volumes in itself. Nevertheless, it suffers from some of the same vices. It is, for example, a victim of the spoils system. During the Pérez Jiménez era, it was a power base for the dictator. Public employees were required to march in parades that, in addition to glorifying national events and achievements, served to express loyalty to the administration. Bureaucrats were also expected to vote for the president. In the 1952 elections of delegates to the constitutional assembly—an election that turned into a presidential campaign for the dictator—government workers were told to turn in their unused ballots to their immediate supervisors.

Despite attempts since 1960 to get a workable civil service

law through the congress, at the end of 1969 no such law had been passed. The 1960 proposal remained in the hands of the congressional committee on social affairs. Part of the opposition to the bill, it has been asserted, came from the ministers themselves. They preferred to have wide latitude in hiring and firing their personnel. In 1965 interested congressmen revived, amended, and reintroduced the measure. The Venezuelan Confederation of Labor also introduced in the same session a similar bill on behalf of its affiliate, the Public Employees Union. Both were tabled. In the absence of congressional regulation, the public administration is governed under an edict issued during President Betancourt's presidency and under provisions of the 1966 Labor Law.

The Venezuelan bureaucracy is better trained and better educated than its Paraguayan counterpart and clearly has a more vigorous role to play. It is organized and can speak on its own behalf as well as use the services of the CTV (Venezuelan Labor Confederation). Top technicians and officials in the ministries and in the numerous autonomous agencies have considerable power of discretion in carrying out government and institute policies. With funds from the World Bank and other lending institutions, the autonomous agencies are a power in themselves. They recruit and train their own staffs, and some are said to be hostile to the political parties.

THE INTELLECTUAL COMMUNITY:
THE UNIVERSITY AND STUDENT ORGANIZATIONS

Latin American students as a rule are intensely political and are therefore important in the arena of national politics, as well as in university politics.

Dedicated to the free and open pursuit of knowledge and, in theory at least, dedicated to the open society, the university regards itself and is regarded as a proper institution to question the tactics and policies of a repressive government. Bolstered by the fiction of university autonomy, which in theory confers upon the institution the unrestricted right to manage its own affairs and restrains the government from interfering in any way in university affairs, faculty and students alike engage in a variety of political activities. If the government is tolerant, it will permit them to take part in peaceful demonstrations and to air their grievances. But often this is not the case. An uneasy regime of questionable legitimacy reacts to university criticism with repression, purges, and, ultimately, closure. They may remain closed for many months as the politicians try to recruit a faculty sympathetic to its view and policies. Repressive action by the government exacerbates the latent hostility that often characterizes the relations between the government and the more liberal university elements. The universities of Venezuela were closed during most of the period between 1948 and 1953 for reasons given above. Paraguayan universities have not been closed so far because they have not posed a serious enough challenge to the government of Alfredo Stroessner.

University autonomy is limited by several factors, the most obvious one being the unwillingness of government officials to observe it in all cases. Then too, the curriculum of the university is, like that of the secondary and primary school system, subject to influence from the national government. The fact that the government controls both curriculum and the power of the purse powerfully conditions the extent of the freedom under which the university operates. Nevertheless, both students and faculty take autonomy seriously. Students like the sanctuary of the university and use it as a safe base from which to conduct their political activity. In order to retain their status as students, some persons regularly fail to complete course requirements and repeat them again and again. In 1963, the administration of Central University in Caracas ruled that students who failed a course three times would not be allowed to repeat it. When this rule was enforced a year later, students paralyzed the university by a thirteen-day strike.

An incident occurred in Venezuela in 1964 that severely tested the relations among the government, the parties, and the university. It involved the principle of university autonomy. In May about 500 agents of DIGEPOL (*Dirección General de Policía*) entered university grounds to recover one of its agents who had been shot by a student during a routine check of the university. University students and faculty alike loudly protested and denounced the police invasion as illegal and unnecessary. The matter was discussed in Congress, where government forces not only defended the action as legal and in the nation's interests, but also criticized the university for permitting criminal elements to operate within its precincts. The government justified its action in ransacking student belongings and confiscating books and pamphlets on the grounds that FALN not only had student reservists among the student body, but also was allowed to offer courses in the use of firearms.[18]

In Venezuela and Paraguay there is little in the way of campus life as it is known in the United States: social clubs, sororities and fraternities, extracurricular activities, and intramural sports. Dormitories are almost unknown. Student organizations are likely to reflect a close association with one of the national political parties; indeed, they are often the party's university arm.

Paraguayan students have organized student groups with party ties. A student group with the ominous name of *Organización Terrorista Estudiantes Colorados* actively supports the Colorado government and is an arm of the party in the university. The Liberal party's student club *Alon,* the Democratic Student Front, the University Federation of Paraguay, and the Christian Democratic Youth of Paraguay are all opponents of the present regime and are as critical of it as the state-of-siege measures and the whims of the president will permit them to be.

In late 1962, the Christian Democratic Youth protested the arrest of one of its members who had courageously asked a visiting Cuban exile before an audience of 500 persons which enemy Paraguay should fight first—the dictator or communism.[19] The president of the University Federation of Paraguay, accused by the police of conversing with CD's student leader, was arrested and tortured. The government released him only after it was deluged with telegrams of protest from forty-seven student federations all over the world. The Federation has called the attention of student organizations in other countries to the farcical nature of elections held during a state of siege. Students sometimes resort to violence as did a member of the

[18] *Hispanic American Report,* 17 (July 1964), 43.
[19] *Hispanic American Report,* 15 (February 1963), 1160.

Federation of Revolutionary Democratic students. He planted a bomb in the capital post office.

Criticism of the government and its tactics reached a new intensity in 1969 when a street vendor died in an Asunción police station after five days of questioning. Students from the National and Catholic Universities immediately protested the incident. One of the student protestors was a second-year medical student at National University who had exemption from the draft as the only son of a Chaco War veteran. The government arrested him and inducted him into the army for a two-year term, declaring that his exemption had been obtained by fraud. Students of the medical faculty declared a strike, which ended in violence as Catholic University students were beaten as they left National University after a sympathy demonstration there.[20]

In Venezuela each of the principal political parties has an organization among the student body and competes vigorously for the elective offices open to students. The ultimate prize is control of the national student organization, the Federation of University Centers. Thus, by permitting and even encouraging the formation of activist political groups with whom many professors are identified, the university participates in the further socialization of individuals and acts as an agency of political recruitment. Many university students begin their careers as politicians in the rough-and-tumble game of university politics.

Elections to the student-faculty committee in the various faculties are normally held annually. The committees then elect members to the all-university body, which in turn is affiliated with the Federation of University Centers.

While Marxism is popular among students, most of them are moderate in their views and affiliate with moderate parties. Extremists are often found in the ranks of FALN, the guerrilla organization. Perhaps the strongest single political force in the Venezuelan student body is COPEI's *Juventud Revolucionario Copeyano* (JRC). It is the main challenge to the far-left elements. COPEI has always been vitally interested in the student movement, having itself originated in a student organization in 1946. *Copeyano* students are more militant and more progressive than

[20] *The New York Times,* May 11, 1969, p. 22.

the old guard in the parent party, and they consider themselves and are regarded as the party's principal driving force.[21] As a militant force, JRC has engaged in street clashes with Communists and members of the Movement of the Revolutionary Left. Although it is the leading student political organization, JRC does not dominate the Federation. Its efforts to do so have been thwarted by coalitions of left-wing student parties in the various universities.

Students are expected to follow the national party's dogma and directives, but do not always do so. In 1964, for example, URD's *Vanguardia Juvenil Urredista* (VJU) objected to the parent party's denunciation of left-wing party activity. In retaliation, URD's national committee ordered the postponement of VJU's forthcoming national convention of student organizations throughout Venezuela. VJU decided to ignore this directive, whereupon the national committee forbade its chairman to participate in politics for a period of one year. This action provoked a motion of censure from the Federation as well as from a labor federation sympathetic to URD.[22]

During the 1964 strike over university attempts to clear the university of perennial repeaters and hangers-on, COPEI supported the university administration while the student arm of the party supported the strike. AD denounced the strike and its students returned to class.

Students comunicate through protest marches, strikes, mass meetings, sympathy demonstrations, tactics designed to provoke security forces and by inflammatory messages and articles in the various student publications, sit-ins, and boycotts. Students played a catalytic role in the overthrow of Pérez Jiménez in 1958. After an abortive attempt by a group of air force pilots to eliminate the dictator, students began to riot in the streets of the capital. Other segments of society joined with the students: workers, ordinary middle-class citizens and even some of the wealthy class. After three weeks of continuing disorder, the army informed Pérez Jiménez that he was through.[23] Thus it can be seen that students can play an important role, not only in

[21] Edward Williams, *Latin America Christian Democratic Parties* (Knoxville, Tenn.: University of Tennessee Press, 1968), p. 189.

[22] *Hispanic American Report*, 16 (November 1968), 996.

[23] Ted Szulc, *Latin America* (New York: Atheneum, 1966), p. 29.

bringing about changes in government, but also in helping to define issues and by providing new blood and ideas. This role is tempered by the fact that ". . . usually the university as an institution begins to turn inward, preparing to meet the demand for professionalism that always arises in times of rapid economic and political development." [24] In Paraguay, students have been an ineffective force, although certainly not a silent one.

THE PROLETARIAN COMMUNITY: INDUSTRIAL AND AGRICULTURAL WORKERS

Venezuela has perhaps one of the strongest labor movements in Latin America. Its power comes not only from the numbers of the total labor force associated with it (about 60 percent), but also from its close and intimate ties with the major parties, particularly with *Acción Democrática*. Because they are so closely associated with the party structures, the labor unions probably have less independence than might otherwise be the case.

Prior to 1945 the labor movement was weak, poorly organized, and had few members. Under Gómez, "the rights of labor and social reform programs were ignored as inappropriate to a philosophy that stressed public works activity and the unhampered private development of the oil industry." [25] A new constitution in 1936 and new labor legislation during the terms of López Contreras and Medina Angarita provided a climate more sympathetic to the labor class.

Today the labor unions have a total of 1.3 million members, more than one-half of which are rural workers and peasants. *Acción Democrática* is largely responsible for the phenomenal growth of trade unions and peasant organizations, both of which are significant bases of its electoral support. Only recently has COPEI begun to share in the benefits of union confidence. Its entry into the principal labor organizations was one of the rewards of coalition partnership with AD. COPEI members now

[24] K. H. Silvert, "The University Student," in *Government and Politics in Latin America, A Reader,* Peter Snow, ed. (New York: Holt, Rinehart and Winston, Inc., 1967), p. 382.

[25] Anderson, p. 211.

share with *Adecos* (the name given to members of AD) the posts of director in several of the large unions that make up the Venezuelan Confederation of Labor (CTV). COPEI seems to be willing to work within the framework of CTV instead of attempting to create a labor union following of its own. It does, however, have a peasant following, the *Frente Campesino*.

After coming to power in 1945, AD began immediately to build a power base by organizing both laborers and peasants. In three years' time, 500 new industrial unions had been established and 13 national federations created. The number of peasant unions rose from 77 to 515. Today the CTV and its affiliate the Venezuelan Peasants Federation (FCV) have respective memberships of 600,000 and 700,000. The association of workers and peasants in the same organization is almost unique in Latin America where the labor force has tended to isolate itself from other social forces. In addition to the giant CTV/FCV, several other smaller organizations exist: the leftist dominated *Confederación Único de Trabajadores* (CUTV), the *Comité de Sindicatos Autónomos,* a Catholic labor union, and a small Communist group. CUTV is a result of one of the party splits within AD. It was organized in 1963 after party dissidents had failed to wrest control from regular party leaders. A similar contest took place in the Peasants Federation and in the Oil Workers Federation (*Fedepetrol*). During the early part of that struggle, the contending wings of the various groups were known by such designations as *"CTV-oficialista"* and *"CTV-no oficialista," "Fedepetrol-oficialista,"* and *"Fedepetrol-no oficialista,"* reflecting the intimate relationship between party and union.

One of the most powerful unions is the 33,000-member Oil Workers Federation. With the aid of a sympathetic government, it has been able over the years to achieve very advantageous working conditions vis-à-vis the foreign oil companies. Not until 1966 was *Fedepetrol* allowed to negotiate a contract with the companies without the intervention of the Ministry of Labor. Its three-year contract called for generous year-end bonuses, liberal pensions, excellent severance pay, and housing and recreation facilities for those working on oil properties in the interior.

Basic goals of Venezuelan trade and peasant associations are similar to those in Latin America in general: good wages and hours, job security, proper working conditions, welfare state, and "distributive justice." In response to such aspirations the Venezuelan Labor Law requires that all enterprises distribute at least 10 percent of their net profits to their employees at the end of each fiscal year. Pregnant women are entitled to leave with pay for a period extending six weeks before and six weeks after childbirth. Work must be performed under conditions that permit normal physical development; that allow sufficient time for rest, education, and legitimate leisure; that afford adequate protection of the health and lives of the workers; and that protect women and children against immoral and other deleterious influences.[26]

Although unions enjoy the right to strike under conditions fixed by law, they ordinarily do not have to do so, for the paternalistic government of AD saw to it that labor was kept reasonably well satisfied. An important function of the labor movement in Venezuela, therefore, has been more political than economic: to defend and uphold the policies of the government.

Because of their mutually profitable associations during the years of AD administration, the government and the labor unions got along very well. There seems to be no reason to anticipate any change under COPEI leadership because it and all other major parties maintain good relations with the principal labor organizations.

Venezuelan peasants and workers, through some of their union officials who hold positions of influence in AD, COPEI, and in the government, can make their views known fairly effectively. Union leaders are also directly involved as members of the state and national legislatures.[27] Already a powerful force to which the government listens respectfully, albeit paternally, the labor movement will increase in importance as it continues to grow in response to the industrialization push.

The economically active population of Paraguay is basically an unskilled labor force and predominantly rural, as the majority

[26] R. Lapervance Parparcen and Armando A. Subero, *A Statement of the Laws of Venezuela in Matters Affecting Business,* 3d ed. (Washington, D.C.: Pan American Union, 1962), pp. 110–112.

[27] Harry Kantor, *Patterns of Political Systems in Latin America* (Skokie, Ill.: Rand McNally, 1969), p. 374.

of Paraguayans make their living from the land. Many of the skilled workers, around whom labor unions are usually organized, left Paraguay during the 1947 civil disturbances and have never returned. As a result, Paraguay even today is in need of such skilled artisans as plumbers, mechanics, electricians, and repairmen. New vocational schools are beginning to supply the need, however.

The labor movement in Paraguay is of relatively recent origin. Prior to 1936 it was virtually nonexistent, because there was nothing to organize. The Febreristas, in their brief eighteen-month span of power tried to stimulate union activity in the small industrial proletariat population. The authoritarian nature of the political system since 1936 put an end to the growth of an independent labor movement.

This was not accomplished without considerable strife. General strikes occurred in 1941, 1943, and 1945. All were vigorous protests by the labor unions over the government's attempt to gain complete control of their organizations. Labor union leaders were imprisoned by the Morínigo regime and sent to concentration camps. His repressive tactics accomplished his objective—labor today in Paraguay is strictly under government control.

One of the few pertinent articles in the 1940 constitution forbade "exploitation of man by man" and declared that social security, safety, and health conditions were to be under the supervision and control of the state. Unlike most other Latin American states, Paraguay did not have a comprehensive labor code until 1961. Until that date, there was no law relating to the organization of unions beyond a statement that they were free to develop under the authority of the National Labor Department. In 1961 all the laws and edicts that dealt with labor were brought together and codified, and conflicting provisions were repealed.

Such rights as the workers enjoy cannot be said to be the direct result of union pressures, for the relation of government to worker has always been a highly paternalistic one. Rights and obligations spelled out in the 1961 Labor Code and the Code of Labor Procedure are those that a benign government has seen fit to confer upon them. These are often more in conformity with advanced codes in other countries than with the realities of the Paraguayan economic system, which is mainly agrarian in nature.

The 1967 constitution reiterates the labor provisions of the 1940 document and includes for the first time in Paraguayan history the right of the worker to strike. The right must be exercised in conformity with "democratic procedures and be exclusively in the defense of workers' interests." General strikes with a political objective, common in other countries of the hemisphere, are illegal and simply do not now occur in the controlled environment. Indeed, the bylaws of the Paraguayan Confederation of Workers (CPT) forbid member unions to engage in any political activity inside the union and eschews political objectives altogether. The labor code requires unions to maintain complete independence from political parties and from all religious bodies. These requirements distinguish Paraguayan labor clearly from Venezuelan labor, where party-union ties are very close indeed.

Under the present code, strikes and lockouts may not be legally called until conciliation procedures established by law have produced no result. Unless the strike has been cleared with the government, an organization feels the heavy hand of the government in the arrest of its leaders. While this situation does not often arise, an example of it occurred in 1962 when union officials at the Quebracho and Agricultural Workers Union were arrested when they called an unauthorized strike to force producers to pay their 1800 workers three months' pay due them. The government plays an active role in all labor disputes. Rarely are there direct negotiations between labor and employers. The Ministry of Justice and Labor has a finger in every labor dispute.

Labor unions may not function at all until they have received the approval of the above ministry. And that approval may be withheld by government officials for almost any reason. Legal status has been granted to about 90 unions, most of whom are affiliated with the Paraguayan Confederation of Workers, the only large federation in Paraguay. CTP claims 92 percent of the 54,000 salary and wage earners who belong to unions. Several minor unions are the International Confederation of Free Trade Unions and the International Federation of Christian Trade Unions.

The close connection between CPT and the government is demonstrated by the fact that CPT holds its annual congresses in Asunción in government buildings such as the auditorium of the Ministry of Public Health. The Ministry of Labor is very much involved in the affairs of the congress in an unofficial way. Paraguayan labor exiles say that government officials exert influence in all the deliberations of the congress. They have called the congresses frauds, dominated by government-controlled puppets. President Stroessner and other high government officials usually put in an appearance at the closing ceremonies, which are sprinkled with goodwill speeches, and on behalf of the government, thanks the workers for their sacrifices. The workers made such a sacrifice in 1963 when they responded to CPT's request to postpone wage demands in support of President Stroessner's "patriotic decision" to maintain the stability of the currency. CPT referred to this act as an example of "deep homage to the motherland and its present greatness." [28] And again in 1964, the CPT withdrew a request for a minimum wage almost as soon as it was presented and accepted instead a much lower increase proposed by the Ministry of Justice and Labor. For this they were severely criticized by Liberals who called it a violation of the trust of the workers. In general, it appears that relations between the government and CPT have been overtly friendly, but marked by labor servility. Opposition groups claim that labor leaders have little ability, and that ignorant workers are being manipulated by ambitious politicians.

The effectiveness of CPT as a political force has been greatly hampered by stringent government regulations and restrictions, and by the slow pace of industrial development, which retards union growth. Although there are some rural workers' organizations, they are even more ineffective than the proletarian unions. The 328,000 agricultural workers, despite the fact that several peasant groups exist, are almost totally ignored by the government. Such labor legislation as does exist applies mainly to urban and industrial workers. The labor code provides for an eight-hour day for urban laborers, but allows a twelve-hour day for agricultural workers.

In Paraguay, labor does as it is told.

[28] *Hispanic American Report,* 16 (June 1963), 401.

THE BUSINESS COMMUNITY:
INDUSTRIAL AND COMMERCIAL GROUPS

The business, industrial, and producing community of Venezuela is represented by numerous organizations, most of which work not only to advance and protect their own interests, but also to contain the labor movement. The most powerful of the lot is the Federation of Chambers of Industry and Commerce (FEDECAMARAS), made up of associations from all sectors of the private economy. It includes banking (The Bankers Association), oil interests (Chamber of Petroleum Industry), agriculture (Ranchers and Livestock Association), and commerce (Caracas Chamber of Commerce). Venezuela is the only country in Latin America in which the private pressure groups are organized into one large association. It is well financed by the elite of the economic system and speaks out not only in its own voice, but through a political arm of the elite called the National Movement of Independents (MNI). MNI was established in 1968 along the lines of the defunct Venezuelan Independent Association, the 1963 political vehicle of industrial, banking and commerce magnates. In political matters, however, MNI was not a united force, for some of its members supported Burelli Rivas for president in 1968 and others opted for Rafael Caldera.

FEDECAMARAS has shown its power over government economic policy on several occasions since 1958. It has been able to exert pressure more effectively than might otherwise be the case because the president of Venezuela does not command a disciplined majority in Congress. Faced by a factionalized legislature, he is unwilling or unable to push legislation to which the large economic interests are hostile.

During 1964, President Leoni announced his intention of bringing Venezuela into the Latin American Free Trade Association (LAFTA), composed of all South American nations but Bolivia and his own country. Business interests were taken by surprise. Although government and business had been discussing the possibility of LAFTA membership for some time, FEDECAMARAS had been dragging its feet because of misgivings about the effects of the move on a country with high, uncompetitive wage scales and a high degree of dependence on oil for its foreign exchange earnings. FEDECAMARAS advocated caution and gradualism in the approach to LAFTA. President Leoni felt strong enough in 1965 to announce at LAFTA's meeting his country's intention to join the organization. Venezuela became a participating member in 1966.

President Leoni was also favorably inclined to Venezuela's participation in a proposed five-nation Andean regional economic bloc. FEDECAMARAS was no more enthusiastic about this venture than it had been about LAFTA, and for over a year engaged in delaying tactics such as requests for new studies on the overall effects of membership. President Leoni was unable to overcome their opposition before going out of office in March 1969.

The new President, Rafael Caldera, is firmly committed to economic integration:

> We look with sympathy to the efforts made towards the integration of Latin America. The peculiar character of our economy, the stability of our currency, the fear of jeopardizing the progress reached and the social gains of our workers, have brought worries as to our participation in the Andean Regional Pact within the Latin American Free Trade Association. In this respect, the position of our private sectors must be seriously taken into consideration, for in a matter of such importance the public and private sectors must go hand in hand, since they jointly constitute the national economy. I feel confident that all obstacles will be overcome and a formula found to this end.[29]

Shortly after taking office he told FEDECAMARAS that joining the Andean bloc was absolutely essential, so much so in fact, that Venezuela would go ahead with integration with or without FEDECAMARAS at the earliest possible moment. That moment had not arrived as of the end of 1970. President Carlos Llera Restrepo of Colombia increased his pressure on President Caldera during the latter's visit to Colombia to bring his country into the bloc. But Caldera needed the approval of his Congress, and it was firmly in the hands of political opponents, the most vociferous of which was AD. Although AD is committed to regional cooperation, it now appears to be more inter-

[29] *Venezuela Up-to-date,* 12 (Spring 1969), 5.

ested in making trouble for the Caldera administration than in living up to its own policy program.

FEDECAMARAS not only opposes; it demands. In the latter part of 1969 it presented the government with a list of demands that included a request for a change of policy to provide better incentives for private investment in the underdeveloped interior of the country, a vigorous drive to counter the declining trend in oil exports, a Venezuelan-owned foreign trade bank, and the maximum encouragement for farmers and cattle raisers.[30]

In November 1969 FEDECAMARAS plunged much more deeply into politics when it attempted to bring about a reconciliation between COPEI and AD. Encouraged by persistent but ill-founded rumors that differences between the two former allies were about to be patched up, FEDECAMARAS approached AD, as well as leaders of most of the other political parties. Its efforts were not well received. AD leaders told FEDECAMARAS that "its role was not that of a super organization coordinating the political parties and telling them what to do." [31] URD was more caustic and charged FEDECAMARAS with meddling in politics and trying to become a political force. This incident reveals a fundamental difference between political parties and FEDECAMARAS about what the role of the latter should be.

FEDECAMARAS undertakes economic studies to justify its economic stands. It has pressured the government for more involvement of private businessmen in working with government officials in "democratic planning." It has sought and obtained high protective tariffs for Venezuelan industries and products. The Chamber of Petroleum Industry and the government exerted great pressure on the United States government in 1969 to persuade it to revise its petroleum policy and allow free access for Venezuelan oil to U.S. markets.

Although the agricultural producers association (FEDEAGRO) is affiliated with FEDECAMARAS, it does not necessarily have all of the same objectives as does the big group, particularly in the matter of industrialization. Oil and industrial workers are paid relatively good wages, enjoy many privileges and benefits, and are paid weekly. Landowners and cattlemen

[30] *Latin America,* July 4, 1969, p. 211.

[31] *Latin America,* November 28, 1968, p. 378.

find it increasingly difficult to obtain the cheap labor they have traditionally relied upon and see further industrialization as a threat to their own enterprises. An industrial society will require many costly things such as more government services, schools, and transportation facilities, all of which will have to be paid by increased taxation. The agrarian elite have never paid much in taxes and are not eager to do so now. Indeed, no one in Venezuela is enthusiastic about taxation.

The Paraguayan counterpart of FEDECAMARAS is FEPRINCO, the *Federación de la Producción, la Industria y el Comercio*. It is, however, far less comprehensive than the Venezuelan body. FEPRINCO makes its views known in a variety of ways. When President Stroessner caught the producing community by surprise by imposing new taxes on personal income, inheritances, and corporation capital and exports, FEPRINCO sent a long letter to the Chamber of Deputies explaining its opposition to the tax measure and its possible adverse effect on the economy. It asked the Chamber not to approve the president's decree until further study could be made. The Chamber, of course, being under the thumb of the president, ignored the request. The organization then sent a committee to the minister of finance asking him to delay the decree. It organized a public debate on the issue and announced that it would form a committee of its own members to study the possible effects of the new tax decree and to make its findings available to the government.[32] Despite all of these moves, the decree went into effect.

While FEPRINCO is better financed than the CTP and represents the wealthier classes, its influence with the government does not appear to be much greater than that of CTP.

Industry in Paraguay consists mostly of small businesses that do business wholly within the country. Most employ fewer than five workers. The largest industry is the meat-packing business. There are also about eight sugar refineries and some minor textile concerns. Industrial unionism is weak in Paraguay because industry is weak.

The economies of both countries are to a significant degree affected by foreign companies owning property or operating

[32] *Hispanic American Report*, 16 (June 1963), 402.

businesses there. Paraguay is particularly susceptible to Argentina interests, which control about three-fourths of its agricultural and manufacturing enterprises. In Venezuela, foreign companies do not own so much property, but, by extracting and processing its valuable resources through concessions granted by the government, they are an extremely important element in the economic system.

The seventeen privately owned foreign oil companies produce 21 percent of the GNP, earn 92 percent of the foreign exchange, and employ about 33,000 persons. The figure for the GNP rises to 28.5 percent if one includes mining. The giants of the oil sector are Creole Petroleum Corporation, a subsidiary of Standard Oil of New Jersey and Royal Dutch Shell, a British-owned company. In one way or another—through income taxes, concession fees, and profit sharing—the oil companies supply the government with two-thirds of its revenue each year. The government and the oil companies have reached an amicable *modus vivendi,* each recognizing and respecting the concerns of the other. A period of anxiety about the intentions of AD, which had been committed to the principle of the nationalization of the oil industry, was ended when that party decided to keep essentially the same arrangements that had prevailed before it came to power, although it did close the door to further concessions. During the Pérez Jiménez regime, the companies profited greatly by his benign attitude toward them. Many new concessions were granted in return for increased flows of revenue into government coffers.

Nationalization no longer seems an attractive alternative to the oil concession policy or to the present arrangements. For one thing, the flood of low-cost Middle Eastern oil has reduced the demand for Venezuelan oil in the world market. Nationalization is not likely to change that. Then too, the oil companies have the expertise and resources to manage the oil industry efficiently and economically. The government receives great profits with little or no effort expended. The oil companies, on the other hand, have derived enormous profits from their operations over the years, and they are not likely to jeopardize them by undue demands and pressures or obstructionist tactics. Indeed, they seem willing to cooperate with the government in trying to reach more advantageous terms in the international market. At the present time, therefore, neither seems threatened by the other, although in the final analysis, the government naturally holds the upper hand. After a year of negotiations with the companies, the government in 1967 got them to yield to a retroactive (to 1958) tax increase that, for the largest two concerns, amounted to $140 million. The companies deal with the government through the Ministry of Mines and Hydrocarbons.

Because the economy of Paraguay is to a large extent dominated by foreign interests, the government is more likely to be sensitive to the need for continued good relations with the foreign owners. Paraguay has neither the funds nor the skilled technicians to embark on large-scale enterprises of its own. Indeed, it seeks to attract further foreign investment and offers advantageous terms to those firms willing to invest in the country.

SUMMARY

In the authoritarian environment of Paraguay, the politics of pluralism are severely limited to the elite of the competing forces in society. Most of Paraguay's citizens have no opportunity to be concerned in matters unrelated to maintaining a minimal standard of living. Agricultural workers, in particular, are in this class. Industrial and urban workers have gone farther along the road to articulating their interests, but have not been particularly successful in realizing their demands. Competing claims upon the government by the relatively few organized groups are almost always settled in a paternalistic fashion. In some cases, government policy with respect to an issue is simply announced without the benefit of negotiation. Since executive supremacy is the cardinal reality in Paraguayan politics, groups compete for the attention and favor of President Stroessner and his cabinet. The supine legislature has little to say about it.

Paraguay's population is lopsidedly polarized into those who have and those who have not. Politics is largely the domain of those who have. Group politics is not at present an important ingredient of the Paraguayan political process.

Venezuela's more democratic environment permits a much higher degree of participation and competition. There are far more organized groups—particularly in industry and commerce —than there are in Paraguay. Politics now concern the active claims of a large organized labor force, well-organized industrial groups, and peasant and student organizations. As is true in Paraguay, all of these groups are dominated by elite sectors who often determine group policy fairly independently. A much closer connection between the organized interest groups and the political parties exists in Venezuela than in Paraguay. Leaders of the various parties work actively to build interest groups among peasants and workers and compete for the loyalties of the pressure groups. Having won them, they are expected to look out for the concerns of the groups.

Although more attention is being paid by political groups to the national legislature these days, the tendency persists to seek conflict resolution from the executive branch of the government. The fragmented nature of the Venezuelan legislature increases the responsibility of the executive in considering the demands of the pressure groups.

SEVEN
STRUCTURES
AND ROLES
IN THE CONVERSION
PROCESS
The national government

We have seen that the state governments of Venezuela are insignificant in terms of power and authority and do not exist at all in Paraguay. Therefore, it is to the national government and its branches that we must turn our attention.

The powers of the national governments in the two countries are extensive, indeed. In addition to those with which the federal government in the United States is endowed, the Venezuelan government has exclusive jurisdiction over low-cost housing, the judicial system for the nation, conservation and development of agriculture, fisheries, livestock, and forests, and the operation and administration of mines, saltbeds, and hydrocarbons. It may also legislate on education, public works, civil, criminal, commercial, and penitentiary codes and procedures, lotteries, racetracks, betting, tourism, elections, nationalization of industries, expropriation, agrarian reform, and many others.

In unitary Paraguay, the central government exercises all the powers authorized in the constitution, powers similar to those enjoyed by the central government in Venezuela.

Both countries subscribe to the doctrine of separation of powers, and thus the powers of the government are allocated among the three branches of government: executive, legislative, and judicial. The thesis of this section is that because of the authoritarian tradition in which Venezuela and Paraguay have developed, the functional separation of powers has not prevented the executive branch of government from dominating the entire political structure. Paraguay has always been a presidential dictatorship; Venezuela, equally so up to the end of the Gómez era. In the present era of coalition government and the emergence of a Congress not controlled by the president's party, the legislature in Venezuela is gaining in importance and influence. The Paraguayan legislature, however, is still an assembly of presidential employees.

THE EXECUTIVE BRANCH OF GOVERNMENT

Venezuela—his excellency, El Jefe Máximo

Before discussing the nature of the office of the presidency in Venezuela, it might be useful to review the careers of several of its occupants. Many of the presidents of Venezuela have been military caudillos: Antonio Páez, José Monagas, Guzmán Blanco, Vicente Gómez, Pérez Jiménez, and others. All of these men exemplify the man on horseback: colorful, vigorous executives, driven by personal ambition and a thirst for power. One of the most interesting of the lot, and a prototype of the Latin American rural, regional caudillo who made good through rude strength was Juan Vicente Gómez, a native of the Andean state of Táchira.

The illegitimate son of a Spanish immigrant and an Indian mother, Gómez is reputed to have fathered about 100 children during his marriageless life.[1] This *táchirense* cowboy, a natural leader, managed to educate himself and became a keen and wily observer of human nature. His political star began to rise when he joined forces with the "Lion of the Andes," caudillo Cipriano Castro, who later made him his vice-president. After usurping the presidency from Castro in 1909, Gómez moved quickly to realize his goals of absolute power and great wealth. He reached both. Through one device or another he came into possession of enormous properties, some of the choicest in Venezuela. Political power rested on his army, which he reorganized, modernized, nationalized, and revitalized, fashioning it into a very effective and loyal base of personal power. Political

[1] Edwin Lieuwen, *Venezuela,* 2d ed. (London: Oxford University Press, 1965), p. 46. See also pages 47–48.

parties were abolished, the press muzzled, his critics silenced with jail, exile, and death, and the legislature reduced to a nonentity. He is said to have personally selected every member of his congresses, the states obediently ratifying his choices. One *gomecista* legislator, stung by criticism about the servility of the legislature vis-à-vis Gómez retorted, "Everyone knows that orders accompanied every bill not to change so much as a comma."

Gómez represents the backwoodsman, rustic caudillo; Marcos Pérez Jiménez the professionally trained military elitist. Like Gómez, Pérez Jiménez was a native of Táchira. He was 21 years old when the dictator died. His mother had been a schoolteacher and his father was a farmer and a tradesman. Pérez Jiménez began his military career when at the age of 17 he entered the military academy founded by Gómez in the city of Maracay. He was a brilliant student and graduated with honors. Later he was sent to an artillery school in Lima, Peru. His military experience and expertise were acquired academically and were primarily of a theoretical nature. Gómez obtained his from the rough-and-tumble game of regional politics in the Andes.

Obsessed with desire for public order, Pérez Jiménez saw his mission as that of saving turbulent Venezuela from herself, in other words to impose authoritarian rule via the military and thus end the "constitutional anarchy" seen in free speech and public criticism of government leaders.

Pérez Jiménez slowly rose to power. Becoming chief of the general staff following the 1945 revolution in which he played a part, it took him seven more years before he reached the presidency. His first step was to assist in the overthrow of President Rómulo Gallegos in 1948. After that, he was successively a member of the military junta and the government junta and then provisional president. He became constitutional president in 1953 at the age of 39. He promptly put into force his authoritarian notions. A constant counselor was Vallanilla Lanz, son of the author of *Cesarismo Democrático*.

Arriving in bulletproof cars and surrounded by officers, Pérez Jiménez and his retinue appeared before Congress and in public ceremonies resplendent in bemedaled military uniforms. Military dictatorship was the rule of the day.

In striking contrast to Gómez and Pérez Jiménez have been the civilian presidents—Rómulo Betancourt, Raúl Leoni, and Rafael Caldera—whose political careers were fashioned through political parties and the electoral process. This is not to say that they were not militant activists, for they were part of the Generation of 1928, which earned its spurs by openly opposing Gómez.

The career of Rafael Caldera is illustrative of the new breed of Venezuelan executives. Author, lawyer, professor, intellectual, and head and founder of COPEI, Caldera was born in the north-central state of Yaracuy. After taking a law degree he went on to earn a doctorate in political science in 1939. He has taught sociology and labor legislation at the Central University of Venezuela and is the author of a widely used text on labor law.

Since 1941, when he was elected to the congress as a deputy from Yaracuy, he has been attorney general, deputy minister of the National Labor Office, and president of the Venezuelan Chamber of Deputies. He ran for the presidency as the candidate of COPEI in 1947, 1958, 1963, and 1969, when he was finally elected. His attitude toward power is contained in his victory statement: "The turnover of power in Venezuela next March will mark the natural birth of a new political regime and not that of a new government born by Caesarian operation." Caldera has been described as an eloquent orator with a strong appeal to Venezuela's growing middle class, and a man who exercises considerable appeal for youth and the anticommunist left.

Presidential powers have always been extensive in Venezuela. How effectively and broadly they are used depends upon the man who occupies the office. In the days of the irresponsible military dictators who had power bases in extraconstitutional sources, they were implemented with little regard for the constitution. The 1961 constitution attempts to saddle the president with some degree of responsibility by requiring approval of other bodies for certain of his actions. Thus the president's powers fall into three categories: those which he may exercise independently through the appropriate minister; those which require the consent of the Council of Ministers or cabinet; and those that call for the concurrence of the congress or its Delegated Committee, a body that functions as a miniature congress when the parent body is not in session. These restrictions are operative in direct proportion to the power and influence of the president vis-à-vis the legislature. It may be repeated at this point that although the presidency of Venezuela still carries with it enormous power, recent presidents have been more responsive to the restrictions than their predecessors. The president swears to uphold and enforce the constitution and all national laws. His willingness to do so when his personal power is in jeopardy depends, as has been suggested, upon the nature of his political socialization. Since 1936, with the notable exception of Pérez Jiménez, the Venezuelan presidents have demonstrated their respect for the rule of law.

The president's independent powers include the right to appoint and remove his ministers, state governors, and all other national officials whose appointment and removal are assigned to him by law; to direct foreign affairs and to make and ratify international treaties, conventions, and agreements; to administer the national finances; to grant pardons; to call meetings of the state governors for the purpose of coordinating national and state administration; and, in his capacity as commander in chief of the national armed forces, to fix their size.

Acting with the advice and consent of his Council of Ministers, the president may declare a state of emergency during which constitutional guarantees may be totally or partially suspended up to ninety days; adopt all measures necessary to preserve and defend the republic in the case of international provocation; issue administrative regulations insofar as they do not change the intent of the law; negotiate foreign loans; make contracts in the national interest; and call special sessions of Congress.

The president needs the authorization of Congress if it is in session, or of the Delegated Committee if it is not, to create new public services or modify and abolish existing ones; to decree additional sums of money to the national budget; and to appoint the attorney general of the republic and the chiefs of the permanent diplomatic missions.

These powers taken in the aggregate bestow a tremendous amount of authority on the president and overshadow the modest grants to Congress. If there is any one section of the

1961 constitution that can be said to reflect the reality of Venezuelan politics, it is that dealing with executive powers. It is in harmony with the Latin American regard for a strong and vigorous executive. The restrictions on his powers are in effect attempts to eliminate the abuses of previous administrations.

Consider, for example, the presidential power to allocate new money to the national budget after it has been passed by Congress. He does this by executive decree from money that has accumulated in the Special Reserve Fund. Large cash surpluses accumulate in the Venezuelan treasury as a result of deliberate governmental practice of underestimating the national revenue. Since 1944, the president, acting upon data supplied by the minister of public finance, has had the power to transfer these surpluses from the treasury to the Special Reserve Fund. It is from this fund that a president may decree expenditures of sums not authorized in the budget. Under Juan Vicente Gómez, large amounts were assigned to "extraordinary expenditures of public service as they occur." Much of the 363 million dollars allocated in this way between 1914 and 1942 found its way into private pockets. It proved to be impossible to account for the money since it was customary to credit the funds in a lump sum without specifying details relative to their expenditure or control.

President López Contreras in 1936 and 1937 authorized additional expenditures totaling 40 percent of the original budget. Figures between 20 and 40 percent can be cited for almost every year since then. During the regime of Marcos Pérez Jiménez there were virtually no effective restrictions on his power to allocate national fiscal surpluses as he saw fit. It is true that he needed the consent of his Council of Ministers, but that body was absolutely subservient to him. Thus, the Special Reserve Fund was for Pérez Jiménez a source of tremendous political power and allegedly of great personal enrichment. The 1961 constitution attempts to remedy the abuses in handling the surpluses by requiring the president to seek the permission of Congress or of the Delegated Committee. It is impossible to say at this point in time how effective a restriction this requirement is. It does seem reasonable to conclude that since the president's party no longer controls the Congress or its Delegated Committee, he may no longer disregard that body in fiscal matters.

Another use of the decree power should be noted. Like most other Latin American executives, the Venezuelan president is authorized to suspend individual guarantees when, in his opinion and that of the Council of Ministers, situations arise that create or could create national or international emergencies. The law requires him to submit the suspension decree to Congress within ten days together with his reasons. A state of emergency in no way affects the functioning or existence of the other branches of the national government. These restrictions have meaning only in the sense that the president is willing to live up to them, or that he does not have the power to violate them with impunity. Both of these conditions are valid today. Presidents Betancourt and Leoni used the decree power to curb terrorism and Communist agitation. President Rafael Caldera will undoubtedly have to also.

The Venezuelan executive has also used his decree power to bring about far-reaching governmental changes without consulting Congress. He formerly could establish new public services or abolish or modify existing ones, provided the Council of Ministers approved. Because he normally controlled the Council of Ministers, this requirement was in no way a restraint. Under the 1961 constitution, however, the executive branch of government has lost its independent right to create, modify, or abolish public services. The president must now seek the approval of Congress, or of its Delegated Committee should Congress be in recess. Venezuelan executives have made repeated use of this important power. President López Contreras created the Ministries of Agriculture and Livestock, and Health and Social Welfare in 1936. The governing junta in 1950 set up the Ministries of Justice and Mines and Hydrocarbons.

A more frequent exercise of the decree power has involved the creation of the so-called autonomous institutes. An autonomous institute is a quasi-governmental body possessing a definite legal personality and properties distinct from and independent of the National Treasury. The establishment of many of these independent agencies involved an initial investment of large sums of public money and the appointment of administrative personnel. In 1946 the Venezuelan Development Corporation was created to stimulate economic growth and domestic investment by providing financial assistance to private business and agriculture. Today it has assets of over one-half billion dollars. During the 1950s many other agencies were founded by the executive. They include the National Institute of Sanitary Works, the Venezuelan Airmail Line, the National Agrarian Institute, the Institute of University City, and the Central Institute of Social Insurance. During the period between the overthrow of Marcos Pérez Jiménez and the adoption of the 1961 constitution, several very important agencies were decreed by the executive. The Venezuelan Petroleum Corporation (1960) is responsible for developing and exploiting Venezuela's enormous oil resources. A companion is the Venezuelan Petrochemical Institute (1961), which plans for the expansion of the petrochemical industry. Perhaps the most ambitious of the agencies is the Venezuelan Guayana Corporation, charged with creating a diversified industrial complex in the heart of the Guayana region in eastern Venezuela. Millions of domestic and foreign dollars are being invested in this mighty undertaking. There are presently some forty-two autonomous agencies operating in Venezuela.

President Raúl Leoni (1964–1969) used his decree powers in yet another field. For example, by executive order he created an experimental University of Caracas to train professional personnel for the economic and social development needs of the country, and modified an existing university by converting the Experimental Center of Higher Education, located in the State of Lara, into the University of the Central Western Region.

Presidential powers are formally exercised through the media of two executive institutions: the Cabinet and the Council of Ministers. Actually, these two bodies are practically identical in personnel. "Cabinet" is the term used to designate the heads of the thirteen executive departments. The Council of Ministers, on the other hand, refers to the formal meetings of these officials under the chairmanship of the president.

Ministers are appointed by the president, are responsible to him, and in practice serve at his pleasure. Under present constitutional arrangements, ministers are partially responsible to the Chamber of Deputies, which has the power to vote a motion of censure against a minister or ministers. The president is required by law to remove a censured minister if the Chamber so directs by a two-thirds vote.

The use of the censure power by the Chamber of Deputies is infrequent. It never happened before the advent of the present era of constitutional government. In June 1963, however, the Chamber of Deputies censured the minister of the interior for ignoring a Chamber order to free a Communist deputy whom the executive branch had detained for alleged participation in the terrorist activities of the last year of the Betancourt administration. The vote of censure was possible because opposition parties controlled the Chamber of Deputies. The censured minister later was replaced.

Although the ministers are the legal agents of the president, they are nevertheless held accountable for all their official acts even when they are carrying out the direct and express orders of the president. All ministers in attendance at Council meetings are jointly and individually held responsible for decisions taken by the Council unless they cast an adverse vote.

Procedurely, the Council of Ministers reaches a collective decision by a two-thirds vote. Deliberations are secret. The governor of the Federal District, appointed by the president, is entitled by law to a seat on the Council and to a voice and vote on all matters pertaining to the Federal District. Each minister is expected to inform other members of the Council concerning matters he intends to discuss and to supply them with pertinent information.

Coalition government, begun in 1959, has considerably diminished the president's control over the ministers of his cabinet. Needing the support of parties other than his own in forming a government, he must now and then defer to their wishes. In President Caldera's cabinet, for example, only five of the thirteen ministries are in the hands of men from his Social Christian party. The rest are manned by political independents, as is the post of governor of the Federal District. Prior to 1959 the ministers were little more than employees. Pérez Jiménez treated his Council of Ministers more as a team of technical experts than as a deliberative body. His weekly Council meetings rarely lasted longer than two hours and were very businesslike. He and his predecessors seldom countenanced contrary opinions and the ministers who offended in this respect were quickly eliminated from the cabinet. The device by which this usually was accomplished was the well-established custom of mass resignation of the cabinet. This action was always publicly held to be a voluntary and patriotic move on the part of the cabinet to give the president a free hand to make the changes he desired. The dismissal of a minister is rarely made openly. In the majority of cases, cabinet resignation *en masse* has been followed by the reappointment of most of the ministers, either to their former posts or to different portfolios.

Between 1936 and the end of the Pérez Jiménez regime in 1958, more than thirty such reorganizations took place, the majority of them occurring in the administrations of López Contreras and Medina Angarita. President Betancourt (AD) also had trouble with his cabinet. The Democratic Republican Union (URD) party forsook him in 1960, and this brought about a major cabinet change. During his five years in office, Betancourt had four different ministers of interior and defense; three of public works, education, labor, and justice; and two of agriculture, communications, and mines and hydrocarbons. Only one of his original appointments in 1959 finished office with him. President Leoni was more fortunate. Although his first cabinet collapsed in 1966 when his coalition partners temporarily withdrew, he managed to finish his term with six of his thirteen original appointments still in the same posts. Several of the other seven served as long as three years before going out of office. A good many of these changes in the Betancourt and Leoni administrations resulted from policy differences among ministers from different parties.

The thirteen ministers of the cabinet have a right to a voice in both houses of the national legislature and in their committees. Furthermore, they must attend either house when requested to do so to give a report or answer interpolations. Every minister submits to a joint session of Congress a long and detailed annual report (*Memoria*) on the activities of his department and an announcement of his plans for the forthcoming year.

Other than observing the constitutional requirement that ministers must have the same qualifications for office as the president, the latter has a free hand in selecting his department heads. No congressional consent is necessary. Prior to 1961 the military fo·ces were always represented. In the case of President Rómulo Gallegos (1948), this was a recognition of the continued importance and influence of the armed forces in the political system. In the case of military presidents, such as López Contreras and Marcos Pérez Jiménez, appointment of military personnel may be regarded as placating power factions within the military establishment, thus making presidential tenure more secure.

Before the Revolution of 1945, presidents often appointed their personal friends to office with little regard for professional competence in the field over which they were to have jurisdiction. This disregard led one Venezuelan observer to lament:

> A poet is chosen to be judge; one who knows nothing of numbers is appointed to be treasurer and a man who is ignorant of geology becomes an inspector of mines. The same thing happens with military, political and administrative officers. It is surprising that until now they have not selected a field marshal to be a hospital physician.[2]

Matters have changed considerably since that was written in 1891. The new agrarian, industrial and economic plans of modern Venezuela call for expertise in planning and a high degree of professional competence and training. The tendency, therefore, has been for the president to seek the best qualified men in his own and other parties to serve in his cabinet and in other appointive positions. The cabinet in office at the end of 1969 included the former president of the National Banking Association, a woman economist, a former official of the International Labor Organization, two former ministers of development under President Betancourt, and several men with congressional experience. One of the five posts held by COPEI went to Caldera's campaign manager, the powerful Ministry of Public Works. In terms of patronage, the minister of public works would be comparable to the postmaster general of the United States. The large number of changes in administrative personnel, however, tends to impair the efficiency of the cabinet, as ministers prior to 1963 were in office hardly long enough to learn the rudiments of their job before they either resign or are removed.

[2] R. F. Seijas, *El Presidente* (Madrid: Imprenta y Lit. Terceno, 1891), p. 72.

Attached to the president's office are two important agencies which are expected to contribute to efficient and effective government. One is the Central Office of Coordination and Planning (Cordiplan), which gives the president technical advice on economic and financial matters connected with long-range planning. The second agency is the Public Administration Commission (CAP) whose primary job is to plan for an efficient and competent civil service. CAP also has a training adjunct in the School of Public Administration that has been providing in-service training for public servants since 1962. The continued stability of the government since 1959 has increased its prospects for success.

A perennial problem in Venezuela in the public administration field has been the turnover of personnel whenever a major change of government takes place. In 1947, for example, according to figures released by the treasury, some 39,000 persons were in government service. Of these about 12,000 had less than one year of service and another 12,000 had less than two years. Only 2130 persons had served more than seven years. Although turnover of personnel and incompetence have not been eliminated by any means, the government is trying to remedy some of the more glaring ills. President Caldera, concerned with long-standing complaints about malfeasance and poor service in government offices, appointed late in 1969 an ombudsman-type official called a presidential commissioner to hear citizens' complaints about inefficiency, graft, illegal use of public monies, undue political influence, and other irregularities in the public service. The commissioner will report directly to the president and his advisors. The office is so new that no evaluation can yet be made of its effectiveness. If the experience of other Latin American countries in combatting the same problems is applicable, the presidential commissioner will be unable to bring about any basic improvement. Greater hope lies in the passage of a strong civil service law that will create a merit system and establish procedures and standards for government offices and autonomous agencies. Although such a law has been drafted and considered several times, it has yet to be approved.

In practice, the individual ministers have been reluctant to require civil service tests for their employees. They do not want to relinquish to a central service commission their power of hiring, firing, promoting, and evaluating employees. After the changeover from President Leoni to Rafael Caldera, there were rumors and even newspaper articles about wholesale firings of personnel from the previous administration—even down to such levels as typists and messengers. In general, the Venezuelans feel that the groundwork for a civil service has been laid, but that the political parties will prevent it from becoming a reality because they need to satisfy their party members with government jobs. Until there are sufficient jobs in industry to make competition for government employment less fierce, this situation is likely to continue.

In spite of these drawbacks, however, the Venezuelan public administration is regarded as one of the better ones in Latin America.[3]

The thirteen executive departments of Venezuelan government are similar to those found in most countries. They are the Ministries of Interior, Public Works, Mines and Hydrocarbons, Defense, Education, Health and Social Welfare, Foreign Affairs, Agriculture and Cattle Raising, Justice, Development, Communications, Public Finance, and Labor. Detailed descriptions of the responsibilities of all the ministries seem unnecessary, but several are of such key importance that they require fuller treatment.

Leading the list is the vital and highly political Ministry of the Interior. So important is this post that it is always occupied by a close and trusted colleague of the president. Upon assuming office in 1969, President Caldera appointed Lorenzo Fernández, one of the founding fathers and a vice-president of COPEI. The new minister had previously been a deputy, a senator and, during the Betancourt administration when his party was in coalition with AD, the minister of development. If anyone is privy to the thoughts of the president, it is the interior minister. He translates the will of the president into decrees, edicts, and messages. As spokesman for the president, he convokes the national legislature into extraordinary sessions and administers security measures when a state of emergency is declared.

[3] Harry Kantor, *Patterns of Politics and Political Systems in Latin America* (Skokie, Ill.: Rand McNally, 1969), p. 377.

The Ministry is also the official channel for communications between the various structures of government, national, state, and local. Thus it is the agency with which state governors most often deal, and it arranges the annual governors meetings. It distributes the *situado* and other federal subsidies to the states. It pays the salaries and expenses of the legislative and executive branches of the government and governs the Federal Territories and Dependencies. Other matters under the jurisdiction of the Ministry of Interior are immigration, registration of foreigners, public monuments, holidays, and the security and police forces. Maintenance of law and order is the responsibility of the Ministry.

Formerly, one of the most political tasks of the minister of the interior was the supervision of elections. Through the use of federal subsidies and control of the electoral machinery, and his command of state governors, the minister was rightly regarded as the key agent in the outcome of elections. This was certainly true through the regime of Marcos Pérez Jiménez when election results were made to conform to the expectations of the dictator. Even in 1969 there were indications that matters had not changed much, despite the fact that elections are now in the hands of a Supreme Electoral Commission appointed by the congress. Rafael Caldera, the candidate of COPEI, accused the AD government of tampering with the electoral process during the long-drawn-out tabulation of results. He complained that election results were being sent to the president and the minister of the interior before being communicated to the Supreme Electoral Commission. Interior's reply that matters were proceeding honestly and smoothly did not silence opposition party claims that the administration was, as usual, controlling the election process. Undoubtedly there were electoral irregularities in the election, and they have prompted a demand for revision of the entire electoral apparatus. About 20 percent of the budgeted income of the government is allocated to interior use.

Another powerful and influential ministry is the Ministry of Public Works. It has great resources at its command and until 1968, when the interior ministry took the lead, spent about 20 percent of the normal budget. In fact, however, it usually spends a good deal more than that, for it is the major recipient of additional allocations from the Special Reserve Fund. Because of its involvement in major construction works, it has far-reaching political and economic influence through its award of lucrative contracts. Its jurisdiction extends to planning, constructing, and maintaining highways, ports, airports, irrigation and flood-control projects, waterworks, public buildings, residential buildings for working classes, urban development, and cartography. Some of its work is carried out through interministerial commissions. Medical centers, for example, are planned jointly by the Ministries of Public Works and Health and Social Welfare. Jails are planned by the Ministries of Public Works and Justice; schools by Public Works and Education.

A good deal of inferior construction goes up and it is completed in a hurry, sometimes to meet anniversaries of events that the administration wishes to commemorate. It begins to deteriorate quickly. This leads Venezuelans to believe, rightly or wrongly, that corruption is rife in Public Works. The Ministry—and the government—has at times seemed preoccupied with grandiose and spectacular projects, such as the construction of a hotel on the top of Mt. Ávila overlooking the city of Caracas. The only access to the hotel is by cable car. Since 1959 policy makers have concentrated on more useful and practical projects: irrigation canals, secondary roads, and country schools.

In a developing and industrializing country such as Venezuela, the government has taken an active part in encouraging and fostering national industries and economic growth. The Venezuelan agency primarily responsible for this activity is the Ministry of Development. The wide scope of its concern can be appreciated by noting some of its component offices: industries, economic information, economic geography, economic investigation, electricity, tourism, census, and legal affairs. The Ministry works closely with the autonomous entities discussed above. In all matters involving the mineral wealth of Venezuela, however, the Ministry of Mines and Hydrocarbons has jurisdiction.

The Ministry of Justice, created in 1950, supervises not only the entire judicial structure of Venezuela, but also the penal systems, Indians missions, and Church-state relations.

In 1968 the Venezuelan government budgeted for a total

expenditure of 8295 million bolívares ($2 billion) and in 1969 for 9280 million bolívares ($2.1 billion). The following table shows the breakdown of allocations by departments.[4]

Table 7–1   Budget allocations for 1968 and 1969

| Departments | Millions of bolívares | | Percent, 1969 |
	1968	1969	
Interior	1826.2	1816.7	19.6%
Foreign Affairs	73.7	75.5	0.8
Finance	658.5	599.3	6.5
Defense	889.3	918.6	9.9
Education	1233.8	1351.2	14.6
Development	201.9	232.5	2.5
Public Works	1804.1	1964.6	21.0
Health and Social Welfare	771.2	802.4	8.7
Labor	112.6	127.4	1.4
Agriculture and Livestock	615.7	614.6	6.6
Communications	320.8	312.7	3.4
Justice	230.0	232.0	2.5
Mines and Hydrocarbons	179.3	196.2	2.1
Unallocated Adjustments	47.9	35.8	0.4
	8965.0	9280.0	100.0%

El Supremo, President of Paraguay

It is not necessary to repeat here the description of the most famous Paraguayan presidents: Dr. Francia and the two Lópezes. All three men exercised power in a highly personal and authoritarian manner. Between 1870 and 1970 only a few men stand out as being anything exceptional.

General Bernardino Caballero was both president (1880–1886) and president-maker until 1904 when a Liberal revolt ended the power of the Conservatives, with whom he was identified. Among the many Liberal presidents who rapidly followed one another during the next thirty-one years, perhaps the most outstanding was Eusebio Ayala (1921–1923 and 1932–1935). He has been described as a man of outstanding intellectual gifts, familiar with the law, Darwin, and Spencer. He also

[4] Embassy of Venezuela, *Venezuela Up-to-date,* 12 (Winter 1968–1969), 13, and 12 (Spring 1968), 25.

found time to travel, to lecture, and to write essays on history and education.[5]

In the new Paraguay—1935 to the present—the political scene has been dominated by Generals Higinio Morínigo and Alfredo Stroessner, both of whom governed under the 1940 constitution, brainchild of yet another general: José Felix Estigarribia.

Although the path to power for almost all of these men was through force rather than the ballot, the law patiently requires that the president must be elected directly by the people through compulsory universal suffrage. Candidates must be natural-born citizens, Roman Catholics, and 40 years of age. The president is forbidden to serve more than two consecutive terms, but President Stroessner has been able, by manipulating Congress, to serve sixteen years so far. An important motivation for revising the constitution in 1967 was Stroessner's desire to free himself from the obnoxious two-term limitation. The new document specifically permits Stroessner to serve an additional ten years, or two more terms.

The powers and influence of the Paraguayan president are preponderantly greater in scope than are those of the Venezuelan executive, and he is far less fettered by constitutional restrictions and political obstructionism than is his Venezuelan counterpart. Indeed, Paraguay has never known anything but heavy-handed executive control. The political culture of the country and also the conditioning influence of its history and leaders have not encouraged the Paraguayans to expect a balanced form of government in which all three branches of government play an effective role. The present constitutional arrangement accurately reflects the basic political realities and intergovernmental relationships.

The president possesses all the powers of the Venezuelan president and more. His appointment powers are vast. Practically every person in public administration depends upon *el presidente* for his job. Since there is no civil service or merit system, a swollen bureaucracy and some 50,000 public employees serve at the pleasure of the president. Almost all of

[5] George Pendle, *Paraguay, A Riverside Nation,* 3d ed. (London: Oxford University Press, 1967), p. 30.

these people are members of the Colorado party, the civilian political power base of the president. The chief executive has a free hand in the appointment and removal of members of his official family. He appoints the members of the Council of State and, with its advice and the concurrence of the Senate, appoints the five judges of the Supreme Court of Justice, the attorney general of the republic, and all diplomatic representatives. With the advice of the Supreme Court of Justice, the president appoints all other judges in the land, including the most lowly justice of the peace. Presidential appointments are always confirmed.

Although members of the legislature are elected by the people of the country in one large electoral district, the president has a great deal to say about whose name shall appear on the ballot and, indeed, who shall ultimately win.

Those whom the president appoints may also be removed by him. The constitutional guarantees of judicial independence and term tenure of the judges, for instance, means very little. The president can and does discharge these functionaries pretty much at will. Legal justification for such acts can always be concocted.

In his role as commander in chief of the armed forces, the president is solely responsible for commissioning and promoting officers up through the grade of lieutenant colonel. Higher ranks need the approval of his obedient Senate. Furthermore, the president determines the size, organization, distribution, and budget of the armed forces, and Congress gives its approval. Persons with military ambitions are thus dependent upon the goodwill of the president for advancement in their chosen careers. With the authorization of Congress, the president may declare war and negotiate peace. In Paraguay, as we have seen, this power is not without meaning. It does not appear in the Venezuelan constitution at all.

Like the Venezuelan president, the Paraguayan executive may use his emergency powers to declare a state of siege in all or part of the land. Unlike his Venezuelan counterpart, he may do so without consulting anyone. He is required to inform Congress within ten days of his reasons for doing so, but that is no restriction. A state-of-siege power in Paraguay, as in all countries of Latin America where it exists, permits the president to suspend some or all of the constitutional rights of the citizens. Article 79 of the 1967 charter, which confers this authority on the president, contains several interesting provisions that point to past abuses. Persons who are suspected of initiating or participating in the events that provoked the state of emergency may be arrested, confined, or moved from one part of the republic to another. They may not, however, be incarcerated in dirty or unhealthy quarters, nor may they be sent to pestilential or unpopulated regions.

The president's fiscal powers are enormous and stem from several sources. First, as chief of state, he has charge of the general administration of the country. Second, he prepares and submits the national budget to Congress for its approval. Third, he collects, invests, and spends the public revenue authorized in his budget. He is required to render a yearly account of his administration, but there is no effective control over him.

When the budget message is received by the Chamber of Deputies, to which it must first be sent, it has absolute priority over all other business. The Chamber must make a decision within thirty days and transmit the budget to the Senate, which must reach its decision in a similar period. If the legislature is unable to agree on the budget in the time allowed, it is considered approved anyway and goes into effect. To reject a budget—an unheard of event—the Congress needs a two-thirds vote in both houses. Neither situation arises, because the president's party controls two-thirds of the seats in both houses of the legislature. The president, therefore, so long as he remains in control of the party, has a free hand in raising and spending the public monies.

Not only is the Paraguayan president the chief of state, chief executive, commander in chief, and chief of administration, he is also in effect the chief legislator. He opens the ordinary sessions of Congress with a message and recommendations concerning the measures he wishes to see enacted. He can convene Congress in special sessions and can prorogue it before the end of its yearly session of five months.

He introduces bills in both houses and through his ministers participates in their discussion at any point in the legislative process. All bills submitted by the executive branch must be disposed of one way or another in the same session. If

Congress does not act upon them, the bills become law automatically upon the adjournment of the legislature. Either way, then, the will of the president prevails.

Another legislative power of the chief executive is his right to issue decrees that carry the force of law. He may do this only during the period between December 21 and April 1 when Congress is not in session. The technical requirement that he consult the Council of State before issuing such a decree has no practical meaning because that body is composed of his appointees and is submissive to him. The stipulation that he submit all decrees to Congress when it next meets for that body's approval, rejection or modification, is hardly more meaningful. Presented with a *fait accompli,* Congress never fails to approve his decrees. The decree power extends to all matters within the jurisdiction of the government and must be considered one of the most useful of the president's prerogatives. The president has used his decree powers to establish government services and autonomous institutes similar to those in Venezuela. The Social Welfare Institute, which oversees the system of compulsory insurance in Paraguay, was created by executive order in 1943 and has been modified similarly several times since then.

Other clues point to the extremely powerful position of the president vis-à-vis the other branches of government. There is, for example, not a word in the constitution about his impeachment or removal from office. The absence of such a provision points to the influence of President Stroessner in the constitutional convention of 1967 and to the political realism of its delegates. Although his ministers are declared to be individually and collectively responsible for their legal actions, it is to the president rather than to Congress that they must account. Congress has no power to censure them, much less cause their removal from office. Ministers submit their annual reports to the president and not to Congress as they do in Venezuela. Again, in constitutional provisions such as these, the Paraguayan people were merely legalizing a relationship that had always existed.

The president of Paraguay possesses a power not given to the Venezuelan leader. On his own authority, he may dissolve Congress for serious causes. What those causes are and when they occur is up to him to determine. One cause is criticism. The president dissolved Congress in 1965 after the legislature had criticized his regime for police brutality. If the dissolved Congress has more than a year left of its five-year mandate, the dissolution decree must call for the election of a new one within three months.

The president carries out his duties through the media of ten government departments: interior, foreign affairs, finance, industry and commerce, agriculture and livestock, public health and welfare, public works and communication, labor and justice, education and religion, and defense. One minister serves without portfolio. The functions and duties of the Paraguayan ministries are similar to those of the Venezuelan government. Generals are always included in the cabinet and they occupy sensitive posts: defense, public works and communication, finance, and agriculture. General Barrientos, who has been with Stroessner since he came to power in 1954, holds down the latter two. There have been remarkably few changes in cabinet personnel since 1957. Ministers, therefore, have time to learn their jobs. Because they are good party members, they can expect a reasonably long tenure. Without an efficient bureaucracy, however, their effectiveness is greatly diminished.

The Council of State is an agency attached to the executive branch of government. The president is expected to consult it before he appoints the attorney general, and to solicit its advice on foreign affairs, economic and financial matters, and on decree laws. Although these provisions seem to add up to some power for the Council, they actually do not. The Council of State is a purely advisory body which gives an opinion only when asked for one. Its members are appointed by the president and include the ministers of his cabinet, the president of the Central Bank of Paraguay, the rector of the Central University, the Archbishop of Asunción, three military officers, and five men representing the fields of agriculture, livestock, industry, commerce, and labor. Despite its impressive membership, the Council of State is of little consequence in the real pattern of power.

The attorney general of Paraguay, a presidential appointee, combines the functions of the attorney general and the prosecutor general of Venezuela. He heads the Public Ministry and is charged with the protection of individual guarantees and constitutional liberties of the citizens vis-à-vis public officials. At the same time he represents the government in all proceedings to which it is a party. By terms of the constitution, he must hold a law degree, have had judicial experience, and have a spotless reputation for honesty. He, too, reports annually to the president rather than to Congress.

Despite the presence of a U.S.-supported School of Public Administration that has been operating since 1959, the Paraguayan bureaucracy is still in a primitive state. Nepotism and inefficiency are rife and presidential favor all important and pervasive. Each of the ministries has its own personnel office and is not subject to any central personnel authority.

In comparing the two executive systems, the conclusion is inescapable that the Venezuelan is more responsible to the needs of the people, is more clearly hedged with effective restraints and more clearly shares its power with the other branches of government. In both systems, however, the executive is still the dominant element in government and is controlled by the elite segments of society.

THE LEGISLATIVE BRANCH OF GOVERNMENT

Venezuela—an assembly of employees?

Before embarking on a discussion of the legislature in Venezuela, it would be well to reemphasize a point made earlier. Prior to 1959, the constitutional provisions outlining the powers and prerogatives of Congress were for the most part meaningless words. The legislature was in no position to limit or curb the executive or, indeed, to exercise its own powers independently of him. For over 100 years, the legislators were little more than personal employees of the president. So low had their state sunk by 1890 that it was caustically written of them:

> Those employees do little else on their own initiative but to erect a statue or approve a decree according honors to the president or to concede him additional titles. In doing so they proclaim to the face of the earth their absolute submission to him who names them, gives them lucrative employment and humors them when they ask for something.[6]

[6] Seijas, p. 20.

In earlier epochs the legislators were expected to give the president unquestioned obedience. They had learned the hard way. In 1848 an unruly Congress tried to impeach President José Monagas. The mob action he angrily instigated led to the death of three deputies in the legislative chambers. This *tour de force* ended a modest trend toward constitutional government; the legislature was made subservient to the president and dictatorial fiat became the law of the land.[7] This situation persisted until the fall of Pérez Jiménez in 1958 and the establishment of a democratic system in 1959.

The changed political climate, the growing sense of responsible government, and the loss of control of Congress by the administration party have made it possible for the legislature to realize more fully than ever before its constitutional powers and authority. Since 1959 it has been an effective and sometimes obstructive partner in the government structure and has been increasing in power vis-à-vis the executive branch. This is not to say, however, that the president and his ministers have lost their dominant voice in political affairs. It does mean that perhaps unfettered domination of the legislature by the president is over at last.

The Venezuelan Congress is a bicameral legislature composed of a Senate and a Chamber of Deputies. The artificial Senate represents the artificial states of the republic, and the Chamber of Deputies represents the people of the several states. Prior to 1961, with the exception of a brief period during which the 1947 constitution was in effect, senators were chosen by the state legislatures dominated by the state governor who was an appointee of the president. This arrangement gave the Venezuelan presidents considerable influence in determining who would sit in the upper house. The Senate now is composed of two senators from each state and the Federal District, elected on the basis of universal suffrage. Senators must be at least 30 years of age and natural-born Venezuelans. In addition to the forty-two senators, additional ones may be won in the states by the political parties on the basis of proportional representation and a national quotient. At the present time there are fifty-two

[7] W. H. Pierson, "Foreign Influences on Venezuelan Political Thought, 1830–1930," *Hispanic American Historical Review,* 15 (February 1935), 18.

senators, twelve of whom owe their seats to proportional representation and the quotient.

Each state is entitled to one deputy in the Chamber of Deputies for every 50,000 inhabitants and one additional deputy for any final fraction that exceeds 25,000 people. Regardless of population, each of the states is guaranteed two deputies. The fixed number of deputies in 1969 was 197. Additional members are added, as in the case of the Senate, by means of proportional representation. At the present time there are 213 deputies. They, too, must be native-born and at least 21 years of age.

The terms of both senators and deputies are five years and coincide with that of the president of the republic. Sessions of Congress extend from March 2 to July 6 and from October 1 to November 30. An absolute majority voting in a joint session can extend the regular session if the legislative calendar demands. The president has the power to call Congress into special session, a right he shares with the Delegated Committee of Congress. There have been numerous special sessions during the last ten years.

Congress may legislate on all matters that are within the jurisdiction of the national government. Each house of Congress has some exclusive powers. As in the Congress of the United States, tax and revenue bills and the budget must be introduced into the lower house, while those involving treaties and international agreements go first to the Senate, which must also consent to some of the president's diplomatic and military appointments.

The Chamber of Deputies alone may censure cabinet ministers. The Senate authorizes impeachment of the president before the Supreme Court if that body has found grounds for such action.

The legislative process followed in Venezuela is almost identical with that of the Congress of the United States, except that in Venezuela only two readings instead of three as in the United States are required before a bill is sent to the president.

Bills may be introduced not only by the executive branch and members of Congress, but also by the petition of 20,000 voters and by the Supreme Court when judicial matters are involved.

The president is required to promulgate the law within

ten days after its receipt or return it with his objections. The elaborate procedures involved in overriding a presidential veto were, until 1969, little more than rational approaches to the problem of containing a willful president. They represented more aspiration than reality. The provisions are as follows. After receiving the law from Congress, the president may ask Congress within ten days to reconsider its action, to amend certain portions of the bill, or to withdraw its sanction of the bill. The two houses of Congress in joint session decide on the points raised by the president. If the results of their reconsideration have been adopted by two-thirds of the members present, the president of the republic must promulgate the bill within five days and may offer no further objections. If, however, Congress reaches a decision by only a simple majority, the president may choose between promulgating it or returning it to Congress once more for a new and final reconsideration. This time, the action of Congress is definitive, even if taken by simple majority vote.

Before promulgating it, the president may raise the issue of constitutionality and ask the Supreme Court for a ruling. If the Court rules in favor of the law, the president must enforce it (Article 173, constitution of 1961).

These procedures were used for the first time in 1969 during a dispute between Congress and the president over a law affecting the president's power to make judicial appointments. In what seemed to be a move to hamper the president and to curb his patronage powers, AD pushed a bill through Congress removing the power to appoint judicial officials below the Supreme Court from the minister of justice to a special committee. The committee was to be made up of the five judges from the political section of the Supreme Court, all of whom are members of AD or URD; two members from Congress, where AD is the largest single party; and two members appointed by the government. President Caldera was adamantly opposed to the bill, and vetoed it. After sending the law to the president, Congress adjourned for the summer. Upon learning of the presidential veto, AD immediately announced it would ask the Delegated Committee to reconvene Congress in a special session to consider President Caldera's action rather than wait until October when Congress would reassemble for its regular fall session. The matter was of some urgency to both sides, as the minister of justice would be appointing the new judges in August.

The Delegated Committee, controlled by opposition party members, convoked Congress into extraordinary session. The bill was repassed with some minor modifications. The president still found the legislation unsatisfactory and again returned it with his objections. Congress speedily overrode the veto once more, whereupon President Caldera resorted to his constitutional privilege of asking the Court to rule on the constitutionality of the law. The Supreme Court, by a vote of 8 to 7 upheld the law and thus administered a severe defeat to the president. For the first time in Venezuelan history, a president had been rebuffed by both his Congress and Court. It now appears that if Congress is firm in its resolve, has the votes, and is willing to carry the battle to the end, its will can prevail over that of the executive, provided the latter observes the rules of the game. Executive power being what it is, the president will not ordinarily let himself be maneuvered into a position in which he risks political defeat by his Congress. The fact that President Caldera found himself in this position in 1969 reveals much about the changed relationship between the executive and Congress and about the changing strengths of the country's political parties.

In recent years, Congress has shown an increasing tendency to take the initiative in proposing legislation. Yet an overwhelming majority of important laws originate with the executive, as is the case in most countries. Even in these days of increased congressional influence and participation in the conversion process, originators of bills will still try to ascertain the attitude of the president toward their proposals. In the authoritarian systems of the recent past, a bill that was unopposed by the president would ordinarily move through the legislature quickly and without much fuss. One to which he objected rarely got far.

In the changed political circumstances of present-day Venezuela, with Congress firmly in the hands of parties unsympathetic to the president, executive proposals often get short shrift. President Caldera has had his legislative proposals amended almost beyond recognition and passed by the Congress despite his objections, or delayed for long periods of time.

President Caldera was particularly dismayed by the failure of Congress in 1969 to approve the oil service contracts that he had submitted. Discussion on the fundamental principles of the regulation of the oil industry and the terms under which the companies would operate had been going on for over six years, reaching back into the administration of former president Leoni (AD). President Caldera presented his legislation to Congress in its 1969 fall session with the expectation that it would be passed and that oil contracts could be signed by December 4. AD, URD, and several minor parties dashed those hopes. A special congressional committee failed to agree on its recommendations by the time Congress adjourned on December 20. Thus a bill to which the administration attached importance and priority second only to the budget failed to win early congressional approval. The legislation was finally approved in a special session in August 1970.

Some of the bills introduced by the congressmen have had the clear intent of harassing the administration. Consider, for example, the threat of AD to introduce legislation that would change the present presidential system into a parliamentary one. Another example is a law, introduced and pushed through Congress by AD, that decreases the authority and patronage powers of the government in the field of labor relations. The law passed by Congress requires the appointment of a union representative on the board of directors of every institute and company in which the government has a controlling voice. This provision can only benefit AD with its strong roots in organized labor, as COPEI has relatively little influence with the unions.

Another power that figures prominently in the relations between the executive and legislative branches of government is that of the purse. Over the years the Venezuelan Congresses have had remarkably little to say about the disposition and expenditures of the public funds. They did what they they were told by the omnipotent president. The 1953 constitution of Marcos Pérez Jiménez carried a not uncommon provision that if Congress had not approved the president's budget by the end of the fiscal year, it would go into effect anyway. That stipulation was removed in the 1961 constitution.

Until 1960, the legislature rarely showed a disposition to oppose the president on fiscal matters. Indeed, they had little opportunity to do so because the budget message was often presented to the legislature so late in the fiscal year that it could little more than give it a most casual perusal. Since 1960, however, Venezuelan presidents have had their troubles with Congress. In 1962, for example, the Chamber of Deputies, controlled by opposition parties, made significant changes in the budget before sending it on to the Senate. It increased the allocations in education and national debt payments and cut defense appropriations by 11 million bolívares. The National Agrarian Institute's funds were also cut by 21 million bolívares. In the latter case, Congress was motivated by the corruption that a Chamber investigating committee had discovered in the Institute. The Senate accepted the changes with little discussion.

Executive-legislative relations on budgetary matters have deteriorated rapidly since President Caldera assumed the presidency in March 1969. Opposition parties spearheaded by AD soon indicated their unwillingness to meet the administration's fiscal demands. The new president found that he had inherited a large public-works deficit from the previous AD administration and discovered that funds for operating the government for the next nine months were almost depleted. His finance minister therefore went before Congress to ask for an emergency appropriation of some 2 billion bolívares, 1.48 billion for meeting ongoing public-works commitments and the remainder to enable the government to meet its operating expenses until January 1970. The opposition-controlled Finance Committee of the Chamber of Deputies slashed the president's request by 40 percent and Congress as a whole went along with the committee report. President Caldera promptly submitted another request for 1.225 billion bolívares before Congress recessed for the summer. The legislature took no action on the request.

When Congress reconvened in early fall for its second regular session of the year, the administration submitted its 1970 budget in the amount of 9.235 billion bolívares, slightly less than the amount requested for the previous year. The budget, however, did not include funds for public works, normally the largest single item in the budget. To cover the cost of public works, the president resorted to the unusual tactic of submitting a supplementary budget of 4 billion bolívares. Both the regular and supplementary budgets were immediately attacked by AD and other opposition groups who feared the supplementary public works budgets would cause a deficit of more than 10 billion bolívares over the next five years. The government was served notice that Congress would hold it within these limits. The administration told the Congress that it expected to raise the additional revenues by a more efficient collection of taxes rather than by the tax reform urged by the opposition leaders. The budget crisis was not resolved before the expiration of the regular term of Congress and a special session was necessary. Not until late December did the Congress finally approve a budget that was 5.8 percent larger than that of 1969.

Congress is thus showing an increasing tendency to use its powers of the purse for what the administration regards as obstructionist purposes. Battles such as the foregoing cause some critics to worry about the survival of the democratic system in Venezuela.

Not only does Congress now have the power to intervene in the budgetary process in its legislative phase, it also has an agency that is entrusted with the control, supervision and auditing of the national revenues, expenditures and assets: the comptroller general of the republic. The comptroller is chosen by a joint session of Congress within thirty days after the beginning of each constitution term. He submits to Congress a detailed annual report concerning the fiscal accounts sent to his office by the agencies of government. No study has been done on the effectiveness of the office of comptroller general in curbing graft and corruption in government, but it seems reasonable to argue that its efficacy would rest on the caliber of the person who occupies it.

The constitution of 1961 attempts to restrain the official conduct of public servants by establishing a Public Ministry, headed by the prosecutor general of the republic. This official, like the comptroller general, is chosen by Congress in joint session. His job is to see to it that the constitution and the laws of the land are observed. His specific duties include those of ensuring that constitutional rights and guarantees are respected both in civil life and in prison, to take care that justice is properly administered, and to see to it that the laws are correctly applied in criminal cases. The prosecutor general may take actions against public officials for abuse of their official positions. All authorities of the republic are required to give the Public Ministry their fullest cooperation as it seeks to carry out its duties. The prosecutor general is required to file a report with Congress each year. He properly belongs to the judicial branch of government.

The duties of the prosecutor general differ from those of the attorney general in that the former represents and defends the people against official wrongdoing while the latter is the spokesman for the executive branch whenever it is involved in judicial proceedings.

Congress is ordinarily in session only six months of the year. Prior to 1961, adjournment meant that a willful president had a free hand in legislating by executive decree. Since 1961, however, a Delegated Committee of Congress acts as a miniature congress during the six-month period that the parent body is not in session and the president is required to seek its approval in certain matters. The Committee is composed of the presiding officers of the two houses of Congress and twenty-one other members of Congress elected by the chambers in joint session. Due regard is paid to the political composition of the Congress in choosing the Committee members. During much of Betancourt's term the Committee membership was evenly divided between the coalition and the opposition parties. An Independent had a tie vote.

The Delegated Committee may call Congress into special session if it deems it necessary. The president needs its approval to modify, create, or abolish public agencies and services and to decree expenditures not authorized by the budget. He may not leave the country without its permission. It may exercise the investigative powers of Congress. Perhaps its most important function is to observe the executive branch to make sure that it respects the constitution and does not interfere with citizens' rights.

The Delegated Committee can be only as effective as its

parent body and because it reflects the party composition of the Congress, the same political differences will be mirrored in it. A Delegated Committee dominated by opposition parties or one in which they have equal representation with administration parties is likely to be more concerned with its role vis-à-vis the executive than would one controlled by the president's party. Even under the former situation the Delegated Committee may find itself hampered in the pursuit of its duties. A case in point is an incident that occurred in September 1963, a time of considerable terrorist agitation in the country. Responding to the murder of five national guardsmen allegedly engineered by the Communist party and the Castro-oriented Movement of the Revolutionary Left (MIR), the president ordered the house arrest of one senator and five deputies suspected of being implicated. They were charged with masterminding the murders.

Article 143 of the constitution permits the detention of members of Congress for a maximum of ninety-six hours in cases of flagrant abuse of their immunity, but requires that they must be released upon the expiration of ninety-six hours unless the Delegated Committee of Congress, or the chamber involved, orders an official arrest and trial. Congress was in recess and thus the matter fell to the Delegated Committee. Unfortunately, two of the arrested deputies were themselves members of the Committee. Several of the other committee members refused to attend its meetings until the arrested members were released and allowed to take their seats. Deprived of a quorum, the Committee was unable to act within the stipulated time.

Instead of releasing the men, however, the president sent several to jail and ordered the trial of the rest by military courts under Article 476 of the Military Code of Justice, a statute that covered rebellion and attempts to incite rebellion. There was nothing the Committee could do except to charge the president with violating the constitution, as he had in fact done.

Although no specific data are available on the ultimate fate of these and other detained individuals, it seems likely that they benefited by the promises made by President Leoni in 1964 to grant amnesty to political prisoners. Nevertheless, the issue of congressional immunity remained a sore point between President Betancourt and his Congress, and it persisted well into the Leoni administration. Congress can never really feel completely secure so long as the president has the power to arrest with impunity its members. Relations between the executive and legislative branches of government thus have not been without their stormy moments.

The Congress that took office in March 1969, is a badly divided one. Eleven political parties are represented, none of which has as much as one-third of the membership of both houses (see Table 7–2). The largest legislative bloc is that of

Table 7–2   Party Composition of the Venezuelan Congress [8]

	Senators	Deputies
Democratic Action (AD)	19	63
Social Christian Party (COPEI)	16	59
People's Electoral Movement (MEP)	5	25
National Civic Crusade (CCN)	4	21
Democratic Republic Union (URD)	3	20
Popular Democratic Force (FDP)	2	10
Democratic National Front (FND)	1	4
Revolutionary Party for National Integration (PRIN)	1	4
Union for Advancing (UPA)	1	5
Social Democratic Party (PSD)	0	1
National Action Movement (MAN)	0	1
	52	213

Acción Democrática, followed by that of COPEI, the party of President Caldera. In its first month of work Congress failed to agree upon almost everything. It took four days of party bickering before the two chambers were even able to choose their presiding officers. Lack of quorums prevented a number of scheduled sessions. Disagreement between the Caldera administration and AD and its partners in Congress over the appointment of the two congressional members to the new Judicial Council delayed the opening of the fall term of Congress for two weeks. Name calling and highly partisan debate characterized the sessions. Because of these difficulties, Congress was attacked from all sides, from within and without, as being an ineffective "do nothing" legislature. Relations between the executive and legislative branches improved considerably in

[8] *Venezuela Up-to-date,* 12 (Spring 1969), 6.

1970 as a result of an agreement between Caldera and *Acción Democrática* to cooperate in matters clearly in the national interest. AD reserved the right to reject any government measure that it considered to be for the partisan advantage of COPEI. The *ad hoc* arrangement did not bring AD into the cabinet, however.

During the Betancourt and Leoni administrations, opposition parties, particularly in the Chamber of Deputies, strongly voiced their objections both to the use by the president of his emergency powers in curbing violence and to the direction and details of his legislative program. The opposition parties have been instrumental in getting Congress to investigate political prisons and charges of corruption in several of the autonomous agencies, and they are beginning to scrutinize the budget more carefully. In Venezuela one may no longer ignore the legislature when considering the pattern of effective power.

The new Congress, containing all shades of opinion from the again-legal Communist party on the left to the supporters of ex-dictator Marcos Pérez Jiménez on the right, may prove that its true function is that of a political forum and meeting place of pressure groups rather than a formulator of laws. In spite of all this, one may no longer ignore the Venezuelan legislature when considering the pattern of effective power.

Paraguay—executive tool?

The Paraguayan Congress has never been of any importance in the political system. Its *raison d'être* has always been to legalize such actions of the president as he sees fit to submit to it. Since the legislature is still largely excluded from the effective pattern of power, it seems irrelevant to enumerate here the powers it supposedly has. The list is very similar to that noted in the section on the Venezuelan legislature.

In 1967 Paraguay discarded the unicameral legislature that had been introduced in 1940 and returned to a bicameral system. A thirty-man Senate has been added to the original sixty-member Chamber of Deputies. On paper the addition of a Senate seems to be a substantial change. Its critics, however, are hard-pressed to find a justification for it and argue that the only purpose it serves is to give the president a few more public posts to distribute among the faithful. Certainly there exists no geographical reason for a Senate, as both it and the Chamber of Deputies are directly elected at large in one great electoral district and thus represent the same constituency. Nor does the Senate act as a restraint on the lower house. Both houses are controlled by the Colorado party, which by law is entitled to two-thirds of the seats in each house by virtue of capturing a plurality of the vote in the last election. Although there have been mutterings of rebellion against the president among Colorado ranks, the president still controls the party and thus the legislature. Legislative terms are for five years and coincide with that of the president.

No practical purpose is served in detailing the internal organization of a powerless body beyond stating that there are permanent committees representing the same fields of jurisdiction as the ministries.

The legislative process is in general similar to that described in the section on Venezuela. Theoretically, any member of Congress may introduce legislation. Members of the Colorado party do not do so unless they have advance assurances that the president is sympathetic. It would be absurd for the greatly outnumbered opposition party members to do so with any hope of success. All important legislation therefore comes from the president, or the agencies controlled by him.

Laws are considered sanctioned when they have received the approval of both houses of the legislature. If the president approves them, he promulgates them in the *Official Gazette* within ten days. He has both a total and a partial veto over laws, but because no legislature has been strong enough or venturesome enough to pass laws repugnant to the president, the power is not used.

The 1967 constitution authorizes a Permanent Committee of Congress composed of six senators and twelve deputies. It shares with the attorney general the responsibility of ensuring the observance of the constitution and of the laws. It is a powerless committee whose duties are primarily housekeeping chores connected with examining election results and making the necessary preparation for holding regular and special sessions of Congress. It is not designed to check the president and does not do so.

The Paraguayan legislature in 1969 remains what it has

always been: a passive bill-passing agency. The Venezuelan legislature, on the other hand, is showing signs of vigorous activity and independent will. Still less than a full partner in the conversion of society's raw demands into policy decisions, it seems at least on the way to becoming a more effective participant.

PUBLIC POLICY PROBLEMS

In terms of public policy, both Venezuela and Paraguay share somewhat the same goals, although their emphasis on them may differ in some cases. Venezuelan public policies over the last decade have reflected the desire of policy planners to diversify the economy in order to decrease its dependence on oil revenues. Thus the government has encouraged the establishment of new industries and the development of its rich iron ore deposits. It has stimulated agricultural development and livestock breeding by a land reform program and inducements to agriculturally inclined immigrants. It has sought to raise the standard of living of its people in order to make them productive and useful citizens. Health and sanitation measures are vitally important in reaching this goal and the government has been active in this field. Considerable time and effort has been devoted to improving the educational system and working conditions for labor.

Paraguay is far less a monocultural country, although its lumber industry is vitally important to its economy. Paraguay is also less concerned with diversifying its economy than with reducing its economic and transportation dependence on Argentina. Thus it invests money in building roads to connect with Brazilian ports. It enjoys an advantageous membership in the Latin American Free Trade Association although some Paraguayan economists are inclined to view somewhat pessimistically its involvement in LAFTA.

Paraguay also encourages immigration, particularly with a view to the settlement of the more habitable regions of the *Chaco*. Several Mennonite colonies were established some years ago.

Other policy problems facing Paraguay are housing programs, unemployment, educational deficiencies and outmoded agricultural methods.

SUMMARY

The institutions and agencies described in this chapter comprise the formal governmental apparatus through which the raw demands of society are converted into statutes, edicts, and decisions; in other words, into the outputs of the system. As we have seen, the governmental structures have been responsive primarily to the policies enunciated by the executive branch of government. For most of the time the two republics have been in existence, the conversion process has reflected the status quo aspiration of the powerful elite forces in society: landowners, military men, Church officials, and aristocrats. This situation still basically characterizes the political system of Paraguay. Venezuela, on the other hand, shows signs that the political, economic, and social aspirations of an ever-increasing number of ordinary citizens are finding channels of expression that ensure a more effective participation by them in the outputs of the system.

EIGHT
THE SPIRIT
OF SPANISH
LAW
The individual and the courts

THE NATURE OF THE SYSTEM

The nature of law, judicial institutions, procedures, and legal philosophy in the countries of Latin America have been profoundly influenced by Spanish principles and practices, as well as by developments in other countries. The existence of judicial review, for example, is due to the influence of North America.

Spain derived many of its legal precepts and values from Rome, which held sway over the Iberian Peninsula for some 400 years. When Roman control ended in 414 A.D., Spain was overrun by the Goths (for 300 years) and then by the Moors (for 700 years). Roman influences managed to survive both these invasions. One major Roman influence was the codification of law. A code is a systematic, precise, detailed organization of all existing law. It attempts to reduce everything to defined categories and specific procedures and standards. An example of such a foundation code in the Spanish background was the great *Corpus Juris Civilis* of the Emperor Justinian, upon which was based the thirteenth-century Spanish code, *Las Sietas Partidas*.[1]

Of importance to the Spanish colonies were two other great codes of law: the *Recopilación de Leyes de Indias* issued in

[1] William S. Stokes, *Latin American Politics* (New York: Crowell, 1959), pp. 465–466.

1682 and its revised edition, *Novísima Recopilación,* adopted in 1805 shortly before the wars for independence broke out. In the *Recopilación* there were 9 books with 6377 laws, classified under 218 *títulos* or subjects: education and religion; judicial organization; administrative, private, naval, and military law; local government, public works, mines, factories, and settlement of new towns; social legislation such as working conditions for the Indians; public finance, commerce, and maritime law; and social relations such as marriage; and attributes, powers, and jurisdiction of royal officials.[2] All new laws and edicts were classified and included in the appropriate section of the code.

The law itself was considered to emanate from the will of the king, the natural ruler, or *señor natural.* The *señor natural* was

> . . . a lord who by inherent nature of superior qualities, goodness, and virtue, and by birth or superior station, attains power legitimately and exercises dominion over all within his lands justly and in accord with divine, natural, and human law and reason, being universally accepted, recognized, and obeyed by his vassals and subjects and acknowledged by other lords and their peoples as one who rightfully possesses his office and rightfully wields authority within his territory. . . .[3]

The king alone could give legitimacy to the law. The principal source of law for the colonies was the king's Royal Council of the Indies, an august body that met regularly with the monarch in his palace to translate the royal will into edict. The notion of law as the expression of the will of the people was foreign to Spanish political philosophy.

For some years after acquiring freedom from Spain, the Latin American republics retained the basic codes under which they had been governed by Spain. When new codes were adopted by them, they were either copies of updated Spanish codes, or were modeled after codes of France, Italy, Germany,

[2] Bailey W. Diffie, *Latin American Civilization,* Colonial Period (Harrisburg, Pa.: Stackpole Sons, 1945), p. 528.

[3] Robert S. Chamberlain, "The Concept of the *Señor Natural* as Revealed in Castilian Law and Administrative Documents," *Hispanic American Historical Review,* 19 (May 1939), 130–137.

or other Latin American countries. Paraguay, for example, adopted in 1887 the entire Argentine civil code. In 1906 the Venezuelan civil code was modified, using Italian and German sources.[4]

Latin American law is organized today under several separate codes such as civil law, commercial and mercantile law, criminal law, labor law, and so on.

In countries with common law foundations, such as England and the United States, judges decide cases by referring to a judicial precedent or line of decisions, as well as upon the written law. Over the years a vast body of such precedents has grown up, based on customs, usage, and the application of reason in settling disputes.

The Latin American judge, on the other hand, relies almost entirely on the codes. His principal task is to ascertain what the law says and how it has been violated and then to apply the appropriate remedy or penalty if guilt is determined. There were, and are, many scholarly commentaries on the law and the codes. One venerable one is that of Juan de Solorano Pereira's *Política indiana* published in 1648. In matters of colonial law, *Política indiana* serves much the same purpose as Blackstone's *Commentaries* on English law.[5] Precedent, however, is not an important principle in Latin America, and case law is ignored almost entirely.

Commenting on the position of judicial precedent in Venezuela, the Supreme Court observed in 1946 that while the essence of jurisprudence consisted of a series of judicial decisions in which a general, uniform, and lasting interpretation of the law was made by the judge, in Venezuela it had only a "scientific authority and was not the source of positive law." The doctrine followed by the Venezuelan judge is that he is not obligated to conform to previous decisions if he finds them contrary to the letter and spirit of the constitution, because he is deciding not by imitation, but by applying the law.[6]

[4] Stokes, p. 467.

[5] Diffie, p. 527.

[6] Venezuela, *Resumen de Jurisprudencia reciente de la Corte Federal y de Casación en 1945 y trimestre 1 de 1946* (Caracas: Tip. "La Nación," 1946), p. 78.

JUDICIAL STRUCTURES AND ROLES

Venezuela

The nationalization of the judiciary   An insight into the operation of the Venezuelan judicial system as a whole prior to its
nationalization can be gained by a review of the arguments
presented in favor of complete national control.

As the national government over the years absorbed more
and more of the powers of the states, the rationale supporting
the existence of twenty separate state judicial structures gradually weakened. The state courts were ultimately left with
little to do but apply national codes in penal, mercantile, civil,
criminal, labor, and fiscal matters. Advocates of nationalizing
the judicial system argued that national codes demanded a coordinated and centrally directed judiciary to ensure uniform
application of national laws.

Advocates also cited the inferior quality of judicial officers
in the various states. The inability of the more rural states to pay
salaries high enough to attract qualified men from the capital
city meant that judges were often persons with a minimum of
legal training. Indeed, the states did not even require their
judges to be lawyers. As a result, judicial posts were often filled
with ignorant, dishonest, and lazy judges.[7] This situation, ag-
gravated by an ever-increasing backlog of cases, brought the
entire judicial system into disrepute.

The advocates of national control of the court system
hoped that federal administration would mean a decrease in
corruption and graft. The venality and dishonesty of many
judges was criticized and deplored by various Venezuelan
students of judicial affairs. Some of these were of the opinion
that corruption and immorality were the greatest obstacles to
the efficient administration of justice. The minister of interior
painted a vivid picture of judicial conduct prior to nationalization. In a letter addressed to the governors of the states, he
asked them to take steps to ensure that the judges in their
jurisdictions

[7] Angel Brice, "Nacionalización del Poder Judicial," *Revista de
Derecho y Legislación* (Diciembre de 1949), 196.

. . . comply with their duty of applying the law with impartiality, without prejudice, and above all, without partisan politics; that judges attend court in conformity with the law and that they do not delay the cases through carelessness, malice, bad faith or disorder in their work; that bonds, bail and other finances be guaranteed by persons of moral and economic solvency and not by individuals who have as their only merit that of being a friend of the judge or of being recommended by one of the parties . . . ; that the judges dispatch their affairs with speed in the interests of social peace, and that the briefs of the case be determined and written in the shortest possible time, eliminating the common practice of postponement; that decisions be handed down within the time limit established by the law, thus ending the evil practice of ignoring the legal limits thereby making necessary a new notification to the parties involved, that appeals be admitted or denied in accord with legal precepts and not, as is frequently the case, through ill-will, passion or vanity of the judges.[8]

National officials also argued that courts, like hospitals and schools, should be placed where they were most needed. Since most litigation in Venezuela ordinarily takes place in the Federal District and about eight of the more populous states, an equal number of courts in the other states was regarded as a costly luxury. An administrative analysis in 1944 revealed that the average cost per case to the governments ranged from $523 in Caracas, to a high of $4300 in the state of Nueva Esparta. The Federal District accounted for 50 percent of the entire judicial business of the Republic at a cost of $253,000 and a personnel force of twenty-four in 1945. The twenty states, on the other hand, spend almost 2 million dollars in handling the other half.

Although the states formally surrendered their judicial power to the central government in the constitutional revisions of 1945, the nationalization of the judiciary did not take place until November 1948, when a presidential decree abrogated all state judicial codes and statutes. Judges were declared federal

---

[8] *Síntesis de las Labores realizadas por la Junta de Gobierno de los EE.UU de Venezuela durante un año de gestión administrativa, 24 de noviembre de 1950–24 de diciembre de 1951* (Caracas: Oficina Nacional de Informaciones y Publicaciones, 1951), pp. 139–141.

employees, and a new Ministry of Justice was created in 1950 to oversee the system.

Whether or not the judicial system has functioned better under the national control has not been determined with any degree of clarity. Judicial processes are still extremely slow. The problem of recruiting good men for outlying posts has not been eliminated. The backlog of cases has been reduced, but by no means eliminated. Two years after nationalization, the minister of justice was calling for an end to the vicious practice of judges collecting more for their services than the judicial code allowed. One decided improvement has been the placement of courts where they are most needed. Thus the Federal District has by far the largest number of superior courts of any of the judicial districts.

The present judicial organization   Jurisdiction in Venezuela embraces civil, mercantile, penal, labor, fiscal, and military matters. The first three categories are exercised by ordinary courts, the latter by special courts. Some of the ordinary courts have jurisdiction in all three of their categories; others may be assigned only one or two, depending on the workload of the court and the size of the district.

The highest court in Venezuela is the nine-judge *Supreme Court of Justice,* one-third of whose membership is elected every three years by Congress for a nine-year term. Judges must be native Venezuelan lawyers at least 30 years of age. They may be removed only for causes set forth in law. The Court is divided into three chambers (*salas*) each of which hears cases in one field: political, civil, or criminal.

The Supreme Court of Justice has the power to try the president of the republic if the Senate authorizes it; it may hear cases involving the constitutionality of national, state, and municipal laws as well as of regulatory and executive acts of the president, and declare them null and void; it may settle jurisdictional disputes between any of the legal divisions of the republic; and, of course, it hears cases arising from the lower courts.

Directly below the Supreme Court are the single-judge superior courts, of which there is at least one in each of the seventeen major judicial divisons into which Venezuela is divided. There are six such courts in the Federal District, and several of the more populous divisions have two or more. Altogether there are now twenty-nine superior courts. These entities have original jurisdiction over cases involving responsibility of judges in inferior courts, and they hear complaints about the work of their judges. They admit lawyers to the bar and hear requests for the legitimization of natural children. They may demand a list of cases pending in the lower courts in order to expedite justice and speed up the judicial process.

Beneath the superior courts are the courts of first instance. There are fifty-one of these tribunals scattered through the seventeen judicial divisions. Courts of first instance have original jurisdiction in almost all criminal cases and in civil cases involving the nation as a party and between citizens when the sum involved is more than 4000 bolívares. Trial is by judge, not by jury. Persons are tried for criminal offenses in the courts of first instance only after they have been indicted by one of the twenty-four courts of instruction. The criminal findings of courts of first instance are reviewed automatically by the superior courts.

In each of the 170 territorial districts of the twenty states there is a district court that hears civil cases involving sums between 2000 and 4000 bolívares. District courts also hear appeals from the decisions of municipal courts. Every town in Venezuela and every ward in the large cities has a court of this latter category to hear civil cases involving sums of less than 2000 bolívares and those involving minor offenses. Municipal courts officiate in such things as marriage ceremonies and validation of contracts.

Court procedure   Judicial procedure in all Venezuelan cases is strictly written and all must be done in the presence of the judge, with the exception of certain cases in which depositions may be brought in and entered into the records.

In civil, mercantile, and labor procedures, the mechanism of the trial generally is as follows. The claimant presents a written claim to the judge listing all the facts called for in the Civil Procedure Code. If the judge accepts the claim, he summons the defendant, who signs a statement upon receiving the summons, acknowledging its receipt on a given day and time. A fixed period then elapses before he must appear in court to answer the charges raised in the claim. If the defendant does not appear on the day specified, the burden of proof is inverted and everything stated in the claim is presumed to be true, unless the defendant should prove the contrary during the course of the trial.

On the day following the answering of the claim, a proof period is opened in which all the evidence is presented. Proof period is followed with a study of the records by the judge, who calls the parties for final statements when he is in possession of all the facts. Decision and sentence by him terminate the case.

Penal procedure is initiated either by an agency of the state or by private accusation. It starts in the courts of instruction, which have the function of investigating and compiling the records of the case. If this court finds sufficient cause for detaining the defendant, his arrest is ordered and the case sent for trial to a court of first instance. There the charges are heard by the judge, and the period of proof, review of the case by the judge, and final statements from the parties follow in sequence and a decision is handed down by the judge.

The relation of the judiciary to the other branches of government   A succinct statement of the self-conceived role of the Supreme Court in the Venezuelan federal system is contained in the 1942 *Memoria* of the Court.

> To ensure that the rule of the Constitution and the tripartite division of the public power may be positive and permanent in our representative and republican system and to maintain the Constitution above the conflicts which could arise in our juridical organization which distributes public power among federal, state and municipal powers, the constituent body created a Constitution which attributes to the Federal Court the role of supreme protector and chief defender of individual rights and guarantees.
>
> The regulatory norms of the life of the state are of two categories: the Supreme Law itself, and those established in ordinary laws. It is obvious that the rules of the last class are, by their nature, subject to the first. Hence the moderating role of the Court is of great importance. . . . It is not strange, therefore, that in this, and in the simultaneous exercise of the

public powers there are conflicts of jurisdiction or interference which require the regulatory action of a supreme organ of national justice.[9]

In its capacity as arbiter of the federal system, the Court has had the constitutional power of judicial review in one form or another since about 1858. It regards itself as the chief defender of the constitution and as such seeks to contain the other powers within their legal limits. Thus the Court, by upholding the concept of limited government, enhances the position of the constitution in the political culture of the country. But its role of defender is seriously compromised by political factors that greatly weaken its power.

The first of these factors is that of the "independence" of the judicial branch. It cannot be seriously argued that the judiciary forms an independent, coordinate, and equal branch of government. The course of events in the years prior to 1961 indicates that up until then it was totally dependent on the executive—a position it shared with the legislature. The Supreme Court, as a structure of public power, was dissolved by the junta that overthrew the constitutional government of President Medina Angarita in 1945. The new Court appointed by the ruling junta functioned until another was elected by the National Constitutional Assembly on July 31, 1947. In the intervening two years, the Court found itself even more limited than it had been. It became a creature of a ruling group that governed the nation without the benefit of a constitution. It was bluntly told in a decree of July 1946 that the validity of acts emanating from the junta could not be impugned before the Court, and that all actions and appeals that might have been initiated or concluded to that effect would be null and void.[10] The junta informed the Court it would render an account of its activities to the National Constitutional Assembly when it met, and to no one else.

The Court elected by the National Constitutional Assembly in 1947 lasted slightly over one year. A military junta success-

[9] Venezuela, *Memoria y Cuenta de la Corte Federal y de Casación,* Vol. I, No. 16 (Caracas: Ed. Bolívar, 1943).

[10] Venezuela, *Memoria y Cuenta de Relaciones Interiores,* 1948–1952 (Caracas: Imprenta Nacional, 1953), Dco. 1, p. 137.

fully deposed the *Acción Democrática* government in 1948 and began to clean house systematically. An early target was the Supreme Court. An entirely new membership was decreed for that body on December 8, 1948. It seems reasonable to assume that the members appointed by it were sympathetic to the new military regime. In the appointment decree it was declared that the *Corte Federal y de Casación* (the Supreme Court) would function in accord with the 1947 constitution as modified by the provisional government and with the Basic Law of the Court enacted on April 22, 1945.

Through its appointment decree of December 21, 1948, the junta effectively assumed control of the judiciary throughout the nation. The highest court, directly appointed by the junta, was required to present to it a list of names for appointment to the superior courts. The superior courts in turn were instructed to present similar lists to the junta for the lower posts in the judicial hierarchy. Since Congress had been dissolved by the junta, it played no part in these elections or appointments. The junta proceeded to name the judges of the superior courts and courts of first instance in all the states and territories under a decree of January 28, 1949. Throughout March and April it completed the appointment of the judicial officers of the lower courts throughout the republic.

It is suggested here that the Supreme Court chosen by the Constitutional Assembly in 1953 was no less dependent on the executive than its immediate predecessor. Although the new constitution stipulated that the Court should be elected by the National Congress, it was, in fact, chosen by the Constitutional Assembly, under a transitory provision appended to the constitution. The Assembly was a pliant tool of the executive, and the constitution it wrote and the business it transacted were in reality nothing but expressions of the desires of the provisional president, Marcos Pérez Jiménez. This being the case, it follows that the Supreme Court of Venezuela prior to the revolution of 1958 was a creature of the executive branch, rather than a coequal with it.

The claim to judicial independence from the executive is now more meaningful since judicial terms no longer coincide with that of the president. In view of the fact that the legislature is becoming a more significant power structure, it may well be that the Court's relations with Congress will assume more importance than those with the executive. Congress holds the power of the purse, subject, of course, to executive will, and the constitution does not forbid a reduction of judicial salaries during a judge's term. Then too, judges may be removed from office "in cases and according to procedure determined by law."

Another factor pertains to the attitudes of citizens and public officials toward the Court. Although the Court considers itself to be the last resort in matters of constitutional law, two incidents will suffice to illustrate the fact that not all citizens and public officials share the Court's view.

As background to the first example, it should be pointed out that the courts, including the Supreme Court, have no power to revoke or revise their decisions or to delay the effects of a decision once the case has been disposed of. This does not mean that there is no right of appeal, but merely that the court with original jurisdiction has no authority to alter its own opinions. Thus the Supreme Court may not review the decision of a case previously before it. The Court pointed out, however, that every court has the legitimate power of rectifying its past mistakes when an analagous case arises.

The first example is contained in an interesting decision handed down by the Court in response to an individual's plea that the Court annul a previous decision in which it had voided the elections of certain senators and representatives. The plaintiff asked the principal members of the Court to disqualify themselves and to call on the alternate judges to decide the case anew. (All elected officials in Venezuela have alternates called *suplentes* who are elected at the same time to fill the office should it be vacated for any reason.) The Court pointed out that to do as the plaintiff asked would be to reduce the Supreme Court to the status of an inferior court and would cause a degeneration of the whole judicial system. The Court thus rejected the plea and told the plaintiff that to grant his request would be to establish the *suplente* judges as a board of review for the decisions handed down by the official court. Such an action would be unconstitutional.

The second example reflects a clear-cut intention of a member of the executive branch to undermine the supremacy and independence of the Supreme Court. In 1939 the attorney general argued that the acts and decisions of the Court—itself one of the public powers—should be no less subject to review and nullification than those of the other two branches of government. He proposed an agency with review powers over the Court.

The Court reacted vigorously to this attack by asserting that the attorney general was merely an organ of a branch of the government to which the Court was an equal and as such he had neither the duty nor right to criticize the acts of the Court. In the opinion of the judges, the suggestions of the attorney general represented an attempt to promote a legislative reform that would allow one of its agencies to revoke the decisions of the Court. Worse still, such an agency would have the power to substitute other decisions for those of the Court. But, said the Court, the constitution gives exclusive powers to the judges to annul acts of the public powers, and therefore no other tribunal is competent to review them. A higher body capable of judging Supreme Court decisions, it argued, would also be a public power whose decisions could be reviewed by a still higher organ. The Court sarcastically asked, "How many courts would have to be piled one on top of the other in an hierarchy without end until judges of infallible flesh and bones might be found?" The interminable process of review that would result from the adoption of the attorney general's suggestion would bring about anarchy and public disorder, said the Court. Nothing came of the matter, and the Court continues to consider itself to be the conscience of the regime and defender of the constitution.

On several occasions the Court has been asked to rule on the constitutionality of various provisions of the national constitution; in effect, to determine whether the constitution was constitutional. The Court has always denied that it had such a power. Specifically rejecting the contention that it could rule on the constitution itself, the Court said

> In all countries, even those governed by flexible constitutions, the basic charter is a law so special that it is granted a pre-eminence superior to all other laws. In countries which have a rigid constitution, as ours does, this pre-eminence reaches its highest value. Here the generic name of law is not broad enough to describe the constitution because the latter is something more: it is a super law, and this super legality makes the

constitution untouchable, even for the legislative power, except through the process of revision and amendment which is provided for in the constitution itself.[11]

The record of the Court over the years in the exercise of its powers of judicial review indicates that it has been more concerned with the growth of national powers and presidential powers than it has with state and legislative powers. One Venezuelan authority sums it up as follows:

> With respect to the municipal autonomy of the Federal District, the Court has often restricted it to the advantage of the governors and agents of the President of the Republic. In the domain of state legislation, it has not only annulled many fiscal and election laws on the grounds that they were contrary to the national constitution, but it has also smothered the feeble attempts of the states to regain some of the autonomy conferred upon them by the constitution. The Court, for example, has denied the states the power to revoke their delegation of authority to the President of the Republic to appoint state governors.
>
> The annulling of laws of Congress is not so common as that of state laws, but in general such annulments deny to the Congress and confer on the president powers which the latter wishes to exercise. In many of its opinions the Court has been guided by political considerations, invoking the doctrine of the supremacy of the constitution to give them respectability.[12]

Until 1969 the principle of judicial review had never seriously hampered the efforts of the executive to put his program into effect. The evidence also indicates that in the very few instances in which judicial review has operated adversely to a national law, it did not seriously modify the distribution of power. Its main effect has been to restrict and limit the autonomy of the states.

All the evidence points to the fact that the judicial branch as a whole in Venezuela has been weak and relatively powerless

[11] Pablo Ruggeri Parra, *Historia política y constitutional de Venezuela* (Caracas: Tip. Americana, 1949), p. 23.

[12] Ernesto Wolf, *Tratado de Derecho constitucional venezolano,* Vol. II (Caracas: Tip. Americana, 1945), pp. 183–184.

to act as a restraint upon the political authorities. Indeed, there are regions in Venezuela where tradition or the persistence of deeply ingrained customs have made it impossible to distinguish between the actions of civil authorities and judicial officers.[13]

In times of constitutional disturbances, such as the period that followed the overthrow of the Gallegos government in 1948, the Court was forbidden to interfere with the activities of the junta. During periods of constitutional government there is little occasion for the Court to pit itself against either the legislature or the executive and it wisely does not do so. It will go to some length to avoid a confrontation with either. In a recent conflict between Congress and the executive, which stemmed from a violation of congressional immunity by President Betancourt and a ban by the president on the Communist and MIR parties, the Court was asked by the president to declare the parties illegal. It sidestepped the issue and after a thirteen-month delay, ruled that while the parties were not illegal, they must be considered inactive until the president rescinded his decree.

The Supreme Court now appears to be caught in a power struggle between the president and an opposition-controlled Congress. *Acción Democrática,* the leading political party in the Congress, has a near majority of the judges and, indeed, all five judges of the Court's political *sala* (section) are *adecos.* In the dispute over the power to make judicial appointments, it appears that the Court may have acted more on partisan than on constitutional grounds in ruling in favor of Congress (see Chapter Seven).

Paraguay

Judicial organization   Almost all of the preceding general discussion is applicable to Paraguay, with the exception that the Paraguayan judicial system has always been national in character.

All judicial officials in Paraguay are appointed by the president. The legislature has no part in the process. Their terms coincide with his, and they may be reappointed for another

---

[13] Venezuela, Congreso Nacional, Cámara de Senadores, *Exposición de motivos y proyecto de ley orgánica del poder judicial,* Vol. II (Caracas: Imprenta Nacional, 1948), p. 1540.

term. Judges are required by the constitution to have legal training, experience, and a "good reputation."

A five-man Supreme Court of Justice is at the apex of the judicial system. Although it has the authority to nullify laws, it never does so. Most of its jurisdiction is appellate.

Below the Supreme Court are twelve courts of appeal, one in each of the major populated departments of Paraguay. There is none in the three desolate departments in the *Chaco*. Next in order are the district courts (similar to the courts of first instance in Venezuela) with original jurisdiction in criminal cases. There are some thirty of these. Over 200 justices of the peace occupy the lowest rung on the judicial ladder. They hear cases involving minor infractions of the law and civil cases involving small sums of money. There are no jury trials in Paraguay.

The constitution also establishes a special Tribunal of Accounts that hears cases involving administrative and fiscal matters in which the government is a party. It serves in somewhat the same capacity as does the office of the comptroller general in Venezuela, although with far less effect.[14]

Court procedure The qualification that the law stipulates for judges hardly compensates for the deficiencies of the system as a whole. A major defect is that all testimony is submitted to the court in writing and on stamped paper that must be purchased from the government. Latin Americans are a litigious people, and the Paraguayans are no exception. Judicial files grow voluminous as cases continue on the docket for long periods of time. Exasperation with the slowness of the judicial process sometimes leads to corruption as litigants seek to influence the judge to dispose of long-delayed cases. The judiciary enjoys little respect in Paraguay.

As a whole, the judicial branch of government is the weakest of the three. Judicial officials, despite the constitutional guarantees of independence and noninterference by the other

[14] For legal provisions relating to the administration of justice in Paraguay see Raul Sapena Pastor and Raul Sapena Brugada. *A Statement of the Laws of Paraguay* (Washington, D.C.: The Pan American Union, 1962), pp. 264–272.

two branches, owe their livelihood to the president and thus are unwilling to antagonize him for fear of removal or of being forced to resign their posts. The judiciary continues to be what it has been for years, a tool of the executive and a sluggish administrator of justice.

Of the two judicial systems, Venezuela's functions with the greater freedom and independence, but this has only been the case since 1959. Before that time it was not much better off than the Paraguayan judiciary.

THE CITIZEN AND THE LAW

The constitutions of both Venezuela and Paraguay afford protection for a full range of individual rights. Venezuela lists them under the categories of individual, social, economic, and political rights. Paraguay lumps them together under a chapter entitled "Rights, Obligations and Guarantees."

The scope of substantive rights, particularly in the economic and social field is of a larger dimension than is that of the United States. In general, however, the civil and political rights and duties closely follow those outlined in the United States Bill of Rights, all of which appear in one form or another, with the exception of the right of the people to keep and bear arms. There are some differences, however.

Citizens in Venezuela and Paraguay are guaranteed freedom of press, assembly, and association only if the uses to which they are put are lawful. The government is authorized to spell out what is unlawful. Paraguay adds a blanket restriction that allows the government great discretion: no form of expression is permitted that "fosters hate or class struggle" among the populace. Anonymity is forbidden in both countries. The Paraguayans' freedom to practice the religion of their choice is unrestricted; Venezuelans may do so only so long as their faith is not contrary to "public order and good customs." All religious organizations, moreover, are subject to the "supreme supervision of the National Executive." Paraguayans are guaranteed the right to learn and teach. Venezuelans are entitled to an education, but only those of "recognized morality and proven fitness" may teach.

In the category of political rights, Venezuelans and Paraguayans are obligated to vote at the age of 18 unless disqualified by other considerations. Voting is free and secret. Paraguay, a country long noted for citizen and party abstention from voting, now makes it a crime to encourage or advocate abstention from the electoral process. Citizens in both countries may organize political parties, groups, and associations under the terms set forth in statutory law. The character of such organizations must be democratic in nature. In Venezuela, citizens may demonstrate peacefully without arms if they meet the requirements laid down in the law.

In the field of procedural and judicial rights, the peoples of the two republics are considered equal before the law, and are assumed innocent until proved guilty. They are entitled to the writ of *habeas corpus* and a fair and speedy trial before a judge. Double jeopardy is outlawed, and extreme and unusual punishment is forbidden. Venezuela sets thirty years as the maximum sentence that a judge may impose. The death penalty may not be imposed under any circumstances in Venezuela. Paraguay forbids it for political causes. Venezuelan citizens may not be banished from the country for any reason, nor may their right to travel freely within or outside Venezuela be compromised. The Paraguayan constitution does not mention travel or exile, and that is realistic because a sizable portion of the Paraguayan people are in exile.

With respect to economic rights and obligations, the Paraguayan constitution says that every Paraguayan home should be located on its own individual piece of land. Paraguayan citizens are obligated to earn their livelihood through their own lawful work. In Venezuela everyone has the right to work. The Venezuelan constitution goes into great detail in matters dealing with reciprocal obligations between state and citizen in areas such as family integrity, motherhood, labor, education, health, economic development, monopoly, land ownership, foreign investments, and many others.

The effectiveness of citizen safeguards in Venezuela and Paraguay responds to several considerations: the willingness and ability of the president to respect them; the ability of the court system to restrain the political officers; the presence or absence of civil controversy and disturbance. Civil rights have suffered more often from the state-of-emergency declarations than from almost anything else. In cases of suspected subversion and conspiracy—and these are easily manufactured by an uneasy regime—the citizens' rights to speak freely and to assemble peacefully give way to political considerations; the public interest, as it is interpreted by the executive, becomes paramount.

There is no point reviewing the record of Venezuela's last dictator, Marcos Pérez Jiménez, in the field of individual rights. It is an unsavory record, to say the least. In pursuit of personal power and enrichment and the establishment of an authoritarian state, he rode roughshod over the liberties of his fellow Venezuelans. Neither Congress nor the Court could stop him.

Although Venezuela has endured a number of states of siege since the days of Pérez Jiménez, the average citizen has been unaffected by the imposed restrictions. Most people enjoy their constitutional liberties. The restrictions are aimed at those who are articulate participants in the political process. The Venezuelan press is perhaps freer today than it has ever been, and it has become an outspoken critic of the government. Organizations of all kinds flourish, and parties are permitted to operate with little restraint. An indication of the more liberal atmosphere that prevails is the legalization of the Communist party in 1969 after more than five years in limbo.

As protectors of citizens' rights vis-à-vis the state, the courts have often found their authority greatly restricted by the presidential right to suspend portions of the constitution when he feels an emergency exists. Nevertheless, if Venezuela continues its present democratic trend, we may expect the rule of law to become more firmly embedded in the political system. As that happens, the courts will take their rightful place as effective structures in the process of government and in conflict resolution.

Civil liberties are less than secure in Paraguay. Indeed, the Paraguayan nation as a whole hardly knows the real meaning of the word "liberty." Paraguayan exiles are constantly referring to police brutality and harassment of opponents of the government. Although there is technically no censorship, the government exercises a heavy restraint on the communication media. Because of the growing liberal opposition to his government, President Stroessner leaves behind a brief period in which he permitted mild criticism of his regime and now requires that all privately owned radio stations broadcast a government editorial twice daily. The government keeps a close watch on *Comunidad,* the troublesome Catholic weekly.

A not uncommon incident occurred in March 1969, when a street vendor died in an Asunción police station after five days of questioning. Although an autopsy was inconclusive, rumors circulated that the man had been tortured to death. The incident provoked responses from the students at the university and the Roman Catholic Church. The government arrested a university medical student who had taken part in a demonstration and revoked his draft exemption, claiming that it had been obtained by fraud. Students from the medical school promptly proclaimed a strike, which led to violence when sympathetic students from the Catholic University marched to the medical school to show their support. Plainclothesmen beat some of the students with clubs and wire whips as they left the university.[15]

Paraguay began the 1970 decade as it had that of 1960—as a police state. In October 1969, the Stroessner administration introduced a bill in the controlled Congress entitled "A Law for the Defense of Democracy and for the Country's Political and Social Order." It replaces an earlier "Law for the Defense of Democracy." While it is in force, Paraguayans will have only such liberties as Stroessner's internal security forces see fit to allow. Among other things, the law empowers the government to impose a three-year prison term on anyone caught reading literature hostile to the regime. Said one commentary on the law, "freedom of the press and the right to hold political meetings will be ended, while the police will be allowed to injure or kill anyone in defense of the political and social order of the state, meaning the Stroessner dictatorship."[16] About the only institutions or groups courageous enough to criticize the

---

[15] *The New York Times,* May 11, 1969, p. 22.
[16] *The Times of Latin America,* November 12, 1969, p. 7.

new law were the Roman Catholic bishops and the Liberal party leadership. The former denounced the measure as a form of "totalitarian absolutism repeatedly condemned by the ecclesiastical authorities in the name of social justice." [17] The Liberal party protested the law and other restrictions in a public meeting that attracted about 500 people.

The list of current and past violations of constitutional rights in Paraguay could be extended indefinitely. Rights are what the president permits at any given time. In the authoritarian environment that exists in Paraguay, the Court and the legislature are powerless to apply even the most cursory limits on the executive branch of the government.

SUMMARY

Venezuela and Paraguay, like all other Latin American countries, have been strongly influenced by Spanish and Roman concepts of law. In addition to the legal precepts inherited from the mother country, they have adopted features derived from other countries as the United States and France. This is particularly true in the area of civil liberties, which are incorporated in the constitutions in much the same fashion as they are in the United States Constitution.

Despite the constitutional guarantees, however, the nature of politics in both countries has meant that individual rights and liberties have often fallen victim to political considerations. Indeed, the constitutions are written in such a way as to make possible the suspension of some of the guarantees by the executive (state-of-siege clause).

The rule of law has never been an operative principle in Paraguay; rather, the rule of men has obtained throughout its history. This observation could be made about Venezuela until the beginning of the last decade. All signs now point to the real possibility that the place of individual rights and liberties is now becoming more secure as the republic responds more and more to democratic influences. This is not to say, however, that the trend is irreversible. Indeed, there are many Venezuelans who worry that the virulence of party politics in the

[17] *Latin America,* September 12, 1969, p. 296.

country may very well discredit the democratic process and provoke a return to authoritarianism.

The citizens of Venezuela and Paraguay have not yet come to regard the courts as genuine protectors of their liberties and rights vis-à-vis the government. Most have come to recognize that the courts themselves may, like individuals, become victims of the political struggle.

NINE
ISOLATIONISM, NATIONALISM, AND INTERNATIONALISM
Foreign policy

CONDITIONING INFLUENCES AND TRENDS

Paraguay

The historical evolution of Venezuela and Paraguay from colony to nation-state, and the course of events since have been discussed in Chapters One and Two. In terms of foreign policy, however, certain points need to be reemphasized here.

Paraguay's image of herself and her view of the world were profoundly influenced by her geographic isolation, not only from the world community at large, but even from most of her Latin American sister republics. Very early in her history Paraguay learned what it was like to be neglected and off the beaten track. Allowed for the most part to shift for themselves, Paraguayans developed a strong sense of independence, nationalism, and even superiority, which sorely tried the patience of Spain in its half-hearted efforts to control the unruly colony. These traits stood the Paraguayans in good stead in the events of later years.

The somber and autocratic rule of Dr. Francia strengthened the nationalistic spirit of the proud people. The dictator's obsession with Paraguay and his hostility toward other countries taught the nation to be suspicious, too, particularly of Argentina. The official foreign policy of Francia was complete noninvolvement in the affairs of the hemisphere and of the world.

For twenty-seven years, therefore, Paraguay lived remote and apart from the rest of mankind. During this solitary period, the people had to be resourceful and self-reliant merely to stay alive, physically and politically.

Official isolation diminished for a time with the ascension to power of the López family. The departure from its hermitic existence, however, brought disaster to the inexperienced country. Francisco Solano López dreamed of making his backward little country a power in southern South America. Egotistical and overconfident about his military and political ability, and personally vain, he set about reaching his goal by creating a well-trained nationalistic army. His dynastic ambitions were thwarted when the Brazilian emperor, Dom Pedro II, politely declined Francisco's offer of marriage with the Princess Isabel. His personal pride piqued, he was more than ever determined that Paraguay should cease being a backwater state at the mercy of his two great neighbors, Brazil and Argentina, and that his country should enjoy a position of equality with them.

His efforts led to the War of the Triple Alliance and brought Paraguay to its knees in the most bloody and fiercely fought war in Latin American history. Six years of war, death, and misery seemed only to strengthen the already deep sense of nationalism and patriotic fervor in the Paraguayan survivors and heightened their distrust and hatred of their neighbors. Paraguay retreated once more into isolation at the end of the war.

During the next sixty-two years, the country was almost completely occupied with domestic intrigue, civil war, and political rivalry between the two parties that had arisen. In 1932 Paraguay once again plunged into war, this time with its northern neighbor, Bolivia, over title to a barren tract of the *Gran Chaco*. The war had larger dimensions for Bolivia, which was desperately seeking a route to the sea via the Paraguay-Paraná river system that ran through Paraguay and Argentina. The defeat of Bolivia, at great cost to Paraguay, ended Bolivia's hopes of an access to the sea except on terms laid down by both Paraguay and Argentina. In 1962 the Paraguayan government concluded an agreement with Bolivia in which both countries pledged to cooperate in reaching a solution to the problems imposed by their landlocked locations.

Paraguay agreed to place at the disposal of Bolivia a river fleet of thirty ships when they were completed.

The first 125 years of Paraguay's national life were shaped by its geographic isolation, its unfortunate location between two powerful neighbors, its strange and powerful leaders, and its subsistence-level economy. Although the first three of these factors forged a unified and nationalistic people, the high cost of the Chaco War and the economic depression caused by it, produced considerable discontent with the domestic political system. The Liberal party was overthrown at the conclusion of the war after thirty-two years in power.

An ensuing period of confusion and government instability seemed likely to end under the firm hand of President Estigarribia. He did not survive to complete even one term, however, and power passed into the hands of General Higinio Morínigo. Before that happened, World War II had broken out and Paraguay's isolation came to an end.

The war improved the country's economic position immeasurably, not because Paraguay had anything of material substance to contribute to the war effort, but because the contending forces were competing for the allegiance, or at the very least, neutrality, of the Latin American republics. Thus the United States plied the country with lend-lease goods, material, loans, and other forms of economic assistance.

President Morínigo was skillful in extracting much in return for little. Paraguay benefited decidedly, for example, when the Inter-American Public Health Service opened a branch office in Asunción in 1941, bringing with it much money and technical expertise.

Despite the financial inducement and material goods sent by the United States and other countries, Morínigo was more sympathetic to the Axis than he was to the Allies. Although he broke diplomatic relations with the Axis in 1942, Paraguay during his regime was a haven for Axis agents and sympathizers. Many pro-German organizations were permitted to operate and recruit members from the Paraguayan population. Not until February 1945, when it was clear to all that the Axis was going to lose the struggle, did he issue a declaration of war against it. Shortly thereafter, he instructed his delegates to sign the Declaration of the United Nations and in June 1945, the Charter of the United Nations. Paraguay's contribution to the war effort was nil.

A prime necessity in Paraguayan foreign policy has been the need to maintain favor in Argentina, which sits astride its life line, the Paraguay-Paraná river system. Argentina is also the principal customer for Paraguayan lumber, tannin extract, and other products. During those periods in which both countries are ruled by dictators, economic considerations rather than ideological ones dominate their relations. Thus, under Morínigo and Stroessner, Paraguay maintained cordial relations with the Argentine dictator, Juan Perón. During the administration of pro-Perón President Federico Chaves, Paraguay and Argentina agreed to an economic union. Perón grandiosely committed Argentina to work for the "greatness of Paraguay and for the happiness of its people," by the utilizations of all "such resources and means as may help Paraguay to consolidate social justice, economic independence, and political sovereignty." [1]

During the sixteen years of the Stroessner administration, Paraguay has gradually involved itself more and more in hemisphere matters and in particular to those of the Plate Region to which it belongs. It has sought to improve its relations with both Argentina and Brazil. Progress in this direction has hit several snags, one political and the other territorial. Argentina was unhappy that Paraguay granted political asylum to the Argentina dictator, Juan Perón, after his ouster in 1955. Perón later left for Panama, Venezuela, and eventually, Spain. A more troublesome issue between Paraguay and its neighbors has been the almost annual launching of rebellions against Paraguay from her neighbors' soil. In 1960 Argentina and Brazil agreed to forbid persons resident in them from encouraging or aiding Paraguayan rebels in any way. Their measures were ineffective, for there was a pronounced increase in such activity the next year. Under the sterner authoritarian political regimes that have prevailed in Brazil and Argentina since the mid-1960s, rebel actions against Paraguay have diminished considerably. The reduction in rebel activity also denoted the more liberal political environment in Paraguay, which Paraguay enjoyed until the fall of 1969. In

[1] Quoted in George Pendle, *Paraguay, a Riverside Nation,* 3d ed. (London: Oxford University Press, 1967), pp. 42–43.

1967, during a state visit to Argentina, President Stroessner and Argentine President Juan Onganía agreed to collaborate in curbing infiltration and sabotage. Cultural and economic pacts also were concluded between the two countries.

There was a territorial dispute with Brazil. In 1966, Paraguay recalled its ambassador from Brazil during a disagreement over the ownership of the Guaíra Falls on the Paraná River, which separates the two countries. The dispute arose when Brazil announced its intention to build hydroelectric facilities at the falls. An agreement between the contestants to establish a study commission eventually restored friendly relations.

Because the Communist party has almost always been illegal in Paraguay, it should come as no surprise that the government takes an exceedingly dim view of the Communist regime of Fidel Castro in Cuba. No diplomatic ties exist between them. Paraguay has more than once charged Cuba with meddling in its internal affairs and of fomenting discord. Paraguay joined with seventeen other Latin American republics in registering a protest with the United Nations when Cuba was host to a convention of world revolutionaries in 1966. The Latin Americans argued that the purpose of the meeting was to plan infiltration and subversion, activities forbidden by the United Nations Charter.

In recent years Paraguay has shown a disposition to abandon altogether the remaining vestiges of its traditional isolationist attitudes and has joined with other countries in the Latin American Free Trade Association. In spite of the fact that it has neither the resources nor strategic importance to be of much consequence in world affairs, it has been visited by a number of distinguished foreign officials, a fact deplored by the exiled opponents of the Stroessner government. They argue that the visits imply official acceptance and approval of dictatorship. Some of those officials who have visited the country are Vice-President Richard Nixon (1958), Ambassador Adlai Stevenson (1961), Prince Philip of Great Britain (1962), President De Gaulle of France (1964), and Governor Nelson Rockefeller (1969). On the occasion of De Gaulle's visit, President Stroessner must have startled the austere and proper French executive when he asserted that in their republican and democratic institutions France and Paraguay were profoundly similar!

President Stroessner has left Paraguay on several occasions to pay state visits to Argentina, Brazil, and in 1968, the United States. His willingness to leave Paraguay for visits abroad demonstrates as much as any single fact his confidence in the stability of his government.

His invitation to visit the United States has been interpreted as a recognition by the United States of Stroessner's military contributions to the Inter-American Peace Force during the Dominican crisis of 1965 and thereafter, as well as an acknowledgment by the United States that politics in Paraguay seemed to have taken a more liberal turn. Gratified by his invitation, President Stroessner emphasized his continued support of the Vietnamese foreign policy of the United States.

Venezuela

During the important formative years of early independence, Venezuela was engrossed in the affairs of state and national building and in the political intrigues of the various power contenders. The period from 1830 to 1848 was remarkably free of foreign difficulties. But as the country began to expand and to borrow in foreign markets to finance internal improvements, it became involved in numerous disputes with foreign citizens and governments over claims and debts. Some resulted in blockade action by the governments whose nationals had been unable to satisfy their claims.

In 1902, for example, the government of Venezuela became embroiled in a controversy with Great Britain, Italy, and Germany. Citizens of these countries had suffered severe economic losses during political disturbances in Venezuela between 1895 and 1902, and many debts remained unpaid. President Cipriano Castro ignored all claims and protests, whereupon the governments of the three European powers instituted a blockade of Venezuelan ports. Their ships inflicted heavy damages on coastal towns before the claims were finally placed before a mixed commission. The award favored Venezuela in that the exaggerated claims of the blockading powers were substantially reduced. The United States reacted sensitively to the blockade, which it considered a violation of the

Monroe Doctrine. To prevent future occurrences of a similar nature, President Theodore Roosevelt announced, in what has become known as the Roosevelt Corollary, that the U.S. would guarantee that the behavior of the small Latin American republics would not provoke the big powers.

In 1895 a dispute broke out between Great Britain and Venezuela over the ownership of two-thirds of British Guiana. During the colonial period no fixed boundaries had been established between the Spanish and English lands. Venezuela argued that the disputed territory was part of the land she inherited from Spain after the war for independence. Britain claimed the land under a treaty with Napoleon. Invoking the Monroe Doctrine and exerting heavy pressure on Great Britain, the United States finally brought the two powers to the arbitration table. In 1899, a tribunal awarded most of the contested land to Great Britain. The award rankled Venezuela, and it never completely relinquished its claims. In 1962, during the administration of President Betancourt, the issue was revived when Venezuela repudiated the 1899 award and once more laid claim to the 60,000-square-mile territory of Essequibo. Both Great Britain and British Guiana rejected the Venezuelan claims, whereupon Venezuela laid the issue before the United Nations. After several vain attempts to get the matter resolved there, Venezuela agreed in a Geneva accord in 1966 to participate in a mixed commission made up of two commissioners from Venezuela and two from British Guiana (which became the independent nation of Guyana in May 1966). The agreement stipulated that in the event of failure to arrive at a satisfactory solution to their dispute by February 1970, the two countries would call upon an international organization to select one of the means for the pacific settlement of disputes set forth in Article 33 of the United Nations Charter. In mid-1970, after four years of fruitless discussion, the two countries signed the Protocol of Spain under which they agreed to shelve the dispute for twelve years without giving up their claims. The Guyanan Parliament promptly ratified the agreement. The Venezuelan Congress, however, was hostile and still had not done so by the end of 1970.

A boundary dispute with Colombia has seriously impaired relations between the two nations. Colombia disputes Venezuela's claim to sovereignty over the Maracaibo region with its rich oil deposits. There were some fears in 1970 that the issue would be resolved through resort to arms.

Venezuela was relatively undisturbed by foreign involvements during the twenty-seven-year rule of Juan Vicente Gómez. Although Gómez personally inclined to Germany during World War I, public opinion seemed to be in favor of the other side. Gómez followed a policy of neutrality. The discovery of oil in 1914 immeasurably enhanced Venezuela's importance in world affairs. Gómez's liberal oil policy encouraged foreign investment and enabled Venezuela to become one of the wealthiest countries in Latin America. As a result, foreign affairs were largely dictated by the development of the oil industry. Gómez labored hard to dispel the dictatorial image abroad of his government. The wealth from oil, his ability to maintain order and stability, and to discharge Venezuela's debts earned him the respect of the governments concerned.

Following the attack on Pearl Harbor in 1941, the Venezuelan government discarded its policy of neutrality and broke diplomatic relations with the Axis powers. It froze Axis funds and impounded their ships, but like Paraguay, did not declare war on them until February 1945. Venezuela's war activities were confined mainly to the protection and maintenance of its vital oil supplies and patrolling sea lanes in the Caribbean Sea.

The country's foreign policy vis-à-vis other Latin American countries has quite naturally reflected the nature of her governments. Under the authoritarian rule of Pérez Jiménez, Venezuela looked more favorably upon the other dictatorships than upon the democracies. Thus, Pérez Jiménez was friendly with Somoza of Nicaragua and the notorious Rafael Trujillo of the Dominican Republic, and he granted asylum to Perón, allowing him to invest sizable sums there. During these same years, the government of the United States conferred upon the Venezuelan dictator its Legion of Merit award, an act greatly resented by most Venezuelan citizens.

Friendly relations with dictatorships ceased under the administrations of *Acción Democrática*. The party had suffered under Pérez Jiménez, and when it came to power the second time in 1959, President Betancourt initiated a policy of refusing to recognize any government that came to power through unconstitutional means (the Betancourt Doctrine). In pursuit of this policy, Venezuela declined to continue relations with Fidel Castro's Cuba and at one time or another with new governments in Peru, Guatemala, Honduras, Brazil, and Argentina, among others.

The change of policy was reflected in Venezuela's strong criticism of the repressive regime of Rafael Trujillo. Early in 1960 President Betancourt had requested the Inter-American Peace Committee to investigate wholesale violations of human rights in the Dominican Republic. Trujillo retaliated by instigating an assassination attempt on the life of the Venezuelan president. For this and other acts, the Dominican Republic was condemned as an aggressor by the OAS under the terms of the Inter-American system, becoming the first Latin American state to be so designated.

Near the end of his term President Leoni referred to the non-recognition policy of AD in the following words:

> We meet our obligations in time. We respect others and we are respected. We are considered a model of democracy in the Hemisphere. We defend our political and economic independence. We maintain our principles, often alone, such as the repudiation of government by force and the usurpation of governments by violence. We do not interfere in the affairs of sister nations, whose people we love and whose well-being or misfortune affects us morally and materially. And we are decidedly against any violation of the individual sovereignty of people, be it from internal subversion or external force.[2]

President Caldera in his inaugural address served notice that he intended to modify the Betancourt Doctrine as well as to resume long-broken relations with the Soviet Union. Said he:

> It seems to me public opinion favors the establishment of relations with countries of political organization and ideology different from ours, for their presence in the world and their influence on economic relations cannot be ignored.
>
> On the other hand, I consider it advisable to change the policy of discontinuing relations with regimes arising from acts of violence against duly elected authorities on this con-

[2] *Venezuela Up-to-date,* 12 (Winter 1968–1969), 8.

tinent. Venezuela cannot continue without relations with peoples united to us by brotherly ties.[3]

Resumption of diplomatic ties with the Soviet Union was delayed because of a disagreement between the two countries over the projected size of the Soviet personnel force in Caracas. The Soviet Union wanted to employ about five times as many persons as the Venezuelan government felt was necessary. On March 28, 1970, diplomatic relations between the two nations were resumed.

REGIONAL ORGANIZATION: THE INTER-AMERICAN SYSTEM

Political relations

The Inter-American system, a unique development in the world, is the product of historical experience, gradual growth of habits of cooperation, and for most of its members, common expectations and problems as well as a common colonial heritage. The twenty-three member states are formally associated under the institutional apparatus of the Organization of American States (members are all of the Latin American states, although Cuba is no longer a participating member, plus the United States, Trinidad, and Tobago), and are bound together by a number of treaties that set forth the principles by which they are expected to conduct their mutual relations, and the common objectives toward which they are striving. All of these are embodied in the Charter of the OAS. It was signed in 1948 and entered into force on December 13, 1951.

The principles and objectives reflect certain basic concerns shared by the Latin American republics and the United States: the territorial integrity and sovereignty of states, the prevention of war in the hemisphere, the creation of methods and mechanisms for the peaceful solution of controversies, the relationship between the more powerful United States and her weaker neighbors, and finally, the political and social nature of the inter-American community and that of its individual members.[4]

[3] *Venezuela Up-to-date*, 12 (Spring 1969), 5.
[4] John C. Dreier, *The Organization of American States and the Hemisphere Crisis* (New York: Harper & Row, 1962), pp. 10–13.

Article 4 of the OAS Charter states the basic objectives:

a. to strengthen the peace and security of the continent;
b. to prevent possible causes of difficulties and to ensure the pacific settlement of disputes that may arise among the member states;
c. to provide for common action on the part of those states in the event of aggression;
d. to seek the solution of political, juridical and economic problems that may arise among them; and
e. to promote, by cooperative action, their economic, social and cultural development.

In pursuit of these objectives, OAS members agree to observe the basic standards of international law, to respect the juridicial equality of each other, to deal in good faith, to observe treaty obligations, and to promote the effective exercise of representative democracy in their own systems and in the organization as a whole.

Intervention in the domestic affairs of any member by another is condemned, as is aggression. An act of aggression against one member is considered to be one against all. The use of force in their international relations, except in self-defense, is renounced. The provisions on war and aggression are also contained in the Inter-American Treaty of Reciprocal Assistance signed in Rio de Janeiro in 1947. It entered into force on December 3, 1948, three years before the OAS Charter became effective. Under the Rio Treaty the American States agree to collective action in meeting any attack on one of its members.

In the forging of this instrument of cooperative action the aspirations of the great Venezuelan liberator, Simón Bolívar, were of seminal influence. At his invitation, delegations from most of the new Latin American states met in Panama in 1826 to consider his proposal for confederation. Although the delegates drafted a treaty of confederation, it was never ratified. Many of the important juridical principles of the present inter-American system, however, were foreshadowed in the 1826 draft treaty.[5]

[5] Dreier, p. 16.

A number of Inter-American Conferences have been held over the years. In 1954 Venezuela was host to the Tenth Inter-American Conference. Democratic Costa Rica refused to attend because of the antidemocratic nature of the Pérez Jiménez regime. Among other things, the Conference reluctantly approved (at the urging of the U.S. delegation led by John Foster Dulles) an anticommunist declaration directed primarily at Communist-dominated Guatemala. The declaration provided for a meeting of consultation among the foreign ministers when the political institutions of any American state were dominated or controlled by the international Communist movement. The member states also agreed to exchange information with each other and to expose communists' movements in their countries. Venezuela and Paraguay, both strongly anticommunist, accepted the declaration with more enthusiasm than did most of the other members who voted for it. The declaration paved the way for OAS action with regard to the Communist regime of Fidel Castro.

The presence of a strong and hostile Communist government in Cuba has been a disturbing influence in the inter-American system and a most trying affliction for its neighbors, particularly Venezuela. The latter has been an active participant in the various inter-American consultative meetings that have considered the Cuban problem. At the seventh meeting of the foreign ministers in San José, Costa Rica, in 1961, Venezuela supported the Declaration of San José, which was directed specifically at the Cuban regime, although the Venezuelan foreign minister resigned his post rather than sign the Declaration for his country. The Declaration condemned extracontinental intervention in hemisphere affairs and warned the Soviet-Sino bloc not to exploit domestic situations for its own purposes. Any American state that accepted such intervention was deemed to have jeopardized the solidarity of the inter-American system. At the Punta del Este meeting in 1962, Venezuela and Paraguay supported the resolution that removed Cuba from participation on the Inter-American Defense Board, a part of the collective defense machinery established under the Treaty of Rio de Janeiro. They also joined with fourteen countries in recommending that all OAS members cease trade in arms with Cuba and, along with twelve others, passed a declaration asserting that in view of the Marxist-Leninst orientation of the Cuban government, its continued participation in the organs of the OAS was incompatible with the democratic principles and aspirations of the inter-American system. Both countries, along with all the other nations of Latin America, supported the United States blockade of Cuban ports during the missile crisis of 1963.

In the years that followed, Venezuela often complained that Cuba was trying to destroy its constitutional system and create an environment conducive to a Communist take-over of its government. A 1965 report of an OAS investigating committee confirmed the truth of Venezuela's often-repeated charges that Cuba was financing, training, and directing guerrilla warfare in Venezuela. The report contained the following observation:

> This support of subversion, which generally takes the form of political aggression, has had positive application in the Republic of Venezuela, the primary objective of Cuba's policy of expansion and ideological penetration in the hemisphere. The vast natural resources of Venezuela, its strategic importance in the hemisphere, and its status as a democratic country were factors that motivated the present government of Cuba to make use of the subversive action of organizations that employ force and violence to overthrow that democratic government.[6]

And in 1967, following a landing of Cuban and Venezuelan guerrillas on Venezuelan soil, another OAS investigating committee appointed at Venezuela's request, reached the conclusion that

> the present government of Cuba continues to give moral and material support to the Venezuelan guerrilla and terrorist movement and that the recent series of aggressive acts against the Government of Venezuela are part of the Cuban Government's persistent intervention in the internal affairs of other American states by fostering and organizing subversive and terrorist activities in their territories.[7]

[6] *Venezuela Up-to-date,* 12 (Summer–Fall 1967), 4.
[7] *Venezuela Up-to-date,* 12 (Summer–Fall 1967), 4.

Venezuela has asked for stronger sanctions than the OAS as a whole has been willing or able to impose on Cuba.

Venezuela reacted somewhat differently to the United States' intervention in the domestic affairs of the Dominican Republic in 1965. The death of Trujillo in 1961 had opened the door to violent partisan politics and by 1965 there had been eight changes of government in the country. Following the overthrow of the Dominican regime in April 1965, the United States landed marines there and argued that intervention was necessary to protect American lives endangered by the civil conflict raging. A few days later it added as a further justification its determination to prevent the installation of another Communist regime in the Caribbean Sea. Favoring a strict application of the nonintervention clauses of the OAS Charter, Venezuela adopted a cool attitude toward the United States' action. In this instance she was more concerned with intervention than with communism. When in an emergency meeting of the foreign ministers, the U.S. requested the creation of an Inter-American Peace Force to share in the burden of the occupation and to widen the legitimacy of the intervention, Venezuela abstained. Paraguay, on the other hand, endorsed the Peace Force and was one of three countries to send troops to the Dominican Republic.

Economic relations: the Alliance for Progress

On March 13, 1961, President Kennedy announced in a speech to the Latin American ambassadors in Washington, D.C., the willingness of the United States to join with the republics of Latin America in a massive effort to improve economic and social conditions of their people. His proposals were formalized at the Punte del Este Conference in August 1961, and were accepted by all the countries present except Cuba.

The Alliance rests upon certain fundamental assumptions and beliefs: revolutionary changes in the economic and social systems can be achieved by reasonable men of good faith working within the framework of democratic, constitutional government. Evolutionary reform is possible without revolution and violence.

In a very real sense, the Alliance for Progress, as this venture is known, is a cooperative venture designed to contain the explosive forces inherent in the maladjusted societies of Latin America and to divert their energies into peaceful solutions to their problems. It was—and is—an attempt to counteract the attractions of Castro's call to action.

The Alliance for Progress is more than a multinational attack on social and economic diseases in the hemisphere, more than a humanitarian response to the revolution of rising expectations. It has as a basic long-range political objective the elimination of dictatorship and the firm and lasting establishment of constitutional government as the basis of legitimacy in all of the cooperating countries. Its political ramifications, therefore, include the expansion of the small class of articulate participants in the political process. Although this ultimate objective is not spelled out specifically in the basic accord that established the Alliance, it can be deduced from the concern for social justice. A society based on social justice is one in

> . . . which the fruits of production are widely and fairly shared, in which the farmer owns his own land and the worker benefits fairly from his labor, in which education and health facilities are available to all, in which equal opportunity and individual dignity have real meaning in the life of the people.[8]

These are precisely some of the major principles upon which the economic and social system of the United States is based. The United States is at present torn by a struggle on the part of *minority* groups to realize these principles. Latin America is torn by a struggle to make the principles applicable to a *majority* of the people.

Hopefully, the major goals of the Alliance for Progress would be achieved through a planned program of cooperative self-help. To that end the United States proposed in 1961 a ten-year program of development that called for an expenditure of $100 billion, 80 percent of which was to come from the Latin Americans themselves and the remainder from the United States government, private investors, international lending agencies, and foreign governments The proposed $80 billion contribution from Latin America was a sizable one, but economic

[8] U.S. Bureau of Public Affairs, Department of State, "The Alliance for Progress," *Foreign Affairs Outline* (June 1964), 5.

experts argued that by attacking the problem of tax evasion, some $3 billion a year could be realized in additional revenue. To do this and to bring about social and economic justice, as well as to increase their ability to share in the financing of the program, Latin American governments were asked to undertake a serious program of tax reform to eliminate widespread tax evasion and improve tax collections. They were expected to draft comprehensive and logical systems of tax laws in order that more of the burden would fall on the shoulders of those who could afford it. Tax reforms should be accompanied by administrative reforms to ensure that increased revenues were properly used for legitimate purposes. Nagging problems in all Latin American countries have been swollen bureaucracies, deficits in public enterprises, and misuse of public funds by corrupt public officials.

Traditionally against taxes in their attitudes, Latin Americans see no reason to pay their taxes to inefficient and corrupt governments. They regard it as proper for them to cheat the government as it is for the government to cheat them. Thus a basic challenge to all of the governments of Latin America is to earn the confidence and cooperation of their taxpayers. Until this is done, administrative reforms and new tax laws are worthless, however scientifically and clearly devised.

A second reform basic to the realization of economic and social justice in Latin America is that of land reform. Under the Alliance for Progress, the Latin American governments commit themselves to attacking

> . . . unjust structures and systems of land tenure and use, with a view of replacing *latifundia* and dwarf holdings by an equitable system of land tenure, so that, with the help of timely and adequate credit, technical assistance and facilities for the marketing and distribution of products, the land will become for the man who owns it the basis of his economic stability, the foundation of his increasing welfare, and the guarantee of his freedom and dignity.[9]

Most of the rural peasantry throughout Latin America own no land at all, are tenant farmers, or worse still, peons who have

[9] *The Charter of Punte del Este,* Title I, clause 6.

almost no monetary income. Peasant land-hunger may very well be one of the most pressing problems facing the Latin American countries. If the answer cannot be found through constitutional process under the stimulation of the Alliance, it might be found through resort to violence. Castro has shown the way.

All governments are expected to cut their swollen military and defense budgets and thus free much-needed revenue for more productive ends such as roads, hospitals, schools, capital improvements, and investments. The Alliance stresses also a desired annual rate of economic growth of at least 2.5 percent, diversification in national economic structures, educational reforms to eliminate adult illiteracy, and by 1970 to assure a minimum of six years of primary education for every school-age child in Latin America.

With these basic concerns in mind, let us now turn to a consideration of the achievements and progress of Venezuela and Paraguay under the Alliance for Progress. A detailed examination of all the facets of development in the two countries is outside the scope of this study, but some results can be noted in several major areas.

Venezuela began a program of land and tax reform before the Alliance for Progress came into being. The reforms were part of the program of *Acción Democrática.* In his final report to the nation in 1969, President Leoni summarized some of the achievements of ten years of AD government. Farm families numbering 160,000 had been given title to and settled on some 3.8 million hectares of land, much of it publicly owned. Agricultural productivity on these lands rose from 80 million bolívares in 1960 to 600 million bolívares in 1967. This was an increase of 650 percent. Overall agricultural production increased at an annual rate of growth of 6.5 percent between 1959 and 1967. Venezuela's record in agrarian reform and production places it among the very few countries in Latin America that have made significant progress in these areas.

Venezuela claims equally dramatic results in its efforts to improve the education system. During the same ten-year period 6427 new classrooms were added to the physical plant to accommodate 323,000 students. The total student enrollment rose from 845,000 in 1959 to more than 2 million in 1969, a rise of 74.5 percent. Illiteracy was decreased from 33 percent of those over 10 years of age to 11 percent by 1968. Annual expenditures on education increased from 10.9 percent of the national budget to 16.3 percent in 1968.

There was little change, however, in military expenditures during the period. In 1965, direct military allocations absorbed 10.2 percent of the budget, while in 1969 they amounted to 9.9 percent.

That the government had not done so well in the realm of tax reforms is indicated by the fact that the minister of finance was asked in 1966 to conduct a study of the fiscal system for the purpose of "framing a harmonious taxation system that will encourage savings and investments, and at the same time, assure enough revenues to carry out the social and economic programs the government has in mind." [10]

Venezuela's GNP has increased at an average rate of 4.5 percent over the past five years, well above the 2.5 percent called for by the Alliance. Food production has risen at an annual rate of 7 percent.

On the basis of such evidence it must be concluded that Venezuela has been an effective partner in the Alliance for Progress and that it has made significant advances in the pursuit of its major goals. It is, however, dissatisfied with some aspects of the Alliance and has called for less financial aid and more cooperation, particularly on the part of the United States in easing her trade restrictions.

With considerably fewer natural, social, and financial resources at its disposal, Paraguay has naturally made much slower progress toward even a minimal realization of the goals of the Alliance. It has had a land reform law on its books since 1936. Opposition of landowners—many of whom were foreigners—and the belief of some of the squatter farmers that the ownership of land might actually be a liability to them, made the law difficult to apply. By 1953 the government seemingly abandoned the plan to divide large holdings into small when it embarked upon a plan of colonization and settlement.[11] Essentially the plan called for the great landowners to encourage

[10] *Venezuela Up-to-date*, 12 (Spring–Summer 1966), 2.
[11] Pendle, p. 61.

peasants to settle on their land and develop it, thus bringing large acreages under production. Landlords were offered a moratorium on property taxes for five years and duty-free imports of all necessary equipment. Under a law passed in 1960, owners of properties in excess of 10,000 hectares are required to colonize 10 percent of their lands if the soil is suitable for farming. They must sell lots to those eligible for the benefits of agrarian farming. The government also began to settle groups of peasants and foreign immigrants such as the Japanese and the Mennonites from Canada. Those who colonize state lands are awarded tracts of land from 20 to 200 hectares free of charge.

By mid-1965, under both public and private colonization settlement projects, the Rural Welfare Institute claimed to have distributed 1.1 million hectares of land to 50,000 family groups in 206 colonization sites. Privately settled communities occupied an additional 1.1 million hectares. In spite of these figures, Paraguay is not regarded as a country that has adequately faced up to its land tenure problem. Its agricultural potential is still barely tapped in spite of the high priority given by the government to agricultural and livestock development.

Paraguay has done nothing about the second objective of the Alliance: tax reform. In 1966, a subcommittee of the Inter-American Committee on the Alliance for Progress (CIAP) urged Paraguay to initiate an integrated program of tax reform, including a realistic appraisal of real-property taxes and the use of sales and consumer taxes. In its 1968 annual review of Paraguay's economic condition, the CIAP's major finding was that tax legislation was absolutely essential if Paraguay wished to ward off financial crisis. At the end of 1969, however, no action had been taken on the CIAP's recommendation. Paraguay is, therefore, depriving itself of badly needed revenue, the lack of which is reflected in all fields of public development, such as in education.

Nevertheless, some gains have been registered in the educational system. Illiteracy has been reduced from 31.4 percent to about 25 percent of those persons 15 years of age and over according to Paraguayan sources. School enrollments have increased from 290,000 in 1958 to almost 400,000 in 1969. Although Paraguay spends about 16.5 percent of its annual budget on education, the physical plant is still far from adequate. Many rural localities are either without facilities at all or are serviced by the barest minimum. In 20 administrative zones of the republic, 627 localities offered only first-grade work; in 650 localities, 2 grades; and in 411 localities, 3 grades. Only 385 communities had schools that offered work through the sixth grade.[12] Paraguay thus has a long way to go before it reaches the Alliance goal of six years of primary education for every child of school age.

Paraguay has done nothing about reducing its military expenditures. The national defense organization and police forces eat up about 22 percent of the yearly revenue.

Economic integration

One of the stated goals of the OAS and the Alliance for Progress is the promotion of the economic development of member states. Article 26 of the OAS Charter commits the members to co-operate as far as their resources and their laws permit to strengthen their economic structures, develop their agriculture and mining, promote their industry, and increase their trade. Title II of the Charter of Punte del Este further elaborates on that objective and outlines concrete suggestions as to how the objectives can be reached.

Under these general guidelines the Latin American republics have set up several economic regional organizations. The Central American Common Market was created in 1952. The Latin American Free Trade Association, embracing the ten countries of South America plus Mexico, was authorized in 1960 by the Treaty of Montevideo. Paraguay was an original member of LAFTA; Venezuela did not become an active member until January 1966.

Faced with the pressure of an ever-increasing population that was outpacing their economic capacities and growth, the signatory nations of LAFTA agreed to work toward the creation by 1972 of a free-trade area among themselves. This objective was to be reached through the process of gradual reductions in and elimination of trade barriers among the participating mem-

[12] *Población, Urbanización y Recursos Humanos en el Paraguay,* D. M. Rivarola and G. Heisecke, eds. (Asunción: Centro Paraguayo de Estudios Sociológicos, 1969), p. 188.

bers, so that by 1972 most LAFTA trade, if not all, would be moving freely. Each year the members meet to negotiate a schedule of concessions that each is willing to grant to the others. Since the beginning of LAFTA there has been a gradual expansion of tariff preferences to LAFTA goods over those imported from the outside.

Paraguay, as one of the least developed countries in LAFTA, enjoys a special status within it. In 1962, for example, LAFTA approved a request by Paraguay for duty-free exports for a number of Paraguayan products for a period of nine years. Since 30 percent of Paraguay's total export trade is with LAFTA markets, and with Argentina in particular, the concession has had real monetary value. In spite of this concession and a few others, economic opinion in Paraguay is divided as to the merits of membership in LAFTA. Some of its small industrial class feel that Paraguay does not have a strong enough industrial establishment to participate advantageously in a free-trade area.[13] President Stroessner, however, has continued to seek closer connections with the economic bloc.

Paraguay's underdeveloped economy and the absence of an even modest industrial complex give it little bargaining power vis-à-vis LAFTA's big three: Argentina, Mexico, and Brazil.

Venezuela remained aloof from LAFTA until 1966, largely because of the opposition of her industrial leaders who felt that tariff reductions and other obligations would adversely affect the growth of its industry and commerce.

LAFTA results have been less than spectacular. About 80 percent of the tariff reductions on some 9800 trade items in effect in 1966 were negotiated in the first several years of the organization's existence.[14] Members appear to be reluctant to make concessions on manufactured goods. At present, the members of LAFTA seem satisfied with relatively modest achievements.

A long-range goal of LAFTA is the creation of a Latin American Common Market. In 1967, delegates from LAFTA

[13] Pendle, p. 72.
[14] Alexander T. Edelmann, *Latin American Government and Politics, the Dynamics of a Revolutionary Society,* rev. ed. (Homewood, Ill.: The Dorsey Press, 1969), p. 285.

and the Central American Common Market met in the Paraguayan capital to discuss the feasibility of a merger between the two blocs. Such a merger would be a great step toward the achievement of that goal. Nothing has come of the plan so far.

In order to speed industrialization of the less developed members of LAFTA, the meeting of American Presidents in 1967 approved the concept of subregional economic integration, with the Andean countries specifically in mind. An Andean group composed of Chile, Ecuador, Peru, Bolivia, Colombia, and Venezuela was contemplated. By mid-1969, however, the basic accord by which the group would function had not been signed by enough members to bring it into effect. For reasons similar to those raised in objection to LAFTA membership, Venezuela has dragged its feet about joining the group. Disparities in relative stages of growth and an unwillingness to expose domestic industry to competition from other member countries have impeded organization progress. The six countries have agreed to the creation of a $100 million Andean Development Corporation to assist in financing industries that can be jointly developed. Its headquarters will be in Caracas. At the end of 1970 Venezuela still had not ratified the treaty.

PARTICIPATION IN INTERNATIONAL ORGANIZATIONS: THE LEAGUE OF NATIONS AND THE UNITED NATIONS

The League of Nations

All twenty Latin American republics were at one time or another members of the League of Nations. They were attracted by the ideal of universality on which the League was based. Their interest began to wane when it became clear that the League was more concerned with Europe than with universality and that the organization would not permit itself to be used in such a way as to counter the influence of the United States in this hemisphere.[15] Paraguay withdrew from the League in 1932 as a protest against League action in the dispute with

[15] John A. Houston, *Latin America in the United Nations* (New York: Carnegie Endowment for International Peace, 1956), p. 4.

Bolivia over the *Chaco*. Venezuela left the League in 1938, giving no reason for its withdrawal.

The United Nations

Both Venezuela and Paraguay, by virtue of their last-minute declarations of war against the Axis in World War II were entitled to sign the Declaration of the United Nations and to take part in the formulation of the Charter. They, along with the other Latin American republics, were original members of the international body. Realistically assessing their impotence as individual members, they formed a Latin American group during the first session of the General Assembly and have voted with near unanimity on many occasions. The United States relied heavily on their votes in its contests with the bloc dominated by the Soviet Union. The importance of the Latin American group has been diluted as a result of the admission of many Afro-Asian states and the new mini-states in recent years.

Although all states are at least theoretically equal in the General Assembly, it is quite clear that a member's voice is listened to in proportion to the audience's estimate of its capabilities and sense of responsibility to the organization.

Paraguay's ability to influence decisions within the Latin American group and in the United Nations at large has been hampered by its small size, its relative unimportance in international affairs and by its inability or unwillingness to meet its financial obligations to the U.N. For many years it paid no assessments at all. In 1964, along with a number of other countries, it was threatened with the loss of its vote in the General Assembly for being more than two years in arrear of its dues. Oil-rich Venezuela has had no difficulty in meeting a much larger assessment.

One indication of a country's power and influence in the United Nations is the posts to which it is elected. Venezuela has been elected to serve four nonconsecutive terms on the powerful Economic and Social Council, one of the six major organs of the U.N., and was a member of the Security Council during 1962–1963. In 1963 its delegate, Carlos Sosa Rodríguez was elected president of the General Assembly. Paraguay has had fewer posts. It was a member of the Security Council during

1968 and 1969 and has served one term on the relatively unimportant Trusteeship Council. Both countries have been members of numerous *ad hoc* committees and subcommittees of the General Assembly.

Paraguay and Venezuela participate in all of the U.N. specialized agencies except the Intergovernmental Maritime Consultative Organization.

During the discussions that led to the Statute of the International Court of Justice, all of the Latin American republics were strongly in favor of compulsory jurisdiction for the Court, feeling that they were more likely to obtain justice in a world court than in the dangerous game of power politics.[16] Venezuela later voted with a majority to accept a subcommittee recommendation to permit optional jurisdiction. Paraguay, however, stood firm and is today one of fewer than forty countries that have accepted the compulsory jurisdiction of the International Court of Justice.

SUMMARY

The ability of a country to carry on an effective foreign policy, to deal forcefully with other nations in pursuit of its national interests, to have its voice listened to with respect in international forums, is, of course, largely dependent upon its domestic capabilities and resources.

In international affairs Paraguay negotiates from a weak position. Its landlocked isolation in the interior of the continent deprives it of strategic importance. Its population is primarily rural, agricultural, and impoverished; one-fourth is illiterate. The economy is greatly underdeveloped and in many areas subsistence farming is a way of life. Valuable mineral resources are almost completely absent. Paraguay, in short, possesses little in the way of the vital financial, social, and natural resources needed to give it some weight in international affairs and in its bilateral relationships. In addition, it suffers from the handicap of being governed by an authoritarian dictatorship that claims to be a democracy. Yet Paraguay has shown by its remarkable military feats in two wars that it will go to great lengths to defend its basic interests.

[16] Houston, p. 57.

Venezuela, on the other hand, has much going for it. It is strategically positioned on the northern rim of South America facing the Caribbean Sea and abutting on the vital approaches to the Panama Canal. The country is rich in enormous resources of oil and iron ore, as well as in generous deposits of other useful minerals. It has a high potential in hydroelectric power, so much so that it contemplates sales to Brazil and Colombia. The evolution of its political system in the direction of democracy gives Venezuela a tremendous psychological advantage in international organizations that are dedicated to the principles of representative democracy. Because of the wealth it derives from oil and iron, it can participate meaningfully in cooperative economic ventures and make a more effective use of funds from international lending agencies.

Paraguay is regarded as a country where little happens and where few changes take place. Venezuela has proved by the enormous activity in all areas of its domestic system that its efforts to bring about real changes are paying off.

TEN
SUMMARY
AND CONCLUSIONS

In the introduction to this book the premise was advanced that despite many similarities in their social, economic, and political structures, Venezuela and Paraguay were at quite different stages in their development at the end of the 1960 decade. The succeeding chapters attempted to analyze the force and factors that have helped to produce this disparity. Thus we discussed their geographic characteristics and location on the continent, their economic and social resources, the nature, source, and ingredients of their political culture, their historical evolution, the nature of their political institutions, and finally some aspects of their political processes.

Utilizing the terms "traditionalism and progress" we described Venezuela as a country that has made considerable progress in spite of the inhibiting forces of traditional structures and attitudes. Paraguay was contrasted as a country that is still dominated by traditionalism in both society and government, and one in which overall progress has been meager.

We can examine progress or the lack of it under several different headings, such as the realization of democratic goals, utilization of national resources, improvement of the economy, and the degree to which the political leadership responds to the demands of the population.

PROGRESS TOWARD DEMOCRACY

Although this volume did not undertake to judge either country primarily on the basis of whether it did or did not have a democratic government and society, that subject inevitably arose in all of the discussions. It did so because the people of both nations have spoken of their attachment to the principles of democracy through the public utterances of their leaders, the writings of some of their intellectuals, and by their constitutional provisions. Alleged observance of both principle and practice of democracy has often formed the basis of an appeal by the political leaders to the population for their support and loyalty. In the minds of both people and leaders, at least outward conformity to democratic institutions and practices is a vital part of a regime's claim to legitimacy. Thus President Stroessner justified a most oppressive law by invoking the prestige value of democracy. His "Law for the Defense of Democracy and the Political and Social Order" is one of the most severe restrictions on the individual liberty of any in Latin America.

Venezuela has made significant progress during the past ten years toward its announced goal of a democratic government, although it has by no means completely achieved that objective. Indeed, there are forces operating in the country that seek to reverse the democratic trends of the past decade, or at least to substitute their own version of the democratic process.

If relatively moderate tensions among competing groups is a requisite for democracy,[1] then perhaps Venezuela might fail this test because of too much tension. Not only has open hostility among the major political parties been evident, but tension, violence, and terrorism have been daily fare for much of society. During the past ten years the Venezuelan government has been under attack by guerrilla and terrorist bands who seek an end to the present form of government. These attempts have been nurtured by such subversive groups as the Movement of the Revolutionary Left (MIR), the Armed Forces for National Liberation (FALN), and the Communist party. Incidents of violence will probably increase, for early in 1970 MIR and FALN

[1] See Seymour Lipset, "Some Social Requisites of Democracy: Economic Development and Political Legitimacy," *American Political Science Review,* 53 (March 1959), 97.

agreed to form a united party and a "single revolutionary army" to carry on the guerrilla warfare.[2] Less-organized elements such as students have also engaged in violence as a means of publicizing their grievances. To meet such threats to the established order, the government has on occasion suspended certain constitutional guarantees relating to freedom of press, assembly, and political activity. Only the resistors, the politically active vociferous citizens are affected much by these suspensions. The ordinary citizens feel no restraint. In seeking to contain the violence, the government regards the use of force to meet force as a legitimate exercise of authority because it is in the defense of the democratic aspirations and institutions of the nation. Although opposition party leaders are usually critical of the government for its handling of the guerrilla problem, most Venezuelans would probably support the state's position. At the end of the decade, then, Venezuela was faced with a determined and disloyal group of dissidents who sought to bring about change through unconstitutional means. It has been suggested that the use of force or threat of force has figured prominently in the political development of Venezuela. What is significant today is that this method of achieving power and bringing about change no longer seems to be regarded as a legitimate aspect of the political process.

It is true that the high incidence of violence casts a pall of gloom over the prospects for an enduring, stable, and democratic government, but the picture is not without its bright spots. For one thing, the persistence of violence has not prevented three national elections from taking place on schedule in spite of threats from such groups as FALN to disrupt the process by firing on citizens who went to the polls (They did not.). The elections have taken place without major incident in a relatively calm and free atmosphere. Charges of electoral irregularities are always made, of course, but Venezuelans seem satisfied that the votes have been counted with reasonable honesty. By adhering to the electoral method of changing power, Venezuelans are showing an increasing commitment to a basic tenet of democracy: citizen participation and consultation.

The prospects for more democracy have also been consid-

[2] *Latin America,* January 30, 1970, p. 40.

erably brightened by one of the most significant political developments in Venezuelan history: the peaceful transfer of power from one constitutionally elected president to another and more importantly, from one party to another. Since 1959, presidential power has changed hands three times, and in 1969 *Acción Democrática* handed over the reins of government to its leading opponent and critic, the Social Christian party. This event should not be underestimated, for it was the first time in Venezuelan history that such a thing had happened. Because of it, leading opposition parties now feel encouraged to entertain the hope, should they win the votes, of being permitted to assume the mantle of power. This expectation can only lead to more participation in politics by persons and groups that previously felt the whole electoral process to be a futile attempt at representation. Although the evidence so far does not support it, all of these developments might lead to more responsibility in government as more parties and their leaders become involved in the process of governing, either as articulate members of the legislature or of the president's cabinet.

Democratic trends have been fostered in other ways: election laws have encouraged many political parties to enter candidates. Since 1959 almost all groups that have sought recognition as political parties have been granted legal status. Thus in 1968, influenced by the prospect for being able to have some say in government and encouraged by the device of proportional representation, some eighteen parties entered the contest. Large numbers of citizens cast their votes, approximately 84 percent of those qualified. A high percent of voter turnout does not, of course, necessarily signify an abiding attachment to the electoral method or to democracy for that matter; indeed, most citizens were complying with their legal obligation. The sanctions for not casting one's vote are such that they pose no realistic threat to lower classes, however, and these people vote in fairly large numbers. Perhaps they do so because they feel both a sense of duty and because they feel their vote is now important. One thing is clear: the voter since 1959 has seen his vote counted and his preference respected. This can only increase his belief in himself as an effective participant in at least one phase of the political process.

Venezuela's march toward a democratic system has been

inhibited by countervailing forces in society and politics. A social, military, and religious elite still cling to an outmoded structure of privilege based upon birth, class status, and educational opportunity. Traditionalism is thus reflected in the enduring preeminence of intellectual and professional notables in the power structure of political parties. Leadership often is acquired on the basis of such ascriptive criteria as illustrious family connections. This is not to deny that brilliant individuals are not recognized for their intellectual merit and their contributions to the national culture. If stature is dependent upon intellectual attainments—as it often is—and such attainments are in turn dependent upon access to the educational system, then the implementation of an educational philosophy that opens the doors to all who would learn and not just to the upper segments of society would be an indication of an intent to democraticize society. The Venezuelan government has succeeded in instituting educational reforms to raise the literacy level of its citizens. Some progress has been made toward liberalizing the university system to permit access by the lower classes, but essentially a university education remains a prerogative of the middle and upper classes.

Other elements of traditionalism are in the process of change. For one thing, the dependent nature of a landless peasantry tied to the economic and political power of the landlord will surely respond to agrarian reform, which has as its basic purpose the distribution of land to the peons. Agrarian reform is decreasing the power of the landlord through expropriation of some of his land. Conferring it upon the landless peasants clothes them in the dignity of ownership, thus increasing the number of people who have an economic stake in the stability of the government. Many peasants have benefited, but few landlords have been affected so far, as much of the land distributed has come from the public domain. Nevertheless, the imbalance of land ownership is being redressed, however slowly.

The Church also is changing as it moves from its traditionally conservative stand to programs associated with economic and social reform. Activist priests have helped to organize labor and peasant groups. The hierarchy has voiced its opposition to authoritarianism in politics and despite its own authoritarian structure, the Church clearly seems to have associated itself with the revolution of rising expectations.

The military establishment has ceased, at least overtly, to interfere in the political process. Yet everyone is sensitive to the fact that the armed forces must be reckoned with in almost every facet of the policy-making process. It is by no means certain that Venezuela will be able to withstand the present strong trend toward military government in Latin America.

All of these developments taken together point to a reasonably healthy political climate in Venezuela. If the present trend toward democracy persists and a government committed to basic social and economic reform can endure, then perhaps Venezuela is on the way to the achievement of a political system in which violence as a way of conflict resolution will diminish, and in which a truly participant society can emerge.

In the 1950s Venezuela and Paraguay were much alike in the realm of politics, both being ruled by dictatorships committed more to law and order than to reform. Venezuela moved from the shadow of authoritarianism with the overthrow of Marcos Pérez Jiménez; in Paraguay the shade appears to be deepening.

There is a temptation to dismiss Paraguay as an unfortunate little republic for which there is little hope. There can be no doubt that the army controls the country; that opposition parties play a farcical role and have no real voice in politics; that so far as one may say there is party government, it is one-party government; and that individual liberties are almost non-existent. Paraguay has few of the ingredients of the democratic system called for in its constitution.

Yet the picture is not all black. Opposition parties were permitted to run candidates in 1968, and although they had little hope of doing much of anything, several of them participated anyway. The Church, long a supporter of Paraguayan regimes, has embarked on a new course, becoming an increasingly active and outspoken critic of the regime. Its role in this area would be stronger if its prestige among Paraguayans were higher. Like the Venezuelan Church, the Paraguayan has begun to show an interest in social and economic progress and has repeatedly reminded the government of this concern in recent years. To this end the Church has been calling for an end to the repressive politics of President Stroessner and for the creation of a state based upon the principles of social justice and Christianity.

Students too are becoming restive under the continued oppression of a government that seeks to silence all dissent. Students are particularly sensitive to criticism leveled at Paraguay by student organizations in other countries, and they are challenging the dictatorship in ways that require a good deal of courage. The Paraguayans, it will be remembered, have never been called cowardly; passive, yes, but not timid.

A military, intellectual, and party elite controlled Paraguay in 1970. At the present time there is little to encourage the belief that power will change hands in the immediate future. Most of the active opposition live abroad; those who live in Paraguay live dangerously.

Paraguayans vote in large numbers. Like the Venezuelans, they have a legal duty to do so. Unlike the Venezuelans, they know they are voting for continuity and the status quo. Elections produce no change in Paraguay.

PROGRESS IN THE UTILIZATION OF NATIONAL RESOURCES

What progress have Venezuela and Paraguay made in using effectively the national resources with which they are endowed—human, material, and natural? And to what degree have their respective populations shared in the benefits at the disposal of the government?

It may be flatly said that Paraguay has made only very modest progress in the effective utilization of its overall resources. A damning fact is that so many Paraguayans choose or are forced to live outside their own country. Some are political exiles, but a sizable number of those who live in Argentina, Brazil, and Uruguay do so because there are greater opportunities there for individual advancement and employment than in Paraguay. Since many of the exiles come from the educated classes or are artisans of the middle class, the country is deprived of their intellectual potential and their skills. The brain drain can have only adverse effects on the development of the nation. Paraguay cannot make intelligent use of its human resources when so many of its people are expatriates.

For those who remain in Paraguay, particularly for the rural population, the government has done little to help them improve their standard of living. The educational infrastructure is expanding at too slow a rate to meet the challenge of the rapidly increasing population. Jobs are not being created nearly fast enough to absorb the growing number of young people—trained and untrained—who are entering the job market each year. For the foreseeable future, therefore, most young Paraguayans are destined to be what their parents were: subsistence farmers or intermittently employed proletarians.

This sorry state of affairs cannot be laid entirely at the door of a callous or indifferent government, although that might be a contributing factor. The lack of adequate revenue to finance programs that could increase the ability of the population to produce and to contribute to economic and cultural growth is perhaps the primary reason for the slow rate of Paraguayan development. Another factor might be the attitude of the population toward the work and sacrifice that is involved in bringing about changes of the magnitude that are required. Some authors believe that many Paraguayans are reasonably content with their lot. Involvement with the government in reform programs might mean an unwelcome increase in their responsibilities as individuals and might restrict them in undesirable ways, such as moving about from place to place in search of temporary use of good land.

Paraguay is hampered in its modest development plans by the poverty of its domestic economy, a poverty that was accentuated by the losses incurred in national wars. The subsoil holds no promise of great wealth, as oil and mineral deposits are minimal. The industrial and manufacturing establishment is in its infancy; the internal transportation system, despite recent additions and improvements, is woefully inadequate for commercial purposes; agricultural methods do not yield enough to feed the country, and foodstuffs often have to be imported. Other inhibiting factors are the antiquated tax structure and an inefficient method of tax collection. The collection of public revenue is affected adversely by the absence of a uniform tax code, the lack of a trained, competent, and efficient bureaucracy, and by a system of farming out taxes to collectors entitled to keep a share of the money they collect. The minister of finance receives and supervises the expenditure of the revenues that are collected. Certain taxes, however, are collected by other ministries and autonomous agencies that disburse them in accordance with the provisions of special laws.

Many people escape paying taxes almost entirely because of the numerous exemptions provided by law. The income tax, which produces about 10 percent of the total yearly revenue of the government, is whittled down by such numerous exemptions as the following: agricultural production, wages of workers, salaries of public officials, income from professional activity, retirement pay, pensions, annuities, inheritances, and gifts or money won in games of chance. Most of these items are taxed in Venezuela. The law also exempts the income of religious, scientific, literary, artistic, and charitable organizations, trade unions, mutual loan societies, and agricultural cooperatives. Income taxes are paid primarily by banks, financial enterprises, investment firms, and commercial, industrial, and transportation concerns.

Paraguay relies to a much heavier extent upon a more traditional source of revenue: import taxes. Import duties make up almost 17 percent of the government's annual income as compared to 7 percent in Venezuela. Much of the remaining income comes from taxes on sales, property, and liquor. The annual budget of Paraguay runs around $60 million. Because the population has an average annual per capita income of less than $200, it is clear that the government and the people cannot expect much from each other. And as to the limited range of its revenue-producing bases and the serious poverty of most of its people, Paraguay is poorly equipped at present to make the most of its limited social and natural resources.

Venezuela is in a much better position than Paraguay to make good use of its total resources. Most Venezuelans remain in Venezuela; even under the repressive regimes of earlier days, the total number of exiles and expatriates was few in comparison with those of Paraguay. The government is encouraging the growth of a scientific and technical class. Many young Venezuelans receive such training abroad and return to their country to put their skills to work. This fact presents the government with a formidable challenge of keeping abreast of occupation demands. The problem of finding employment for large numbers of young workers each year is almost as pressing in Venezuela as in Paraguay. Venezuela is in a more advantageous position to meet this and other challenges because of the wealth it derives from its oil and iron reserves. Indeed, in terms of social and economic development, the economies of Venezuela and Paraguay began to diverge in the second decade of this century when oil was discovered in Venezuela. The wealth released into the economy as a result of that event provided the government with large and steady revenues and enabled it to begin many needed development programs. More than wealth was needed, however. Intelligent leadership committed to the wise investment of the money and to the welfare of all of the people was an essential requirement. The equitable distribution of the common wealth of the country in services and facilities also had to await the birth of genuine political parties motivated by national rather than particular concerns.

Although the Gómez regime adopted the policy of "sowing the oil," that is, of investing the proceeds in domestic improvement projects, real progress in this direction did not begin until after the dictator's death in 1935. Since then the government has used oil income to change the face of the republic. Superhighways, secondary roads, schools of all types, hotels, dams, and hospitals have been built all over the country. Though still not enough, more and more people are benefiting from better employment opportunities, government services (health, education, old age benefits, and so on), and from government development programs. Venezuela has been remarkably successful in negotiating advantageous contracts with the foreign oil companies, and has come to rely very heavily upon them for money to run the country. The dominance of oil in the economic system can be seen from the fact that the companies normally provide about two-thirds of the government revenue each year in the form of royalties and income tax. Indeed, the companies pay about 80 percent of the total income tax collected. Venezuelans with an income of less than $2640 a year are not required to file a tax return. As the majority of Venezuelans earn less than this (the average annual per capita income is about $800), most citizens escape paying the tax.

Oil companies often are expected to bear new tax burdens to make up for deficiencies in the revenue structure or to pay for new undertakings. It is far easier, for example, for the government to impose tax increases on foreign companies doing business in Venezuela than it is to increase and collect taxes on Venezuelan citizens and business concerns. The creation of new domestic taxes or an increase in an old one almost always results in a flight of capital from the country. The point has been made that Venezuelans and Paraguayans, like most Latin Americans, are not meticulous in honoring their tax obligations. Indeed, tax evasion is thought to be the rule rather than the exception. Evasion becomes a serious problem for a country like Paraguay, which lacks a major revenue-producing source directly under government control. In Venezuela the effects are less severe because of the oil wealth. So long as the government can collect adequate funds from the oil and mining companies, it will probably make little effort to improve its tax structures or to insist on the payment of taxes legally due it from its own citizens. If one considers the payment of taxes as a major form of citizen support for the system, then Paraguay and Venezuela would rank low.

Until recent years Venezuelans were reluctant to invest their capital in domestic enterprises, preferring to put their funds in land, savings accounts, or in foreign stocks. In part, this reluctance was due to a cultural inheritance that placed a prestige value on land ownership and in part, among those with capital to invest, to a lack of confidence in the ability of the government to maintain an environment stable enough to protect domestic investments. These attitudes are now changing as a result of agrarian reforms, and forceful initiatives by the government to encourage new industry, both domestic and foreign.

Venezuela's extractive capabilities cannot, in the final analysis, be considered apart from their dependence upon oil and mineral resources. In a modern age of increasing demands and expectations, these capabilities have yet to be adequately tested.

PROGRESS IN THE DISTRIBUTION
OF GOODS AND SERVICES

How are government revenues distributed and who benefits by them? The government has at its disposal not only money, but jobs, honors, services, economic opportunities, and military and tax exemptions.

We have argued previously that the military establishment in both Paraguay and Venezuela always receives a healthy portion of the government's annual revenues—about 10 percent in Venezuela and 17 percent in Paraguay. It is true that the armed forces use some of their allocation in civic-action programs (road building, for example), but most of it goes toward keeping an up-to-date and expensive defense apparatus that considers itself an integral part of the political and policy-making process. In neither country does the military organization really earn its keep in terms of protecting the nation from external aggression. It is, of course, used to combat internal threats. So long as either country is under the protective umbrella of the United States, however distasteful that may be to them, neither needs a military force of the magnitude it has.

Of prime importance to every political system is the scope and range of its educational structure. Paraguay now spends in the neighborhood of 15 percent of its income on educational institutions. In its 1969 budget, Venezuela allocated 14.6 percent. In terms of money spent, however, that means that Venezuela expended $300 million as compared with Paraguay's $63 million. Venezuela's massive effort to improve its whole educational posture is affecting ever larger numbers of children and even adults who wish to take advantage of the opportunity to become literate. Inefficient use is made of the facilities that do exist in Paraguay, as 50 percent of the dropouts occur between the first and second grades. Paraguay's problem is not only one of money and facilities, but also one of parental attitudes and student attendance, neither of which is high among the majority of lower-class citizens.

In other areas of citizen welfare, Venezuela spends about 9 percent of its annual government income on public health measures, while Paraguay allots about 6 percent. Venezuela spends another 6.6 percent on the related areas of agriculture and livestock; Paraguay spends less than 2 percent. In the area of public works the discrepancy is somewhat greater. Paraguay spends in the neighborhood of 4 percent of its revenue on physical improvements such as roads, dams, schools, irrigation projects, and port facilities; Venezuela expends about 21 percent. Many of Paraguay's improvements have benefited only the residents of Asunción. Projects such as the installation of a water supply system, a telephone system, the international airport, and schools are designed for the metropolitan populations. Rural towns and villages have changed very little because of government planning.

The *campesino* of the Paraguayan countryside has been the object of government solicitude in one respect: land reform. There is reason to believe that the distribution of land to the peasants has not been as extensive or as successful as government figures would seem to indicate. Venezuelan figures are perhaps more reliable. They reveal a rather extensive program of land reform. The acreage distributed to the rural farmers is a matter of some pride to the Venezuelan government.

One of the most sought after favors that a government can bestow in a society where employment opportunities are limited is a position with the administration. Critics of President Stroessner assert that his 50,000-man bureaucracy is far larger than Paraguay needs and that it is a personal labor force that forms a part of his power base. Government jobs go only to members of the president's party. In the granting of government employment, therefore, only the Colorado half of the population are effective competitors.

Political patronage based upon ascriptive criteria is also a primary feature of the Venezuelan system. No political party now commands a majority voice in the government, and this complicates the process of distributing government favors. Surely one of the prices the president has to pay to get other parties to cooperate with him in a coalition is to permit their ministers to have some say in the disposition of government jobs.

The evidence presented in this book supports the conclusion that Venezuela not only has more in the way of resources than does Paraguay, but that it is somewhat better organized and equipped to make a more equitable distribution of its services, jobs, and favors. A larger percent of the Venezuelan population share in and benefit from the national wealth.

PROGRESS IN RESPONDING TO THE DEMANDS OF SOCIETY

In evaluating progress in the responsiveness of the two systems to citizen demands, one must consider such things as the status and stage of development of political parties and pressure groups and their ability to present demands in a meaningful way; the resistance of entrenched elite elements of the power structure; the groups and institutions and regions to which the political structure responds; and the policy areas that the regime regards as important.

During most of their histories, Venezuela and Paraguay have been controlled by family dynasties, military heroes, personalist caudillos, landholders, and to a degree, by churchmen. Most of these came from the aristocratic stratum of society or from the more rugged and plebeian military apparatus. Generals Gómez and Antonio Páez, both peons in their origin, were hardly persons with whom the aristocracy cared to associate, but they were of the power elite. Unlettered men might occupy the presidential palace, but conservative aristocratic forces resisted any significant changes. Thus for many years the two systems responded only to a small, wealthy, educated, and articulate class whose demands and differences provided the grist of the policy mill.

This situation prevails to a considerable degree in the Paraguay of 1971. A highly responsive political system will ordinarily have an effective and competitive party system and a distinct set of interest groups, both of which provide access to the policy makers. It should be apparent by now that while Paraguay has political parties, only one really counts. Interest groups are paternally regulated and their respective demands are granted at the discretion of the executive. There is little give-and-take in the legislative halls. Military and ruling-party objectives are paramount.

A system truly responsive to the various forces in and demands of society accomplishes conflict resolution through the orderly processes of legislative debate, judicial and administrative interpretation, and executive deliberation, as well as through party competition. For reasons given in earlier chapters, it seems reasonable to conclude that the Paraguayan system has a low degree of responsiveness, a fact previously related to the relatively few demands made upon it by its simple agricultural society. As the population becomes more urbanized and more economically diversified, the inability or unwillingness to respond to increasing demands will be a serious affliction unless more adequate response mechanisms are developed.

Venezuela has become more responsive to the inputs and demands of its society, although paternalism still characterizes the relations of citizen and government to a degree. Because *Acción Democrática* organized and sought the support of peasants and workers, it has had to be responsive to their needs if it wishes to retain their electoral support. Its land reform program and its industrial development plans have been pushed in spite of the resistance of the conservative landowners. Politics in Venezuela is more and more responding to the needs of the majority lower-class population.

THE CITIZEN AND SYMBOLIC VALUES

Finally let us turn to an index of some importance in the evaluation of a political system: the degree to which people identify with or react to the symbols of the system. Although Venezuelans and Paraguayans may dislike a given regime, many of them are willing to participate in political ceremonies that demonstrate their emotional attachment to the historical traditions of their country. When they seek to overthrow an unpopular regime, their reasons are often cast in terms that reflect their belief that the government in question has been disloyal to these traditions.

Paraguayans dwell on the military achievements of their soldiers and heroes during two hard-fought wars. The past is ever-present in the form of statutes to Dr. Francia and in particular to Francisco Solano López. History books acceptable to the Ministry of Education proclaim the greatness of the Paraguayan people and the nobleness of their achievements. Political leaders identify with these sentiments and capitalize on the patriotic and nationalist sentiments of the Paraguayan people.

Presidential speeches are given wide publicity, as are the official inaugurations of any new material accomplishment: schools, hospitals, and roads. National holidays and days commemorating the various achievements of the regime in power are celebrated with impressive ceremonies. The celebration of the *Día de la Raza* (Day of the Race) ties the individual members of the nation together as well as symbolizing their membership in the larger Spanish community. The presence of government officials at important religious ceremonies and festivals, as well as the attendance of Church dignitaries at political events, have created the illusion of mutual respect between the two forces and has given the regime an aura of legitimacy it might not otherwise have. The breakdown of this friendly custom in recent years is a danger signal that some of the traditional relations in the political order are in disarray.

Venezuela's rallying point is its great liberator, Simón Bolívar, a native of Caracas. So great is the reverence in which this man is held that all political leaders feel compelled to pay homage to him. Reference to his ideals and aspirations and achievements constantly appear in literature, textbooks, celebrations, and speeches. Whatever else the Venezuelans may disagree on, they are one people in honoring their past heroes and glorifying their heroism in the service of their country.

With the exception of the regime of Marcos Pérez Jiménez, the Venezuelan leadership in the past several decades has endeavored to increase the symbolic value of democracy in their country. Thus they stress the democratic nature of their political system, emphasize the dignity and worth of the individual, hail elections as the epitome of the democratic process, and proclaim their firm and undying attachment to the principles of representative government. On the basis of achievement, however, only in the last decade can the government truly claim to be the champion of the democratic order and the common man. For a people who cherish ideals, the beginning of its realization is a satisfying thing indeed.

CONCLUSION

It must be said that the overall performance of the two political systems is directly related to the distribution of their respective populations. Two-thirds of the Venezuelan people are now classed as urban; one-third of Paraguay falls into this category. The urban trend of its population and the development efforts of the Venezuelan government in the direction of more industry and economic diversification will undoubtedly create new pressures and problems for the system. Fewer people on the land will necessitate better farming techniques, more government assistance in terms of such things as subsidies, distribution facilities, and more secondary roads. The increasing concentration of people in urban communities will result in more vocal demands for larger numbers of schools, hospitals, welfare programs, and services of all kinds. As these things materialize, the attractiveness of urban life will lure larger members of the rural population to the cities.

If all the pressures and demands are to be met, the government must have adequate domestic resources, a sympathetic and trained corps of experts with the vision to anticipate future needs and with financial support to achieve them, all of which Venezuela either has or is developing. Residence in urban communities generally brings with it a greater political awareness, and this awareness may in turn lead groups heretofore excluded to increased participation in the political process.

If the process of converting inputs into outputs remains relatively open and responsive and adequate channels to policy makers exist, and if the power elite is reasonably responsive to the demands of a growing society, there is a good chance that a transitional system such as Venezuela may achieve its goal of a participating democracy.

At the present time Venezuela certainly seems headed in that direction. Its political structure is becoming increasingly specialized—the legislature, for example, actually legislates instead of waiting for the nod from the executive. Although still subject to a considerable degree of regulation, parties, interest groups, courts, and legislature are beginning to acquire more autonomy. The conversion process in Venezuela is developing in such a way as to include more significant roles for structures other than the executive branch.

Venezuela has a homogeneous culture based on Catholic and Spanish values, both spiritual and moral. This is not to say that no alienation exists. The existence of MIR, FALN, and the Communist party, as well as other disaffected groups and their willingness to resort to violence are indications of the depth and quality of opposition to the system. Conditions in Venezuela in 1970 seem to point to the fact that the majority of the people identify with the political system and its leaders and structures. Very few Venezuelans today are in political prisons or in exile.

The story is somewhat different in Paraguay. There, present conditions point to the continuation of authoritarian system. Subsystem autonomy is very low, indeed. Courts, legislatures, parties, and interest groups are all at the mercy of the executive. Even the Colorado party and the armed forces have lost ground to President Stroessner. In this state of affairs, the conversion process is largely preempted by the executive branch of government, where major conflict resolution almost wholly takes place. Minor grass-roots conflict resolution involves local party officials, priests, and minor government officials.

The majority of the Paraguayan people, while aware of the government and the political infrastructures, are not sufficiently involved in the political process to be called participants. They are subjects. All are members of one or another of the two principal parties or of the newly arisen ones, but they are deferential to the elites that control them.

Paraguay has one of the most homogeneous peoples and culture in Latin America, yet it has one of the largest alienated groups. Since Paraguayans are highly nationalistic and very devoted to their country, the large number of them who live outside Paraguay tells us something about their attitudes toward the present political system and the economic opportunities in their homeland. Even inside Paraguay increasing alienation is taking place as students and Church members are challenging the regime.

When, and if, the Paraguayan population begins to accelerate its movement to urban centers, the present political edifice will make it difficult to respond within the framework of democratic government to the pressures that the movement will create. The extremely limited nature of all its resources will make their allocation far more difficult that would be the case in Venezuela, where they are more plentiful. The magnitude of the task of modernizing the economy and of assuring equitable allocations of goods, services, and opportunities among competing groups and individuals may well create the rationale for the continued existence of authoritarian government in Paraguay for years to come.

In almost all categories, therefore, Venezuela ranks well ahead of Paraguay. In all fairness, it must be added that even if Paraguay had the will to improve its abilities, it is sorely handicapped by factors that have nothing to do with its aspirations and over which it has little control. Venezuela is blessed with an abundance of advantages, Paraguay with practically none.

ADDITIONAL BIBLIOGRAPHY

Adams, Richard N. *The Second Sowing.* San Francisco: Chandler, 1969.

Aguilar, Luis E., ed. *Marxism in Latin America.* New York: Knopf, 1968.

Alba, Victor. *The Latin Americans.* New York: Praeger, 1969.

Alexander, Robert J. *The Venezuelan Democratic Revolution.* New Brunswick, N.J.: Rutgers University Press, 1964.

Bailey, Norman A. *Latin America in World Politics.* New York: Walker and Company, 1967.

Bonilla, Frank, and José Michelena, eds. *A Strategy for Research on Social Change,* Vol. 1 of *The Politics of Change in Venezuela* (Cambridge, Mass.: The M.I.T. Press, 1967). This book is particularly useful for the student because it contains a wealth of material on such aspects of the Venezuelan social and political system as nationalism, the bureaucracy, the rural farmer (campesino), and an evaluation of the elites.

Edelmann, Alexander T. *Latin American Government and Politics.* Rev. ed. Homewood, Ill.: The Dorsey Press, 1969.

Fagen, Richard R., and Wayne A. Cornelius, Jr., eds. *Political Power in Latin America, Seven Confrontations.* Englewood Cliffs, N.J.: Prentice-Hall, 1970.

Friedman, John. *Venezuela: From Doctrine to Dialogue.* Syracuse, N.Y.: Syracuse University Press, 1965.

Gilmore, Robert L. *Caudillismo and Militarism in Venezuela 1810–1910.* Athens, Ohio: Ohio University Press, 1964.

Groves, Roderick T. "Administrative Reform and the Politics of

Reform: The Case of Venezuela," *Public Administration Review,* 27 (December 1967), 436–445.

Hassan, M. F. "The Second Four-Year Plan of Venezuela," *Journal of Inter-American Studies,* 9 (April 1967), 296–320.

Lambert, Jacques. *Latin America: Social Structure and Political Institutions,* trans. by Helen Katel. Berkeley, Calif.: University of California Press, 1967.

Lieuwin, Edwin. *Arms and Politics in Latin America.* New York: Praeger, 1960.

————. *Generals vs. Presidents.* New York: Praeger, 1964.

Lipset, Seymour M., and Aldo Solari, eds. *Elites in Latin America.* New York: Oxford University Press, 1967.

Marsland, William D., and Amy L. Marsland. *Venezuela through Its History.* New York: Crowell, 1954.

Masur, Gerhard. *Nationalism in Latin America.* New York: Crowell-Collier-Macmillan, 1966.

Meyer, Gordon. *The River and the People.* London: Metheun, 1965.

Nava, Julian. "Illustrious American: The Development of Nationalism in Venezuela under Antonio Guzmán Blanco," *The Hispanic American Historical Review,* 45 (November 1965), 527–543.

Nisbet, Charles T., ed. *Latin America: Problems in Economic Development.* New York: The Free Press, 1970.

Peattie, Lisa. *The View from the Barrio.* Ann Arbor, Mich.: University of Michigan Press, 1968.

Raine, Philip. *Paraguay.* New Brunswick, N.J.: Scarecrow Press, 1956.

Ray, Talton F. *The Politics of the Barrios of Venezuela.* Berkeley, Calif.: University of California Press, 1969.

Reh, Emma. *Paraguayan Rural Life: Survey of Food Problems 1943–1945.* Washington, D.C.: Institute of Inter-American Affairs, Food Supply Division, 1946.

Ronning, C. Neale. *Law and Politics in Inter-American Diplomacy.* New York: Wiley, 1963.

Serxner, J. J. *Acción Democrática of Venezuela, Its Origins and Development.* Gainesville, Fla.: University of Florida Press, 1959.

Sigmund, Paul E., ed. *Models of Political Change in Latin America.* New York: Praeger, 1970.

Taylor, Philip B., Jr. "Progress in Venezuela," *Current History,* 53 (November 1967), 270–274.

Tugwell, Franklin. "The Christian Democrats of Venezuela," *Journal of Inter-American Studies,* 7 (April 1965), 245–267.

Von Lazar, Arpad, and Robert R. Kaufman, eds. *Reform and Revo-*

lution: Readings in Latin American Politics. Allyn and Bacon, 1969.

Wise, George S. *Caudillo: A Portrait of Antonio Guzmán Blanco.* New York: Columbia University Press, 1951.

Zook, David H., Jr. *The Conduct of the Chaco War.* New Haven, Conn.: Bookman Associates, 1960.

INDEX

Absolutism, 42, 94, 142
Acción Democrática (Venezuela), 78–88, 117, 125, 134, 184, 195, 197, 200, 215, 225, 228–229, 231–236, 240, 242, 250, 253, 268, 276, 277, 306, 308, 309, 313, 314, 346, 355, 367; labor movement and, 269–271
Achuagas, 36
Acosta, Cecilio, 151n, 171
Acosta, Cesar R., 23n
Agrarian Leagues (Paraguay), 227
Agriculture, Paraguay, 19, 20, 26, 32; Venezuela, 13, 14–15, 16, 19, 21, 30
Alexander, Robert, 232n
Alliance for Progress, 352–358
Almond, Gabriel A., 28n, 122n, 138n
Alon (student club), 266
Aluminum, 12
Andean Development Corporation, 360
Andean highlands (Venezuela), 14–16
Anderson, Charles W., 250n, 251n, 269n
Angel Falls, 10
Annual income (*see* Income, annual)
Anticlericalism, 108–109, 252
Aprista party, 225

Arawaks, 35
Arcaya, Pedro Manuel, 149n, 155n, 167n
Arciniegas, German, 153n
Area, Latin America, 1; Paraguay, 16; Venezuela, 9
Argentina, independence movement in, 56
Armed forces (*see* Military)
Armed Forces for National Liberation, (FALN), 86, 134–135, 235, 251, 266, 267, 365, 366, 381
Asunción, Paraguay, 19, 20, 22, 123
Asunción, founding of, 31–32; local government, 204
Audiencia, 43
Authoritarianism, 97, 120, 121; democracy and, 148–152
Authority, Spaniard's concept of, 140
Ayala, Eusebio, 89, 297–298
Ayolas, Juán de, 32
Aztecs, 35

Bankers Association (Venezuela), 275
Barria, Jorge, 255n
Barrientos, General, 302
Barrios, Gonzalo, 87, 233
Bauxite, 12
Belaunde, Victor A., 46n

Bernstein, Harry, 82n
Betancourt, Rómulo, 73, 80, 85, 86, 125, 126, 133–134, 285, 288; cabinet and, 291
Betancourt Doctrine, 347
Bolívar, Simon, 46, 58, 167, 168, 349
Bonaparte, Joseph, 56
Bonaparte, Napoleon, 56
Boves, 58
Brice, Angel, 321n
British Guiana, boundary dispute, 71
Bureaucracy, as an interest group, 262–264
Burelli Rivas, Miguel A., 234
Busey, James, 170n
Business community, interest groups within the, 275–280

Caballero, Bernardino, 74, 75, 77, 297
Cabildo, 44
Cabinet, Paraguay, 302; Venezuela, 289, 291, 292
Caldera, Rafael, 85, 87–88, 131, 135, 228, 285, 288; biographical sketch, 285; cabinet, 290; concept of democracy, 151; congress and, 206–209; hostility of Acción Democrática toward, 200, 231–232; inaugural address (1969), 230, 347; Latin American economic integration favored by, 276; military establishment and, 260–261; National Student Union and, 228; Social Christian party and, 228, 230
Candidato único, 75
Captaincy-general, 43
Capuchins, 51
Caracas, Venezuela, 15, 16, 123; Chamber of Commerce, 275; founding of, 30; University of, 30, 73, 84, 265
Caribs, 35
Caritás, 253
Carobobo, Battle of, 58
Caroní River, 10
Caserío, 189
Castro, Cipriano, 71–72, 73, 112, 124, 283, 344
Castro, Fidel, 86, 180, 343, 347, 350
Catholic Church, as cultural agent, 146; as socializing agent, 105–109; education and the, 49, 107–

108; in Latin America, 2–3, 47–55; in Paraguay, 4, 51–55, 59, 61, 105–109, 251–256, 369–370; in Venezuela, 4, 50–51, 54, 57–58, 59, 65–66, 68, 70–71, 84, 105–109, 229, 252–256, 368–369; politics and the, 145–148, 229, 251–256; publications, 108, 209; women and the, 100, 105
Catholic University (Paraguay), 107, 108
Cattle, Paraguay, 18, 19; Venezuela, 13, 15, 16
Caudillos, 4
Causa Rehabilidora, 214
Censorship, 207–208
Central American Common Market, 358, 360
Central Institute of Social Insurance (Venezuela), 289
Central Office of Coordination and Planning (Venezuela), 293
Cerro Bolívar, 12
Cesarísmo democrático, 148–149, 150
Chaco (Paraguay), 18–19
Chaco War (1932–1935), 18, 70, 76, 77, 88, 261, 340–341
Chacras, 118
Chalbaud, Delgado, 83, 159–164
Chamber of Deputies (Venezuela), 289–290
Chamber of Petroleum Industry (Venezuela), 275, 277
Chamberlain, Robert S., 319n
Chaperone system, 141
Chaves, Federico, 92, 342
Children, role of, 100–101
Christian Democratic party (Paraguay), 128, 216, 220, 225–227, 238, 239, 240, 256
Christian Democratic Youth of Paraguay, 266
Church (see Catholic Church)
Citizens, demands of, response to, 377–378; law and, 333–337; symbolic values and, 378–379
Ciudad Guayana, Venezuela, 12
Civil service, 293–294
Class structure, during colonial period, 40–41; Paraguay, 22–25, 26, 33–41; Venezuela, 22–25, 26, 33–41
Coal, 12
Coffee, 14, 15
Colonial period, in Paraguay, 31–

56; in Venezuela, 29–31, 33–56; political organization during, 42–47; religious influences during, 47–55; social structure during, 33–41

Colonias, 204

Colorado party (Paraguay), 74, 91, 92, 93, 104, 125, 127–130, 137, 180, 203–206, 216, 219, 222–224, 238, 239, 247–248, 261, 266, 299, 315; founding of, 215–216; paper, 209; patronage and the, 262; structure, 238

Columbus, Christopher, 29

Comité de Sindicatos Autónomos, 270

Committee for Independent Electoral Organization (Venezuela), 228

Communications, face-to-face contacts, 210; Paraguay, 20, 22, 97, 206–211; Venezuela, 206–211; violence as, 211; *See also* Newspapers; Radio stations; Television stations

Communist party, Paraguay, 91, 227, 343; Venezuela, 84, 85, 86, 125, 134, 135, 215, 217, 232, 235–236, 312, 365

Compadrazgo, 101, 115, 117

Compañías, 204

Compromise, Spaniard's reluctance to, 142–146

Comunero revolt, 33

Comunidad (Church paper), 209, 210, 254

Confederación Unico de Trabajadores (CUTV), 270

Confederation of Latin American Christian Trade Unions, 255

Conferences, Inter-American, 350

Congress, Paraguayan, 314–316; Venezuela, 303–314

Conquistadores, 30, 32, 35, 48

Conservative oligarchy (Venezuela), 213–214

Conservative (Colorado) party (*see* Colorado party)

Conservatives, Paraguay, 297; Venezuela, 67, 68

Constitutionalism, 165–185

Constitutions, as instruments of power, 180–185; as panaceas, 171–172; as political instruments, 177–178; as symbol of restraint, 178–180; as vehicles for person-

alismo, 172–177; foreign influences in, 167–170; symbolic significance of, 170–171

COPEI (*see* Social Christian party)

Corregidor, 43

Cotton, Paraguay, 19; Venezuela, 13

Council of Ministers (Venezuela), 289, 290

Council of State (Paraguay), 302

Courts, Paraguayan, 331–333; Venezuelan, 321–331

Creole Petroleum Corporation, 279

Criollo class, 41

Crow, John A., 58*n*

Cultures, political, ingredients of, 138–185

Cumanagota Indians, 29, 35

Currency, 21

Curriculum, 111–112, 265

Davis, Kingsley, 146*n*

De Gaulle, Charles, 343

Delegados, 203, 206

Delegated Committee of Congress (Venezuela), 311–312

Democracia solidarista, 149–150

Democracy, authoritarianism and, 148–152; in Latin America, 151; in Paraguay, 34, 121, 137, 149–150, 151, 365, 369–370; in Venezuela, 27, 34, 96, 121, 141, 148–152, 154, 365–369; progress toward, 365–370; solidary, 149–150

Democratic caesar, 148–149, 150

Democratic National Front (FND), 234

Democratic party (Venezuela), 79

Democratic Popular Force (FDP), 234

Democratic Republican Union (URD), 85, 125, 215, 228–229, 234–235, 240, 242, 268, 277, 291, 306

Democratic Socialist party (Venezuela), 235

Democratic Student Front, 266

Demonstrations, 211, 267, 268

Departments (Paraguay), 203–204

Development, of Paraguay, 28–93; of Venezuela, 28–93

Development, Ministry of (Venezuela), 296

Diamonds, 12

Diffie, Bailey W., 39*n*, 47*n*, 319*n*, 320*n*

Dirección General de Policía (Digepol), 265
Directorio Revolucionario del Partido Liberal, 218
Discovery, of Venezuela, 29
Dix, Robert H., 251*n*
Doña Barbara (Gallegos), 14
Doyle, Sir Arthur Conan, 10
Drier, John C., 348*n*, 349*n*
Dulles, John Foster, 350

Economy, Paraguay, 4–5, 7, 19–21, 278–279, 352–360; Venezuela, 4–5, 12, 21–22, 278–279, 352–360
Edelmann, Alexander T., 359*n*
Education, as a class determinant, 24–25; as socializing agent, 109–115; church and, 49, 107–108; Paraguay, 6, 61, 76, 357–358; political recruitment process and, 124–126; Venezuela, 5, 71, 355–356
El Dorado, 30
Elections, in Paraguay, 153–156; in Venezuela, 153–156
Electoral process, Paraguay, 247–248, 249; Venezuela, 241–247, 249
Elite, 120
Elite (Venezuelan periodical), 209
Encomienda system, 37–38
Estigarribia, José Felix, 89, 149, 261, 298, 341; constitutional changes made by, 176
Europe, influences on Latin America, 1, 3, 23
Exports, Venezuelan, 12, 13, 21
Executive branch of government, Paraguay, 297–303; Venezuela, 283–297

Family, as socializing agent, 98–105; extended, 101–102; nuclear, 100–101
Fatalism, 142–143
Father, role of, 99–100
Febreristas, 89, 90, 91, 92, 128, 149, 216, 218, 219, 220, 224–225, 232, 237, 238, 239, 240; labor movement and, 272
Fedepetrol (*see* Oil Workers Federation)
Federación de la Producción, la Industria y el Comercio (FE-PRINCO), 278
Federal War (Venezuela), 67, 152

Federalism, 152; inter-governmental relations and, 202; judicial structure and, 201–202; municipalities under, 192–193, 198–201; states under, 186–198; Venezuela and, 67, 70, 186–203
Federalist Papers, 152
Federation of Chambers of Industry and Commerce (FEDECAMARAS), 275–278
Federation of Revolutionary Democratic Students, 267
Federation of University Centers, 267–268
FEI (*see* Independent Electoral Front)
Ferdinand VII, King (Spain), 56
Fernández, Lorenzo, 294
Festivals, religious, 106
Fiestas, 106
Filial obligation, 99
Fluharty, Vernon, 167*n*
FND (*see* National Democratic Front)
Foreign investments, 278–280
Foreign policy, Paraguay, 339–344; Venezuela, 344–348
Fortoul, José Gil, 172*n*
Francia, José Gaspar, Rodríguez de, 33, 60–62, 70, 74, 102, 109, 112, 124, 140, 149, 155, 158, 166; foreign policy, 339
Franco, Rafael, 89, 91, 224–225, 261
Freedom of the press, 208
Frei, Eduardo, 228
Frente Campesino, 270
Frente Electoral, 215
Frente Electoral Independiente, 215

Gaceta Oficial, 206
García Calderón, F., 105, 146
Gallegos, Rómulo, 14, 81–82, 124; council of Ministers and, 291–292; overthrow of, 284
Generation of 1928, 125, 285
Geography, Paraguay, 4, 7, 9, 16–19; politics and, 6–19; Venezuela, 4, 7, 8, 9–16
Godparenthood, 101, 115
Gómez, Juan Vicente, 70, 72–73, 77, 78, 122, 124, 140, 144–145, 148, 283; biographical sketch, 283–284; constitutional changes made by, 172–174; foreign policy, 346; labor movement and,

269; political parties under, 214

Goods, progress in distribution of, 375–377

Government, executive branch of: Paraguay, 297–303; Venezuela, 283–297; judicial branch of: Paraguay, 331–333; Venezuela, 321–331; legislative branch of: Paraguay, 314–316; Venezuela, 303–314; Paraguay, 4, 6, 60–64, 203–206, 241; Venezuela, 4, 5, 64–69, 186–203, 241; *See also* Local government; National government

Governors, state (Venezuela), 187–198, 206

Gran Colombia, Republic of, 59

Guahibos, 36

Guaíra Falls, 343

Guaraní (language), 4, 25

Guaraní Indians, 32, 37, 48, 52, 61, 110, 112

Guayana Corporation, 12

Guayana highlands (Venezuela), 10–13

Guri Dam, 10

Guayana, 345

Guzmán, Antonio Leocadio, 66, 104, 213–214; Liberal party organized by, 213–214

Guzmán Blanco, Antonio, 67, 70–71, 73, 104, 122, 140, 214, 283; Catholic Church and, 252; constitutional changes made by, 175; on federalism, 152

Haciendas, 4, 102; as socializing agent, 115–119

Hadley, Paul E., 222n, 223n, 224n, 225n, 227n

Hall, Edwin T., 141n

Haring, C. H., 44n, 113n

Hautart, François, 148n

Heritage, Hispanic, 138–185

Herring, Hubert, 13n, 45n, 52, 72n

Hicks, Federick, 104n, 129, 204n, 205n, 221, 238n

Hitler, Adolf, 91

House of Trade (Spain), 43

Houston, John A., 360n

Hydroelectric power, 10

Ideologies, 120; politics and, 148–152

Illiteracy, Paraguay, 109, 207, 357; Venezuela, 5, 86, 109, 207, 356

Incas, 35

Income, per capita: Paraguay, 5, Venezuela, 5, 373–374; national: Paraguay, 5, Venezuela, 5, 16

Independence movement, Paraguay, 57, 60; Venezuela, 57–60

Independent Democratic Union (Venezuela), 235

Independent Electoral Front (FEI), 158–159, 175

Independent National Union Bloc, (Venezuela), 235

Independent Revolutionary Front, (Venezuela), 215

Index (Catholic Church), 49, 54, 108

Indians, conversion of, 48; Cumanagota, 29, 35; in Paraguay, 18, 25, 35, 36–38; in Venezuela, 15, 25, 35–36, 39, 41, 56; Jesuits and the, 51–54; population statistics, 2; Spain and the, 35–38; *See also* Aztecs; Guaraní Indians; Incas, Mayas

Industry, Paraguay, 19–20, 278; Venezuela, 5, 10, 12–13, 21

Inquisition, 47, 49, 54

Institute of University City (Venezuela), 289

Instituto de Formación Demócrata Cristiana, 230

Intellectuals, 124–126; as a pressure group, 264–269

Inter–American Conferences, 350

Inter–American Development Bank, 20

Inter–American Peace Force, 344, 347, 352

Inter–American Press Association, 208

Inter-American Public Health Service, 341

Inter–American system, 348–360

Inter–American Treaty of Reciprocal Assistance, 349

Interest groups, 250–281; bureaucracy, 262–264; Catholic Church, 251–256; industrial and commercial groups, 275–280; intellectuals, 265–269; military establishment, 256–262; proletarian community, 269–274

Interior, Ministry of (Venezuela), 294–295

International Confederation of Free Trade Unions (Paraguay), 273

International Court of Justice, 362
International Federation of Christian Trade Unions (Paraguay), 273
Investments, foreign, 278–280
Iron ore, 12, 21
Isabel, Princess (Brazil), 340
Isolationism, Paraguay and, 339–341, 343

Jane, Cecil, 34n, 139n, 140, 142n
Jesuits, 49, 51, 52–54
Judicial system, 313–338; nature of, in Latin America, 318–320; structures and roles: Paraguay, 331–333, Venezuela, 201–202, 321–331
Junta de Gobierno, 207
Juntas, 56
Juntas comunales (Community boards), 188–189
Justice, Ministry of (Venezuela), 296
Juventud Revolucionario Copeyano (JRC), 267–268

Kantor, Harry, 204n, 271n, 294n
Kennedy, John F., 352

Labor Force, Paraguay, 19, 38; Venezuela, 19, 21
Labor movement, Paraguay, 271–274; Venezuela, 81, 269–274
Labor unions, direct action by, 133; Paraguay, 90; socialization process and, 119
Land ownership, Latin America, 115; Paraguay, 20–21, 118–119, 356–357; Venezuela, 5, 14
Language, 4
Lanz, Vallanilla, 148–149, 284
Lares, Eduardo Picón, 150n
Larrázabel, Wolfgang, 85, 125–126, 234
Latifundios, 4, 20, 115
Latin America, area, 1; countries in, 2; cultural influences on, 1–2, 3; definition of, 2; generalizations about, 3; political development, 3; population, 1, 2, 3; religion in, 2–3
Latin American Common Market (proposed), 359
Latin American Free Trade Association (LAFTA), 275–276, 316, 343, 358–360

Law, citizen and the, 333–337; Latin American, 318–320
League of Nations, 360–361
Legislative branch of government, Paraguay, 314–316; Venezuela, 303–314
Leo XIII, Pope, 147
Leoni, Raúl, 73, 86–87, 125, 134, 285, 288, 289, 355; cabinet and, 291; Latin American Free Trade Association and, 275–276; military establishment and, 165, 259–260
Levi Ruffelini, Carlos A., 218
"Levirales," 218
Lewis, Paul H., 225n
Liberal party, Paraguay, 74, 75, 89, 90, 91, 92, 104, 128, 129–130, 205, 209, 216, 218, 219, 222, 224, 237–238, 266, 297; Venezuela, 66, 68, 71, 214, 235
Libertad, La, 209
Lieuwin, Edwin, 23n, 84n, 213n, 253n, 283n
Limestone, 19
Line of Demarcation, 47
Lipset, Seymour, 365n
Llaneros, 13
Llanos (Venezuela), 13–14, 18
Llera Restrepo, Carlos, 276
Local government, Paraguay, 204–206; Venezuela, 192–193, 198–201, 206
López, Carlos Antonio, 62–63, 104, 109, 112, 140; constitution of, 169
López Contreras, Eleasar, 78–80, 122, 124, 150, 153, 287, 288; cabinet and, 291; Council of Ministers and, 292
Lost World, The (Doyle), 10
Lott, Leo B., 132n, 174n
Lower class, Paraguay, 23, 26; Venezuela, 23, 26
Lumber, 18, 19

Machado, Gustavo, 125
Madariaga, Salvador de, 99, 144n
Mañach, Jorge, 108n, 255n
"Mañana complex," 144
Maracaibo, Venezuela, 16
Maracaibo Basin (Venezuela), 14, 16
Martz, John D., 78n, 236n, 237n
Marxism, 267
Mayas, 35

McKorkle, Thomas, 189n, 203
Mecham, J. Lloyd, 61n, 66n, 71n, 105, 106n, 168n, 180n
Medina Angarita, Isaías, 78–80, 122; cabinet and, 291; concept of democracy, 151; labor movement and, 269
Medina Silva, Pedro, 135
Medinistas, 215
Mennonites, 18
Mérida, Venezuela, 15
Merkl, Peter, 105n
Mestizos, in Latin America, 38; in Paraguay, 25, 38–40; in Venezuela, 25, 39–40
Middle class, Paraguay, 22–23, 26; Venezuela, 22, 23, 24, 26
Militarism, politics and, 157–165
Military, role of the, 122–124, 256–262
Mind, Spanish, 139–145
Minifundios, 20, 115
Missionaries, 50
Missions, 50, 52–53
Molas López, Felípe, 155
Monagas, Gregorio, 66
Monagas, José Tadeo, 66–67, 122, 283; constitutional changes made by, 174–175; impeachment attempt, 304
Monagas family, 65–68
Monasteries, 49
Monroe Doctrine, 345
Morínigo, Higinio, 89–92, 140, 261, 298, 341; electoral democracy rejected by, 153–154; labor movement and, 272; Liberal party outlawed by, 216; relations with Argentina, 342
Morón, Guillermo, 33
Morse, Richard M., 42n
Movement of the Revolutionary Left (MIR), 86, 134, 232, 235, 268, 312, 365, 381
Movimiento Familiar Cristiano, 253
Movimiento Nacionalista Revolucionaria (Bolivia), 232
Movimiento Popular Colorado, 223
Movimiento Social Demócrata Cristiano, 225
Mulattoes, 16, 39
Mundo, El (Venezuelan newspaper) 209
Municipal government, Paraguay,
204–206; Venezuela, 192–193, 198–201, 206
Municipios, 188
Munro, Dana Gardner, 69, 71n
Mussolini, Benito, 91

National, El (Venezuelan newspaper), 209
Natalicio Gonzalez, Juan, 91
National Agrarian Institute, 289
National Civic Crusade (Venezuela), 88
National Democratic Front (FND), 87
National Government, executive branch of, 283–303; judicial branch of, 318–338; legislative branch, 303–316; Paraguay, 203–206, 282–283, 297–303; Venezuela, 186–203, 283–297
National Institute of Sanitary Works (Venezuela), 289
National Movement of Independents (MNI), 275
National product (GNP), Paraguay, 5, 19–20; Venezuela, 5, 19, 21, 279, 356
National Student Union (Venezuela), 228
Nationalism, 121; Paraguay, 26, 61, 64, 103, 112, 339; Venezuela, 112
Nationalist Civic Crusade (CCN), 227–228
Natural resources, Paraguay, 19, 26; progress in utilization of, 370–374; Venezuela, 10, 12, 21, 26
Negroes, Paraguay, 25, 38; Venezuela, 16, 25, 30, 39, 41, 56; population statistics, 2; See also Slaves and slavery
Nepotism, 101
Newspapers, Catholic, 108; Paraguay, 207, 208–210; Venezuela, 207, 209
Nichols, Byron, 119n, 130, 209n, 219n, 220n, 223n, 238n, 239n, 248n, 262n,
Nixon, Richard, 343

Oil, Paraguay, 18, 19; Venezuela, 12, 14, 16, 21, 73, 82, 231, 277, 279–280, 373–374
Oil Workers Federation (Venezuela), 270

Ojeda, Alonso de, 29
Ongania, Juan, 343
Opus Dei, 253
Organización Demócrata Cristiana de America (ODCA), 229–230
Organización Terrorista Estudiantes Colorados (Paraguay), 266
Organizaciones Independientes, 215
Organization of American States, 347, 348–352, 358
Oriental (Paraguay), 19
Orinoco River, 10
Orinoco steel mill, 12

Páez, José Antonio, 13, 58, 65–66, 68, 69, 122, 124, 140, 148, 283
Paraguay, area, 16; colonial period, 31–56; consolidation of state and nation in, 70, 73–77; contrasts between Venezuela and, 4–6; currency unit, 21; development of, 28–93; evaluation of state and nation in, 60–64; geographical regions of, 16–19; homogeneity in, 26, 33; independence movement, 57; location, 7, 9; origin of name, 31; population, 16; relations with U.S., 62; settlement of, 31–32; *See also* under name of subject concerned
Paraguay River, 16
Paraguayan Confederation of Workers (CPT), 273–274
Paria Peninsula (Venezuela), 16
Parparcen, R. Lapervance, 271*n*
Participation, political, 126–135
Party system (*see* Political parties)
Paternalism, 250
Patria (Colorado party paper), 209
Patronage, 129, 298–299
Pattee, Richard, 146*n*
Pearl fishing (Venezuela), 16
Peasants, 23, 25
Pedro II, Emeror (Brazil), 340
Peer groups, socialization process and, 119
Pen, Emile, 148*n*
Pendle, George, 6, 16*n*, 18*n*, 76*n*, 89*n*, 176, 298*n*, 342*n*, 356*n*, 359*n*
People's Electoral Movement (Venezuela), 87, 233
Per capita income (*see* Income, per capita)
Pérez Jiménez, Marcos, 83–85, 88, 122, 124, 125, 132, 133, 140, 143, 283, 287; authoritarian charter of, 184; biographical sketch, 284; Catholic Church and, 252; *cesarismo democratico* and, 149; constitutional changes made by, 177; Council of Ministers and, 290, 292; elected to Senate, 227; inaugural address, 140; Independent Electoral Front and, 158–159; military establishment and, 258; overthrow of, 268; Social Christian party and, 229
Perón, Juan, 342
Personalism in politics, Venezuela and, 45, 68, 73
Personalismo, constitution as vehicle for, 172–177
Petroleum (*see* Oil)
Philip, Prince (Great Britain), 343
Pierson, W. H., 67*n*, 304*n*
Plata Basin, 32, 63–64
Pluralism, oligarchical and institutional, 250–281
Política indiana, 320
Political cultures, ingredients of, 138–185
Political participation, 126–135
Political parties, 213–249; communications and, 210; contemporary milieu of, 216–222; historical perspectives, 213–216; Paraguay, 74–75, 77, 88–93, 117–130, 215–216, 222–227, 237–241; socialization process and, 119; Venezuela, 66–67, 77, 78–88, 130–135, 213–215, 227–237, 239–240
Political recruitment, 121–126
Political socialization, 85–121
Politics, Catholic Church and, 145–148, 229, 251–256; during colonial period, 42–47; economic bases of, 19–22; geographic bases of, 6–19; idealogies and, 148–152; militarism and, 157–165; of consent and command, 153–156; of power and restraint, 165–185; Paraguay and, 4, 6, 63, 73–77, 88–93, 95, 103–104, 125–130, 136–137, 215–216, 222–227, 237–239; social bases of, 22–25; theology and, 145–148; Venezuela and, 4, 5, 66–68, 70–71, 77–88, 93–94, 95, 103–104, 125, 130–135, 136, 213–215, 227–237
Poppini, Rollie, 227*n*

Popular Alliance (Venezuela), 235
Popular Democratic Force (Venezuela), 126
Popular Electoral Movement, 235
Popular National Vanguard (Venezuela), 235
Population, Latin America, 1, 2, 3; Paraguay, 16, 25; Venezuela, 9, 25, 39
Powell, G. Bingham, Jr., 28n, 122n, 138n
Power, constitutions as instruments of, 180–185
Powers, Francis Jr., 147n
Powers, presidential, Paraguay, 298–302; Venezuela, 285–289
President, office of, Paraguay, 297–303; Venezuela, 283–297
Pressure groups (see Interest groups)
Prieto Figueroa, Luis Beltrán, 87, 233, 235
Proletariat, labor movement and the, 269–274; Paraguay, 23, 269–274; Venezuela, 24, 269–274
Public Administration Commission (Venezuela), 293
Public Employees Union (Venezuela), 264
Public health services (Venezuela), 191–192
Public Ministry (Venezuela), 310–311
Public policy, problems of, Paraguay, 316–317; Venezuela, 316
Public Works, Ministry of (Venezuela), 295–296
Pueblo, El (paper), 209
Puerto Ordaz, Venezuela, 10, 22

Quintero, José Humberto, 253

Radical Liberals (Paraguay), 224, 238, 239
Radio stations, Paraguay, 207; Venezuela, 207, 212
Ramos, Samuel, 139n, 143n
Ranchers and Livestock Association (Venezuela), 275
Recruitment, political, 121–126
Reducciones, 52
Regional organization, 348–360
Regionalism, in Paraguay, 122–124; in Venezuela, 45, 68, 102, 122–123

Regions, geographical, Paraguay, 16–19; Venezuela, 8, 9–16
Religión, La, 209
Religion, in Latin America, 2–3; influence of the Church in Latin America, 47–55; Paraguay, 4, 18, 51–55; Venezuela, 4, 50–51, 54
Renovación, 92, 218, 219
República, La (Venezuelan newspaper), 209
Residencia, 44, 45
Revenue, government, distribution of, 375–377
Revolution of 1935 (Venezuela), 80–81, 93–94, 133
Revolution of 1945, 93–94
Revolutionary Party of National Integration (PRIN), 235
Rice, 13
Rights, human, 333–337
Rippy, J. Fred, 74n
Rivas, Burelli, 275
Rivas, Ulises Picón, 68n, 175n
Rivero, M. Marques, 190n
Rockefeller, Nelson, 343
Rolon, Raimundo, 155
Roman Catholic Church (see Catholic Church)
Roosevelt, Theodore, 72, 345
Roosevelt Corollary, 345
Rosas, Juan Manuel, 62
Royal Council of the Indies, 42, 43, 44
Royal Dutch Shell, 279
Royal Guipuzcoa Company (Caracas), 30–31
Ruggeri Parra, Pablo, 330n
Rural Welfare Institute (Paraguay), 357

Schaeffer, Wendell G., 36n
School of Public Administration (Venezuela), 293
Schools, as socializing agents, 109–115; Church, 107–108
Schurz, William S., 39n
Segovia highlands (Venezuela), 15
Seijas, R. F., 196n, 292n, 303n
Service, Elman R. and Helen S. 22n, 23n, 24, 25n, 37n, 51, 100, 103, 105, 106, 111n, 112n, 113n
Services, progress in distribution of, 375–377
Sierra Nevada de Mérida, 14–15
Silvert, K. H., 171n, 269n

Siso, Carlos, 39*n*, 152
Situado constitucional, 190
Slaves and slavery, in Latin America, 35; in Venezuela, 30, 36, 66
Social Christian party (COPEI), 85, 87, 130, 195, 197, 215, 228–234, 236–237, 240, 242, 253, 256, 267, 268, 277, 290, 292, 308, 313, 314, 367; labor unions and, 269–270, 271
Social structure, during colonial period, 40–41; Paraguay, 22–25, 26, 33–41, 95–121; Venezuela, 22–25, 26, 33–41, 95–121
Socialist party (Venezuela), 215
Socialist Workers party (Venezuela), 215
Socialization, political, 85–121
Society of Jesus (*see* Jesuits)
Solano López, Francisco, 63–64, 104, 109, 112, 140, 158; foreign policy of, 340
Solorano Pereira, Juan de, 320
Somoza, Anastasio, 346
Sosa Rodriguez, Carlos, 361
Spain, Indians and, 35–38; Latin America and, 34–35, 42; Paraguay and, 31–56; Venezuela and, 30–56
Spaniards, in Latin America, 34–41; in Paraguay, 35–41; in Venezuela, 35–41; political views of, 129–145; values of, 139–145
Special Reserve Fund, 287
Standard Oil of New Jersey, 279
State and nation, consolidation of, 70–77: Paraguay, 72–76, Venezuela, 70–73; evolution of, 60–69: Paraguay, 60–64, Venezuela, 64–69
States, federal system and (Venezuela), 186–198
Steel, 12
Stefanich, Juan, 149
Stevenson, Adlai, 343
Stokes, William S., 155*n*, 318*n*, 320*n*
Stroessner, Alfredo, 6, 92–93, 124, 125, 127, 128, 130, 135, 137, 140, 180, 298; Catholic Church and, 253–255; censorship and, 208; Colorado party and, 216; constitutional changes made by, 176–177; foreign policy and, 342–344; labor movement and, 274; military establishment and, 261–262; patronage and, 262; political parties and, 217–219, 222, 223, 225–227; taxes and, 278
"Stroessneristas," 223, 224
Student organization, 264–269
Subero, Armando A., 271*n*
Suffrage, 126–128
Supreme Court (Venezuela), 201–202
Supreme Electoral Council (Venezuela), 241–242
Szulc, Tad, 120*n*, 268*n*

Tannenbaum, Frank, 40*n*, 116, 117
Taxation, Paraguay, 278, 357, 371–372; Venezuela, 189, 192, 278, 356
Taylor, Philip B., Jr., 136*n*
Teacher Federation (Venezuela), 132
Technology, 5
Television stations, Paraguay, 207; Venezuela, 207, 212
Tello, James, 30*n*
Theology, politics and, 145–148
Thomas, Alfred B., 171*n*
Time, Spanish attitude toward, 144
Timotes, 35
Tobacco, 19
Topography, politics and, 6–19
Transportation, Paraguay, 20, 97; Venezuela, 7, 10, 12, 22
Tribuna, La (Paraguayan paper), 209
Trujillo, Rafael, 346, 347, 352

Ultimas Noticias (Venezuelan newspaper), 209
Unemployment, in Venezuela, 5, 86
Union for Progress (Venezuela), 235
Unión Nacional, 215
Unión Nacional Paraguaya pact, 218
Unión Republicana Democrática (*see* Democratic Republican Union)
Unitary system of government (Paraguay), 203–206
United Nations, 361–362
United States, Paraguay and the, 62
Universal, El (Venezuelan newspaper), 209

Universities, 113–114; Catholic, 107
University Federation of Paraguay, 266
Upper class, Paraguay, 22, 26; Venezuela, 23, 24, 26
URD (*see* Democratic Republican Union)
Uslar Pietri, Arturo, 58*n*, 65*n*, 126, 207, 234
Uslar Pretri, Jr., 45*n*

Values, Spanish, 139–145
Vanguardia Juvenil Urredista (VJU), 268
Venezolano, El (newspaper), 213
Venezuela, area, 9; colonial period, 29–31, 33–56; consolidation of state and nation in, 70–73, 76–77; contrasts between Paraguay and, 4–6; currency unit, 21; development of, 28–93; discovery of, 29; evolution of state and nation in, 64–69; independence movement, 57–59; location, 7; negroes in, 2; origin of name, 29; population, 9, 25, 39; public debt, 22; regions of, 8, 9–16; settlement of, 29–31; similarities between Paraguay and, 3–4, *See also* under name of subject concerned
Venezuelan Airmail Line, 289
Venezuelan Confederation of Labor, 264, 270
Venezuelan Development Corporation, 288–289

Venezuelan Guayana Corporation, 289
Venezuelan Peasant Federation, 81, 270
Venezuelan Petrochemical Institute, 289
Venezuelan Petroleum Corporation, 289
Viceroyalties, 43
Victory Front, 234
Villalba, Jovita, 125, 234, 235
Violence, 133–135, 154–156; as communications, 211
Visita, 45
Visitadors (inspectors), 44, 45
Voting (*see* Suffrage)

Wagley, Charles, 95–96, 97*n*, 98*n*
Wald, Haskell P., 116*n*
War of the Triple Alliance (1864–1870), 24, 25, 63–64, 70, 76, 77, 102, 158, 340
Warren, Harris Gaylord, 31*n*, 40*n*, 41, 47, 54, 64*n*, 150*n*, 155*n*
Watters, Mary, 50, 51*n*, 106*n*
Wife, role of, 100
Williams, Edward, 226*n*, 229*n*, 230*n*, 236*n*, 268*n*
Wolf, Ernesto, 145*n*, 158, 169, 172*n*, 193*n*, 330*n*
Women, role of, 100, 103, 104
Worcester, Donald E., 36*n*
Work, Spanish attitude toward, 143
World Bank, 264
World Union of Christian Democracy, 230
World War II, Paraguay and, 341; Venezuela and, 346